LADY SYBIL

Best wishes,

LADY SYBIL

Empire, War and Revolution

Simon Boyd

HAYLOFT PUBLISHING LTD

First published by Hayloft Publishing Ltd., 2017

A CIP catalogue record for this book is available from the British Library

ISBN 978-1-910237-29-8

Designed, printed and bound in the EU

Hayloft policy is to use papers that are natural, renewable and recyclable products and made from wood grown in sustainable forests. The logging and manufacturing processes are expected to conform to the environmental regulations of the country of origin.

Hayloft Publishing Ltd,
a company registered in England number 4802586
2 Staveley Mill Yard, Staveley, Kendal, LA8 9LR (registered office)
L'Ancien Presbytère, 21460 Corsaint, France (editorial office)

Email: books@hayloft.eu
Tel: 07971 352473
www.hayloft.eu

Frontispiece image: Sybil with her young family, Harry and Molly

To my nieces and nephews and great niece and great nephew

Contents

List of Plates

Introduction

What led a young English woman to travel to St Petersburg, capital of Russia, in the middle of the First World War, to set up a British Red Cross Hospital? The Anglo-Russian Hospital was Britain's gift to its Russian ally, intended to show off the best standards of modern British surgery and nursing. The young woman was Lady Sybil Grey, second daughter of Albert fourth Earl Grey and Countess Alice Grey. She was born before cars, telephones and aeroplanes existed, and lived to see the start of the Space Race. A child of the late Victorian age, she witnessed the great social changes of the Edwardian era and the First World War, the opening up of greater opportunities for women to work, the eventual coming of women's franchise, the Second World War and the end of Empire.

When she set out to Russia at the age of 33, she had already travelled widely. She had visited Europe; she had hunted big game in the Congo; she had spent nearly seven years in Canada which she passionately loved, while her father was Governor General there, and in early 1914 she had travelled round the world with her parents.

During her time in Russia she enjoyed the hectic social life of the court; was wounded at the front; helped shelter one of the murderers of Rasputin; met the Tsarina and witnessed the Russian Revolution. She showed her courage when she faced the mob that broke into the Anglo-Russian Hospital during the Revolution, pointing guns and bayonets at her while she sought to calm the situation.

She was adventurous, loved travel and learning about new places and people. She was passionately interested in politics (a passion inherited from her father), chronicling the collapse of the Imperial Russian regime in relentless and vivid detail. She was in the audience of the Duma (Russian parliament) both for the Tsar's triumphant first visit in 1915 and for the last session of the Duma before the February 1917 revolution, when a left-wing critic excoriated his government – 'You're leading this country into revolution and you'll even make a mess out of that.'

Above all she was observant – her letters and diaries are vivid records, not just of the events that occurred but of the feelings they stirred in her. She had an eye for unusual stories, with vivid depictions of exotic happenings such as a midnight's entertainment with the Russian gypsies.

She was funny and amusing, commenting with a dry wit on people and events, and occasionally playing practical jokes. But she was nevertheless a deeply serious person, and saw her job in Russia as a patriotic duty to help promote Britain's interests in wartime.

She wrote regularly to her mother, Countess Alice Grey, describing life in Imperial Russia and her mother responded with news of the home front. Perceptive and entertaining, the tone of their correspondence darkens as bereavement and the death of friends and family in World War I begins to hit home. There is the gradual realisation that 'life will never be the same again.'

Sybil went on to command the Women's Legion, one of the first uniformed detachments of women serving with the British Army in France, providing ambulance and staff car drivers .

She had a restless enquiring mind, eager for new experiences and she loved travel. She was naturally a woman of action and thrived on physical challenges like salmon fishing in the wilds of Canada. She saw herself as the equal of men and must have relished her independence and the opportunity for her to serve her country in charge of the Anglo-Russian Hospital in Russia and of the Women's Legion in France.

After her extraordinary early life, we see her settle down to marriage and motherhood, with two children when she was in her early 40s. Still she did not give up her love of travel and challenges – and her later correspondence tell of her journeys to South America, Canada, South Africa and Kenya.

She was determined and personally brave, facing down the mob which invaded the Anglo-Russian Hospital during the Russian Revolution. She was good at relating to people and always gave them the feeling that their concerns mattered to her. Even in old age she remained very young in spirit and her great nephews and nieces and grandchildren felt no age gap between her and them. She admired strong women and felt that she herself had many masculine qualities, but she remained attractive and feminine and a devoted mother.

There are intriguing puzzles – how did the loss of her beloved elder sister affect her; what was the significance of her friendships with women and men; why did she marry so late (aged 40) in an age when early marriage was expected; how did she react to the loss of her independence; was hers a happy marriage?

She was sensible and practical, with the wisdom and judgement to see people and courses of actions clearly – in Russia her friends referred to her as 'the Grey Fox' and lamented her departure – 'Now no-one will clear our minds for us as you did'.

Above all she was a great and loyal friend – she had a huge circle of friends, who remained devoted to her throughout her life. One of her nieces spoke for them all: 'Her intense love of, and enthusiasm for, life and people and their concerns gave a special patina to everything she said and did – so that being with her was always a refreshment and stimulus, and one was warmed and revitalised and somehow made to glow by her flame.'

The book spans 80 years of huge change in Britain and the World, from before the First World War until the time of the Cold War. It draws on Sybil Grey's letters and diaries, and those of her mother, to give first-hand, vivid insights into people, events, living conditions and profound changes in Canada, Russia, Africa and above all in Britain, through the life of a remarkable woman.

Prologue: A Journey to Russia

When Lady Sybil Grey set out for Russia on 5 October 1915 she was 33 years old, unmarried, brave and very determined. She had brown hair, grey eyes and her War Office passbook recorded her height at 5 foot 8 inches. The First World War had already raged for more than a year and she had trained as a Voluntary Aid Detachment nurse. She was travelling with three companions to establish a British Red Cross hospital to nurse Russian wounded soldiers in the Russian capital Petrograd, the new name for St Petersburg, 2,000 miles away from home.

She was understandably nervous, not just about the hazardous journey but also about successfully filling the role of setting up and administering the hospital. The route out to Russia involved a two-day crossing of the North Sea, menaced by German submarines which were ferociously sinking both British and neutral shipping – the torpedoing of the liner *Lusitania* had shocked the world only five months earlier. After arriving at Stavanger, they would travel by train in a huge arc north eastwards across Norway, Sweden and Finland, before arriving in Petrograd. Sybil wrote to her parents:

> My beloved ones, I can hardly believe that I have really left you all and have started. It seems such a dream. I shall miss you all too horribly. Russia is such a long way, or it seems so when one has never been there, but I expect when one has travelled there that one feels it is no distance at all, like Canada.
>
> It is a wonderful chance and it is up to me to prove myself worthy of it. I do hope I shall. I feel awfully frightened. Anyhow if I don't I shall have only myself to blame, if that is any consolation. It really is extraordinary luck having such a chance, how thrilling and exciting it ought to be.
>
> Oceans and oceans of love,
> God bless you both, do look after yourselves.

The second daughter of Albert 4th Earl Grey and his wife Countess Alice Grey, Sybil was already a seasoned traveller – before she was 20 she had visited Europe – Italy, France, Germany and even Malta. She had spent almost seven years living with her parents in Canada where her father was Governor General; she had travelled with them to southern Africa where she hunted big game in the Congo. And she had accompanied them on a four-month trip around the world, in early 1914, before the First World War, visiting Ceylon, Australia, New Zealand, Tasmania, Fiji and Honolulu, before crossing the United States and returning home.

Brought up as one of five children in a wealthy family at Howick Hall, a large country house on the north east coast in Northumberland, she nevertheless was used to 'roughing it' on occasion – she loved going on fishing expeditions in the northern wilds of Canada and in New Zealand. She had grown up confident of her own abilities and judgement.

On their voyage across the North Sea, their neutral Norwegian ship the *Irma* was clearly identified day and night – the Norwegian flag was painted on the side of the ship, illuminated by powerful electric lights, its name and nationality picked out in letters two feet high in fluorescent light on the top deck.

Sybil had time to reflect on the train of events which brought her there. A little over a month before she had received a letter from Lady Muriel Paget, the organiser of the Anglo-Russian Hospital:

> I'm afraid there would not be the remotest chance of persuading you to come to Russia to help organise and run a field base hospital? If you could you would be the perfect person in every way and I should like to write pages putting every reason why you should do it – nothing has been done to help nurse the Russians, etc, etc, etc. We propose to take a fully equipped unit of 200 beds and to maintain it six or eight doctors, 22 nurses etc

The idea of sending a British military Red Cross hospital to Russia was the brain-child of Lady Muriel Paget who had heard of the terrible casualties on the Eastern front. It was intended to help counteract widespread disillusionment in Russia about the commitment of Britain, its ally in the First World War. The Anglo-Russian Hospital was promoted by the British Government and its embassy in Petrograd. It was funded by public subscription – the King and Queen headed the list of subscribers, and many British towns contributed on condition that their municipal crests were displayed above the beds of wounded Russian soldiers. Money also came from the British dominions – the government of Canada donated £10,000. A large and prestigious committee nominally controlled the Anglo-Russian Hospital under the chairmanship of Lord Cheylesmore, and included the Prime Minster H. H. Asquith, Sybil's cousin the Foreign Secretary Sir Edward Grey, and 80 other dignitaries.

Lady Paget knew that Sybil would jump at the challenge of setting up the hospital. Sybil wrote to her mother, Countess Alice: 'I would naturally love to go. I think you will sympathise with my feelings for I am certain you would feel the same were you in my place. I think it would be a wonderful experience and extraordinarily interesting.' But she had first to find a replacement to take on her current role in charge of the convalescent hospital that had been established at her father's seat at Howick Hall.

With her parents' blessing, Sybil accepted the job in Russia and set about preparing for her new role, meeting the leading staff members – Dr Andrew Fleming in charge of the medical team and the Matron, Sister Irvine Robertson.

Her appointment was not greeted with unanimous approval. *The British Journal of Nursing* denounced it on 16 October:

> The nursing profession we think has a right to know why a young untrained girl is to be placed in this responsible position, when a very experienced woman has been selected as matron and a staff of 24 certificated nurses has been engaged.
> The reply to this question will no doubt be as usual – that the trained matron will be in charge of the hospital, and that their duties do not clash. Bitter experience proves that it is most difficult to maintain nursing discipline under this system of

dual control, and that when an untrained lady of title – backed by social influence – is in supreme authority in a military hospital, disorganisation in the nursing department is inevitable … Let us hope the committee of the Anglo-Russian Hospital will consider this defect in its organisation before it is too late.

By that time Sybil Grey and her advanced party were already on their way to Russia.

In fact, Sybil was a good choice to lead the advance party to establish the hospital. Her background fitted her perfectly to interact with members of the Russian elite (many of them aristocrats like herself) and the fact that she was young, attractive and good company also gave her natural advantages in getting people to do things. She had undertaken some training herself as a Voluntary Aid Detachment auxiliary nurse. She spoke fluent French (the preferred foreign language of the Russian court). She was hard-working, unflappable and above all realistic. Faced with a foreign capital city in which there was a very limited choice of suitable buildings, she accepted the offer of the first floor of a royal palace as the location for the hospital, in the face of objections from her head doctor: 'Dr Fleming has got to realise that we have to make do with what is offered, even if it isn't ideal. Beggars can't be choosers, and this is war not peace.'

As, her brother-in-law, 'Jonah' Jones, wrote in her obituary 50 years later, 'Little did they know. By her coolness, her imperturbable common-sense, her charm, her warm human sympathies and above all her unself-regarding devotion to duty, Sybil Grey made an outstanding success of her job.'[1]

Her companions on the outward journey were Dr Andrew Fleming, aged 45 with long experience of running hospitals in Rhodesia, but with a 'colonial' style of management which antagonised his fellow doctors so much that later Sybil would have to demote him; the young Countess Olga Poutiatine, half English and half Russian, who would be their translator as well as acting as a support nurse; and Ian Malcolm, a friend of the Greys and MP for Croydon, who was a member of the Cheylesmore Committee.

As they steamed into Stavanger early in the morning of 7 October, Sybil noted: 'a very pretty little town, the sun just penetrating through the mist so that a big gasometer high on the hill looked picturesque. Red and green and white coloured wooden houses down to the water's edge, with steeply gabled roofs.' They then continued on up the fjord to Bergen which they reached at 4:15pm. The water and sky were a deep blue and the narrow fjord was bounded by low stony hills and heather, rising to higher hills in the distance. Sybil and her companions were reminded of the west coast of Scotland.

At Bergen she telegraphed a message home: 'To: Grey, Little Mill: Splendid passage, love, Sybil Grey.'

They then boarded a train for Christiania (the former name of Oslo, capital of Norway), for a twelve hour journey arriving early in the morning. On the train they had their first Russian lesson from Countess Olga.

---

1 Quoted in *The Forgotten Hospital* by Michael Harmer (1982).

At Christiania they changed trains and breakfast baskets were brought on board: 'a curious collection of unappetising things for the early morning – shrimps, German sausage which we don't have to eat, and heavy-looking stuff like Yorkshire pudding on rounds of bread. We all ate the little rolls of bread and still felt hungry.'

Sybil was well used to travelling long distances, having crossed Canada three times with her father and having travelled right up to Dawson in the Yukon, Canada's most northerly outpost. The party spent nearly the entire day trying to learn the Russian alphabet and looking out of the window: 'The country reminded me very much of Canada. A great many lakes and fir trees – with silver birches mixed in all along this part of the line. As far as colouring went, they were at their best, a beautiful gold. It looked very prosperous farming country and I saw several fields of winter wheat beginning to grow.'

On arrival at Stockholm in Sweden, they were met by the assistant of Crown Prince Gustaf Adolf of Sweden and by Mme Wallenberg, wife of the Swedish Foreign Minister. Crown Prince Gustaf's English wife, Princess Margaret of Sweden, was a member of the Connaught family who were good friends of the Greys. Dr Fleming and Countess Olga stayed at the main hotel while Sybil Grey and Ian Malcom were invited to stay at the castle with the Crown Prince and his family.

The next day they set off by train for Finland. Passing through wooded country with fast flowing rivers, Sybil observed 'a certain number of small farms, little painted wooden houses mostly painted brick red. The people one saw at the stations all looked rather mournful and depressed.' She noticed the traditional way crops were harvested: 'they have a curious way of drying their corn and wheat in this country – it is all raised above the ground on poles so that a field of cut corn looks like a regiment of tall men dressed in straw advancing on you.'

Sybil was beginning to understand how different Russia would be, and was perhaps worried about how well she would cope

Their language lessons continued: 'Most of today we been struggling with Russian, it is frightfully difficult. The different intonations are so hard to get hold of – but if I am in Russia for seven or eight months I hope I shall be able to talk a certain amount.'

Sybil had a keen eye for the new and unusual and gave an amusing account of mealtimes at station stops along the way, where the train would stop briefly to allow passengers to eat:

> Everybody rushes out of the train and crowds into a small room where there is a big table crammed with food, hot and cold. Very well cooked potatoes and excellent rolls, scones and bread, meat of all kinds, hors d'oeuvres, coffee and tea etc. One elbows one's way to the table, snatches a plate and fork and knife and grabs the food that looks most tempting, and then provisions in hand fights one's way through the zoo to a quiet corner and chair, every known language being talked.

Passengers could eat as much as they liked (or were able to in such a short time) and paid 1 Kronen 50 – not quite two shillings.

On 11 October, a crisp fine morning with a keen frost on the ground, they reached Haparanda on the north Baltic coast, the Swedish border with Finland (then a Grand Duchy and an autonomous part of the Russian Empire). The Customs examined everything and even strip searched some passengers in the open air. In her diary Sybil said, 'It was amusing to see some four or five men putting on their shirts, waistcoats, ties and coats outside in the sun.' But many years later she remembered the incident in a harsher light, with one poor woman having her bare skin relentlessly scrubbed for an hour by the paranoid Russian border police searching for spies: 'The poor woman was not only undressed but put into a bath and scrubbed hard all over with lemon and ammonia as the authorities had got it into their heads that she was a famous and beautiful spy – and that she was carrying messages in invisible writing on her back.'

The *Laissez Passé* documents carried by Sybil's party meant that their baggage was not opened. Tornio, the town on the Finnish side of the border was crowded with Russian soldiers – it was the town where exchanges of severely wounded prisoners, the *grand blessés*, took place between Germany and Russia.

Sybil had told her parents on the crossing that she was frightened but she probably didn't share the full extent of her fears. What if everything went wrong and she was cut off by advancing German armies, thousands of miles from home in a war zone? Would she be able to cope? In fact when it came to it, she would surmount both being wounded at the front and later face danger and uncertainty of the Revolution, when Russia did indeed spiral down into chaos.

Perhaps the dangers and uncertainties also attracted her – they were a way of escaping the circumscribed and restrictive norms of life for a young English woman at that time, even though her class gave her a far greater range of choice than most of her contemporaries. The war and the dangerous trip out to Russia represented for her as for many women a route to new experiences, the chance to serve her country and take on a real and testing job for the first time.

On 12 October, they set off on the final day of their journey, Sybil for the first time adding the Russian date, 29 September (Russia still used the Julian calendar which lagged thirteen days behind the Gregorian calendar used by the rest of Europe). They studied Russian, read the latest Sherlock Holmes mystery and arrived at Petrograd just before midnight, stepping down onto the platform at the Finland Station where Lenin was to make his appearance on the stage a year and a half later.

What fitted Sybil to take on this role? Her connections with the topmost levels of society were certainly important, but so too were her strength of character, her determination and, her confidence in dealing with people of all kinds. She was able to both listen and learn and act decisively; she was interested in people, places and politics, and was brave in a crisis. And she had a strong sense of duty and was passionately committed to the mission that the Anglo-Russian Hospital was setting out to deliver. These qualities were demonstrated when she had to protect the hospital and its staff from harm during the chaotic days of the Revolution. She learnt many of them from her parents and her upbringing.

PART I

Howick Hall, engraving 1926, from the author's collection.

1

Family and Early Life

Sybil was born on 15 July 1882 and grew up in the family home, Howick Hall on the wild Northumbrian coast and it remained her spiritual home throughout her life, a place of beauty and peace. A large Georgian house of honey coloured sandstone, its north side faces the drive, with wings to either side accessed by curving single storey quadrants, and flanked by trees. To the south, the house looks out over gardens, leading down to a burn and fields. There is a tradition in the family of establishing arboreta, and Howick's Silver Wood is spectacular. The Long Walk takes one to the nearby rocky shore and beyond that, some miles to the north, lies the fishing village of Craster and the stark silhouette of ruined Dunstanburgh Castle perching on its headland. Although it can be mild in summer, in winter the sea on this coast can be fearsome. Wrecks were common there in Sybil's day – the loss of the French trawler, *Tadorne*, with five of its crew, in March 1913, is commemorated in Howick Church.

Speaking to a meeting of the Women's Institute over 60 years later, Sybil said:

> I personally was very fortunate for I was born of well-to-do parents and lived in a lovely house and park – but what mattered far more than that was that I was one of a devoted family with five children and we had wonderful parents. My father[1] was an exceptional man, clever, caring and altogether delightful, who tried to teach all his children that the greatest happiness in life was to try and serve others.

She described her childhood in 1882, and how radically it differed from the modern world of her 1950s audience:

> Can you imagine a world without telephones, without motorcars, with only very few two-horse buses which went at the rate of about four or five miles an hour – without radios, television, cinemas, gramophones. All I had when I was a child was a music box which played two or three set tunes by clockwork.

And she remembered how happy and self-reliant children were even without modern media and excitements:

> Children had to make their own amusements, they had to use their brains and imaginations and act their own games – quite unlike the modern child who can in many homes often turn a knob and sit entranced in front of television. But what fun we children had and how happy we were living in a world of our own imaginations.

---

1 Albert 4th Earl Grey (1851-1917). He married Alice Holford in 1877. They had five children of whom Lady Sybil Grey was third.

But that young imagination could conjure up terrors at night time:

> When I was young we did not have electric light in our house until about 1910. I went
> to bed along a dark passage, and the gaslight threw dark shadows that seemed to clutch
> at me in my headlong flight to bed. I think I must have been a timid child, because I
> was well into my teens before I stopped taking a flying leap into bed, to avoid whatever
> monster lay under the bed reaching out and catching me by my ankle.

FAMILY

The daughter of Albert, 4th Earl Grey and his wife Countess Alice, Sybil was the
middle one of five children – Sybil's elder sister Lady Victoria Grey (always known
as Vera) born in 1878 was four years older than her, and her brother the Hon.
Charles Grey was two and a half years her senior; the younger members of the family were her sister Lady Evelyn (Evy) nearly four years younger than Sybil and the
baby of the family, Lilian, who was nine years Sybil's junior. The society in which
she grew up at the end of the Victorian era was far removed in its values and concerns from that of Britain today. The family was positioned at the apex of a social
world that included the aristocracy, the gentry and court circles. Her grandfather,
General Charles Grey,[2] was Personal Secretary to Queen Victoria, which meant that
he spent much of his time with the Royal family either in Windsor, where he had a
home in part of Windsor Castle, or visiting Balmoral, Sandringham and Osborne
on the Isle of Wight. He would presumably also accompany Queen Victoria abroad
– for example on her winter excursions to Nice in the south of France.

Sybil's paternal aunts, Countess Louisa Antrim (Auntie Lou) and Countess Mary
Minto (Aunt Mary),[3] were both ladies-in-waiting to Queen Victoria. 'Auntie Lou'
was married to William Randal McDonnell, Earl of Antrim,[4] of Glenarm Castle on
the coast near Belfast. His nickname was 'the Buzzard' and he had a reputation as
a bully – faced with a plebiscite on Irish Home Rule he locked his tenants in Glenarm village hall, placed the keys and a loaded pistol on the table and offered to
shoot anyone who voted the wrong way. Aunt Mary was married to the altogether
more stately figure of Gilbert Elliot-Murray-Kynynmound, 4th Earl of Minto,[5]
(Sybil's 'Uncle Rowley'), who preceded Sybil's father as Governor General of
Canada, and who went on to become Viceroy of India. A third aunt, Lady Victoria
(Auntie Tora) was married to the Hon. Lewis Dawnay.

Sybil's uncle on her mother's side, Sir George Holford,[6] was a mild mannered
bachelor, Equerry to Prince Albert Victor, Duke of Clarence – the scandal hit grandson of Queen Victoria. He must certainly have been a difficult charge for Sir George
Holford to look after. After Prince Albert Victor's early death aged 28, Sir George
Holford went on to be Equerry to Edward Prince of Wales (later Edward VII) and
subsequently to Queen Alexandra.

---

2 Gen. Charles Grey (1804-70)
3 Countess Louisa Antrim (1855-1949), Countess Mary Minto (1858-1940) and Lady Victoria Dawnay (1846-1922) were the three sisters of Albert, 4th Earl Grey.
4 William Randal McDonnell, 6th Earl of Antrim (1851-1918)
5 Gilbert Elliot-Murray-Kynynmound, 4th Earl of Minto (1845-1914)
6 Sir George Holford (1860-1926), son of Robert Stayner Holford and brother of Alice Holford.

Albert, 4th Earl Grey, at Howick.

On her father's side, Sybil was descended from one of the great aristocratic political families of north east England, which had been centrally involved in Liberal politics for nearly a century. Her great grandfather, Charles, 2nd Earl Grey was the Liberal Prime Minister who brought in the Great Reform Bill which cleared away the abuses of the eighteenth century 'rotten boroughs' and gave the first real extension of the electoral franchise. Her father, Albert, 4th Earl Grey, moulded many of Sybil's opinions and beliefs with his intense commitment to the Empire.

On her mother's side she hailed from the Holford family, which had made its money by supplying fresh water to London via a specially built canal. Her maternal grandfather, Robert Stayner Holford,[7] was an extraordinary man. An MP for a Gloucestershire seat, he was a very rich landowner, but more than that he was a true multi-talented 'Renaissance man'. He was an art lover and connoisseur who amassed one of the most important collections of Italian art in private hands in Victorian England, specialising in the art of the Renaissance through to the then 'modern' pictures of the Pre-Raphaelites, as well as collections of china and rare books. He commissioned the building of two splendid houses – Dorchester House in London and Westonbirt in Gloucestershire – to house this collection; and he was a notable collector of trees and plants, establishing what has now become the national arboretum at Westonbirt. Sybil's mother, Alice Holford, grew up at home in these two houses.

The Grey family owned a great deal of land, especially around Howick, but great landed estates were often short of cash as they cost a lot to upkeep and generated relatively little in rents. The Greys were encumbered with a very large mortgage, estimated at £250,000 in 1900, taken out partly to fund the lifestyle and commitments of a life in politics, and so were always in need of money. The Greys had land and titles, the Holfords had money and taste – it was a match made in heaven!

All of this was of course of little interest to young Sybil, growing up as a high spirited youngster with her brother and sisters, at home in the country at Howick Hall, or staying at her uncle's house, Dorchester House in London, with its big garden off Park Lane. Her energy was spent in riding and caring for her ponies, Chuckles and Giggles; in biking through the park at Westonbirt; or in swimming on the shore at Howick; and in playing tennis, croquet and hockey on the lawns.

Sybil was brought up in large houses and she would have been used to a world centred on the family. A big house like Howick was a world of its own, with a complete retinue of servants to look after every aspect of running the house and meeting the family's needs – from a complex mix of cooks, kitchen maids and still room maids who helped prepare the food, to the Earl's personal valet and the Countess's lady's maid, to the butler and footmen, and to the groom, stablemen and coachman in charge of the horses which were the only means of transport for riding and pulling carriages. The estate also employed an estate manager, carpenters, gardeners and other labourers on the land. A country house like Howick was an interdependent world – the family in the big house knew all the servants and their families well and Sybil would have been used to visiting tenants on the estate on holidays, on

---

7 Robert Stayner Holford (1808-92).

Boxing Day when the family literally took round boxes of food and other presents, and on church festivals such as Easter. Sybil would have knowns all the tenants' children, who were invited to a Christmas party at Howick Hall and an Easter Fair held at the vicarage. The family had a keen sense of responsibility for the wider community that served the house.

There would have been a routine of weekly church services at the church in the grounds of Howick and possibly daily prayers at the Howick involving both the family and the servants. At Easter the pews would be decorated with primroses and at Harvest Festival the church was laden with all manner of fruit and produce.

The upbringing of girls in the 1880s and 1890s was very conventional and the education they received quite restricted. Sybil and her sisters would have had lessons at home in a 'schoolroom' set apart for the purpose, taught by a governess. Subjects studied would include the '3Rs' (reading, writing and arithmetic), and at an older age the 'liberal arts' and 'humanities', history, geography, with French probably taught by a French governess – someone called Amie is mentioned frequently, and their cousins, the Parkers, were taught by a governess named Mlle. Roberti. The arts – music, dance and water colour painting – were all standard. All the Grey sisters were taught to sing and to play the piano. When they visited the Holford family houses of Westonbirt and Dorchester House, they would have been able to immerse themselves literally in the great art of Renaissance Italy which hung on the walls – the incomparable Holford collection.

By contrast, the education given to her brother Charlie was quite different as befitted the son of the family – being sent off to Eton and then to university at Cambridge. For all their advantages, her sister Evy was later to write to her friend Elsie Reford in Canada in 1907: 'men have very many chances we don't have.' In London, when not having lessons in their 'schoolroom', Sybil and her younger sister Evy would go to dancing and swimming classes with other children. At home in Northumberland, they were very active, riding their bicycles and their ponies, and playing hockey and croquet matches with their friends and neighbours. Sybil was by nature a tomboy – not wanting to be confined just to more ladylike pursuits – instead enjoying the robust outdoor life which girls of her social class had available to them – riding her pony furiously around the 'Shoulder of Mutton' near Howick, hunting, fishing and even occasionally shooting – practising with pistol and rifle with her mother and siblings.

Her parents and grandparents were huge influences on Sybil. Her father, Albert Grey, was a man whose political and social interests coalesced around his philosophy of optimism and commitment to serving others. He was a gifted speaker, able to give impromptu and persuasive speeches on many issues. An admirer of the Italian thinker, Mazzini – who advised that one's every action should be conducive to the general good 'and if it is not, desist' – Grey was a lifelong advocate of proportional representation, a keen admirer of the workers' co-operative movement, interested in garden cities and church reform, and above all he was inspired by the ideal of Empire.

He was also an impulsive figure, who sometimes dissipated his energies in a plethora of schemes and causes. His own chosen biographer, Harold Begbie, said of him 'He was so prolific a genius of ideas, fancies and imaginations that he could not narrow his sympathies to the needs of practical politics… He was not quite serious enough in an age in which democracy had begun to think seriously indeed.'

Faced with the apparent gulf between Grey's ambitions for change and his lack of impact on national politics, Begbie suggested that he was essentially too civilised and open hearted a man, without the ruthlessness and lack of principle to be a career politician. 'He never became a notable leader of men, never in any degree swayed even a fraction of the multitude.'

Decades later, Albert Grey had his own explanation:

Robert Stayner Holford
(Holford Collection, author's photograph)

I do not profess to be a party politician; I have no parliamentary ambition. My work is outside Parliament – promoting movements for the good housing of the people, for reconciling the interests of capital and labour through the application of principles of co-partnership to industrial enterprise.'

And he spoke of his ambitions for constitutional change:

For re-enfranchising the individual elector by making his vote effective through proportional representation; for federating the United Kingdom on lines which will lead to that ultimate organic union which appears to be essential to its future maintenance. I wish to work for increasing the strength of the Empire, and improving the conditions of the people, and not through coercion but by general consent.[8]

Sybil's mother, Alice, brought a more realistic and prudent strain to her daughter's make-up. The daughter of Robert Stayner Holford, she was a keen gardener and botanist who knew the Latin names of all the species of flora she encountered. She instinctively distrusted politics and tried to keep her husband Albert as far away as possible from the stress and strains of London which she blamed for his increasing

---

8 Earl Grey speaking to an audience in New Zealand in March 1914, reported by *The Auckland* newspaper (in the University of Durham Special Collections).

ill health. She was artistic – her letters and diaries are studded with tiny pen and ink sketches of people, places and plants. From her mother and from her maternal grandparents, Robert Stayner Holford and his wife Mary Anne Lindsay, Sybil inherited her love of art and of travel. There are a number of iconic images of R. S. Holford – a photograph of him in middle age, swathed in a brocaded black cape, with large brimmed black hat, looking like something between a nobleman and a stage villain; a painting of him in old age as Sybil knew him, at Westonbirt, showing him with a skull cap, posed almost like a Venetian Doge; and a marble effigy of him on his tomb in the small chapel at Westonbirt, with his hands piously clasped in prayer, like a sixteenth century knight.

PASSIONATE POLITICS

Sybil and her siblings were born into a family with a tradition of liberal political reform and action, and politics remained a lifelong interest of hers. In 1894, when Sybil was twelve, her father, Albert Grey inherited the Earldom from his uncle, and took his seat in the House of Lords. That was of course no bar to involvement in national politics, and Grey had many interests in the progressive tradition of the Liberals, but above all he was dedicated to the ideal of the British Empire. It is difficult now to understand how all embracing this devotion to the Empire was. Albert Grey saw the Empire as the fount of all progress. A friend and political associate, Moreton Frewen, summed up Grey's 'impossibly inflated view of the Empire' [9]:

> He loved it as the most beautiful thing under heaven… Under the British flag, wherever he journeyed, he found men of English speech living in an atmosphere of liberty and carrying on the dear domestic traditions of the British Isles. He saw justice planted there, industry and invention hard at work unfettered by tyranny of any kind, domestic life prospering in natural conditions, and our old English kindness and cheerfulness and broadminded tolerance keeping things together… the Empire wasn't a word to him. It was a vast, almost boundless home for honest men… but what gave him his real passion for the Empire was the knowledge in his heart that here was room provided for British genius to expand forever and ever… He loved the Empire. It was for him the supreme achievement of British genius.

Grey's vision of the Empire was big. He was a founder member in 1885 of the Imperial Federation League, which aimed to set up an Imperial Parliament to which the great dominions (Canada, Australia, and New Zealand) would send their elected representatives, adding their voices to the deliberations about the Empire's direction. The Empire was then almost at its height, covering about a quarter of the Earth's surface, and ruling a fifth of its population – an empire where the sun truly never set. Sybil inherited her father's devotion to the Empire, even if she inherited her mother's more practical and down to earth attitudes.

Albert Grey had originally succeeded his father as a Liberal MP for South Northumberland and started out as an admirer of Gladstone. But the Liberal Party

---

9 Quoted by G. Sims, *Paladin of Empire*.

faced a great watershed which split the party – the question of Irish Home Rule. In the early 1880s the Liberal Leadership, particularly Gladstone, had become ever more aware of the demands of Irish Nationalists for self-government. Gladstone's support for Irish Home Rule was partly due to hard political calculation – the 1885 election delivered a result where the Irish Nationalists held the balance of power and Gladstone needed their votes.

The Liberals who opposed Home Rule formed the Liberal Unionist Party, a separate party which went into coalition with the Conservatives, and ultimately merged with them nearly 20 years later. They did so for a variety of reasons: opposition to Irish nationalism, self-interest if they held land in Ireland, and above all commitment to the British Empire, and determination not to allow the United Kingdom to be fragmented by Irish independence.

Albert Grey was deeply committed to the Empire, and this and his family links to Anglo-Irish aristocracy – the Earl of Antrim was his brother in law – led him and his cousin the Earl of Morley to leave the Liberal Party. It must have been a great wrench to leave his friends and colleagues in the Liberals, including his cousin and close neighbour, Sir Edward Grey, a rising star of the Liberals who went on to become the longest serving Foreign Secretary of the twentieth century.

It is easy to see this break up as a straightforward division between the more progressive, forward looking Gladstonian Liberals and their more conservative brethren, concerned to protect their interests in Ireland. The case of Joseph Chamberlain[10] shows it was more complex. Chamberlain was one of the most visionary and progressive of the Liberal leadership and a towering figure in British politics. A self-made businessman and a pioneering Mayor of Birmingham, he was particularly active in slum clearance, provision of public gas and water services, and improving public health. He built libraries, swimming pools and new public parks. As an MP, he led campaigns for universal male suffrage, land reform, free public education, disestablishment of the Church of England and protection for the trade unions, all in advance of their time. But like Grey, he was a committed believer in the British Empire and feared that Home Rule would lead to Irish independence and the breakup of the United Kingdom. Chamberlain was one of the key breakaway leaders of the Liberal Unionists who later served as Colonial Secretary in the Conservative-Unionist coalition government.

With men like Chamberlain on one's side, leaving the Liberal Party must have felt less like a renunciation or betrayal of liberal values, and more like joining a mission to save the United Kingdom and her Empire. Grey and Chamberlain both held progressive views, but ultimately their belief in the absolute primacy of the British Empire marked them out as men of the late nineteenth century, not as forerunners of the twentieth century.

Politics was always discussed at home, and Sybil would have grown up with a regular succession of national figures from the worlds of politics and society visiting the family at Howick and in London. One can see from her later letters to her father

---

10 Joseph Chamberlain (1836-1914) a British politican and statesman, who was first a radical Liberal and then a Liberal Unionist.

in particular that Sybil became deeply interested in and involved with politics. And the new realignment of British politics, with a coalition of the Conservative and the Unionists, placed Grey and his family at the heart of developments and debates on political issues during the Conservative-led governments of the 1890s.

The period saw great changes which formed the backdrop to Sybil's childhood and adolescence. On the international scene, the Scramble for Africa, where European Powers competed to bring Africa under foreign imperial rule. At home the decade saw the continued rise of the trade union movement (first legalised in 1871) and the beginnings of the Labour Party which grew out of the Labour Representation Committee in 1899. Another new force was also beginning to rise – the Suffragettes. The National Union of Women's Suffrage Societies was founded in 1897 and began a long campaign for votes for women – interrupted by the First World War. Innovations and inventions were slowly beginning to change peoples' lives – the telephone had been invented by Alexander Graham Bell in 1876, and electric light in the houses of the rich was just beginning to be used (it didn't reach Howick Hall until 1911). The first petrol engine car, invented by Carl Benz, made its appearance in 1885, three years after Sybil's birth.

She recalled seeing her first motor car when she was about fifteen:

> I was bicycling up a hill in Northumberland when suddenly coming over the top I saw this strange horseless vehicle. I was so thrilled that I didn't look where I was going and my bicycle got in a rut and wobbled and wobbled right across the road in front of the car – which probably was not going more than ten or twelve miles an hour – anyhow I rolled off into the ditch and was saved.

Within the Grey family, the years before the millenium saw a series of joyous events – the birth of Sybil's two younger sisters – Evy in 1886 and her baby sister Lilian in 1891; and the arrival of her first cousins Guy Benson and Rex (Reginald) Benson, sons of her Aunt Evy Benson, in 1888 and 1889 respectively.

Queen Victoria's Golden Jubilee, held on 20-21 June 1887, celebrated 50 years of her reign, with the Queen travelling through London in an open topped landau to Westminster, and appearing on the balcony of Buckingham Palace to acknowledge the crowds. Sybil aged five was too young to see it but might have heard about it.

2
Youth (1892-1895)

Sybil's early letters, describing her life at Howick, show an exuberant youngster interested in all aspects of her life. Full of misspellings and brimming with enthusiasm, her sentences flow on without punctuation sometimes for several pages.

1892

On 16 July 1892, the day after her tenth birthday, she wrote to her mother to tell her about the presents she had received. 'I am writing without the letter being corrected as you whiched' – evidently Alice Grey was trying to make sure Sybil learned her spelling. Sybil told her gleefully: 'I got a beautiful golden watch from Uncle Henry[1] and a very nice blotting book from Aunt Helen and a beautiful paper cutter from Uncle John and very nice little French book from Amie and two lovely French books from Jeanne and her aunt, and a slate from Evy to draw on and a very nice book from Mr Green and a boat from Maggie Pope.'

Uncle Henry and Uncle John were her very elderly great uncles – Howick was the home of Henry, 3rd Earl Grey, aged nearly 90; Uncle John, aged 80, was the Rector at Houghton le Spring, County Durham, and Aunt Helen was his wife. It is not clear who Amie was – probably a French governess; similarly we don't know the identity of Jeanne but she may just possibly have been Jeanne Marie Langtry, illegitimate daughter of the actress Lillie Langtry reputedly by Prince Louis of Battenberg, who was brought up in Paris. Jeanne Langtry, a year older than Sybil, became a close friend and later married the Conservative MP Ian Malcom who accompanied Sybil to Russia. It seems just possible that Sybil and Jeanne may have known each other from childhood.[2]

Sybil continued: 'We had a beautiful birthday cake with ten candles. Mr Green, Mrs Pope and Bertie and Maggie Pope came to tea, we had a game of crickit after tea and amussed ourselfs very much.' Mr Green was the local vicar at Howick.

1　Uncle Henry and Uncle John were both brothers of Albert Grey's father, Sir Charles Grey (1804-70) – all of them sons of Charles Grey, 2nd Earl Grey, the Prime Minister (1764-1845). They were both approaching the end of their lives. Henry George Grey, (1802-94) was 3rd Earl Grey. Howick was his home. He had been a Whig MP, a Privy Councillor, Secretary of State for War and Secretary of State for the Colonies. He was reportedly quite a fiercesome old man. The Rev. the Hon. John Grey (1812-95) was Rector at Houghton le Spring, County Durham. His second wife was Helen Spalding – Aunt Helen.

2　It is not clear how the Greys knew Jeanne Langtry and her mother. A possible connection could be that Sybil's cousin, Elizabeth Bulteel, was lady in waiting to Princess Beatrice of Battenberg, sister in law to Prince Louis of Battenberg, Jeanne's reputed father, (another rumour suggested the Prince of Wales was her father). Earl Grey and Ian Malcom were corresponding by 1905.

Studio portrait of three children, London – presumed to be, left to right – Charlie Grey, Sybil Grey and Victoria Grey, probably mid-1880s (Boyd family collection).

Later that year in November, she wrote to her father two days before his 41st birthday: 'Many happy returns of the day. Yesterday I was riding with Evy, but Zulu was very fresh and was kicking a good deal, and as I was going down a hill, he kicked me off – Evy had a great triumph over me.'

1894

Two years later, in May 1894, while their parents visited Rhodesia, Sybil and Evy stayed in Ireland, at Glenarm Castle, home of their uncle and aunt, William Mc-Donnell, 6th Earl of Antrim and his wife Lady Louisa. Their children were Lady Sybil McDonnell (six years older than Sybil Grey, who was probably a heroine for the younger girl), the heir Hon. Randal McDonnell (Lord Dunluce) and Angus Mc-Donnell[3] (one year older than Sybil). Glenarm was a 'Gothicised' Castle built of grey stone, with four pepperpot towers on the coast of Antrim, 34 miles from Belfast. Louisa Antrim was Lady in Waiting to Queen Victoria.

Sybil's visit to Ireland was her first adventure away from home, at the age of twelve, to a part of Britain which in some respects felt like a different country. Sybil described their trip to nearby Castle Garron, perched on a hill overlooking the sea. 'The castle is all black and very ugly outside, no one was living in it; it is very fine with lots of armour about and some cannons that were used at the battle of Waterloo, there is a lovely view, from the windows we saw the sea and on one side a very big

3 Sybil's cousins Lady Sybil McDonnell (1876-1959), Hon. Randal McDonnell (1878-1932) and Angus McDonnell (1881-1966) – children of the Earl and Countess of Antrim.

hill all covered with gorse, it made it look very pretty.'

They collected sea shells: 'Evy and I are beginning a collection of all sorts of shells, Sybil has a big collection and has given us some, and she has two shells worth a pound. If you find any shells will you bring them home for our collection, if you please, if you can get one of the nautiluses, they are very precious.'

Sybil also looked forward to visiting her baby sister Lilian on her return: 'We are very pleased to think of seeing Baby[4] in London.'

An early family photograph at Howick. Henry, 3rd Earl Grey, is seated holding a cane. Behind him is Albert Grey with Charlie on his back. Alice Grey is in front, presumably with Sybil, the infant Evy and Victoria (Vera) at the rear, with an unknown woman – perhaps Nana. (Howick Hall Trustees)

Two months later they were back at Howick. On 13 July 1894 (just before her twelfth birthday) we have a picture of her as she was driven down from Howick to Alnwick in a small open carriage called a 'victoria', pulled by two horses called Teddy and Snipe: 'It was a lovely day and we enjoyed the drive very much, the hedges were beautiful with all the dog roses. Aunt Baba gave me five shillings to buy what I liked for my birthday. I bought a book called *The Reign of Terror* it is about the French Revolution in 1790 made into a story. I have begun it and it is very interesting. I bought a little book for Baby and we got three nice pails for the sand, one red, one blue, and one brown.'

---

4 Lilian Winifred Grey, the youngest of the five children of Albert and Alice Grey. She was born on 11 June 1891 and died in April 1895, just short of her fourth birthday.

Did Sybil remember buying the children's book on the French Revolution when she faced a real revolution in Russia 23 years later?

1895

1895 was the year that Oscar Wilde's play *The Importance of Being Earnest* opened in London and Tchaikovsky's *Swan Lake* premiered in St Petersburg.

It was the year when Sybil Grey's youngest sister, Lilian, died on 7 April just two months short of her fourth birthday. The little girl died of stomach complications (perhaps an obstruction of the gut, a family affliction) at Westonbirt – her death was registered at the nearby town of Tetbury. This tragedy must have profoundly affected young Sybil, nearly aged thirteen, and particularly her mother. The whole family would have been in mourning and attended her funeral at Howick in Northumberland where Lilian is buried.

It was also the year in which Earl Grey's passion for Empire received practical recognition in the offer of the position of Administrator of Rhodesia (effectively governor of the territory). His uncle Henry had been the Secretary for the Colonies in 1846-52, and Albert Grey had inherited his uncle's interest in seeing the colonies and great dominions well governed by men of integrity and with a mission to improve the lands they ruled. He had a visceral belief in the great mission of the British Empire – to civilise the world and to spread the benefits of English rule and customs, constitutional law, trade and civilisation throughout the world.

Shortly before his death in 1917, Grey told his biographer, Harold Begbie: 'England should be proud to lead the world's march of progress. As the centre of a vast Empire it is her duty to lead the van of civilization. She must always be ahead of other nations… To her, more than any other country, it seems to me that the fortunes of God are committed.'

Benevolent as it was in intent, this was very much a vision of a white man's universe, where indigenous peoples were assumed to be the lucky beneficiaries of British rule.

One of the key influences on Albert Grey was Cecil Rhodes,[5] founder of Rhodesia. Rhodes was a visionary committed to imperial expansion, through his creation the Chartered Company which effectively ruled and owned Rhodesia. He was a financier, a trader, sometimes a bully, always a man of action, and one who was not deterred by legal niceties or territorial boundaries in achieving his goals. In London society 'Albert Grey's approval of any scheme was virtually considered a guarantee of respectability'[6] and in 1889 Rhodes invited Grey to join the board of the British South Africa Company, which had just been granted a charter by Queen Victoria to administer Rhodesia.

A key associate of Rhodes's was Sir Leander Starr Jameson,[7] the Administrator of Southern Rhodesia. Jameson was an extraordinary and charismatic figure – a

5 Cecil Rhodes (1853-1902) founder of Rhodesia.
6 Quoted in Graham Sims, *Paladin of Empire*, about Albert 4th Earl Grey's period as Administrator of Rhodesia.
7 Footnote on page 14.

'What is my Country?' was a favourite maxim of Albert 4th Earl Grey. This probably hung in the school room at Howick. Millais' 'Boyhood of Raleigh' hangs above it.
(Howick Hall Trustees)

doctor and quite a small man, he was nonetheless a man of action, stamped with the same determination as Rhodes and committed to aggrandising the company's field of influence. In late 1895, Jameson embarked on a daring and disastrous course of action that was to bear his name – the Jameson Raid.

The British in South Africa and in Rhodesia had long resented the Boer free state of the Transvaal, which with its capital Johannesburg had recently become a centre of gold mining. Rhodes and Jameson conspired to invade the Transvaal, on the pretext of protecting Englishmen (Uitlanders) there. The British Government, although sympathetic to their aims, never actually sanctioned the raid. On 28 December 1895, Jameson went ahead and led a small armed force into the Transvaal. The British Government sent messengers ordering the raiders to withdraw immediately. Jameson and his party ignored this and pressed on, but all their plans unravelled and they were surrounded and captured. Jameson was sent back to Britain, tried and briefly imprisoned for treason. The escapade did great damage to Rhodes and the standing of the Chartered Company, whose buccaneering ways had encouraged the disaster.

Rhodes sought for someone who could take over the job of Administrator but who would nevertheless be acceptable to a critical Government in London. Albert Grey was the ideal candidate and he accepted the job.

---

7 Sir Leander Starr Jameson (1853-1917). After his disgrace and imprisonment, Jameson returned to Africa and ultimately became the Prime Minister of Cape Colony. He was the inspiration for Rudyard Kipling's poem *If*. He remained one of Earl Grey's oldest and best friends, dying just three months after him in November 1917. He incidentally also served as Vice Chairman of the Anglo-Russian Hospital's Committee.

3

1896 – A Year of Growing Up

The year 1896 was one of great changes for Sybil, aged fourteen years old, in which both her parents went to Africa, prompting her to grow up and become more independent. It was the year in which her father started his job as Administrator of Rhodesia. In May, the family moved out of Howick Hall, and stayed with relatives in the south of England, and in due course Alice Grey and her eldest daughter Vera sailed out to Africa in August 1896 to visit Albert in Rhodesia. The family was away from Howick Hall for some months, so Sybil had to live for a prolonged time with cousins, having to fit into new family groupings and environments, without relying on her parents.

Howick

The year began with Lady Mary Parker and her brother Jacky (John), the younger children of Sybil's Aunt Minnie (Lady Margaret Parker), staying for a couple of months at Howick. Mary was half a year older than Sybil and was accompanied by her French governess Mademoiselle Roberti.[1] Sybil delighted in showing her cousins her home. They fished on the pond with Donald, the head gamekeeper, and Sybil helped her cousin Mary to learn to ride: 'Mary and I ride nearly every day, she always rides Chuckles and I ride Giggles, she rides much better now, she goes much faster than at first and enjoys it immensely. I am glad to say that Giggles has not once got away with me.'

Sybil wrote enthusiastically of how she had invested her pocket money: 'I have got my money out of the bank and have put it into the stores.' The previous year, her father, a great supporter of the Worker's Co-operative movement, had set up the Howick Co-operative stores, dedicated to improving the welfare of its members, to paying fair wages and giving all the shoppers a dividend sharing of the profits. It supplied local villages around Howick with groceries, drapery, hardware, boots and shoes, furniture and fishing tackle, and continued in existence until the 1960s.

On 9 April she greeted the news of her father's arrival in Africa: 'We are so pleased to hear that you got quite safely to the Cape and that you are quite well.' Once more she included an eclectic mix of news: 'My black ewe has got twin lambs, one black and the other white. Berrington Nell has a foal. Evy can go alone on a

---

1 Aunt Minnie (or Minny) was Sybil's mother's sister Margaret (née Holford), married to Albert Parker, 3rd Earl of Morley. Lady Mary Parker (1881-1932) was her daughter and Mlle Roberti was Mary's governess. Jacky was their youngest son, John Parker (1886-1955). Their two other sons were Edmund Parker (Viscount Boringdon, later 4th Earl of Morley, 1877-1951) and Montague Parker (known as 'Monty', later 5th Earl of Morley, 1878-1962).

bicycle now.' The picture we have in these letters is of a young girl, absorbed by riding her pony and by life in and around Howick Hall.

On Easter Monday the local vicar, Mr Green, held a party for the village children in the field behind his house, with games and presents and tea: 'We all went down in the carriage to the village, we played all sorts of games with them. I had nine wooden Easter eggs with some chocolates, that I got from the Army and Navy Stores, and little toys inside them, which I gave to the others on Easter.'

The village children were understandably mainly interested in the sweets: 'They ate most of the chocolates and gave me back the eggs with the toys inside.' It was springtime and the church was decorated with flowers: 'the pew ends had daffodils and periwinkles in little moss pots, it was very pretty.'

Visiting friends in Alnmouth they were introduced to a new game: 'We played pat-ball, four people played, two on each side, there is a big pole with a ball on a bit of string hanging to it and whichever side gets the ball round the pole first wins, it is great fun.'

Sybil and her brother Charlie competed as to who could row fastest: 'I rowed Charlie round the pond in seven minutes and a half and he rowed around in four minutes, then I rowed round again in five minutes, then we pulled up the nets and there was a tench in one of them. Charlie took it and put it in the fountain.'

She was teaching both her mother and Mary to ride bicycles: 'Mary can get on and off now alone. Mother has improved a lot. Charlie and I went in front of the carriage the other day on bicycles, we went to the Low Stead and Long Houghton. Mother got on at Richardson's Lodge and bicycled home.'

On 25 April, their cousins, Mary and Jacky Parker finally left for home, so they all had a day off school: 'In the morning we played pat-ball, bicycled, hide-and-seek and climbed trees, it was great fun. Charlie, Evy and I went in the waggonette to see them off at the station, they have been here nine weeks to the day; I was very sorry to see them go.'

On their own once more, Charlie and Sybil rode their ponies energetically around the country: 'This morning Charlie and I went out riding, Charlie on Chuckles and I rode Serena; Serena was very fresh and bucked a lot but we met Graham we then went all into the Shoulder of Mutton and galloped round as hard as we could. Last Monday Charlie and I rode, we jumped the jumps.'

The family also indulged in some target shooting: 'The other day we shot at the target with a rifle and revolver. Mother and Charlie hit the bull's eye but Vera and I did not. Evy bicycles at a tremendous rate, goes down the hills and everywhere, she is not a bit afraid.'

She described her paternal grandmother, Lady Caroline Grey, aged 82, being wheeled down the rocky path to the sea: 'Granny has been twice down to the sea, since she has been here, in the bath chair, her footman pulls the chair and Wilby pushes it.' And she reported the progress of the Stores and its 'divi': 'There are 96 members in the Stores now. The last three months they have got five more pounds each month.'

On 1st May, she greeted the news that her 'Darling Daddy' had arrived in

'Bulanwayo'. She accompanied her mother to Newcastle where Countess Alice was to make a speech for the Lifeboat Saturday movement, Britain's first on-street charitable collection. It was named after a disaster on the Lancashire coast in December 1886, when a lifeboat had capsized while trying to rescue a German boat in a terrible storm – thirteen out of the lifeboat's sixteen-man crew were lost.

Sybil described the visit to Newcastle: 'At three o'clock we went in the Mayor's carriage to his house where the meeting was, there were lots of ladies and some gentlemen also. Mother did her speech very well and at half past four we had an excellent tea, we each had a cup of very good chocolate, we then went away.'

She related to her father their continued fishing exploits: 'Charlie got home from fishing just in time for luncheon, they had caught 26 trout at Burnmouth; at four o'clock Charlie and I went to Burnmouth in the little cart, we found Donald there, we caught another dozen, making 38 fish in one day, we were delighted.' Fishing was to become one of Sybil's greatest passions, particularly salmon fishing in Canada to which she returned time and again.

They paid a final visit to all the people in Howick village, telling her father: 'Frank Bickerton is much better; Mrs Foreman and Miss Thompson told us how much they liked your shawls. The Stores took £143 in a fortnight the other day.' The family was 'very busy packing' for what proved to be a ten month absence from Howick.

London

On 6 May they arrived in London, where they were to spend the next two months. They stayed at Dorchester House, the home of her uncle Sir George Holford.

London's great new attraction was the Big Ferris Wheel erected that year at Earls Court. Gleefully Sybil wrote to her father: 'In the evening from the nursery window we can see the big wheel all lighted up.' Three hundred foot high and with forty cars, the wheel broke down one evening with all its passengers still on board. Sybil wrote: 'Last Friday we heard that the big wheel had stopped and that there were 75 prisoners in it. It stopped at 7 o'clock in the night and they could not get it to move till 12 o'clock next morning.'

A resourceful lady passenger let down a reel of cotton, to which those on the ground tied a rope, enabling her to haul up baskets of provisions. Each person who was stranded was later compensated with five guineas. Sybil was envious of the adventure: 'How I should like to have been there.'

They called on the Keppels, the family of the Earl of Albermarle, relatives of Sybil's maternal great great aunt, Susan Keppel (née Trotter). This was the family into which Alice Edmondstone[2] had married in 1891 when she wed the Hon. George Keppel, son of the 7th Earl of Albemarle. However, seven years later Alice Keppel met Edward, Prince of Wales (later King Edward VII), the 56-year-old heir to the throne and soon became one of his favourite mistresses. She was great grandmother of Camilla Parker Bowles, second wife of the present Prince of Wales.

Sybil was growing up quickly. She told her father,'I am quite as tall as mother

---

2 Alice Keppel (née Edmondstone, 1868-1947).

now'. She was weighed and measured and found that she had grown two inches in height in eleven months, and was aghast to learn that she had put on a stone in weight. 'I could do without the stone's weight I can assure you. If I go on getting heavy at this rate, by the time you come back none of the horses in the stables will carry me.'

On the Queen's birthday, Sybil, Evy and Nana went to St James's Park to watch the Prince of Wales come back from the trooping of the colours: 'There were lots of people waiting for him and also some men on horseback. Uncle George[3] was with the Prince; and he saw Lord Lonsdale who was in the background on horseback, take up a man by his collar and carry him holding him up near the saddle, to a policeman about 30 yards off. Lord Lonsdale had seen the man pickpocketing.'

Their life in London was packed with activity: 'This morning Evy and I went to the swimming class. I had a lesson in diving it was great fun and I enjoyed it thoroughly. Evy and I are going to a sort of drawing class every week. The park is always full of bicycling – there were three bicycle accidents at Hyde Park Corner the other day and one person was badly hurt.'

Sybil had a keen sense of humour. She gave an account of how, alone in Dorchester House without her mother and elder sister Vera, she had to receive an unexpected visitor from South Africa whose name she failed to catch. 'The door opens and Hindmarsh announces 'Lady ... ', we could not make out the name. Mother and Vera were both out so I had to talk to this African lady. Naturally my dear brother and sister did not think of helping me in my conversation, so I had to rattle away for ever so long. At last the door opened, Oh horror! not Mother and Vera but Jenny Lindsay,[4] not knowing the dear lady's name I could not introduce them, Oh how awkward! Then arrives Hilda Keppel, then Aunt Minny, no Mother, no Vera, dear dear, then comes in Uncle Morley. At last comes the hostess, Oh what joy. They were all filed up and introduced to Lady Bower, that was her name.' Sybil's voice and her bubbling sense of humour come across very clearly.

She gave a dig at her over-pious Aunt Louisa, who was given to going to church twice on a Sunday: 'Last Sunday Mother, Vera, Evy and I went to church at Chapel Royal, we met Aunt Church, I mean Louisa.'

Her mother and sister were waiting for a telegram from her father to confirm that they could visit Rhodesia: 'Vera and Mother are on pins for your answer to their telegram as to whether they may go on 19th of June, they get more and more depressed every day.' Sybil had obviously heard that conditions in Rhodesia were getting tough with dwindling food supplies; 'I hope you're not eating rat pie and roast snake at Bulawayo.'

Rhodesia

The country that Earl Grey had gone out to administer was largely the creation of one man and named after him – Cecil Rhodes. Rhodesia was administered and effectively owned by the British South Africa Company, which raised its own troops

---

3 Sir George Holford was an equerry to the Prince of Wales.
4 Lady Jane Lindsay – a cousin, daughter of Sybil's great aunt, Margaret Lindsay.

and had fought and won a war against the Matabele, the largest tribal grouping in the territory. Rhodesia was prized for its agriculture, particularly tobacco, and minerals. Most of the good agricultural land had been sold off to white settlers after the First Matabele War in 1893.

There was a natural assumption of the superiority of the white man's civilisation and that the British Empire brought the benefits of Christianity, education, law and stability, and modern agriculture and commerce. Rhodes embodied this attitude in a colourful remark he made to Grey in Bulawayo: 'Have you never realised that you might have been a Chinaman or a Hottentot, or that most degraded of all men, a Mashona? … But you are not, you are an Englishman and have consequently drawn the greatest prize in the lottery of life.' [5]

Earl Grey went out with a number of aims. First of all, he was there to uphold the interests of the company and ensure that Rhodesia was developed, particularly its agriculture and mining. He was also intent on modernising the administration which was haphazard and devil-may-care under his predecessor, Jameson. But he was also concerned to govern as far as possible for the benefit of the native peoples and to help in their development as part of the British Empire. He would be limited in achieving these aims by the state of the country.

On arrival in Southern Rhodesia, Grey was immediately faced with another rising by the Matabele, the Second Matabele War. There was also the problem of rinderpest, a disease of cattle that threatened to incapacitate Rhodesia's transport, heavily dependent on ox-carts. Grey remained in the southern town of Bulawayo and tried to address the growing problems of disease and the threat of famine. Sybil wrote to her father half humorously: 'I hope you won't get rinderpest – or any other kind of pest!' [6]

By May 1896, however, Grey was enjoying his role. He wrote to his wife Alice: 'The administration has now been handed over to me, and I am in sole command, and I find to my surprise I really enjoy having power. I don't think that I have made a mistake so far and I have scored some good points, but it is very easy at any moment to take a false step.' [7]

To his teenage son, Charlie, he light heartedly boasted: 'I am thoroughly enjoying myself here – I am far and away the hardest worked man in the country, but I enjoy the excitement of responsibility… Fancy my being a Commander-in-Chief and riding out with my staff to inspect my Army… quite the Duke of Cambridge!' [8] It soon became evident that the native rebellion was not going to be easily quelled. The rebels had withdrawn into the Matopos hills near Bulawayo from where they could organise guerrilla style attacks and avoid pitched battles. Grey wrote home: 'They are like a running partridge in a big turnip field, very difficult to find.' [9]

---

5 Quoted by Albert Grey in his book, *Hubert Hervey: student and imperialist*, and also by G. Sims, *Paladin of Empire*, (1970)
6 Sybil Grey, 9 April 1896, University of Durham archive.
7 Quoted by Graham Sims, *ibid.*
8 Quoted by Graham Sims, *ibid.*
9 Grey to his daughter, 22.v.1896 (quoted by Graham Sims) *ibid.*

The guerrilla war continued, mining and other industries were paralysed and the company grew daily nearer to bankruptcy. A harsher tone came into Grey's voice: 'Three patrols are out hunting the rebels who disappear into the bush. Our efforts to catch them are not very successful. Until we do catch them and thoroughly convince them that this country is to be the country of the white man, and not of the black man, we must go on hammering and hunting them. They still believe that every single white man in the country in the long run will be   killed.'
[10]

The belief that large swathes of Africa could be permanently run for a white ruling elite persisted until the 1950s in East Africa, and in Rhodesia and South Africa until the 1980s; but such views feel very uncomfortable nowadays.

London

Back in London, young Sybil was enjoying the excitement of new experiences. In early 1896, the first screening of a moving picture film in Britain was given by the Lumière brothers, Auguste and Louis, at their Cinématographe Theatre. The films were made in France and its colonies. It was a sensation and a repeat showing was given in May 1896 at the Polytechnic Institute in Regent Street, London, the capital's first public cinema.

On 26 May, Sybil was taken to see it and wrote a breathless account: 'The other day I went out driving with Auntie Minnie and Mary. Auntie Minnie took us to the Politechnique[11] to see the photographs that move, you know like real life. It was delightful, the first thing we saw was a French cavalry stables and the soldiers bringing out their horses to drink, we longed for one of the horses to kick but they would not; the second was some black people dancing about and playing in the streets with a crowd round them, and a bicycle flew past; then there came the train running into the station and all the passengers getting in and out and all the bustle of a station. Then we saw a small vessel going against the wind and waves pushing it back; then we saw the launching of a big vessel, and a conjuror and several other things, it was delightful.'

The Lumière brothers specialised in short clips of film of about a minute each, blended together in a medley. The experience of film was so new that some audiences leapt to their feet in terror as the train appeared to hurtle towards them in their seats!

Sybil also enjoyed a trip to the zoo with her cousin Guy Benson, eldest son of her Aunt Evy: 'We saw the lions fed and the seal, we saw the two little polar bears and lots of other animals, it was great fun. On Monday afternoon Evy and I went to Aunt Evy's and pasted pictures on a screen with Aunt Evy, Guy, Rex and Daisy

---

10 Grey to his son, 15.vi.1896 (quoted by Graham Sims) *ibid.*
11 In August 1838, the Polytechnic Institute opened at 309 Regent Street. On 21 February 1896, the Lumière brothers' Cinématographe was demonstrated – the first public showing of moving pictures to a paying audience in Britain.

[Margaret],[12] we got pretty messy I can tell you.'

Her sister Vera and Mother were overjoyed at having received a telegram saying they could go out and visit Earl Grey in Rhodesia. But the realisation that her mother and elder sister were about to leave suddenly struck Sybil: 'It is dreadful to think that Mother and Vera are really going today week, I can hardly believe it, they are going to say goodbye to Charlie on Sunday, we are all beginning to feel a little low.'

But she was naturally positive and upbeat and reported the latest news that the Prince of Wales's horse, Persimmon, had won the Derby. 'Uncle George went and he came back radiant with joy, he said that thousands of people cheered at the top of their voices for a quarter of an hour they were so pleased. I wish I had been there to hear it.'

On the 4 June, the whole family went to the Military Tournament where they met up with her cousins the Parkers and the Bensons. They were treated to a wide range of spectacles: 'We saw Lance and Sword, the lance on horseback and the sword on foot; I think the infantry won the most often, it was very amusing indeed.' Then they witnessed a parade of the 'Sons of the Empire' – men from regiments right across the British Empire and beyond, Australians, Africans, Chinese from Hong Kong, and even Japanese. 'It was most interesting to see all the different uniforms, some of them were splendid, it was very pretty indeed.'

After the Imperial parade there were displays of horsemanship. 'Then we had the musical ride of the Royal Scots Greys which was very pretty indeed; we also had three tug of wars which were thrilling and then we had the Galloping of the Guns between posts, also the men trying to knock off the other side's hats with wooden swords, it was most amusing. Then we had wrestling on horseback, there were six red and six whites and the whites got five reds off; then the four remaining whites threw themselves on the remaining red man at once, one pulling his leg, another his arm, a third his back and so on, and they could not get him off. At last they pushed him off the back of the horse but he slipped under the horse's neck and with his hands round its neck and his feet round also, at last they got him off but he was tremendously cheered.'

There was a final display of imperial derring-do, which harked back to the Afghan wars of the 1830s and 1870s which had seen Britain pitted against the indomitable Afghan tribesmen: 'They had the sham fight between the English and the Afghans, it was thrilling.'

Sybil graphically lingered over a gory accident behind the scenes at the tournament: 'The champion swordsman of England was instructing a Captain Johnson, and he got too near and in making a straight backwards swing cut his eye right out.'

---

12 Sybil's cousins, the children of Sybil's aunt Evy Benson (née Holford, 1856-1943) and her husband Robin [Robert] Benson (1850-1929) – Guy Benson (1888-1975), Rex [Reginald] Benson (1889-1968), Con [Constantine] Benson (1895-1960), Daisy [Margaret] Benson (1892-1976) and Lindy [Rosalind] Benson (1899-1982).

Westonbirt

They visited her Uncle George's other home in the country. Westonbirt lies a few miles from the small market town of Tetbury, in the rolling Gloucestershire countryside. You go through the gates, down the drive, turn a corner and the house lies before you. At first sight it looks a little like a diminutive Castle Howard, with a central tower and wings, but Westonbirt is only a fraction of the size and is very compact. Built in 1895 by Sybil's grandfather, Robert Stayner Holford, to house his incomparable art collection, it was designed on neo-Elizabethan lines by architect Lewis Vulliamy.

The house is built in sandstone, with a grand entrance and a central tower over a rectangular hall, lit from above by a high glazed roof. A gallery runs all the way round the first floor, with bedrooms leading off it, some of the walls of which are hand painted by Robert Holford's wife Mary. The walls of the principal downstairs reception rooms are covered in expensive silk, and R. S. Holford kept his library of rare books at Westonbirt. In the 1890s the house would have been hung with exquisite pictures, ranging from Italian Renaissance masterpieces from the school of Leonardo, Titian and Sustermans, Dutch old masters by Rubens and Van Dyck, and pictures by Velazquez, Poussin and Byrne Jones.

For all its grandeur and nostalgia for a pseudo Elizabethan style, the house was built with the latest modern conveniences of electricity and central heating, and constructed around a steel frame which proved extremely strong and stood the test of time. The outside of the house is emblazoned with the family crest – the head of a greyhound – carved on the walls. On R. S. Holford's death in 1892, Westonbirt

Westonbirt, the glass houses where the arboretum was nurtured. By kind permission of the Holfords of Westonbirt Trust.

had passed to his son Sir George Holford.

The house is set in park land with splendid mature trees. Robert Stayner Holford's philosophy was that there should be no strict demarcation between the garden surrounding the house and the parkland and finally the arboretum into which it merges. The lawns spread down from the house, with a number of fine old trees, including a great cedar growing near the orangery. A small family chapel lies shadowed with trees to the side of the lawns, with memorials to R. S. Holford and his wife Mary, his son Sir George Holford and his son-in-law, Robert Benson.

Alice Holford had grown up at Westonbirt and so it was no surprise that she visited Westonbirt with her daughter Vera and the rest of her family just before setting off on a long and potentially hazardous journey to Africa.

Sybil wrote to her father: 'Here we are at Westonbirt, oh it is so lovely. We came down here yesterday afternoon from London. We had tea as soon as we arrived and then Mother and Aunt Evy and David and Uncle George went for a bicycle ride whilst Vera and I marked out the croquet ground, we two then had a game. Then when they got back they all tried all sorts of things on the bicycles, we none of us went in [till] 20 minutes past 8.'

'David' was David Lindsay,[13] heir to the twin Earldoms of Lindsay and Balcarres, ten years older than Sybil and her cousin on her mother's side. As well as her Uncle George and his wife Susannah (known as 'Tottie'),[14] her cousins the Bensons were also there.

The womenfolk, Mother, Aunt Evy, Vera and Sybil were given a lesson in basket making sitting out on the lawn. 'It was my first lesson. I think it is great fun making them. I wish you could see us under the big tree near the house all making baskets with a small basin of water beside each of us where we dip our wickers in to wet them, that is with what we make the baskets, and one table with peaches in the middle. Uncle Robin came out in his bath chair and talked to us whilst we were making our baskets.'

They were sitting under the great cedar which still stands near the orangery today.

Newells

Sybil's mother, Vera and Uncle George Holford left for Africa in late June, Alice and Vera each being presented on departure with a silver whistle and compass by Uncle Morley. Sybil and Evy spent much of July until early August at Newells, a country house at Lower Beeding near Horsham which belonged to her maternal grandmother, Mary Holford, widow of Robert Stayner Holford. It was one of the family homes Sybil knew (including Dorchester House and Lockinge near

---

13 David Lindsay, 27th Earl of Crawford and 10th Earl of Balcarres (1871-1940). He had a varied political career, beginning as junior Lord of the Treasury in Balfour's Conservative government (1903-05), and as President of the Board of Agriculture and Lord Privy seal in the wartime Liberal led Coalition government under Asquith, and later as First Commissioner of Works and Minister of Transport in the post-war Coalition government under Lloyd George.
14 Susannah [Tottie] Graham Menzies (née West Wilson) later Lady Holford (1865-1943).

Wantage) which now no longer exist.

Newells subsequently became the HQ of the Canadian Division before D-Day in World War II, then a boys' boarding school in 1947 and was destroyed by fire in 1968. Surviving rather grainy photographs show an attractive three-storey Victorian house with steeply pitched roofs and high chimneys, a croquet lawn and terraces and sheltered by trees. It was set in its own small estate which included stables, kitchen gardens and some woodland.

Sybil wrote to her father on 3 July: 'We are at Newells with Aunt Minny and B and of course Granny'. 'B' was Aunt Minny's eldest son, Edmund Parker, Viscount Boringdon (hence 'B'), Sybil's first cousin. Nineteen years old, 'B' was physically weak and suffered from dyslexia. His career at Eton came to an abrupt end after only two years, following an attack of scarlet fever. His head master wrote of him: 'Spelling ludicrous; even in words of one syllable the order of letters is often reversed.'[15] Clearly however he must have been a very engaging character as Sybil was very fond of him.

Particularly in such privileged circles, young Victorian girls had relatively little to keep them occupied. They played a lot of croquet and enjoyed the garden: 'On Sunday we all went to church in the morning and afterwards we went into the kitchen garden and ate strawberries and then we sat in shade of the wood and had a game of proverbs, it was grand fun.' After yet more croquet games against Charlie, B and Evy: 'we four children accompanied Granny into the wood, she went in her bath chair drawn by the pony; we had a delightful walk and we saw a tiny tiny baby rabbit which we caught but we put him down again, he was such a darling.' In the evening they were expected to dress for dinner, even at the age of fourteen.

Charlie, being a boy, of course returned to school at Eton, leaving his two sisters cooped up at home. One senses their isolation and boredom when Aunt Minnie told them she was going to bring B back – 'We nearly jumped up to the ceiling with joy.' The return of Sybil's favourite cousin was clearly a red letter day. She worked hard in the garden all afternoon until Aunt Minnie and B returned, when they celebrated with tea and a series of games of croquet until dinner time.

Sybil sent good wishes and advice to her father: She had been surprised to hear of the high cost of food in Rhodesia: 'Do you buy a quart of milk for 10s? I would go without if I were you.' But she ended: 'Goodbye dear Father, I wish I was with you very much indeed. I send you no end of love from your loving daughter.'

They visited a local 'attraction' at Leonardslee House, Lower Beeding; as always Sybil was interested in the prodigious and extraordinary: 'Today we are going to see Sir Edmund Loder's Museum, he has got the biggest elephant tusks in the world and a very long boa constrictor and beautiful bush elk which does not exist anymore and plenty more, we are longing to see them. I hope you are quite well in very good spirits and not eating too many cabbages at the prices of 5/6 each and eggs at 3/- each, it comes a bit expensive. It has been glorious weather.'

The next afternoon they watched a cricket match 'between Newells and some other village, Newells was beaten.' Sybil had a consuming interest in cricket which

15 Source Wikipedia article on Edmund Parker, 4th Earl of Morley.

lasted all her life. During July she attended the first day of Eton and Harrow cricket match at Lords, keeping a full record of the score, the runs and the bowling averages of both sides, and sending them in a letter to her father. Harrow went in to bat first, scoring a total of 236, whereas Eton disappointed Sybil by only managing 112 for six wickets by close of play the first day. She commented: 'So you see Eton did well at first but then there was a rot. I hope we shall do better tomorrow.'

Saltram

In August 1896, Sybil and Evy went to live at Saltram, home of her uncle Albert Parker, 3rd Earl of Morley[16] and his family – his wife Margaret Parker 'Aunt Minny', and their children Edmund, Viscount Boringdon ('B'), Montagu ('Monty'), Mary and John ('Jacky'). Sybil and Evy were to remain at Saltram until the end of January 1897, while Charlie was at school at Eton.

Saltram House, exterior 1860s, by kind permisson of the National Trust.

Saltram is a marvellous place. A magnificent white Georgian mansion just outside Plymouth in Devon, set in a 500 acre estate of woods and parklands, overlooking the estuary of the River Plym. The Parker family had owned Saltram since 1712, and had hugely reshaped it, grafting a Palladian façade onto what had originally been a Tudor manor house. The house is large and imposing and its interior and contents are still largely original, a fabulous time capsule of the Victorian era. It includes a splendid neo-classical saloon in blue and silvery grey by Robert Adams,

---

16 Albert Parker, 3rd Earl of Morley (1843-1905), Liberal and later Liberal Unionist politician.

hung with chandeliers and thought to be one of his finest interiors; a superb country house library lined with leather bound volumes, where Sybil and her cousins acted out plays for the servants; bedrooms with Chinese wallpapers (commissioned directly from China at great expense); and a huge kitchen equipped with roasting spits and copper pots and pans and an iron kitchen range, installed in 1895 just before Sybil's arrival.

The very Spartan and undecorated corridor in the servants' quarters retains the set of electric bells indicating each of the family's bedrooms and reception rooms – the entrance hall, the library, the velvet room, Lady Parker's room, the tapestry room etc.– which rang to summon assistance. Throughout the house the Parkers displayed an exceptional collection of paintings, particularly family portraits by Sir Joshua Reynolds. The family's rooms, with their ornate decoration, rich silk wall-coverings, collection of fine furniture and paintings, clearly designed to impress and set off the Morley's possessions, are in sharp contrast to the much more utilitarian passageways and rooms of the servants' quarters, which are painted in a dull brown colour known as 'drab'.

Outside are the stables – an impressive collection of loose boxes built around a central courtyard, where Sybil and her cousin Mary Parker must have regularly saddled up their ponies. A long broad front drive leads through parkland towards Plympton, while the back drive takes one to 'Stag Lodge' where the back gate is flanked by the stone statues of two stags.

The garden has wide lawns, a fine orangery, an obligatory folly, shrubberies and imposing trees, and the 'Melancholy Walk' with its burial plot for family pets. It is easy to forget how relatively close Plymouth is – a few miles away across the river – because although it can be seen in the distance from the back drive, Saltram seems to exist in a world entirely of its own of woods and rolling fields. But one can approach Plymouth closer by taking a track through woods smelling of wild garlic to the river bank at 'Saltram Beach', down along the muddy salt flats that gave the house its name. Here, Plympton is just across the river and Plymouth a few miles upstream, beyond the cast iron Laira Bridge built by the 1st Earl Morley in the 1830s.

The 3rd Earl, Albert Parker 'Uncle Morley', had been a Liberal politician, holding the office of Under Secretary of War between 1880 and 1885, before he broke with Gladstone over Irish Home Rule, and like Sybil's father joined the Liberal Unionists. Deputy Speaker of the House of Lords, 1889 to 1905, Albert Parker should not to be confused with the more prominent Liberal politician also called Morley (John Morley, 1st Viscount Morley) who was a lynch pin of the Liberal Government from 1905-15, and who had worked his way up from more modest circumstances.

Sybil wrote at least ten letters to her parents from Saltram over a period of over five months. She described a bicycle riding competition at Tavistock which was won by the person who came in last! 'The 'tortoise race' had two heats in it. The race was to bicycle one hundred yards and whoever got in last won, but you were not to put your foot down or go out of your track or you were disqualified; our track was nine yards, I came in second at the first heat as I did not start slow enough. The two firsts and two seconds of the heat had another race. I started much better and just got in the last, so I won. I was delighted, my prize was a very pretty little green velvet pin cushion with gold round it.'

She was very envious of her brother Charlie, who was leaving to go up to Howick: 'I heartedly wish I was with him though we have great fun here. We went shooting with him in the morning, we had three ferrets, two keepers and a dog. We had great fun and Charlie shot four rabbits and six rats; after lunch he went out again for half an hour to shoot near the house.'

She and her cousin Mary received their rather provisional education from a governess in a schoolroom on the top floor. One day their lessons were disturbed: 'Whilst we were at a lesson we heard a band coming up the drive. We flew to see what it was, and found it was the foresters' fête, about 30 people in all, carrying flags and a big banner, green bands over their shoulders with silver tassels to show they belonged to the Foresters' Committee. And a little boy walked in front carrying the Union Jack; they came to the front door, the band played and they wanted money for their club – I gave them two shillings, Evy one, Nana one.'

The servants held a picnic and Sybil and Mary went along too: 'There were about 30 in all, they were very merry indeed, they sang songs and all sorts of things.'

Horse riding took pride of place among her interests and activities. Her Uncle George had sent a pony from Westonbirt to Saltram, enabling her to ride along the headlands overlooking the river and sea. 'Last Saturday I went out riding with the coachman. When we got to the top of the Staddon Heights, it was a beautiful view, though a little misty – we saw all over the sound right over Mount Edgcumbe and all over Plymouth and the sea the other side.'

When she went to be measured and weighed at the stables, she was in for a shock finding she was nearly as heavy as her older cousin: 'B was weighed first and he weighed 10 st. 11 lbs. I weighed 9 st. 9 lbs., when I came here I weighed only nine stone, I can't believe that I have gained nine pounds in a little over three weeks, not months, but they are government weights and all the others are right, is it not dreadful to think of it!!!' She consoled herself that Mary weighed three pounds more than she did: 'When we got home we were all measured with a horse measure in Uncle Morley's study. I measured 5ft. 6in. and Mary the same, so she is heavier than I am for our height.' Photographs of Mary Parker show a tall, broad featured girl with long blonde hair, fashionably dressed with shoulder pads.

Sybil gives little vignettes of their daily life: 'On Monday morning we went to find mushrooms; we got some beauties. In the afternoon it rained and we played battledore and shuttlecock, it was great fun. In the evening we all had a game called honesty, which is most amusing. Aunt Minny is dreadfully occupied with all the garden party arrangements. On Wednesday we taught Mademoiselle Roberti to bicycle in the garden, Mary and I held her on and she could not keep her feet on the pedals for some time which was very unlucky, and she laughed so much that she could not do anything, but after a little while she managed to keep her feet on and then she went much better.'

Then we come to a sustained story of a riding expedition which turns into a hunt for her cousin Mary Parker who gets run away with. It shows how Sybil can tell a vivid narrative, with pictures of her Uncle Morley galloping along in search of his daughter, and the conversations they have with strangers in their west country dialect during their search.

It began with Uncle Morley, Sybil and Mary setting out to ride to Membland, a nearby country house. 'Directly Mary got out of the stables, her little grey pony bolted and she ran away along the park and out of an open gate into what they call the lane. Uncle Morley and I did not like to follow at once as we thought that we should excite her animal so we only galloped after her when she had turned a corner.'

Arriving in the lane they found no sign of Mary: 'When we got out of the park we were at the Stag Lodge we had nothing to tell us which way she had gone as there were three roads all going in different directions.'

They tried each road in turn: 'We saw a man at the gates and we asked him if he had seen a young lady on a grey pony, "No Sur I have coom up from the Laira Bridge[17] and I have seen nobody," so that decided that she did not go that way and Uncle Morley went up the high road towards Hardwick till he met a man to say she was not that way, then we turned and went down the last road.'

'We cantered along the high road for some time, each corner we expected to see Mary, but we did not. Then we got to a place where they are making the railway. As we cantered past we shouted 'Seen a young lady on a grey pony? "Yes Sur passed over the bridge and went along that road," Was she going fast said Uncle Morley, "Pretty smart Sur." We at last found her coming along the road at a walk, a man had stopped her.'

They returned home in the late afternoon just in time to change for church: 'We arrived five minutes late which was rather dreadful as our seats were right up in the front and the church being full it was not amusing to pass between everybody.'

Rhodesia[18]
In Rhodesia, the war to put down the Matabele rebellion continued unabated, further complicated when the despised Mashona also rebelled. It meant huge costs to the administration which had to pay both for the company's own forces as well as the British Government troops sent from South Africa, at a time when the country's agriculture was in crisis.

At the end of August, Countess Alice Grey, by now in Rhodesia, wrote to her children (Sybil, Charlie and Evy) back home: 'A determined effort has to be made to bring this war to a close... starvation stares the country in the face... feeding the Army's horses and mules would alone necessitate the arrival of over 1000 wagons of mealies in the next two months before the rains – besides the food needed to feed the population.' And she was not sure when they would return home: 'I feel if Albert's worries increase that I shall long very much to remain here and see him

---

17 The Laira is the tidal estuary of the Plym near Saltram.
18 This section based on Graham Sim's account in *Albert, 4th Earl Grey: Paladin of Empire*.
19 Lady Alice Grey to her children, 28.viii.1896, *ibid.*

through the worst of them.'[19]

Grey and Rhodes were keen to negotiate peace with the Matabele quickly, using Rhodes' contacts and prestige, in order to avert a famine and to enable the natives to go back on the land and sow new seed for the following year. They were delayed by clashes with Sir Richard Martin, representative of the British Government, who believed that only he should be responsible for peace negotiations and the surrender of the Matabele. Eventually, two months of patient and persistent negotiation by Rhodes paid off in bringing the rebellion to an end. Grey met the warriors at an Indaba on 13 October, urging them to return to their land, warning them it was useless to fight the English and promising them fair treatment.

Grey then set about reducing the number of imperial troops which the government had sent to deal with the rebellion. He also brought in a new native policy, to help re-establish some link between traditional tribal structures and the government, paying the chiefs a small monthly salary of £5 and making them responsible for the conduct of their people, dealing with minor disputes, collecting native taxes and helping ensure that native labour was available for both public and private works. A native commission was also set up to hear their complaints and bring them to the attention of the government.

Grey realised that land was also an issue. The government wanted the tribes to go back to farming, but much of the best land had been given or sold to white settlers after the 1893 war, and the remaining government land was poor and inadequate to meet the needs of the tribesmen. He therefore began negotiating a system by which the natives would contract with white landowners and become tenant farmers, to allow them back onto the land to plant and harvest vitally needed crops.

Saltram again

Meanwhile, at Saltram, a disparate collection of house party guests arrived for a week's shooting. They included her uncle Sir George Holford, her father's cousin Bessie (Elizabeth) Bulteel,[20] Admiral Freemantle[21] who couldn't shoot straight – Sybil dismissed him contemptuously 'such a swell down', General Hume and finally Mr Vivian and his wife Lady Jane Vivian. Sybil liked Mr Vivian – 'he is a very nice man and a deadly shot, never wounds but whatever goes in his reach came down plomb; I wish you would ask him to Howick to shoot, it is always nice to have a good shot.'

She relished the shoot: 'At half past eleven, Aunt Min, Bessie B, Mary, Evy and I all sallied forth to see them shoot Hardwick Wood; the beaters went down the wood in three lines with a good bit of space between them. In the Stag Lodge road stood Mr Vivian with Aunt Min, Bessie, Mlle Roberti and Evy behind him; a little farther off General Hume stood, also an excellent shot, and the Admiral stood in the high road just about 60 yards in front – he was in the best place but he was put there because he never hit a bird and all that he missed went over to the other two.

20 Elizabeth Bulteel (1832-1916), granddaughter of Charles, 2nd Earl Grey, and Lady in Waiting to HRH Princess Beatrice of Battenberg. A distant cousin of Sybil's.
21 Admiral in charge of Portsmouth.

Then Uncle George was in the field higher up and there were four outsiders shooting, two of them excellent shots. Well, Uncle George shot 38 birds at that stand and he had fired off 92 cartridges, while Mr Vivian they say shot 116 birds at that one stand and hardly ever missed, that was good was it not. Then we went to lunch at the Stag Lodge.'

A family photograph shows Stag Lodge, the ground heaped with dead game birds and a very satisfied gathering of 'guns', family and beaters. The day's bag was large even by the standards of the time at a big country house: 'Pheasant cocks 422, hens 238, making altogether 638 birds, fourteen hares and four rabbits, a tame pigeon and a partridge.' (Sybil's arithmetic seems to be faulty, as the number of pheasants shot appears to be 660).

Stag Lodge shooting party, 1894. Lady Morley and Earl Morley are fourth and fifth from the right of the photograph. By kind permission of the National Trust.

That evening Bessie Bulteel, lady-in-waiting to Princess Beatrice of Battenberg, played the piano for the household in the schoolroom: 'Aunt Min, Uncle George, Uncle Morley, Mlle Roberti, Amie, Mary, Evy, Jacky and I were the company played to. She played some very pretty things and we enjoyed it very much.'

Sybil ended the letter to her father: 'Now listen attentively, this next week or the week after we are going to write and send you our Christmas letters with not to be opened till Xmas on them and mind you do not.' She added rather enviously: 'Aunt Evy and the Benson family are to stay at Howick till the end of January.'

She was pleased to hear that her mother and Vera had left Salisbury on their way back home but was sorry that as a consequence her father was now alone: 'You must feel very low and dull without them and I am very sorry for you, but of course I am very pleased myself that they are coming home sooner.'

A week later, on 18 December, Sybil was excited at the approach of Christmas. She had bought presents for the family: 'I will tell you what I have got: *Robbery under Arms*[22] for Evelyn, Aunt Minnie says it is a delightful book. A very good knife for Charlie with 'Howick' engraved on it, he said he wanted one badly. One of Dickens' books for Nana and a little sort of glass thing for your dressing table for Amie. Two pocket books for B and Monty, a paint box for Jack and last of all a pocket ink stand for Mary.'

Mary Parker had just celebrated her fifteenth birthday and they got a day's holiday off their school routine at Saltram: 'These are her presents: from Aunt Minny she got two beautifully bound volumes of Molière with very good engravings, from Uncle Morley a silver whistle and compass at the end like Mother and Vera were given just before starting in the train on the way to Southampton, then from Mademoiselle Roberti 'Corniel'[23] bound just like Molière. I gave her a very pretty frame, Evy furniture for her doll's house and Amie a little silver frame and Mrs Wethy a very pretty silver thimble.'

In the morning they went for a walk in the wintery countryside: 'It was a glorious day, Mademoiselle Roberti, Mary, Jack and I all went out for a long walk, it was very, very slippery as it had rained all last week. The last two nights it has frozen hard, so you can think in what state the roads were in. We went to see the canal and it was frozen so hard that throwing a stone hard at it did not break it. We have written in all haste for our skates and we hope to have some fun.'

In the afternoon they had tea with Aunt Minny: 'We had a glorious tea, such a cake it was, sponge with chocolate on one side and sugar on the other, it was very good and we had crackers with fireworks in them and we had the fireworks in the dining room – they were most amusing.'

It was an age when families read books aloud to each other, so Aunt Minny read them *Peter Simple*,[24] a story of a young British midshipman in the Napoleonic Wars. 'We all like *Peter Simple* very much. Then we all went to dinner, little ones too, and after dinner we played Rubicun Bezique,[25] Mary and Aunt Minny against B and I – we played four games, and B and I won three of them. Evy and Jacky played the fool and were quite wild – wild fits of laughter the whole evening – and Aunt Min said it was a good thing they had drunk no wine for she would have thought it that. They went to bed at ten and Mary and I at half past ten.'

---

22 *Robbery Under Arms* is a classic Australian novel by Rolf Bolderwood (a pseudonym for Thomas Alexander Browne). It was first published in serialised form by *The Sydney Mail* between July 1882 and August 1883.

23 Pierre Corneille was one of the three great seventeenth-century French dramatists, along with Molière and Racine.

24 An 1834 novel by Frederick Marryat about a young midshipman's journey from adolescence to adulthood.

25 Bezique originated in France in the early nineteenth century as Bésigue. It was extremely fashionable in Britain in the early twentieth century.

Her next letter was to her mother, presumably now in Cape Town waiting to embark for the journey home. Sybil had grown much more independent over the year and she reproached her mother: 'It is the first time in my life that for Xmas we are not all together at Howick, what a pity that we have broken the rule but it cannot be helped. Charlie is at Howick, I wish he was here or rather that I was there.'

But Sybil was delighted that her mother and sister's ship, the SS *Dunvegan Castle*, would soon land nearby at Plymouth: 'How delighted we shall all be to see you.'

In her letter to her father she told him how she wished they were all together at home at Howick, 'but it cannot be so I will not moan', and she gave a round up of the news. Her Uncle Morley had lumbago; her brother Charlie had gained a distinction at Eton for his verses; the Parker's middle son Monty[26] had arrived home from France 'quite the Frenchman'; the Howick stores were reported to be doing very well indeed. 'All the frost is thawed now. Aunt Minny is reading us the *Prisoner of Zenda* every evening. This evening a band from Plymouth is coming to play and the choir come to the house and sing carols.'

She spent Christmas in a state of high excitement at the thought of the imminent return of her mother and Vera, and the prospect of at last going back to Howick.

---

26 Montague Parker, second son of Albert Parker.

4

1897 – The Year of Jubilee

The previous year had been a crucial time for Sybil who was growing up fast. She was now fourteen and a half years old and for the last five months she and Evy had lived with relatives, completely without their parents who were both overseas in Africa. Sybil's confidence had grown in the course of the year, and she felt confident of her own abilities and was willing to criticise her parents for their decision that for the first time the family should not be together over Christmas.

Over New Year, Sybil, Evy and her cousins Mary and Jacky went by train to an elaborate children's fancy dress party at nearby Port Eliot, the home of Henry Eliot, the Earl of St Germans, and his family. She told her mother:

> Mary was dressed in your Karmandy peasant dress, Jacky as a mattadore (I do not know if I have spelt it right, I mean a Spanish bullfighter), Evy as a Roman peasant in Mary's old dress, and I as a Neapolitan peasant. We got ready directly after lunch, had tea at four and then showed ourselves to the servants and we went in the carriage to Plymouth to catch the five o'clock train.

The Parker and Grey children were dressed in improvised fancy dress clothes and were thoroughly upstaged by the children of the host family who were magnificently attired.

> Lady St Germans came in dressed very smartly (it is her house) with John who is five years old, he was dressed as a courtier of Charles' the first time in yellow satin with a sword. Then in came Eliot, the St Germans' oldest son, he is at Reigate, he was in a bright blue suit with gold and powdered hair and so on, it was very pretty indeed (he was a courtier of Louis the 16th King of France's time). There were about 35 children there. One little boy of four was dressed as a General of the Coldstream Guards about a hundred years ago, it was quite perfect. Oh how we enjoyed ourselves.

The dance was a 'cotillion' – a courtly eighteenth century dance which involved dancing in a square formation and choosing partners:

> Presents went round and you took one out and presented it to whoever you wished to dance with. We had polkas and waltzes and all sorts of dances. There were lots of different amusing ways of finding who you were to dance with. We danced all the time and enjoyed it very much. We got home at a quarter to 11, after having enjoyed ourselves thoroughly.

A couple of weeks later, the family acted out the *Bengal Tiger*, an old comic play, for all the servants and stablemen. They staged it in Saltram's splendid library:

Evelyn was the first to go in, she had a long skirt on and her hair done up. Charlie followed her (reading the newspaper) he was her brother; then Mary, the housekeeper, took a letter in, she was in a dark blue rather old-fashioned dress with an apron and a cap on; her hair was of course done up, it was also made grey with powder. Aunt Minny was Miss Yellowleaf, she was dressed in a smart dress with a shawl over it in an old-fashioned way and her hair brought down over her ears, a bit of black ribbon over her forehead with a brooch in the middle, and an old fashioned hat trimmed with yellow satin and black satin, she did look funny. Jacky was dressed as my Indian servant with a turban on, he looked very nice. I had a pair of flowery chintzy sort of trousers on, bedroom slippers, flowery waistcoat, Uncle Morley's old dressing gown, and eye glasses. Aunt Minny had painted wrinkles on my forehead. But it went off very well and the servants laughed a good deal.

At last, on 29 January, suffering from a heavy cold, she triumphantly described how they all trooped down early in the morning to Plymouth to meet her mother and Vera on their return:

Aunt Min, Mary, Evy and I drove to Plymouth to await the Dunvegan's arrival. We first of all went and got tickets to allow us to go on the tender and then we met Charlie who had slept at Plymouth as the Dunvegan was due at five in the morning. The Donald and Currie office told us that they had had headwinds from Madeira and that he could not tell when she would come in – he said that the last boat was 30 hours late.

They went to the Royal Hotel[1] to wait until the ship arrived. Aunt Minny read to them and they went for occasional walks, but were restless waiting for the message that the ship had been sighted. 'At one o'clock we all had lunch, then Aunt Minny read to us and then Aunt Minny, Mary and Evy went out for a walk and they left Charlie and me on guard telling us that if any news came we were to take a fly and go straight to the Hoe where they were going to walk to.'

At last, at 3.30 the great news came:

Charlie jumped up and left everything pell-mell, papers lying all over the room and so on. Charlie got me a fly which I got into and drove full speed to the Hoe whilst Charlie walked to the tender. I met them halfway coming home, then we all drove to the tender.

When their boat neared the *Dunvegan*, a snowstorm began, preventing them getting alongside. 'When we did get up to her we could not see Mother and Vera anywhere on deck. We were rather disappointed but they soon came up, we were quite delighted to see them, they looked very well indeed and Vera said that the voyage home was delightful. We went to the saloon to have some tea. We were two hours on board and enjoyed it thoroughly.'

They finally landed in a blizzard and returned to Saltram. Sybil was pleased: 'It was delightful having them back again, we had a very noisy dinner and we all went to bed at 11 o'clock.' The next day, they caught up on news from home and abroad:

We talked all the morning and in the afternoon we went out for a walk. It was a lovely

---

1 The Royal Hotel no longer exists in modern Plymouth, and the Grand has become a block of flats.

day and as Vera had never been to Saltram it gave her a good impression of the place.

Coming home they rehearsed the *Bengal Tiger* once more in order to act it that evening to Mother, Vera, Uncle Morley and all the servants. 'They had all seen it before but they laughed just as much the second time.' This was the last letter she wrote from Saltram.

London

A fortnight later, back in London at Dorchester House, Sybil told her father of the move: 'We arrived here a week ago from Saltram. I was very pleased to come up. I think that Mother and Vera are looking very well and pretty.'

Her mother and Vera had decided to hold a 'Drawing Room' reception at Dorchester House – these were formal afternoon receptions at which women showed off their finest gowns: 'On Wednesday after the drawing room a lot of people in court gowns are coming here to tea, Auntie Tora,[2] Aunt Evy and several others, it will be most amusing to see them.'

Sybil longed to return home: 'I am so glad that we are going soon to Howick it is such a long time since we left. It is nearly a year since you went, I do hope you will come home soon.'

Her sister Vera was enjoying herself very much indeed back in London. Sybil gave a Victorian teenager's modern view of the city. 'There are a good many smart ladies in London now… I have not seen any motor cars in the streets or park yet but several people have, I think they must look very ugly.' How different London must have looked before the advent of cars!

She had heard that her father had missed having letters from his children. On 26 February she wrote: 'After that delightful letter from you to me about "the frown upon the Administrator's face when he saw no handwriting in his children's hand," I feel I ought to write you a nice letter, so I will try.' She described the family's Sunday visit to the Chapel Royal, with her Auntie Tora (Lady Victoria Dawnay), Uncle Lewis and Aunt Louisa (Lady Lousia Antrim), and then visiting Lady Sybil McDonnell, Aunt Louisa's daughter, who was about to get married. Sybil was unimpressed by her cousin Sybil's husband to be, Vivian Hugh Smith: 'Vivian came in whilst we were there, I had never seen him before; I think he looks nice but nothing wonderful.'

She described, too, the drawing room reception that Mother and Vera were holding at Dorchester House, associated perhaps with the forthcoming wedding:

Tuesday was the day before the drawing-room so of course Mother and Vera went to see their gowns and bouquets were all right. Wednesday – the great day. At 11.30 the hairdresser came and did Vera's hair first and put in the veil and feathers and so on and I was watching the proceedings and doing innumerable messages; the bouquets arrived at a quarter to one and I was sent to fetch them on the way down. Mother's was very pretty made of lilies of the valley and flame coloured tulips; Vera's was only lilies of the valleys but very very pretty.

2 Lady Victoria Alexandrina Grey, (1846-1922) sister of Albert, 4th Earl Grey. She married Lt.-Col. Hon. Lewis Rayan Dawnay.

Soon Granny arrived, then Mrs Green and Aunt Helen. At 1.30 Mother and Vera appeared, Mother was looking very well with Granny's tiara and Vera I thought was very pretty in white of course. Aunt Evy came in to show herself before going to the drawing. It was a very pretty gown of red, green and gold. Mother's gown was white satin embroidered at the bottom with silver piètas and the train was of a very pretty white rich stuff and embroidered with gold and lined with satin of a light blue. Mother's dress I thought was the prettiest.

While Mother and Vera entertained their guests, Charlie took Sybil and Evy to see a stage show given by the 'illusionists' John Maskelyne and George Cooke, famous for dramatic wizardry like 'The Floating Lady', who gave regular performances at the Egyptian Hall, Piccadilly. Some of the finest magicians of the day were among the performers, and they were also involved in projections of very early cinema.[3]

When we got home Mother and Vera were already there and a lot of other people; there were altogether nine 'trains' – I mean nine ladies in court gowns – and about 35 other people to look at them, it was most amusing to look at them all...

In early March, Sybil faced two milestones in her young life – the wedding of her first cousin Sybil McDonnell and the imminent departure of her old nanny, Nana:

Tomorrow is Sybil's wedding, just think of it; it is to be at two o'clock. We are very unhappy as Nana is going to leave us and go to the Duke of York[4] to take his children. She is going to leave us on the 17th which is very sad, we are all very low at the thought of her going, she has now been with us eighteen years, she is very low about going poor thing. I wish she was not going. But of course it is good place for her and I ought to look on it on the bright side.

It was obviously a great honour for Nana to become the nanny of the children of the Duke of York, who later became King George V. George and his wife, Princess Victoria Mary of Teck (known as 'May') had married in 1893. Their first son, Edward (who as Edward VIII later abdicated the throne) was born in 1894, and their second son George a year later. Princess Mary, their third child, was born in April 1897. So Nana was taking over the care of the young royals at a very early stage in their lives. She probably got the job partly through the Greys' long standing contact with the royal family – Sybil's grandfather had been Secretary to Queen Victoria and Aunt Louisa and Aunt Mary were ladies in waiting.

They enjoyed the entertainment in London: 'Last Saturday, Mother, Vera, Charlie, Evy and myself went to the pantomime. It was very amusing indeed and there was an excellent juggler in it who did wonderful things. Evy had never seen a pantomime before so it was quite a new sort of thing for her she liked it very much.'

On 12 March 1897, the great day came when she returned to her Northumberland home:

We have at last arrived at Howick, we have been away ten months, I have never been away for so long at a time. I am delighted to get back, the only thing that spoils coming

3 Source: Who's Who in Victorian Cinema (website).
4 The future King George V, second son of Edward VII.

Dorchester House, the drawing room, © The Holfords of Westonbirt Trust.

back is Nana leaving us so soon, she goes on Tuesday and today is Friday. Is it not very sad that she is going, but I suppose it is a very good place to get.

Vera, Charlie, Evy and Sybil gave their nanny a gold watch chain as a leaving present: 'a very pretty one which goes once round the neck and then hangs, it has red enamel beads about three inches apart all down it. Mother gave her very pretty dark blue and gold links, and Granny gave her a very pretty ring with five pearls.'

Back at Howick after their long absence, the Grey children visited friends and neighbours: 'We went in the little pony cart with Uncle Robin's pony, we went round by the Red Stead and saw Graham and Mrs Graham, he says all the horses are very well also my sheep; then we went on to the Grange and saw Mrs Ronaldson, Lina, Heta and Tim,[5] they are all very well and very pleased to see us back.'

Sybil still playfully reprimanded her father: 'Do you know that in nine days it will be a year that you have been away, it is shameful and if you do not come home at once I shall come out and fetch you myself – (private: a thing I should like very much to do). Everybody here thinks you have been away quite long enough.'

---

5 The 1891 Census for Howick Grange lists the following: William Matthewson (coachman, domestic servant), Mary Matthewson (wife), James J. Ronaldson (head, living on own means), Harriet Ronaldson (daughter, born about 1864), Lilian Ronaldson, nickname 'Tim' (daughter, born about 1868), Jane Armstrong (servant), Annie Cairns (servant), Mary Wood (servant), Isabella Dixon (servant).

On 19 March she wrote again. 'We do enjoy your letters so. The only thing you never mention in them is when you are coming home. I do hope it will be soon.'

Thrilling news had arrived of one of Earl Grey's escapades in the veldt: 'How exciting it must have been to go with the police and storm the fortified kraal. Mother was not altogether quite pleased with you for going.'

Sybil described a visit to their tenants on the Howick estate: 'Mother, Vera and I went down to the village to pay visits. We saw Mrs Farmer, old Frank Bickerton and Jane Turner. Jane has been very ill indeed lately but she is much better now; she asked me if I remembered that she told you to run away if there was any fighting but I am afraid that you have not done her bidding. I think we are all going to see the new Mrs Craster this afternoon in the little cart.'

A week later, on 26 March, she upbraided her father for not telling them that he had been ill: 'Well, so who told Mother nothing about a fever attack that somebody had and only said that he had had a bilious headache? Oh fie, fie for not telling his wife the truth but we heard it through a certain little bird' – presumably via one of her father's aide-de-camps.

And she related a lighthearted hockey match involving the family, their friends and neighbours in Howick and Alnwick:

> Well yesterday we had a big hockey match on the grass. The Ronaldsons got up the match and Howick played Alnwick in the Shoulder of Mutton. This is the Howick team: Bob, Lena and Tim Ronaldson (Bob was our Captain) and Captain Rose a friend of theirs and an excellent player, then Mother, Vera, Evy and I and Mr Green, that makes nine.

Three other members of the Howick team failed to turn up.

> The Alnwick team was: Captain and Mrs Scott, Mrs Bremer, Mr and Mrs Jervis, Mr and Mrs Williams, Mr Lever, Jack Tate, two Tate girls and another man – so they had twelve and we had only nine, but they gave us two of theirs, Jack Tate who was no use and a Tate girl.
>
> Mother kept goal all the time so she did not get hot but she played very well indeed. I was a forward wing so I did nothing but run most of the time, you see I was to be always a little in front of the ball on the side so if there was fighting for the ball in the middle of the ground one of our side could hit it to me on the side so that I should take it up the side of the ground to the goal. Unfortunately we were beaten by one goal. It was most amusing.

Practical jokes were much in vogue and the Grey sisters certainly indulged in them. Sybil described an elaborate joke they played on their friend Lilian Ronaldson (nicknamed 'Tim'), who was preparing to go out to India to marry her fiancé, Mr Goodwin, a soldier. They sent her a package, enclosing a neighbour's visiting card (used without her knowledge):

> We have had great fun this week in making April fools. We made Tim[6] a beautiful one. We sent her a little parcel beautifully packed and addressed to Miss Lilian Ronaldson, Alnwick, and in the inside was a little pink cardboard box and a visiting card of Mrs

---

6 Evidently 'Tim' is a nickname of Lilian Ronaldson.

Bosanquet's with "Best wishes for all future happiness," written on it. Inside the box was a little green leather case and inside the case a neat little bit of paper with this written on it: "April fool from Vera, Sybil and Evy". They told us that everybody roared with laughter, they were at breakfast and Bob laughed so much that he could not eat anything afterwards.

They turned the screw, getting more mileage out of the joke:

We also made a fool of her in another way for we wrote her a letter from a 'Mrs Stoner', saying that she was going to India to join her husband Captain Stoner, and she proposed to chaperone Tim on the way out. Tim answered the letter and refused the offer. And she wrote to Mr Goodwin[7] her future man and asked him if he knew the Stoners as we had put in the letter that Mr Goodwin was an old friend. Bob looked through the Army List all yesterday morning to see if he could find Captain Stoner's name – of course he could not. But it was a great success and they all were taken in by it.

She gave a picture of their everyday life: Evy increasingly liked riding with her, Sybil fished the pond and Mother was improving her bicycling: 'she can get up little hills now and down decently big ones.' Animals were also dear to her heart: 'There are two dear little puppies in the kennels, spaniels, both dark brown and one has little white legs, they are three months old but they already carry little baby rabbits very nicely.'

The family picked daffodils to decorate Howick Church and also to send to London for a charity in the East End. 'Yesterday Mother and I got a clothes basket full of daffodils and we have sent them packed in a hamper to Mr Barnett, Jude's Vicarage, Whitechapel,[8] London, for the poor people, I hope he will like them.'

The local vicar, Mr Green and his wife, gave an Easter Fair and tea for the Howick village children. Bob Ronaldson and Sybil's brother Charlie acted as clowns and Sybil described the fun:

They came to the show in my little cart and the pony, with a large gold placard stuck up in the front of the car with "Messrs Broal & Co, Bookmakers" embroidered in red on it. Besides themselves in the cart it was full of cricket bags, hat boxes and I do not know what else which they called their luggage. They were dressed in dust sheets all done up for the occasion, with animal heads and moons and stars cut out and stuck on in different stuffs red, blue, black and yellow. Their faces were powdered all over with flour and they had cochineal on their faces in beautiful red designs.

They played the fool beautifully. 'They had in a hat box some little silver paper

---

7 Lieutenant General Sir Thomas Herbert John Chapman Goodwin (1871-1960), known as Sir John Goodwin, was a soldier and medical practioner, who served in India on the North West frontier, and in France in World War One. He was Governor of the Australian state of Queensland between 1927 and 1932. He married Lilian Isabel Richardson. They had no children.

8 Canon Samuel Barnett (1844-1913) was an East London clergyman who, between 1872 and 1893, held the living of St. Jude's parish in Whitechapel. In 1892 he became canon of Bristol Cathedral, a post he kept until 1906 when he became canon and sub-dean of Westminster Abbey. Barnett is perhaps most famous, however, for founding the university settlement movement and being Head of one of the first settlement houses: Toynbee Hall, a position he would keep for over twenty yuears (1884-1906), source Lucinda Matthew Jones.

balls which were filled with flour and when they threw them [at] somebody the paper broke and they got all the flour over them.' Sybil's Mother had bought eleven shillings worth of sweets and crackers at the Stores in the morning, and the family tied them up in little parcels. The clowns threw these packets of sweets and crackers around to all and sundry. 'We stayed amusing the children till 5.30 and then we went home – we began cheering as we left and the children took it up at once and cheered better than any of us have heard them cheer before.'

Rhodesia

We left Earl Grey struggling to put down the uprising by the Shona people, having settled the earlier rebellion by the Matabele.

The suppression of the Mashona took time. The tribes were headed by chiefs who were believed to be spirit mediums and thought themselves invulnerable, attacking and burning the kraals of friendly natives. The British mounted infantry conducted operations against these guerrilla fighters, attacking the kraals of the rebels. Earl Grey himself was sometimes involved in police raids. One of his aides, Mr. Howard, wrote to Lady Grey, apparently with an element of tongue in cheek exaggeration: 'You would be shocked at the fierceness of Lord G. He rides through the veldt seeking whom he may shoot and has to be restrained from committing most inexcusable murders. His Honour was everywhere a rifle in hand, blazing away now and then with the best of them.'[9] It was certainly a curious turn of events for a man who was never cut out to be a soldier.

Earl Grey tried to encourage the Shona to surrender by a policy of leniency in murder prosecutions, prosecuting only the actual murderers and not the leaders who had instigated the killings. But the Shona fought on doggedly and the rebellion was only ended after Grey's return to England. In other areas, Grey was not able to reform the civil service administration of Rhodesia, partly because of the military emergency and partly because he lacked the experience of civil service practice to institute reforms. The author of Grey's obituary twenty years later in *African World* said: 'Grey was perhaps not the best man who could have been chosen to deal with such complex problems – racial and administrative, political and economic. He was too accessible to casual influences and momentary impressions.'[10] He nevertheless steered Rhodesia through a perilous time and helped restore the reputation of the Chartered Company and of the territory it ruled.

London

That summer saw Queen Victoria's Diamond Jubilee, celebrating 60 years of her rule. It included a review of the Fleet at Spithead at which over 165 warships saluted her son, the Prince of Wales. It culminated with the Queen's triumphal parade through London on 21 July.

Sybil was an eyewitness to both events and left excited accounts of them. Sybil, her mother and her sister Evy watched that Tuesday morning as the Queen

---

9 This section is based on Graham Sims' *Paladin of Empire.*
10 Quoted in G. Sims, *ibid.*

processed from, Buckingham Palace to St Paul's Cathedral in an open carriage drawn by eight horses. She wrote to her father:

> At about ten o'clock the colonial procession passed us, most of them looked very well indeed and they received a hearty reception, especially the Rhodesian Horse with Mr Gifford at their head. Then came the Queen's procession headed by Captain Ames of the 1st Life Guards, the tallest man in the army – he is six foot eight inches and just behind him were four of the tallest troopers of the 1st Life Guards and they looked small beside him. The procession was very beautiful and Lord Roberts looked magnificent on a little white Arab... When the Queen came the cheering was tremendous, she looked so nice and well and was bowing right and left, she had a lot of white lace about her front which made her look very bright. The cream coloured horses looked splendid in their purple and gold trappings.

They spent the afternoon at the zoo and in the evening set out on foot to see the illuminations. Grosvenor Square and Berkley Square were prettily decked with lights but the crowds were too great for them to get into Piccadilly.

The following Saturday Sybil was asked if she would like to see the Review of the Fleet – 'I nearly jumped out of my skin with excitement.' Sybil, her mother, Aunt Evy, Vera and her cousin David Lindsay set off from Waterloo by special train on the two hour trip to Spithead. It was packed and it was all they could do to get seats in a compartment kindly lent them by Lord Dudley. When they arrived, they embarked on separate Cunard liners which sailed out to meet the fleet carrying dignitaries – Alice, Vera and David boarded the *Campania*, the boat carrying Members of Parliament, while Sybil and Aunt Evy went one better and sailed on the *Danube* (the House of Lords boat):

> At 10.30 we glided out of the dock as the fleet was five miles off. It was perfectly calm and we passed the *Campania* who followed after us as it was the House of Commons boat, we waved vigorously to Mother, David and Vera as we passed. At about 11.30 we got in sight of the fleet – it was lovely and we went up through the line of our own men of war, there were five lines of them each five miles long all decked with flags, it was quite beautiful.

The huge flotilla, including over 30 battleships and some 60 cruisers drawn from just the Home Fleet, clearly demonstrated the might of the Royal Navy and the Empire.

During the Jubilee, Dorchester House displayed double rows of lighted candles in every window and four dozen Chinese lanterns on the trees in the garden. Her uncle Sir George Holford gave a splendid ball there in July, attended by both the Prince of Wales and the Duke of York. Sybil's mother and Aunt Evy acted as hostesses. It was one of a number of balls given to celebrate the Queen's Jubilee – the most famous being the elaborate Fancy Dress ball given at Devonshire House on 2 July, with the Duchess of Devonshire dressed as Empress Marie Theresa and attended by a galaxy of London society.

Sybil described the preparations for ball held at her family's home:

> It was rather an exciting day as we had to get everything ready for the ball that night.

We arranged all the flowers for the two libraries and the two sitting rooms upstairs –
the rooms did look so nice, and as for the tent all along the terrace [it] was lovely quite
lovely, all the tables were laid and the three royal tables in the middle had the most
beautiful erections of red roses on one table, pink on the other and white on the third.
The flowers at the bottom of the staircase and all the rest were done by Goodier quite
beautifully and the lighting all over the ballroom, the supper tent and the hall was beautiful.

The guests began to arrive:

At half past ten we were all dressed and then half an hour later people began to come
steadily but never too many at once. When about 50 people had arrived, TRH the Duke
and Duchess of York arrived and Mother had to go off with the Duchess into the ballroom, but she soon gave her over to Aunt Evy to talk to and went back to the top of the
staircase to go on receiving people. At 12.25, TRH the Prince and Princess arrived with
Princess Victoria of Wales accompanied by Aunt Alice as lady in waiting; the Duke
and Duchess of Teck arrived pretty early.

Sybil and Evy danced until dawn. 'Of course it was more amusing as the old pomps
left as well as the Royalties, but the Prince and Princess of Wales did not go to bed
till after three in the morning. We went to bed at a quarter to five after having enjoyed the ball very much indeed. Everybody said it was the best of the season.'

A week later she burst into a peal of joy: 'Hurrah, Hurrah, at last you have started
from the Cape and in less than no time you will be in bonny old England again,
how delightful it will be to see you again. I hope you will have a good passage and
attend every meal and also have nice people on board. Howick is longing for your
return as well as its inmates.'

Sybil ended with the words: 'I hope this is the last letter I have to write to you
for a long time.'

Earl Grey finally returned at the end of the summer, and this letter was indeed
the last she wrote to him in Africa. There are no more extant letters from Sybil for
the remainder of 1897 or for 1898, but we can imagine the family's joyful celebrations when Earl Grey did rejoin them.

5

Young womanhood: Italy – first trip abroad (1898-1901)

The year 1898 saw births and deaths which epitomised the end of an older era and the start of a new. Chief among the deaths was that of William Ewart Gladstone, four times Prime Minister, on 19 May at the age of 89. He had inspired the young Albert Grey who most probably attended his funeral in London. Artists and writers of the Victorian era who also died in 1898 included Edward Burne-Jones the Pre-Raphaelite romantic artist collected by Sybil's grandfather, and Lewis Carroll, creator of the Alice books. Births, heralding a new age included the singer Gracie Fields, the dancer Ninette de Valois, Henry Moore the sculptor and C. S. Lewis the writer.

On his return, Earl Grey busied himself with managing his estates and its finances, which were in constant need of attention. As a large landowner of estates which did not yield very large rents or income, and with a colossal overhang of debt which had built up over the years (the family had a mortgage debt of about £250,000 in 1900), he faced an endless uphill task to 'make ends meet', at least in the context of his class and the circles in which he moved. His dilemma was not that uncommon – other great landowners had to sometimes move out of their houses and let them out – for example Edmund Parker, the 2nd Earl of Morley had let Saltram to tenants and moved abroad with his family in 1861 in order to pay off the massive debts left by his father. The family of Sir Lawrence Jones, father of Sybil's brother in law 'Jonah', was to do the same with their family seat at Cranmer Hall in Norfolk, moving to Switzerland for several years when Jonah was in his early teens in the late 1890s – Jonah found it a liberating experience.

Albert Grey made continual attempts to improve his finances by investment in all sorts of concerns, usually ending disastrously, sometimes as a result of the advice he took from family members.

Grey was appointed Lord Lieutenant of Northumberland from 1899 to 1904 – the King's representative in the county. The family would have been involved in attending many ceremonial occasions; they would also have entertained a great deal at Howick. Sybil (aged sixteen in July 1898) and particularly her sister Vera (aged twenty) would have had an important part to play in the family's public events.

Grey was a man who was naturally given to sudden enthusiasms and to backing sometimes unpopular or impractical projects. This is reflected in some memories of Grey by people who knew him when as Lord Lieutenant he was involved with Northumberland County Council. An observer sympathetic to Grey, but aware that his character needed explaining, wrote[1]:

> Lord Grey had always been a man of varied fads and sympathies. He has been well described as a man of impulsive enthusiasm, an opportunist-idealist, a man of great public spirit, of keen intelligence and passionate patriotism. There have been complaints that his sympathies are too alert and numerous. Fanciful and fantastic proposals used to be put forward by him on the Northumberland County Council.

A more trenchant critic of the contradictory aspects of his character wrote: 'He is a Liberal who supports Conservatives, a Temperance reformer who runs pubs, a Free Trader who takes the chair for Mr Chamberlain, a Peace Crusader who promoted the Boer War;' but the writer concluded generously or perhaps ironically: 'Really what it amounts to is that Lord Grey has thought keenly about everything, and that all these activities are merely a sign of his many sidedness.'

The politics of Britain in the late 1890s saw a Conservative Government in coalition with the Liberal Unionists, led by Robert Gascoyne-Cecil, 3rd Marquess of Salisbury. Salisbury was Prime Minister three times (1885-6, 1886-92, 1895-1902). He was the first Prime Minister of the twentieth century and the last to lead his Government from the House of Lords.

Son of a family that had held high office since Lord Burghley in the reign of Queen Elizabeth I, Salisbury was instinctively conservative, voting consistently against the extension of the franchise, opposing even the conservative Benjamin Disraeli's proposed extension of the suffrage to working class men in 1867, and Gladstone's Reform Bill of 1884 which would have extended the vote to two million rural workers. However, he was not completely insensitive to the need for change. As Prime Minister, in 1885 Salisbury introduced the Housing of the Working Classes Bill to alleviate the desperate conditions of the urban poor. In coalition with the Unionists, his government promoted a number of radical reforms, such as establishing democratic county councils, measures for the provision of small holdings for rural workers and the extension of free, compulsory education to the entire country. Joseph Chamberlain, the Unionist leader, wrote with some surprise: 'I have in the last five years seen more progress made with the practical application of my political programme than in all my previous life. I owe this result entirely to my former opponents and all the opposition has come from my former friends.'[2]

In foreign policy, Salisbury preferred to hold Britain aloof from the alliances that the European powers spent much time in forming – a policy that became known as 'splendid isolation'. However, he finally ended this policy through the Mediterranean Agreements with Italy and Austria, and the Naval Defence Act of 1889 which authorised the spending of an extra £20 million on the Royal Navy, then the biggest ever expansion of the navy in peacetime.[3]

Chamberlain was Secretary of State of the Colonies in Salisbury's third government, 1895-1902, and wanted to use the Colonial Office to expand and popularise the Empire. He wished to foster closer links between Britain and the white settler

---

1 Quoted by Graham Sims in his book about Lord Grey, *Paladin of Empire.*
2 Wikipedia entry on Chamberlain.
3 Source: based on Wikipedia.

colonies (especially Canada, Australia and New Zealand), and reform the empire as a federation of Anglo-Saxon nations. Chamberlain stated: 'I believe that the British race is the greatest of the governing races that the world has ever seen… it is not enough to occupy great spaces of the world's surface unless you can make the best of them. It is the duty of a landlord to develop his estate.'[4] Earl Grey certainly agreed with these views and they represented the prevailing opinion and mindset which existed when Sybil was growing up and forming her own view of the world.

Italy

In April 1899, Sybil went on her first foreign adventure, to Florence in Italy. She was visiting her great Aunt Margaret Lindsay,[5] widow of Alexander Crawford Lindsay, 25th Earl of Crawford and 8th Earl of Balcarres.

Margaret Lindsay lived for most of the year at the Villa Palmieri, at Fiesole, overlooking Florence, which had been bought by her son, James Lindsay, 26th Earl of Crawford, in 1873. The Villa Palmieri was a place of legends. A large patrician villa atop a hill, of a deep orange ochre colour, set amid dark cypress trees, it was stocked with Lindsay's fine collection of Italian sculptures and paintings. It had been built in the fourteenth century, and was owned by the Humanist scholar Marco Palmieri in the fifteenth century. It featured marvellous sun drenched gardens which swept downhill towards Florence in a series of five descending levels, with an elaborate lemon garden at the bottom. These gardens were reputed to be the setting of Boccaccio's *Decameron*, where young aristocrats retreated from the Black Death raging in Florence to tell stories, and which Boccaccio had described as 'Paradise on earth'.

A big retinue of relatives were staying there during Sybil's visit in 1899. In addition to Sybil's great aunt Margaret Lindsay, who owned the villa, there was the Hon. Frederick Wood Meynell, a cousin of the Greys, his wife Lady Susan Lindsay, and his children Francis, Robert ('Bob'), Everard, Charles and Mary. Another cousin was Margaret Aline Majendie (usually just called 'Aline'),[6] granddaughter of Margaret Lindsay, together with her mother, Lady Margaret Majendie ('Cousin Minnie') who owned Hedingham Castle. Aline was ten years older than Sybil who looked up to her. Margaret Lindsay's sister, Mary Anne Holford (Sybil's grandmother), was also staying at the villa, though she also had her own suite of rooms at one of Rome's prestigious hotels. Mary Holford plainly loved Italy, and may well have encouraged her husband, Robert Stayner Holford, to scout there for paintings for his magnificent collection of Italian Renaissance art.

Finally there were guests who visited for lunch, particularly the Connaughts. Prince Arthur, Duke of Connaught and Strathearn, was third son of Queen Victoria. He was married to Princess Louise Margaret of Prussia, great niece of the first Emperor of Germany, Wilhelm I. Their children were Princess Margaret Victoria, like

---

4 Quoted in Wikipedia on Chamberlain.
5 Margaret Lindsay (1824-1909).
6 Aline Majendie was a granddaughter of Margaret Lindsay, and a distant cousin of Sybil's. She went on to marry Field Marshal Francis Wallace Grenfell.

Sybil born in 1882, Prince Arthur Frederick (known to Sybil as Prince A), Princess Victoria Patricia (known as Princess P, and sometimes Princess Patsy). The family was partly German – their family name was Saxe-Coburg-Gotha, famously changed to Windsor during the First World War on the orders of King Edward VII. The Connaught's were enjoying a holiday break in Italy, before setting out on what was perhaps an annual visit to the family home at Coburg, in northern Bavaria.

Sybil gave a description of the luncheon visit of the Connaughts: 'They arrived 12.30 and left 3.15, pretty decent isn't it. We had a room for our lunch, that is to say, the young people: Aline, myself, Prince A, Bob, Princess P, King – that was the proper order for ages. We had a much jollier lunch than the big people. Prince A is very nice he has such a nice face but he is not very strong. I expect he has grown too much. He is not allowed breakfast and is given soup, port wine and glasses of cold water at all hours of the day.'

Sybil, a budding photographer, visited the famous Boboli Gardens, at the foot of the hill beneath the villa. 'They are beautiful; I am going to take my camera there some of these days.' Sybil must have been stunned by Florence, perhaps the most perfect Renaissance city in Italy, with its Duomo and Baptistery, its royal palaces and galleries, and the River Arno flowing through its centre.

In mid April she wrote to entreat her mother to come out and spend Whitsuntide in Rome. 'Granny told me that she would pay for your rooms and all that, your only expense would be to come out and go back. Mother darling if you love me come. I am sure you would like to see Rome and we should be so happy together, oh it would be almost too good to be true.'

One evening the household went to see the famous entertainer, Lepoldo Fregoli in Florence. Fregoli was a 'quick change artist' known for his extraordinary impersonations of famous people and his exceptionally fast changes of role. He had toured Brazil, Spain, the United States, and London in 1897 which he took by storm. Sybil described their outing:

> Last night we went to Frigoli at L'Aremona Nationalle. We had to see a stupid little play first of all which thank heavens did not last long. Then on came the Great and Marvellous Frigoli. He entertained us for two hours. He is marvellously clever, we were all astounded with him. On an average, for we timed him with great care, Frigoli took six seconds to change – he would be a man with whiskers and he would go out of one door and come in at the other in six seconds as a woman, a fat old woman with grey hair. He was good.

Fregoli entertained them with a bewilderingly varied series of impressions:- he played all twelve different characters in a play, he danced, he was a clown, a conjuror who flunked his tricks, he sang falsetto in the character of a German lady. 'He was Bismarck, Victor Emmanuel, Garibaldi, Fauré and others. The Florentines are very critical but they were immensely pleased with him. Then he conducted the orchestra like all the different composers – he made himself up exactly like them and conducted as they did.'

About a fortnight later, on 5 May, Sybil wrote again to her mother describing her last view of Florence: 'It was a lovely evening when we left Florence, Jenny took us to the station and saw us off. The sunset on the hills was lovely; altogether the hills, woods, old castles and all helped to make it enchanting, and then at several places along the line there were huge patches of that big light blue iris growing wild; that would have pleased you I think.'

She was now staying in Rome with her grandmother[7] at the Hotel Bristol. Her father and sister Vera were due to visit: 'Every hour is bringing closer Daddy and Vera's arrival, oh what a welcome I will give them! I shall dance the whole day that they arrive.' She promised her mother that she would dress up warmly when going round visiting cold churches. She had heard nothing from her brother Charlie, and ended with: 'Why does not the Boy write to me? I am longing to hear what he is doing.'

There are no further letters in 1899. We can only imagine Sybil's delight in taking her father and sister around Rome, showing them to the Coliseum, the extraordinary Pantheon, and the Roman Forum, as well as the vast basilica of St. Peters with its huge square, and the Castel Sant'Angelo lowering over the banks of the Tiber. She returned home with them after their visit, and presumably spent the summer and autumn at Howick, or in London, or with relatives at Westonbirt.

1900

The turn of the century was clearly an important event for Sybil and for the country, whether she was at home in Northumberland or up in London. There must have been celebrations of the birth of the twentieth century, with firework displays and bands and parties, both in the capital and across the country in places like Newcastle and Alnwick in Northumberland. The new century saw important changes – in politics the year began with the founding of the Labour Party (originally called the Labour Representation Committee) in February, and culminated with the victory of the Conservative and Unionists parties in coalition at the 'Khaki election' in December. The year saw the outbreak of the Second Boer War, beginning with alarming and unexpected British reverses at Ladysmith and at Spion Kop, followed by British victories at Mafeking and Pretoria later in the summer.

It was the year that Sybil turned eighteen, and in which she would normally have been expected to become a debutante. Young ladies from rich families 'came out' for a 'season' – their introduction to society. Frances Campbell-Preston (Sybil's niece) described it in the 1930s as 'a series of parties – in fact an upper-class marriage market'. The season would begin in London at the annual Queen Charlotte's Ball, at which dressed in their finest gowns the young debs would curtsey to the Queen (later generations curtseyed to a cake!). It continued with society balls at great houses, with the chance of meeting with lots of marriageable young men. Frances Campbell-Preston wrote 'It was great fun. I was in love all the time and I never stopped dancing.'[8]

Another feature of society was the country house party, with a select guest list staying for the week or weekend. Some were linked to balls of the season, but by

---

7 Mary Anne Lindsay (died 1901), wife of Robert Stayner Holford.
8 Article by Frances Campbell-Preston (source online).

and large they were social events in their own right – some just held for family members, others with a much broader guest list including the rich and famous.

There is a wonderful album of country house parties attended by the Greys. It includes photographs of houses and houseguests, their signatures and occasionally jokey cartoons and comments. The album covers nearly 30 visits to country houses across three and a half years from June 1900 until December 1903, predominantly in the autumn of 1903. It also has pictures of visits to Canada in 1902 by Vera Grey, and to Malta in the winter of 1902 to 1903 by Vera and Sybil.

It includes a roll-call of important families and great houses – family names such as Cavendish, Harewood, Astor, Percy, Lambton and Balfour – and houses such as Cliveden, Garrowby, Drummond Castle, Bamburgh Castle, Patshull and Greystoke. It was also a window into life with a wide range of relations – the Mintos, Holfords and Greys, at Minto Hall, Westonbirt and Howick. The album belonged to either Vera or Sybil.

Upper-class Edwardian society was a close-knit elite, with many great families knowing each other very well and intermarrying. But it was also changing and opening up to a much wider range of people from the wealthy middle class who were also welcomed at these house parties.

The next series of letters come from Sybil at the family's rented London house at 1 Connaught Place, just around the corner from Marble Arch. She rode every morning in Rotten Row, the sandy avenue leading through Hyde Park. On 29 June, she wrote to her mother who was visiting Germany, outraged that a neighbour, Mr Blenahasset, should mistake her as being weak or foolish:

> He said to me, 'I heard of you in the row the other day.' I said that we rode every morning but did he hear anything particular. Yes, he said, 'I heard that you shrieked! The person who told me looked round when they heard the shriek and saw it was you.' I was horrified, I said it was a base slander and asked him to tell me who told him, but he wouldn't, he said that I did not know the person, but they knew me well by sight. I wonder who else they will tell this story to. I am very much annoyed, because I don't usually ride along the row shrieking.

Sybil was offended that anyone would think of her as weak or silly, shrieking with excitement or alarm. And she took the offender to task for spreading the rumour.

She outlined the activities planned for the following few days: Princess Victoria (daughter of the Connaughts) was coming to luncheon – and Sybil and Vera decided to take her on to see Lord Rowton's houses a new chain of hostels built in London, by the Victorian philanthropist Lord Rowton to provide decent accommodation for working men. Following that they were due to go to the opera, where Aunt Lou had been given the Queen's box.

They were staying at Buckhurst Park in Sussex, the house rented by the Bensons from the Sackvilles (the family of Lord De La Warr). As well as her cousin Angus McDonnell, Sybil mentions for the first time Arthur Grenfell, who was to become Vera's husband and a major influence in Sybil's life. Her cousins, the Bensons, had moved to Buckhurst in 1899 and it became a wonderful family home, with its own golf course and cricket pitch put in by Robin Benson for his sons, Guy, Rex and Con, as well as beautiful gardens. In her book on the Bensons, Jehanne Wake describes family life at Buckhurst:[9] 'If the gardens were the perfection of Buckhurst, music was its joy. All the Benson children were musical, and their talent was fostered by their father's deep love of music and his musical parties, a feature of Buckhurst.' A patron of the Royal College of Music, Robin Benson would regularly invite a college quartet to stay and play from Saturday until Monday. Rex Benson was able to play the piano by ear – Sybil wrote admiringly: 'A song or tune has to be whistled to him once and he can immediately play it, a very great gift.' Rex would often lead the singing from the piano deep into the night, with the young people seated in circles on the floor.

The Benson family are immortalised in a series of charcoal sketches by the fashionable artist John Singer Sargent. They show Robert Benson and his wife Evy, and their sons Guy, Rex and Constantine ('Con'). The portraits show three very similar young men, all with the Benson features, but conveying their individuality – the sensitive, rather shy Guy Benson, the more assertive set chin of Rex and the self-possessed Con.

Her cousin, Aline Majendie, visited Sybil in London, devastated by the death in the South African War of the young Second Lieutenant, the Hon. Charles Cavendish,[10] killed at Diamond Hill near Pretoria. The young man was perhaps Aline's fiancé or relative. 'She did not want to stop in London for a night because she dreads meeting any of her friends as she says that she is so changed since she saw them, before Charlie Cavendish was killed.'

The young soldier's father, Lord Chesham, is also described as 'absolutely broken hearted, quite an altered man.' The personal tragedies and losses of the Boer War have nowadays been forgotten, eclipsed by the much greater loss of life in 1914-18.

Meanwhile her sister Vera was honoured to be chosen as the only young woman to meet the Duke and Duchess of York during their visit to Patshull Hall, the Earl of Dartmouth's home in Shropshire. Nana, the Grey's old nanny, had recently gone to work for the Yorks. 'Evy heard at the dancing class from a cousin of the Dartmouths that Vera is going to be the only girl to meet the Yorks and that they had not succeeded in getting a single young man. Vera was just a little depressed when she heard this.'

Sybil kept her mother up to date with developments in London, and relayed the news that the family had decided to keep the lease for the Connaught Place house for another year. She also informed her mother: 'My money is going very fast, I am very much afraid that I shan't be able to hold out this year.'

We have another of Sybil's wryly observed stories. The weather was excruciatingly hot ('127 in the sun, 85 in the shade') and Vera had entered for a swimming competition:

---

9 Jehanne Wake, *Kleinwort Benson: the history of two families in banking* (OUP, 1997).

10 2nd Lieutenant the Hon. Charles William Cavendish (1878-1900), 17th Lancers, was killed in action at Diamond Hill, near Pretoria, South Africa, 11 June 1900, aged 21. He was the son of Lord Chesham.

At about 12 o'clock we went to the Bath Club to see Vera compete for the gold medal. The place was simply crowded, the result being that everybody used their handkerchiefs very freely. Vera did everything quite beautifully and was only beaten by Lady Constance MacKenzie by three marks, Lady Constance got 27 and Vera 24.

The result did not come as a surprise:

Vera did not expect to get the gold medal, she got the silver one, as Lady Constance who is as strong as a horse has been swimming every day for two hours. She bathes for the whole of the year round and remains for two hours in the sea; she even bathes, in Scotland, when there is snow on the ground.

Lady Constance was the daughter of the Earl of Cromartie and was born in the same year as Sybil. She was independent and unconventional, and became a superb dancer and sportswoman. A decade later, her entry in *Every Woman's Encyclopedia* for 1910-12, read:

Lady Constance has earned the reputation of being the most unconventional and daring personage in smart society. She has carried everything before her as a swimmer; has explored parts of India in which no other white woman has trod; has lassoed cattle in Texas; started the fashion among women of wearing a kilt for shooting and fishing in the Highlands, and of riding astride in Rotten Row, while she appeared at the Palace Theatre, London, in a series of the classical dances made popular by Miss Maud Allan.

Photographs of the young Lady Constance show a confident, rather round faced girl, with long dark hair, in a tweed jacket and tie, smiling at the camera.

That afternoon Sybil, together with Vera, her father, her aunts Tora (Victoria) and Lou (Louisa), and cousins Mary Parker and Sybil Smith, went to a royal garden party. 'We had great fun there. There were about 6,000 people. I saw the Queen three times quite quite close, she looked so well and so bright, but very hot poor dear. I was delighted to see her so close because I have never seen her except during driving through Hyde Park where she and the Princess were driving in a low victoria.'

Before going on to a dance later that evening, Sybil and her cousin Angus McDonnell enjoyed a dinner alone: 'Father dined out, and Vera dined with the Jeunes, so Angus and I had a little tête-à-tête, we played piquet after dinner and then joined the merry dancers at 10.30. Angus and I never enjoyed ourselves more, I don't think Vera did either. We danced till four and were last to leave the house.' Angus and she were obviously attracted to each other and enjoyed each other's company. It is clear that Sybil was hugely enjoying the novelty and entertainment that London had to offer.

There are several photographs of Angus McDonnell, showing him skating at Government House in Ottawa and earlier on at Glenarm Castle, sitting on an 'Otto Dicycle', an early type of cycle with huge wheels either side of the cyclist and tiny rear bogies to keep balance.

The family were worried at having no news of her cousin Guy Payan Dawnay, son of her Aunt Victoria and her Uncle Lewis Payan Dawnay, who was serving with the Coldstream Guards in the war against the Boers in South Africa. As it happened, Guy Dawnay was safe and served with distinction in South Africa and then later at Gallipoli in the First World War. Another cousin, Monty Parker, second son of Uncle Morley and Aunt Minny, was also serving in South Africa: 'Aunt Minny had a long letter from Monty the other day, he said that he was quite well and was enjoying himself very much.' On his return home from South Africa, Monty was treated to a hero's welcome by the little town of Plympton, near to Saltram.

By this age, Sybil was already a confirmed aficionado of the game of cricket, and she remained a firm supporter all her life. She described the drama of that year's Eton and Harrow cricket match, a contest between the two premier schools. It is still played today at Lords where one can hire a nineteenth century stage coach as an exclusive grandstand from which to watch the game from the boundary line. Sybil described the mounting tension of a match that at the start looked like a straight forward win for Harrow:

> The anxiety was awful and it aged us all ten years. I don't think that I have ever seen a more exciting thing.

Harrow had begun with a mere 125 runs to make to win and with a comfortable two and a half hours to do it. But after making only 35 runs, they fell apart:

> Cookson, the Captain, was bowled! Their best bat, Mr Alex Brown's brother, was bowled by the last ball of the over and the first three balls of the next over took three wickets, so that was four wickets in four balls running. Nothing can describe to you the wild enthusiasm and joy when the fourth wicket fell, we absolutely stood up on the coaches and roared!! ladies too!

The result came down to a single ball:

> Well all the wickets went down and the last man came in and seven runs to make to win. We were all absolutely trembling with excitement and then as each ball was bowled, you heard 'Hush' go round the ground and then absolute dead silence, one could have heard a pin drop; then an absolute roar 'Well played', 'Well fielded', then they made a four and they had equalled us, would it be a tie? – then another stroke, and they won.

She concluded: 'I never was so excited; I hope I shall never be more so.'

The following week, on 21 July, her father and Vera set out for Patshull Hall, to where the Duke and Duchess of York were staying as guests of the Earl of Dartmouth. This was presumably the occasion when Vera was 'the only girl to meet the Yorks.' Two relatively new additions to Vera and Sybil's circle of friends were Arthur Morton Grenfell,[11] 26 years old, and his younger brother, Francis Octavius Grenfell, aged 20. Arthur would shortly become Vera's husband and play a major part in the future of the Grey family.

It was a hot summer: 'Yesterday it was 95 in the shade; it was rather funny driving through the Park as most of the horses had on sorts of hats (straw with holes

---

11 Arthur Morton Grenfell (1873-1958). He was married first to Lady Victoria (Vera) Grey – Sybil's elder sister – and later to Hilda Lyttelton.

for their ears and a red puff on the top) and the coachman and footman in straw sailor hats.'

While Vera visited Patshull, Sybil went to stay at Elibank, an elegant house on the Thames at Taplow, belonging to the Grenfell family. She described an excursion on the River Thames near Taplow with friends and relatives:

> I met the Dawnays at Maidenhead. All the Dawnays (except Alan and Guy), B, Captain Tryon, Mr Beckwith, Mr Thornton, Mrs Howard and Colonel Follet. We took three big boats, three of the men could not row as they had bad arms, two of them having [been] shot in the arms, so B and I rowed one boat, Vera and Colonel F another, and Uncle Lewis the third.

Her relatives in the party were her cousin 'B' (Edmund Parker), Uncle Lewis (Hon. Lewis Payan Dawnay, husband of Sybil's Aunt Victoria), and presumably some of Uncle Lewis's children Marion and Margaret. The injured men had clearly been wounded in South Africa.

They started at Maidenhead and rowed upstream: 'We rowed right up past Cliveden to Cookham, had tea there and then rowed back to Mr W.G.'s backwater and had dinner on the bank by his boathouse. Angus joined us to dinner.'

Angus is of course her cousin, Angus McDonnell. Sybil concluded:

> After dinner the rest rowed back to Maidenhead and Angus and I walked up the hill to Elibank. There was no object in going up to London that night so both Angus and I slept at Elibank and came up early next morning. I had breakfast at 9 o'clock with Madeleine at Harley Street.

Angus McDonnell was clearly a close friend. When Sybil travelled with her father to the Yukon, nine years later, she made a special arrangement to stop their train to meet Angus near Banff in the Rockies where he was working. There is really almost no evidence at all of what might now be called Sybil's 'love life' before she married at the age of 40. It seems that she and Angus were attracted to each other, but Angus ended up marrying another woman, Ethelwyn Sylvia Arthur Jones, known as 'Susan', in December 1913.

Returning to Northumberland on 27 July, Sybil rejoiced in the beauty of the Howick garden: 'It is a joy to be here and everything is so green and beautiful. The terrace is very pretty – the roses are a dream.' She painted her mother a picture of the garden's glorious variety and colour:

> The crimson rambler on the terrace wall is glorious although not fully out yet, but I am afraid that most of the tea roses will be over before you come back. The two big herbaceous borders in the old garden are very pretty and are almost too full. The delphiniums are very fine, and also the sweet williams, beautiful. The sweet peas are only just begun, but there are some very pretty different colours. The Japanese irises are not half so good as last year but perhaps it is a little early for them. The carnations are not out yet, but there are thousands of buds and they look very strong and healthy.

Her sister Evy had ambitions as a pianist and Sybil reported on the programme her governess had mapped out: 'Miss Westall wants me to ask you how much you want Evy to do till you come back. She proposes that she should do two hours of regular music and an hour of French and German. Evy is practising now and then we are going to play tennis at the rectory.' Sybil found Miss Westhall altogether too sentimental for her taste: 'There is only one thing that annoys me in her and that is that everything is, "sweet".'

1901

1901 saw Sybil's change from adolescence to young womanhood. The year heralded great changes to the life of the nation, beginning with the death of the old Queen Victoria on 22 January and her funeral at Windsor on 2 February. The Queen was nearly 82 and had been on the throne for almost 64 years. In many ways she literally embodied what it meant to be British, and her death must have left most of her subjects with a great personal sense of loss. We don't know whether Sybil and her family were in London when the Queen died, or whether she was at Howick. Earl Grey was most probably one of those invited to the funeral in St Georges' Chapel, Windsor Castle, as his father had been the Queen's personal secretary. His sister, Louisa Antrim, was invited but was unable to attend as she was in Canada where her brother-in-law Earl Minto was Governor General.

Another landmark was the 1901 Census. On the day of the census, 31 March, the Grey family, or at least part of it, was living at Howick Hall. The return for Howick Hall lists the family members as Alice Grey ('head of household'), Victoria (Vera) Grey and Sybil Grey. Clearly Earl Grey, Charlie and Evy were all somewhere else, perhaps in London. The Howick return lists a further seventeen people living at Howick Hall, including a cook (Annie Jeffery), three lady's maids, three laundry maids, four housemaids, a dairy man, a stillroom maid, a scullery maid, a butler (Malcolm McCullen), and two footmen.

As well as the complement at Howick Hall, there were people living in other houses and dwellings of the estate, who were plainly employed at Howick. There were six men living at the Howick stables – headed by the coachman, William Meecham, and the second coachman, Charles French, together with four stablemen. The farm steward, John Butterfield and his family of four, lived at Howick Red Stead; Donald Campbell, head gamekeeper and his family of seven, lived at 3 Howick Village; William Shaw, under gamekeeper at 1 Howick Village; and John Urquhart the joiner at 2 Howick Village. There was also Thomas Foreman, the sawyer, and his family; Archibald Copland the caretaker at Howick Grange; and Henry Richardson, another joiner, and his family, at South Lodge. James Thompson, sawmill labourer, lived at the Pasture House with his family. The estate was plainly very well served, and others in the Howick neighbourhood also played a part.

However the greatest change in Sybil's life was the marriage, in July, of her elder sister Vera to Arthur Morton Grenfell. The wedding took place on 23 July in St George's Church, Hanover Square, well known for society weddings – a London ceremony would have catered for more guests than one at the bride's home at Howick in Northumberland.

The groom's family, the Grenfells, were a distinguished military family –

Arthur's uncle, Lieutenant General Francis Wallace Grenfell,[12] was Governor of Malta (1899-1903). Arthur himself was one of thirteen children, nine of whom were sons (hence the names Septimus, Octavius and Nonus for the seventh, eighth and ninth). Many of the brothers were professional soldiers, and five of them were to die on active service. The eldest son, Pascoe St Leger Grenfell had been killed in the second Matabele War in 1896. His younger brother Reginald du Pré Grenfell had died earlier of fever aged 22 in 1889 whilst serving in India with the 17th Lancers. The seventh son, Robert Septimus Grenfell was killed at Omdurman in 1898, aged 23. Two more sons were to tragically die in battle in the First World War – Francis Octavius Grenfell and his twin brother Riversdale Nonus Grenfell – as did two of their cousins, the poet Julian Grenfell and his brother William (Billy) Grenfell. There is a memorial to all these young Grenfells[13] in the cloisters at Eton College where they went to school.

Born in October 1873, Arthur Grenfell was a larger-than-life charismatic and flawed character. He was an inveterate risk taker, but was not a soldier (except during the First World War). Instead he was merchant banker and entrepreneur, and his career encompassed both great success and personal bankruptcy. Listing his profession in the 1901 Census as 'merchant', he was living at 17 Hans Road, Kensington, with three other members of his family – his sister Maria Grenfell ('musician'), his older brother John, aged 31 and his youngest brother Riversdale ('Rivy'), aged 20.

Arthur was constantly scouting for profitable business in different countries. This took him to Rhodesia in 1902, just after marrying Vera, where with Earl Grey he looked at investing in the copper mining industry. He was a successful partner in the private bank of Chaplin, Milne & Grenfell and involved a series of increasingly ambitious business deals culminating in personal bankruptcy after his failed attempt to take over the Canadian Grand Trunk Railway in 1913.

Already in August 1902, Robert Benson (Earl Grey's brother in law and himself a banker) warned of the very large debts Arthur had clocked up – £65,000 in 1902 – musing: 'how did he get in so deep before he realised?' – and blaming 'old experienced brokers who let young men run up big accounts, and omit to advise or dissuade… and the knife in at the end.' Arthur's business dealings were always on a knife edge. The archive of Earl Grey's papers at the Durham University Library include a succession of letters regarding Arthur's business crises, beginning in 1902 and coming to a head with the Canadian failure. Far from being a welcome source of commercial and entrepreneurial expertise coming to the aid of Earl Grey, Arthur Grenfell was often a source of financial difficulty and embarrassment to the family.

It is no surprise to find that, as a soldier in the First World War, Arthur was said to be personally fearless, despite being badly wounded while serving with the Royal

---

12 Field Marshal Francis Wallace Grenfell, 1st Baron Grenfell (1841-1925), Governor of Malta. He later married Sybil's cousin, Aline Majendie.
13 Francis Octavius Grenfell (1880-1915) and his twin brother Riversdale Nonus Grenfell (1880-1915) and William (Billy) Grenfell (1890-1915).

Buckinghamshire Hussars in France, where he was mentioned in dispatches three times. There was no doubt a link between his courage on the battlefield and his willingness to take on risky business transactions. He must have been personally a very entertaining and engaging character, somebody who stood out from the crowd.

Following their wedding, Arthur and Vera settled down at Butler's Court, a house given them by Lord Grenfell, in Beaconsfield. They went on to have three children – Sybil Vera Grenfell[14] (known as 'V') born on 21 July 1902, Reggie Grenfell, born in 1903, and Harry Grenfell, born in 1905.

Before this, another event occurred which must have caused Sybil great sorrow – the death in early spring of her grandmother, Mary Anne Holford (née Lindsay) whom Sybil had known since she was a little girl and with whom she had stayed in Rome two years before. This would almost certainly have involved the whole family in returning to Westonbirt, Mary Anne's home for so many years, to see her buried in the chapel in the garden there.

---

14 Children of Lady Victoria (Vera) Grenfell and Arthur Grenfell: Sybil Vera ('V') Grenfell (1903-90), Reggie Grenfell (1902-93) and Harry Grenfell (1905-85).

6

1902: Germany and Malta

The year 1902 saw two forays by Sybil into Europe, the first an enigmatic trip with her father to Germany, and the second a formative visit to Malta with her newly married sister Vera.

Germany

In the summer of 1902, Sybil visited Germany with her father. The letters she sent are fragmentary (giving no dates and unsigned) but it is clear that they visited Darmstadt and the schloss of Grand Duke Ernest Ludwig of Hesse, a grandson of Queen Victoria. Sybil wrote: 'It is very big and full of reception rooms. A lot of very good furniture, glass and china and some good pictures. There is a magnificent Holbein there, worth any amount of money. The top floor is where the Grand Duke lives, when he lives there which is very rare, as he has a summer Palace just outside Darmstadt.'

The Grand Duke, who was homosexual although married to Princess Victoria Melita, herself also a granddaughter of Queen Victoria, came to dinner at the British Legation. Sybil watched him, fascinated: 'We were only eight at dinner and I sat opposite him and watched him with the greatest amusement, never stops talking for a moment. He talks at a great pace and shakes his hands in your face and wriggles about and roars with laughter.' The Grand Duke's sister Princess Alix of Hesse, was the wife of Tsar Nicholas II, whom Sybil was to meet later in Russia.

They were also presented to members of the von Eulenberg family. Philip Prince of Eulenberg and Hertefeld, was one of the closest advisers of Kaiser Wilhelm II. Also a noted homosexual, he was a colleague of Bernhardt von Bulow, Foreign Minister and then Chancellor of the German Empire.

During the visit, Sybil was asked to help open a public park:

There were a lot of people there and it was very hot. They had a big camera and a regimental band. I was presented by the committee with a beautiful bouquet of white roses and carnations, very heavy, and Countess von Eulenburg a red bouquet, more suited to her years. Then we were all moved out into the middle of the ground to be photographed, I standing with a mallet at the hoop. I had given up my sunshade [parasol] as I thought I was at once to hit off the ball to open the ground, but not a bit of it I had to wait while the Burgomaster Von Marse made a long, and excellent, I believe, speech. No sunshade and 96 in the shade, I was not altogether happy. But with that consummate skill which is natural to me, at the appointed moment I gracefully hit off the ball and immediately the National Anthem was played!

There are other engaging glimpses from this visit – Earl Grey and Sybil, coming back from a visit to small town near Darmstadt, stopped at the top a hill and gazed at the view of the plains below them, lying on the grass for three quarters of an hour while Earl Grey smoked a cigar and Sybil read a novel.

They travelled by train and Earl Grey exhibited a very devil-may-care approach to safety – on one occasion he jumped into a train just as it set off, accidently leaving Sybil and the rest of the party behind to catch the following one. On another occasion, he attempted to lead the party across the tracks to catch their connection on the opposite platform, and was prevented by railway officials who insisted rightly on their walking round by the foot bridge – again missing their train, Earl Grey blustering and threatening to report the officials to their Emperor.

Sybil evidently had some German – she spoke of herself laughingly as 'a scholar of German', and on her visit to Malta she found her attempts at speaking Italian came 'peppered with a lot of German words'.

It is not explained why the Greys travelled to Germany, but the answer may lie in the fact that Sir Alfred Egerton was a member of the party. As well as being British Ambassador to Greece, he was Comptroller of the Household to HRH Duke of Connaught. The Connaughts were friends of the Greys and were close relations to the Duke of Saxe-Coburg Gotha. The Greys certainly met some very influential and well connected people in the course of their visit.

Malta

Sybil's next great adventure was a visit to Malta over Christmas 1902, with her recently married sister Vera, and Vera's sister in law, Florita Grenfell. (The Grenfells specialised in selecting Latin American names for their daughters – Florita Catherine Grenfell, Juanita Gertrude Grenfell, Maria Dolores Grenfell, and Maraquita Masini Grenfell – all sisters of Arthur. Their grandfather, Vice Admiral John Pascoe Grenfell, had served in the Brazilian Navy).

The three young women travelled out via Italy, arriving in Malta at the start of December 1902, to stay with Florita's uncle, General Francis Wallace Grenfell, the Governor of Malta, at his magnificent palace.

Malta was the main base of the Royal Navy's Mediterranean Fleet, its largest and most prestigious squadron, comprising ten first-class battleships – double the number of the Channel Fleet – and a large number of smaller warships. The British, under Admiral Sir John ('Jacky') Fisher, had just begun a much overdue modernisation of the Navy, with improved training, gunnery practice and a programme of rapidly building the new Super-Dreadnought class battleships in response to Germany's creation of its High Seas Fleet. He also introduced the use of torpedoes and turbine engines, as well as better rations for sailors.

Although Sybil did not yet know it, her family was soon be associated with another important figure who influenced the Navy at this time – Lord Selborne, who was to become father-in-law to her brother Charlie when he married Mabel Palmer, Selborne's daughter, in 1906. From 1900-05, Lord Selborne was First Lord of the Admiralty, and he saw the developing threat of Germany's new High Seas Fleet in stark terms: 'The German Navy is very carefully built up from the point of view of a new war with us,' he told the Cabinet in 1902. He went on 'Our stakes are out of all proportion to those of any other Power. To us defeat in a maritime war would mean a disaster of almost unparalleled magnitude in history. It might mean the destruction of our mercantile marine, the stoppage of our manufactures, scarcity of food, invasion, and disruption of Empire.'[1] The colossal expansion of the German Navy, begun in 1898, was the personal project of Kaiser Wilhelm II and of Admiral Alfred von Tirpitz, and was proceeding at breakneck speed, putting Germany on a collision course with the British Empire.

However, to the young Sybil and her friends in 1902, Malta presented an unparalleled opportunity for endless enjoyment. As the Governor's guests they were invited to all the balls, functions and trips on the Navy's warships and to the Army's dinners and sporting gatherings.

Even today, Valletta looks like a small corner of Britain set down on a rocky island in the Mediterranean, with streets of sandstone Georgian houses which could well grace Bath, together with red Royal Mail post boxes and telephone boxes. The Grand Harbour is one of the largest protected anchorages in the world. In Sybil's day it was full of Royal Navy 'men of war' (as warships were known) and Valletta's fashionable houses would have been home to senior Navy and Army officers and their families.

On 6 December, Sybil related their journey out via Sicily, en route for Malta:

We arrived at Reggio[2] from Naples at nine o'clock on Thursday morning. Lovely day and beautiful scenery, the sea the most lovely colour. We got into a little steamer at Reggio to cross to Messina. It took about 40 minutes but it was quite calm and very pretty so we enjoyed it. Directly we landed a grubby unshaven man, not in any uniform, came up and began to talk in bad English. He put our things in the train and asked for our tickets which we gave him. Then he began to walk away with them, we got rather nervous and followed him hurriedly and also explained that we were 'affamé', so he took us out of the station, put us in a cab, got on the box and drove off and we began to wonder whether he was a brigand and whether we should spend our next night on the top of Mount Etna, also how much money you would feel inclined to pay as ransom, when Vera's pretty little pink ear reached you by post. However he was no ruffian and took us to another station where we had coffee and very uncooked eggs, but as we were really hungry we thought them good.

The light-hearted joke about Vera's little pink ear being cut off sounds very much like Sybil's sense of humour – Vera was much too preoccupied about her looks to have thought it funny.

As they travelled by train across Sicily, Sybil revelled in the hot sunny summer's day with its delicious breeze. The sea was dark, dark blue and all the orange trees, vines and mountains made the countryside look most attractive. Mount Etna was covered with snow and clouds on the top, so they couldn't tell whether or not it was smoking.

---

1 Margaret MacMillan, *The War that ended Peace*, (2014), page 106.
2 Reggio di Calabria.

At Syracuse they were taken on board a boat sent by Lord Grenfell to collect them: 'He had brought over for our comfort on board rugs, cushions, a chicken, a bottle of hock, champagne, brandy and whisky – tea, butter biscuits, cake – and a letter to the captain to say he was to look after us. So we were well provided for. It was as calm as it could be and very warm so we stayed on deck and read till it was dark and then sat and talked till half past six.'

The captain gave them a first-rate dinner of champagne and snipe which was their undoing:

> We ate more than was good for us. We then retired to a big and charming cabin and thought we would go to sleep till 12.50 when we landed. However we began rolling and before many minutes there was a catastrophe in Vera's quarter, so she was on the sofa and I was in the upper berth feeling quite well lying down, but not very well standing up, so all I did was look down with compassion every hour or so when she had a particularly bad ten minutes and say, 'Poor darling how I wish I could help you,' and then turn over and go to sleep again.

They arrived in Valletta at 1 a.m. to be greeted by Florita's husband Major Guy St Aubyn and were taken to the Palace, where Lord Grenfell plied them with more chicken and champagne: 'We got to bed by three. Our rooms lead out of each other on the first floor – nice big rooms with painted ceilings. We had breakfast in bed and Florita[3] and Lola came and saw us and we only appeared for luncheon.'

The Governor's Palace in Malta was very impressive, with a magnificent interior, particularly the entrance hall with its display of arms and armour. One of the first buildings built in the new city of Valletta, founded by Grand Master Jean de Valette in 1566, the Palace was enlarged and developed by successive Grand Masters to serve as their official residence. It became the Governor's residence under the British and is now the seat of the President of Malta and the house of Parliament.

Sybil was bowled over by its magnificent architecture and accoutrements – the tapestries, the painted canvas ceiling, and the suits of magnificent armour from its armoury standing round the walls:

> It is a very big house, and like the Italian houses is built around a courtyard with trees and palms in it. The dining room is gigantic and there are endless drawing rooms and reception rooms, the ball room is beautiful. Frescoes and painted ceilings everywhere. The council room is all covered with glorious tapestry which is in perfect preservation only about four bits and worth over £60,000. Then there is a long corridor round three sides of the house looking out onto the courtyard.

She sketched a plan of the courtyard and the surrounding colonnade, and she explained the history of the magnificent collection of arms. 'The armoury is a high room with a plain ceiling and walls 300 hundred feet long. The walls are covered with armour and men in full armour all the way round the room.' A visiting British expert told them that it was the finest collection of armour he had ever seen. 'Some

---

3 Florita Catherine Grenfell, daughter of Pascoe du Pré Grenfell, and elder sister of Vera Grey's husband Arthur Morton Grenfell. She was married to Guy St Aubyn and died in 1925.

of the suits all inlaid with gold and which belonged to some of the most distinguished Grand Masters stand beside a picture of their owner in full armour which
makes it much more interesting. Each Grand Master as he died left his suits of armour to the collection.'

The collection of arms had been cleverly disguised to prevent conquering armies
from looting it: 'Most of the suits were painted black, which was done to prevent

The Governor's Palace in Malta, © de Wesselow Collection.

Napoleon seeing how valuable they were and removing them; however now there are only about 20 that have still got to be boiled and cleaned.'

They were given an easy first few days, with no guests for lunch or dinner: 'Last night after dinner we had ghost stories, some of them excellent and very bloodcurdling. We were thankful that our rooms were together not at all ghostly.'

Sybil looked forward to the variety of entertainment they were promised:

> We see that we are going to enjoy ourselves wildly. There is a children's dance fancy dress cotillion on the 23rd here and Vera and I are going to be two of the leaders. New Ping Pong tables arrive today, so far in that direction I have been victorious.
>
> We are going out in one of the torpedo destroyers one of these days and have endless delightful plans in prospect. There is a lot of golf here and we are sorry we didn't bring our clubs. I think we shall do a good deal of riding. I am very well and taking my medicine.[4] Mondays and Thursdays we always go to the Opera.

She had dinner with the 'Victor Stanleys' – a prominent naval officer and his wife, in their house overlooking the harbour. 'Such a pretty sight it was, looking down on all the men of war and their lights. We all enjoyed our evening immensely.' She was particularly attracted to one of the amusing young officers, Commander Adolphus Williamson, nicknamed the 'Quail' in the Navy.

On Sunday they went to the military church: 'I must say I do like a band in church. Afterwards we were introduced to the Blundells, she is about 24 is very pretty and looks much older. Two of the 60th[5] lunched with us, both very nice.' The 60th Royal Rifles was the regiment which Governor Grenfell had joined as a young ensign in 1859 and were part of his retinue in Malta.

In the afternoon they all went to San Antonio for the afternoon and tea: 'Lord Grenfell, Doris Vivian, Captain Farmer and I riding and the rest driving. I rode a pony called Up John, extremely quiet and like an armchair, even you would have loved it. You canter along the roads here quite happily and it doesn't feel a bit hard. Riding home at about 5.30 was quite delicious and the most beautiful sunset.' San Antonio was the San Anton Palace at Attard, in the centre of Malta, nowadays the official residence of the President of Malta.

She sketched the planned future events:

> This morning I played a round of golf with Doris Vivian. The links are in the ditches but rather amusing although you hardly ever get a decent lie. This evening a dinner party and opera, tomorrow a ball here in the Palace about 300 people. Thursday opera, Friday a man's dinner here; and we dine with Captain Craddock on his ship and dance afterwards. The Children's Cotillion[6] is on 23rd and we are very busy getting ready for it. Vera, Mrs Stanley, I and another woman lead from different doors, we each have a man and two Middies (midshipmen) to help.

---

4 Around this time Sybil had a suspected case of breast cancer, which she referred to in a letter to her own daughter Molly decades later in the 1940s. It happily proved not to be cancer, but may account for why Sybil was concerned about her health all her life. The medicine may have been for this.

5 General (later Field Marshall) Grenfell was originally commissioned in the 60th Rifles.

6 A cotillion is a type of patterned social dance that originated in France in the eighteenth century. It was originally made up of four couples in a square formation.

The cotillion involved preparing decorations and gifts, including ribbons and 'favours', and crowns for the dancers, and a great final set piece:

> The last figure is to be a great surprise. The lights will be turned out and a ship be drawn in by six cadets who have just come out and who are none of them over fourteen and commanded by the smallest Middy here. The boat and the rigging is to be entirely out-lined with electric light and all the presents to be inside. This is to be kept a dead secret and we talk of it as 'the snowball'. I think it ought to be great fun.

Three days later, on 11 December, she wrote again:

> The Polo Ground is playable for the first time in three weeks, hence great excitement throughout Malta. You heard that they had terrible rains three weeks ago and the Polo Ground was four foot under water, a pony drowned and six men very nearly drowned.

Her life was a hectic round of social events and sports which she enjoyed hugely. The dances and dinners were essentially military affairs, involving the 60th Rifles and the cream of the Mediterranean Fleet:

> I have just come in having been out much later than I expected. The ball here was most amusing and we did enjoy ourselves, good music, beautiful floor, and very good dancers. Of course all the uniforms made it look very bright. We had four Admirals and Flag Captains etc. The Commander in Chief Admiral Sir Compton Domville is shorter than Florita and in his uniform looks like a little Eton boy with a short jacket and grey hair. They all went away at about one o'clock. Vera enjoyed herself hugely.

They spent the next day preparing crowns and badges for the cotillion dance, but they spared time for some shooting practice:

> This morning Vera, Florita and I went and practised shooting with a rook rifle, there is a ladies club here and there is a match on the nineteenth, the Army against the Navy. We each have a man partner, Vera is Navy and I am Army so we have to practise hard at that, besides which Lord Grenfell has competitions at which he gives cups.

The shooting competition against the men's teams was a challenge which Sybil took on with gusto and at which she proved surprisingly good.

On 14 December she wrote: 'Yesterday it blew a hurricane and poured and now today before breakfast, I see it is still pouring. They have never known such weather in Malta.'

She described a memorable dinner and dance on the the flagship, *Andromeda*: 'We each had a beautiful little menu with a ship hand painted on it and our initials done by one of the officers and very well done.' After dinner they danced on the Quarter deck the sides of which were covered in with flags.

> It is not a good deck for dancing, all sorts of obstacles in the way, but oh! how we all enjoyed ourselves; we had lancers and every sort of dance. There were two men too many, so of course two had to dance together. Captain Blundell became a lady and was absolutely killing. He wore my cloak which although it was a foot off the ground did very well, and a scarf on his head. After that he danced with a broom and then sat it on a chair and began to talk to it, I don't think I have ever laughed so much in my life!

She told her mother their plans until they were due to leave Malta:

> We go to San Antonio about second of January. On the 20th of this month [December], the 60th women and children come and have tea in the Armoury and we have to get them an Xmas tree. There is not a single night now till we go away that we haven't a dinner party except Tuesday when Vera and I dine with the Blundells. Vera wore her white gown with orange last night and it was much approved of.

Her sister Vera was over the moon, having heard from her husband Arthur, who was in Rhodesia with Earl Grey looking at business opportunities in the Copper Belt:

> Vera received three letters from Arthur[7] this morning and is therefore very happy. He was very optimistic about the copper.

Sybil was practising hard for the shooting competition:

> The competition is tomorrow. Five Army couples against Five Navy ones. Captain Farmer is my partner and we were both on the bull this morning, therefore I tremble to think of tomorrow. Florita was also very good this morning which is more than I can say for her partner.

Her upbringing involving regular field sports, with occasional practice with a revolver or a rook rifle, stood Sybil in good stead in the coming competition; she was naturally a good shot and was very competitive.

Arrangements were being made for a charity ball: 'It is to be 7s/6d a head, and fancy dress or uniform, a 'calico ball' so that nobody can have an excuse for not turning up.' The term 'calico ball' meant that the dresses had to be made of cheap material.

Vera and Florita were going to the ball dressed as Vivandières – a name for camp followers of the French Napoleonic Army, so slightly saucy. Sybil said: 'I think their dresses will be very pretty. I am sending you a bad drawing of it. It will be made of red twill, the facings and bands on the skirt are white and black three-cornered hats.'

She herself was going more demurely dressed: 'I am going to be a Gainsborough lady. Florita is lending me a big black hat and I shall have a little white dress made and blue sash.' Sybil sketched Vera's costume and photographs taken at the time show it was a very good likeness.

Vera had heard again from Arthur in Africa, with a thrilling story of camping in the wild: 'Vera has received another long letter from Arthur by the second post. He says that one night lions came to the camp and in the morning they found that two lions had been within six feet of him and he had never woken!'

The next day, 19 December, she painted an attractive picture of the two sisters writing letters together:

---

7 Arthur Grenfell and his father-in-law, Albert Earl Grey, were evidently in southern Africa, probably in the Northern Rhodesian copper belt. Earl Grey had been Administrator of Southern Rhodesia (1896-7) and Arthur Grenfell was a financier and speculator who was interested in copper as an investment.

Vera is writing to you opposite me at the same table and I feel we shall say the same things. Another lovely day but windy and so Florita and I are anxious about our shooting which comes off this afternoon.

The sisters were so close that they were literally thinking and writing alike. After this holiday they would never be so close again as Vera became more involved with motherhood – her youngest (little Vera) had been born five months earlier.

As Christmas approached, Sybil gave a resumé of her hectic social life:

As you will have gathered from our letters we are enjoying ourselves wildly. This week we are frightfully busy, what with Xmas trees, children's cotillions, toys to be taken to all the hospitals and crèches, balls dinners etc. There are such a lot of charming people here – the 60th officers are all delightful, and charming sailors abound. Captain Stanley, one of Lord Derby's sons is very nice, and has a charming and pretty wife. He is doing our boat for the cotillion, which is going to be the greatest thing ever seen in Malta.

Today we are going to have our rehearsal, the dance is next Tuesday.

On Boxing Day, they did their duty helping with charity events for the men:

Vera and I went to early service at eight and then directly after breakfast we went and cut bread and butter for a tea of about 500 soldiers and sailors. They pay 6d each for that and they have a most excellent tea and cigarettes and a concert lasting four hours!! and they love it, it is a first-rate thing as it keeps them out of the pubs. We then went to church at the Baracca where the soldiers simply bawled *Hark the Herald Angels Sing.*

It was warm Mediterranean weather, unlike Boxing Day back home:

After luncheon, we went and watched polo at the Marsa for a little, most glorious afternoon not a breath of air and not a cloud; we went to G. O. C. Lane's tea and Xmas tree; and from there we went on to the soldiers and sailors and gave them tea and worked hard carrying lots of boiling tea for over an hour. Some of the sailors were too amusing and didn't mind what they said. We got home just in time to dress for dinner, a big dinner of 38. We had a very jolly dinner and the uncle [Gen. Grenfell] made a most amusing speech at the end and made us all roar with laughter. After dinner about 70 other people arrived and we danced till about one o'clock.

And she appealed to her mother for more money:

I meant to tell you but always forgot, could you send me out a little more money. I am afraid going through Italy made it very expensive as they do not allow you pounds of luggage so we had to pay a great deal overweight besides sleepers, meals, tips etc., and the two nights in Paris. I have about 35 shillings left which will about pay my washing and stamps, but I shall have none left for coming home and tips.

On 4 January 1903, she thought of how her mother would love the life they led in Malta:

I would give anything to have you here this morning in this heavenly place. Lovely garden, you can sit there this morning without a jacket, birds singing like the middle of summer; you sit in the shade with the noise of a fountain playing quite close and if you get hungry you simply put up your arm and pick an orange warmed and sweetened right through by the sun, and ever so many lovely roses out all round, oh how you would love it. I simply shiver to think of you with cold east winds and snow.

Sybil, in fancy dress for the ball, Malta, 1902 (de Wesselow collection).

She gave an enthusiastic description of the shooting competition between the men's and ladies' team, showing her considerable ability as a marksman. 'Mr Stanley had got up the man's team of seven and Mr Raikes the women's of seven. They each shot for their respective sides. The match was seven shots and a sighter at 50 and 80 yards.'

If the men thought they would win easily they had reckoned without the skill and competiveness of the ladies:

Of course most people expected the men to beat us into a cocked hat, however we had some good shots on our side and were determined to make a fight of it. When we had all shot except the two leaders who hadn't shot at the 80 range, we counted up and found that the ladies led by one point. We didn't dare tell Mr Stanley and Mr Raikes for fear of making them nervous and we watched with breathless anxiety their shooting and we knew that we were beaten unless Mr Raikes made a bull with the very last shot, which he did. Wild excitement as it made us equal so we thought, but when it was all added up again we found that we had just lost. The totals were this. Men 437 points, Women 435. A good match wasn't it.

Sybil was one of the top scorers:

I won a prize given by Mr Baird for the top ladies score in all the 50 yards, and Mr Raikes gave a prize to the lady who made the biggest score at the two ranges combined, which I thought I had also safely won. I led when there was only one lady's total still to come in and she had to make 32 out of a possible 35 at the 80 range to beat me, so we all thought it was a certainty and bother the woman she made 31, so we tied and had to shoot it off three shots and a sighter at 50, and she just beat me.

There was a flurry of activity and final preparations for the children's cotillion dance. Sybil was still very much Vera's younger sister, ending the letter: 'Vera is yelling for me to go and make paper whips for the boys [for the cotillion] so I suppose I must go. We really are horribly hurried.'

The dance itself seems to have gone off without a hitch, although there is no description of the event.

On the final evening at San Antonio, they had a splendid dance after dinner, Sybil commenting on the fashion of dancing:

The club room is a very big and pretty room and was frightfully crowded, but it was great fun. One always has to dance here holding up one's skirt with one hand otherwise you run the risk of ending the evening minus your skirt. Some hold it a little high, with two women on Friday night I saw above the knee!!

It was all frivolity and frippery, but in the background there was tragedy – another family, the Farrants, one of whose two daughters aged 20 had fallen ill with acute appendicitis, which became inoperable. The girl died and her parents and twin sister bore their loss as bravely as possible – 'The girl is heartbroken poor thing as she has never been really parted from her sister and they have always slept together, and everybody says how very pretty and charming she was.'

Sybil could not have imagined that a mere four years later she and her family would be plunged into the same abyss of loss and desolation.

7

Canada – first love

Canada was Sybil's home for much of the next few years, from 1904 to 1911. She went there with her father who was appointed Governor General of the Dominion in succession to his brother-in-law, Earl Minto.

Sybil fell in love with Canada, and like all first love it remained with her for a lifetime. She was awed by its size – 41 times the size of England, Scotland and Wales together, but with only one fourth of the population. Standing in Ottawa, the capital of Canada in the province of Ontario, you were nearer to London than to Vancouver on the Pacific coast.

She recorded its diversity – the confident and established eastern cities of Ottawa and Toronto, the traditional French enclaves of Quebec and Montreal, the new cities such as Winnipeg proud of their growth and development, and the recently laid out northern towns such as Prince Rupert, with its neat pegged out plots and 'corduroy roads' (made of logs lashed together). She watched it grow and change visibly; she was fascinated with its human stories, and with the social achievements and industries of every place they visited.

Many years later, speaking to a Women's Institute audience in England, she took them on an imaginary journey across the country – using photographs and her graphic recollections. She described the great variety of places that she had seen: 'Quebec with its steep narrow streets where you hear little else spoken but French and where the buildings are all of French eighteenth century architecture, streets with convents and monasteries where monks and nuns walk in their habits with an assurance unchanged since the days of Cardinal Richelieu.' She went on: 'Here you still find a French civilisation that is hardly changed since the days of Louis XVth and which does not remotely resemble the France of today.'

She described Quebec as one of the most magnificently situated cities in the world – standing on a high bluff 300 feet above the St Lawrence, at that point a mile wide, overlooked by the Heights of Abraham.

She recalled the rural province of Quebec, filled with French speaking peasants who mostly lived in wooden houses and earned their living in small family holdings or in lumbering. During the winter months, when the snow was many feet thick on the ground, the women did a lot of weaving. 'Many have immense families. I remember my father stopping one day at a log cabin and asking the woman how many children she had. She replied, with a charming smile: "Ah, the kind God has been very good to me – he has nine and I have seven".'

She described Ottawa, the capital, with its Federal Houses of Parliament perched

*Earl Grey and Countess Alice Grey by William James Topley
(Library and Archives of Canada).*

on a bluff and down below the river filled at springtime with great logs which had been floated down from the forests upstream, gathering in great log jams. Lumber men in scarlet shirts cleverly balanced on the logs and manoeuvred them down the river with poles.

She showed pictures of Montreal with its high buildings, the original skyscrapers, and she remembered the provincial capitals such as Edmonton, capital of Alberta province, three times as large as Great Britain but with only three quarters of a million inhabitants – commenting that their building such a fine provincial parliament 'shows the unbounded belief in their own greatness and future.' She next showed them Winnipeg, capital of Manitoba, gateway to the prairies and the wheat country. Situated halfway across Canada from east to west, it was built in absolutely flat country on two big rivers.

Speaking to her English audience in the early 1950s, she commented:

> When I first knew it 44 years ago, Winnipeg was a small but go ahead town, now it is a most imposing and attractive great city. Most of the grain in Canada passes through it. Even in those far off days it had a belief in its future greatness for the town was laid out in great broad avenues with four lines of trees in every street, and with grass verges between the avenues. The houses, some of stone but many of wood, all painted in the gayest colours, are built 30 feet back from the sidewalk, nearly all standing in their own little piece of ground; there are no fences of any kind between the houses or in front of them, but instead flowers and mown grass, so you can imagine what an attractive street scene it makes.

She recalled: 'Everyone knows everybody else's business, for practically all over Canada in the summer the inhabitants sit out on their verandas in huge rocking chairs, watching the world go by.'

After Winnipeg, the prairies began, with mile upon mile of Manitoba followed by mile upon mile of Saskatchewan, a vast flat country with horizons that seem to stretch a hundred miles away. Beyond Saskatchewan lay Alberta, still completely flat, punctuated with great wooden towers of grain elevators alongside the railway stations and grain castles (silos), the country's insurance against famine.

In a country where east and west were separated by 3,000 miles, the climate and way of life of the people varied immensely.

> In the maritime provinces on the east coast, the climate is much like it is here in England, whilst British Columbia in the west has a lovely climate – frost and snow are practically unknown there. The rest of Canada has anything up to five months of snow – when it can reach 40° below zero in Ottawa, that is 72° of frost (using the Fahrenheit scale).

In the Northern Territories, 70 below was often experienced. The summers were usually hotter than in Britain – 100 degrees in the shade being not unusual.

She spoke of the winter, when Canadians kept their houses very warm and dressed up tremendously in order to go out. She told her neighbours in the little village of Burley in Hampshire,

> If you went out to tea with a friend in Burley Street, and it was 20° of frost or below,

you would put on another pair of knickers, over stockings and overshoes, a leather or fur coat, and a woollen hood or scarf covering as much of your face as you could. And if a stranger suddenly ran at you and started rubbing your nose with snow, you would know he was not assaulting you but that he had noticed your nose was white and frostbitten and he was offering first-aid.

She remarked: 'Luckily the cold is very dry and is often accompanied by brilliant sun and no wind – and under those conditions you really feel the cold less than you do in this country on a damp or windy day. It is only when there is a wind that it becomes unbearable in Canada.' In the cold, the air was in fact so dry that static electricity was generated – 'nobody would dream of carelessly touching the electric switch to turn on the light without first running their hand up the wall – otherwise you would get quite a nasty shock up your arm.'
  She told the story of a party game they played:

At Government House in Ottawa we used to light the gas with our fingers. There was a gas jet at the end of a long corridor and for fun we used to stand in a long line of say a dozen people all holding hands. A thirteenth person would run, shuffling their feet along the passageway to generate electricity, and would touch the out-stretched hand of the last person in line, the electric shock going through the line of twelve, and at the same instant the person at the end nearest the light would touch the jet sharply with their finger and thus would light it.

Sybil's sister Vera (Lady Victoria Grenfell) (Library and Archives Canada)

A cousin of hers (perhaps Angus McDonnell) boasted that he would light the jet with his very pointed nose – 'he succeeded but he burned his eyebrows off.'
  Two years before, her elder sister Vera had visited Canada during the governor generalship of her uncle Earl Minto, and gave a vivid account of the winter in Canada: 'The country is looking at its prettiest, every little tree twig being covered with frozen snow, long icicles hanging from all the windows and all round the roof. I long to walk along the street with a long pole and knock them all off.'
  Skating was the craze in winter: 'Skating has begun in earnest... At the skating parties they do nothing but valse... I was so encouraged that I at

once tried a rocker with Mr Evans, with the result that I came down and had a black eye for two days.'

She preferred skiing 'I like skiing much the best – it is lovely feeling to start at the top of the hill and go flying down and glide right out onto the river.' Skating remained a national obsession. Indeed, Evy Grey, Earl Grey's youngest daughter, actually won a national skating competition, competing in a waltz on the ice in 1910.

The reality of existence for the settlers on the great mid-western plains and in the northern forests of Canada was very different from the comforts of Ottawa:

> In winter they would be snowed up for months and in those days there was no telephone, radio or wireless. One heard of cases where there were perhaps no children and the farmer had to go on his snowshoes for urgent supplies to the nearest town, necessitating him being away for several days. His wife left completely alone, surrounded on all sides with mile upon mile of white and complete silence, with nothing to do but think. No wonder they would unpick a jersey they had just knitted and then knit it up again, and quite a few lost their reason.

Sybil by Topley (Library and Archives Canada)

Sybil continued her travelogue across Canada, reaching Calgary, the capital of Alberta, the pioneer city of the west. She wrote: 'Once a year the cowboys come down from the ranches and the Rockies and ride in the great stampede. Bronco busting, ten gallon hats, steer riding, all the paraphernalia of the Wild West movies come to life.'

By 1950, Calgary had grown from a few log huts to a great modern city. Sybil said: 'If I lived in the prairies I would choose to live in Calgary, for although at least 40 miles away one looks at the foothills of the Rockies. I've seen them from Calgary in the early morning light, cold and grey, and as the sun rises the tops become pink and then red.'

She described a journey through the Rockies: 'that superb range of mountains with its turbulent rivers, its canyons, its glaciers… snow-capped mountains on every side, deep ravines, rivers a wonderful turquoise colour, poplar trees turning every shade of yellow and gold, and added to this the thrill of seeing bear, moose and elk.'

Having crossed the Rockies one arrived in British Columbia 'perhaps of all provinces of Canada the most attractive, the land of fruit orchards and of vast forests with gigantic trees.'

Above all, Canada won Sybil's heart with its wild places – its trackless forests, its great lakes, its mighty rivers and the Rocky Mountains. She described a personal epiphany –'the most wonderful experience of my life' – while travelling by boat up the Pacific West Coast to Skagway on the way to the Yukon in 1909:

> Passing the Sitka Archipelago, we stopped and a friend and I were rowed to the shore and walked off into the primeval forest. It was like entering some vast cathedral – the trees went straight up a hundred feet without a branch and were all from 150 to 200 feet high. There was a subdued light with occasional gleams of sunlight forcing their way through the heavy canopy of green foliage at the top. The moss on the ground was inches thick, so that our feet made no sound and there was no undergrowth. We neither of us spoke as we walked a mile into this forest, 200 miles away from civilisation, and lay down on the moss.
>
> I was struck with a feeling of deep awe and then I realised what it was, it was silence, complete utter silence. There was not a breath of wind, not a bird not an animal, just a silence that enveloped you as if it were a cloak that one could almost touch so powerful was it. I was almost afraid to breathe and I knew that this was something quite new, something that in one's ordinary life one could never experience. Two lines of poetry of Robert Service's[1] came to me: 'Have you stood in a mighty mouthed hollow that's plumb full of hush to the brim?' Well I was in a mighty forest that was plumb full of hush to the brim, and the marvel of it remains with me to this day.

Finally, Sybil declared: 'If I were a young man now I think I would emigrate to Canada, that land of sunshine and illimitable possibilities, where if you are prepared to work hard and turn your hand to anything, you can hardly fail to succeed.'

Governor General

Earl Grey had been recommended for the appointment as Governor General by his brother-in-law, Gilbert Elliott-Murray-Kynynmound, the Earl of Minto (who was Governor General from 1898 to 1904). Initially he had been hesitant about accepting the post. His daughters, Vera, Sybil and Evy, wrote telling him they would never speak to him again if he turned it down, adding 'Evy thinks this may be your chief reason for refusing!' The post required considerable personal wealth on top of the governor's stipend – Earl Grey was lucky enough to be funded by his wife's aunt by marriage, Harriet Loyd-Lindsay,[2] Lady Wantage (Sybil's favourite great aunt Harriet).

The Grey family had long associations with Canada. Not only was the Earl of Minto Governor General before him, but nearly 70 years before, his grandfather's son-in-law, John Lambton, 1st Earl of Durham,[3] had served as Governor General in the late 1830s. 'Radical Jack' Durham had put down a rebellion of the Quebecois

---

1 Robert Service, Canadian poet (1874-1958), sometimes called the Bard of the Yukon.
2 The Hon. Harriet Loyd-Lindsay (c.1838-1920). She was married to the Crimean War hero Brig. Gen. Robert Loyd-Lindsay, VC.
3 John George Lambton, 1st Earl of Durham, (1792-1840), son in law to Charles, 2nd Earl Grey, and who assisted him in bringing in the Great Reform Bill of 1832.

Parade for Edward VII's funeral, Ottawa, (Library and Archives Canada)

with an iron fist, but he was also remembered as the author of the Durham Report, which proposed that the great Dominions should have their own legislatures and be governed in the interests of their peoples.

Not everyone welcomed Earl Grey's appointment. Liberal cabinet minister John Morley (not Grey's brother-in-law, Earl Morley), commented acidly to a friend in Canada: 'Have we sent you a sufficiently superb windbag to rule over you in Ottawa? I hope Laurier will keep H.E.'s claws clipped.'[4]

Earl Grey was chosen for the post partly on the strength of his service in Rhodesia. He was committed to the ideal of the Empire and to extending, deepening and consolidating it through the idea of an Imperial Parliament in which self-governing dominions such as Canada and Australia would participate as equals with Britain in deciding the destiny of the Empire within a federal structure. He was a founder member of the Imperial Federation League which argued for the creation of a federation of the colonies and dominions of the British Empire.

This meant that Grey came out with the intention of promoting much greater integration of Canada within the Empire at a time when Canada was beginning to turn its thoughts toward self-government. Already it had its own legislature – a bicameral parliament – and its experienced and very able Prime Minister, Sir Wilfrid

---

4 Source *Rideau Hall,* by R. H. Hubbard, page 99.

Laurier,[5] was determined to maintain Canada's path towards greater independence. The two men had occasionally tricky but a very cordial relationship, and they avoided conflict. The *Canadian Encyclopaedia* comments that 'it was fortunate for Canada and Britain that, in this difficult transition period in Imperial relations, a Governor General of Grey's energy and charm was associated with a Prime Minister of Laurier's strengths and patience!' In fact, Grey and Laurier became firm friends.

On arrival, Grey was welcomed by each province and major city that he came to on his journey to Ottawa. The Province of Nova Scotia expressed the hope that he would appreciate 'the instincts of freedom and equality which prevail in this Dominion'. Grey was adroit and careful to respond positively and sympathetically to all these greetings. He was also careful to respect the separate historic tradition of French Canadians, replying to them and thanking them in their own language when he visited Quebec and Montreal. He told the city of Montreal 'I come from an island where, for centuries, the strain of French descent has been regarded as the most precious inheritance bequeathed to us by our Fathers.'

In his book on Rideau Hall (Government House in Ottawa), R. H. Hubbard, wrote: 'In Canada Grey found full scope for his imperial zeal, his oratory and his charm with people. In a period of material prosperity, he became not only the country's best advertising agent but also its spur in improved pursuit of higher things.'

On arrival in Quebec in late 1904 he took up the cause of the preservation of walls and battlefields, which came to fruition during his time as governor with the establishment of a monument to the battlefields and to the decisive victory of Wolfe over Montcalm on the Heights of Abraham in 1759, which had delivered the whole of French Canada into British hands.

He travelled widely, beginning in 1905 with official visits to Quebec and Montreal. He also made the first of several visits to the United States (he visited again in 1906, 1907 and in 1911). In the summer of 1905 he visited Toronto and went fishing at the remote island of Anticosti at the mouth of the St Lawrence, where it is nearly 90 miles wide from shore to shore. He was accompanied on this expedition by Evy and Sybil, whose first experience it was of salmon fishing in Canada's wild and mighty rivers. They sailed there in the yatch *Bacchante*, whose captain presented them with an album of photographs of the trip.

Earl Grey also journeyed west to inaugurate the new provinces of Saskatchewan and Alberta which were received into the Confederation of Canada in September 1905. In Winnipeg he urged citizens to have 'the best schools, the best churches, the best music, the best newspapers and the best literature in the Dominion'. He championed sport, instituting the Grey Cup for (Canadian) football, and encouraging hockey, skating and curling.

Visiting British Columbia in 1906, his enthusiasm reached its peak as he conjured up visions of the province developing an international fruit industry and he wrote to Laurier about the suggested export of electric power to the United States. On a visit to Newfoundland he declared himself in favour of its annexation to Canada (it finally ceased to be a separate Dominion and joined the Confederation

5 Sir Wilfred Laurier (1841-1919).

Yacht Bacchante, Anticosti (Library and Archives Canada)

in 1949). Less realistically he suggested that Bermuda and the West Indies should also be incorporated in Canada.

He energetically promoted cultural matters, arranged music and drama festivals, and helped establish the National Gallery. His guests at Government House included writers such as Rudyard Kipling, Ernest Thompson Seton, Rider Haggard and Stephen Leacock. He invited Conan Doyle to write a history of the Canadian Mounted Police – Doyle declined the commission.

Among his other causes were the introduction of reindeer into Labrador, a tuberculosis campaign, civil service reform and introducing a winter carnival for Montreal.

In 1908 the Quebec Tercentenary, the greatest event of his governorship, commemorating the establishment of the first settlement at Quebec by Samuel de Champlain in 1608, took place for a whole week in the presence of George Prince of Wales. Grey spoke of its objective being 'harmonising and unifying the two great races which together make up the nation of Canada' and of promoting imperial unity. He was involved in discussions with the United States on improving boundary cooperation. He was also involved in initially promoting and then restricting the use of Asian labour in the west of Canada.

The Greys lived at Government House (Rideau Hall), overlooking Governor Bay on the Ottawa River. A grey stone mansion, it had been built by a Scottish entrepreneur, acquired by the government and added to by successive Governor Generals (Grey himself added a little wing for his study). Much of the building was taken up for public events and receptions (the reason why successive governor generals added new rooms for their personal use). It looked like many another country house that might be found dotting the Northumberland landscape, so the Greys must have felt thoroughly at home. It is situated out to the east of the city on a wooded promontory called Rockliffe.

The Governor General would make a journey of a few miles in to Ottawa, where the Parliament Buildings stood on another promontory, with its central debating chamber, impressively high clock tower (the 'Peace Tower') modelled on Big Ben, and the chambers of the Senate and House of Commons. Here lay the centre of ceremonial and political power. I believe that Sybil's interest in politics and power, which she retained all her life, began in this microcosm in which her father had one of the most eminent roles. Ottawa was the place where the elite of Canada's social and political world resided, but it remained essentially a windy 'lumberjack' town, where the great timber logs were floated downriver to be transported to Britain which was hungry for Canadian timber. So Parliament must always have looked a little out of place in an otherwise unadorned city.

When they visited Quebec they stayed at the Citadelle, the great fortification above the city. Quebec was entirely different to English speaking Ottawa – founded in 1608 it had been the capital of Nouvelle France for over 150 years until it was taken by the British in the battle on the Plains of Abraham that left both French and British commanders mortally wounded. The only walled town in America north of Mexico, it remained essentially French in architecture and culture, with its proud motto 'je me souviens'. Government House in Quebec was located at the centre of the Citadelle, with its circle of deep defensive enfiladed ditches, a killing ground where besieging troops could be cut off and destroyed. Still a functioning army base to this day, it has a very different feel to the ceremonial pomp of Ottawa – Quebec is a place with the sense of having experienced the sharp end of Empire, where the British had once conquered and held down a subject French population by force. Both Ottawa and Quebec would have impressed themselves on the young Lady Sybil – the reassuring pomp of Ottawa and the reality of military power in Quebec.

The Greys were of course involved in much ceremonial. Two years before, Vera had described the St Andrews Day ball given for Earl Minto (her uncle Rolly) and his wife at Montreal:

> We were marshalled into the hall, first six men in full Highland dress playing the pipes. We walked through a long hall lined with a guard of honour of the Royal Scots, to one of the reception rooms where we stood whilst Uncle Rolly and Mary received the principal guests. Then the procession formed up again and we passed down some steps into the most splendid ballroom I have ever seen, bigger by far than the Buckingham Palace one and hung all round with flags. At the farther end there was the throne with a big canopy and a band on top of the canopy. About 500 people, so there was always heaps of room. It was very amusing and I enjoyed it immensely.

The Grey's period at Government House was one in which there was less formality and the Governor made himself very accessible.

The first few years of the Grey's existence in Canada were ones of prosperity and happiness. But then in January 1907, a little over two years after their arrival, tragedy struck – Sybil's elder sister, Vera (Lady Victoria Grenfell) fell ill. It all happened very unexpectedly. Vera had accompanied her husband Arthur Grenfell on a business trip to Central America. Returning from Mexico to Ottawa, she almost immediately fell ill. To start with it was assumed to be a bad fever but it became evident that she was suffering from typhoid. Still the Greys assumed that she would pull through, but she continued to decline and after a terrible illness lasting 26 days she died aged only 28, leaving her husband and three young children.

Her family were stunned and grief stricken. Her mother Alice wrote to a friend: 'I am still unable to realise that it is true that we have lost beloved Vera, and that we shall never see her again with these earthly eyes of ours, or touch her.' Her younger sister Evy wrote: 'I think the door will open and Vera will come in – or I shall find her in some room. You see I never thought she would die.'[6]

There is no record of Sybil's thoughts or feelings, but she must have been devastated. Vera had always been there for her, sometimes yelling at her to do things, but always close to her heart, addressing her in letters as 'Dear Sybikins'. She was Sybil's other half. The Grey's comfortable and cosseted life as Canada's 'first family' must suddenly have felt empty and meaningless. But of all the family, Sybil was best placed to render her dead sister a last service. The body made a final progress from Ottawa to the coast on a Canadian Pacific Railway train garlanded with flowers and green branches, and was loaded onto a ship to be carried back to England for burial. Sybil accompanied her sister on her last journey, with her to the end.

---

6 Letters written by Countess Grey and Lady Evelyn Grey to Elsie Reford, 1907, (from the Reford collection.

8

Vice-regal visit to the Yukon (1909)

Sybil's next set of letters and diaries cover the summer of 1909, nearly two and half years after the death of her sister Vera. During that time of course Earl Grey and his family continued their public roles in Canada despite their loss, and Sybil also travelled backwards and forwards between Britain and Canada. It is difficult to know her state of mind, partly because in all her surviving letters she never wrote once about Vera's death, a void which itself perhaps speaks of the extent of her loss. Her relationship with the rest of her family, particularly her mother and young sister, deepened and she always remained very close to her father and brother. She may have taken it upon herself to an extent to fill the gap left by her elder sister. She was devoted to her young niece Vera and to her nephews Harry and Reggie, and it was she who invited her friend Hilda Lyttelton (four years her junior) to Canada and introduced her to Arthur Grenfell – they married in February 1909.

Some beautiful glass negative photographs were taken of the Greys in Ottawa. An early one shows quite a tubby, fresh-faced young Sybil, in a shiny satin dress perhaps before a grand occasion, taken in about 1905-06. Another set shows a much thinner Sybil and her sister Evy in 1911. Sybil sits reading, her face turned away from the viewer, apparently lost in thought.

In the intervening years Sybil may have been depressed by the loss of the sister she had treasured – Earl Grey, writing in 1909, perhaps reflected this earlier depression when he wrote that: 'the sight of Sybil happy, eager and sympathetic makes my heart leap for joy.' But she was not a person to allow events and circumstances to overwhelm her. She matured, partly through accompanying her father on some of his trips across Canada which she traversed three times. She perhaps became more thoughtful and serious and brilliantly filled the role of companion to her father on his vice-regal trip to the Yukon in 1909. She retained her sense of humour but was now more concerned with bigger questions – particularly the way that the Dominion her father governed was developing and its future potential. She was also sensitive to the natural wonders and almost spiritual quality of the great primeval wilderness of the Pacific West Coast.

As well as perhaps filling her dead sister's place in the Grey family, she became friends with other women – for example Elsie Reford, about ten years older than her, who perhaps helped fill a void in Sybil's world left by the death of Vera. Another friend from this time was Aileen Roberts, daughter of Field Marshal Lord Roberts, twelve years older than Sybil, who became a close friend and confidante. And it could even be that Sybil consciously or unconsciously resolved to fulfil some of the potential that had been denied to both her own mother and to Vera by the restricting customs of the time, which saw early marriage as the natural destiny of women.

Sybil Grey, 1911, by Topley, (Library and Archives Canada)

Vice-regal visit

Two and a half years after the death of Vera, Sybil, her father Earl Grey, Lord Harry Lascelles[1] (his ADC) and her friend Lady Sybil Brodrick,[2] both about Sybil's age, left Ottawa on their own special train on the first leg of the epic journey. It would take them right across the continent to Vancouver, then up the beautiful Pacific West Coast to Prince Rupert, and on to Dawson City in the Yukon, which a mere ten years before had been capital of the Klondike Gold Rush.

They left Countess Alice Grey in quarantine in Ottawa, recovering from a bout of scarlet fever. For weeks she'd been isolated in her bedroom – Sybil had even bought a pair of megaphones so as to be able to talk to her mother from the garden below her sickroom! Her sister Evy stayed behind to look after her mother.

On 29 August 1909 they set out from Ottawa: 'The train was very comfortable, two cars and a baggage wagon.' The ends of such trains had an open platform with seats for observing the passing scenery. Sybil described how the two young women sat there: 'reading, talking and admiring the scenery which is wild and desolate, mostly burnt forest land with rocks and one big lake after another. We had lovely evening lights as we went along the shores of Lake Superior.'

As it was an official vice-regal tour, they were supplied with abundant information at every stage of their journey, by the officials and dignitaries of each town they visited. Sybil was a good listener and kept detailed notes – she was genuinely interested in everything from the process of railway construction to the hydrology used for mining in the Yukon, and from city development to the economics of wheat and fruit farming. Mr Skelly of the Canadian Pacific Railway explained how railway tracks were laid, their gradients, the calculation of how much tonnage could be transported and the problems besetting construction – for example 'musk egg' where unstable ground caused subsidence and undermined the line.

Winnipeg

Sybil was surprised to be asked by one of the wives of the dignitaries to speak to the girls of Winnipeg: 'She said the girls here do nothing but gamble, smoke and drink, not a very complimentary thing to say about one's town.'

They toured the town and an experimental farm outside. Sybil had been to Winnipeg three years before and was impressed by how much had changed. 'There are many new streets with good houses and beautiful green lawns with avenues of trees bordering the sidewalk, where three years ago was nothing but prairie.' The town had grown from 42,000 to 250,000, and land values had shot up by more than 26 fold.

They travelled on through the prairies, stopping to be shown more experimental farms, until they reached Moose Jaw, and continued through the night to Calgary at the edge of the Rockies. 'At 5 a.m. I woke father and Sybil. The latter dressed

---

1 Lord Henry Lascelles, subsequently 6th Earl of Harewood (1882-1947). He later married George V's daughter, Princess Mary, in 1922.
2 Lady Sybil Brodrick (1884-1934). She was the daughter of William St. John Broderick, 1st Earl of Midleton. She was a lifelong friend of Sybil Grey.

but father came in his pyjamas and dressing gown to the observation car. It was really beautiful – the sun was rising and shining on the foothills of the Rockies, making them a bright pink and they toned in with the pink clouds above.'

At the next station Sybil Brodrick ill-advisedly got off the train to photograph Sybil Grey and her father sitting on the end: 'She took so long focusing that the train started without her, with the result that she fell against the step, barked her shins, nearly broke her camera and dropped her shoe.' Earl Grey jumped out of the moving train 'at peril of his life' and retrieved it for her. Sybil Brodrick would continue to be accident prone, suffering from problems with her illnesses and toothache.

Sybil made arrangements to meet her cousin Angus McDonnell at Laggan near Banff – he was working nearby. 'No sooner did his train come in than he ran jostling along platform, pipe in mouth, carrying his grip sack.' They walked eight miles to

Evelyn Grey, 1911, by Topley, (Library and Archives Canada)

the Lake Louise Hotel. She was sorry that Angus had to leave that evening to return to his work at Sicanus. 'The Canadian Pacific Railway has not given him any more work and he rather wants to return to Virginia – I hope he doesn't.'

Having crossed the Rockies, they reached British Columbia and visited a fruit farm on the Learmouth estate, where 200 acres were already under orchard and a further 700 waiting to be developed. Sybil noted the problems of growing the young trees and irrigating them. 'It takes four men six weeks to irrigate 200 acres and costs about $300. They say that when an orchard is nine or ten months old one might make from $100 to $400 net profit per acre. That remains to be seen.'

Another cousin, Arnold Keppel, two years younger than Sybil, visited and told them of the insecurity of casual workers on such fruit farms. He himself had been working on a farm for $15 a month while paying $20 for his food and lodging. He moved on to a second orchard where he received $25 per month and his board, but his new employer had to discharge two of his men as he was hard up and couldn't pay their wages. 'Arnold had talked to quite a few fruit growers and had come to the conclusion that most rather wished that they were out of it. Quite a different tale to what we'd been hearing all the morning.' Arnold had decided to quit fruit growing and was thinking of sheep farming instead!

Vancouver

On 5 August, they arrived in Vancouver to be met by the Lieutenant Governor of British Columbia, James Dunsmuir and his wife. Dunsmuir was one of several great entrepreneurs, born into poverty in Scotland, who had emigrated and built up huge fortunes – in his case in machinery and industry, to become the richest man in British Columbia. Other towering figures who had similarly worked their way up from nothing in Canada included George Stephen,[3] later Lord Mount Stephen, owner of the Canadian Pacific Railway, and Donald Smith,[4] Lord Strathcona, governor of the Hudson Bay Company and president of the Bank of Montreal. Both sons of crofters in their native Scotland, these men were among the Empire's foremost entrepreneurs, philanthropists and politicians. They were all friends and acquaintances of Earl Grey.

In the afternoon the Greys embarked on a government boat, the *Quadra*, to take them up the coast to Prince Rupert. They progressed up the Inside Passage along the Pacific West Coast. 'We sat out on deck reading part of the morning but it was quite cold. Most of the day we were steaming through absolutely calm waters that

---

3 George Stephen, 1st Baron Mount Stephen (1829-1921). Mount Stephen was born in Dufftown, Scotland, where he began work as a stable boy. He emigrated to Canada at the age of eighteen. He and his first cousin, Donald Smith, from a similar humble background, worked together to build up great business empires, creating the Canadian Pacific Railway, and becoming major philanthropists, building hospitals in Montreal and London. Mount Stephen gave his fishing lodge at Grand Metis to his niece, Elsie Reford.

4 Donald Smith, 1st Baron Strathcona, (1820-1914); like his cousin, George Stephen, emigrated from Scotland. He worked for the Hudson Bay Company, becoming its president, and also embarked on a political career, as well as becoming President of the Bank of Montreal. Both men formed social ties with the British Royal family by the end of their lives.

much resembled a big river with mountains on either side densely wooded right down to the water's edge, with no sign of the habitation of man.'

At five o'clock however they reached Queen Charlotte's Sound, four hours of open sea, where the boat began to pitch about, bringing on Sybil's habitual seasickness. 'I stuck manfully to the jigsaw puzzle I was doing until I was overcome and had to make a very hurried exit.'

The Greys on a train in Canada. Earl Grey, centre, is flanked by Sybil and Countess Grey with Evy on the extreme right, (Durham University)

Prince Rupert

The next day they reached Prince Rupert. 'The town is on a hill with a commanding view over all the harbour which is a most magnificent one, infinitely better than Vancouver. The harbour looks like a huge lake with a number of beautiful wooded islands in it.' Prince Rupert was a town literally in the process of being born:

> The site of the town is there but as the lots were only being sold on 25th of May, the town is more or less imaginary, although there are countless wooden houses being built everywhere – all the town is laid out in avenues and streets on the New York system. At the present moment everywhere you get wet morass and roots of trees, and then a cleared patch with a house, and then more wet ground with tree trunks, but this is the West not the East so houses grow up like mushrooms in the night and the Prince Rupert of today is not recognisable a week hence.

The next morning they continued up the coast, passing through a large school of porpoises which Lord Harry tried in vain to shoot.

'We caught sight of a high glacier at about 4pm and slowly approached it all afternoon until it unfolded itself into a whole range of mountains with glaciers, the sun lighting up the peaks.' They had reached the Wrangle Narrows – a 30 mile long channel just big enough for a ship – where they had to wait until the next day to navigate the narrow passage.

Here on a deserted stretch of coastline they went ashore and walked into the forest where as we've seen Sybil experienced her epiphany, lying in silence on the floor of the great forest. It was a response which we would now perhaps characterise as something between a near religious sensibility and modern environmental concern for nature. Sybil wrote: 'We felt so immeasurably far away from the world where all is hurry, bustle and striving for life – and it all seemed so petty and small in this grand silent forest. How I understand the love of the Silent Places and how it must grow on one.'

Skagway

Arriving in Skagway they were met by Mr Graves, an Englishman, President of the White Pass and Yukon Railway, and Major Wood and Major Snyder of the North West Mounted Police, who showed them round the town. It had been called 'the Gateway to the Golden North' during the Klondike gold rush of less than a decade before. 'It is now practically deserted from what it used to be in 1898 and 1900. There are only about 800 inhabitants now to the 10,000 of those days.'

Sybil related its history graphically as it was told to her. When the first gold rush stampede began, Skagway had been disputed territory as to whether it was part of Canada or the United States – with the result that there was no jurisdiction and it was completely lawless. 'The consequence was that the town was a sink of iniquity, and all the people who were wanted in America and other countries congregated there, and the town was wide open.' A tall handsome, well-spoken soap peddler called Jefferson Smith, 'Soapy Smith', was uncrowned King of Skagway and his word was law. Smith raised a private army of some 400 men and astutely offered his 'volunteers' to the American president to fight in the Spanish American war.

The offer was refused with thanks and the President's letter was framed and hung up in Smith's gambling and drinking bar. Sybil says: 'Soapy Smith belonged to the criminal class who had brains. He seldom took an active part in crimes of violence, which he regarded as the work of underlings, but he held the town in terror for two years and robbed nearly everyone.'

Smith's nemesis came in 1898 with the arrival of the railway men, a rallying point for the majority of the townspeople who favoured law and order. Things came to a head when Soapy's men robbed a young man of $3,000 in gold dust which he was bringing back from the Yukon. The citizens of Skagway notified Smith that the money must be returned. When this failed to happen, the citizens held a mass meeting and formed a vigilance committee with Mr Graves as its chairman. Soapy Smith's men attempted to disperse the meeting which was guarded by only two railway man, Reid and an Irishman called Murphy.

Suddenly Soapy Smith himself appeared, armed to the teeth with a couple of big revolvers, a cartridge belt and a double barrelled Winchester repeating rifle, followed by fourteen of his men forming a bodyguard. Sybil took up the tale:

> Soapy shouted to the crowd to go to bed and then went up to Reid and told him to be gone. When Reid did not move, he hit him over the head with the barrel of his rifle. Reid put up one hand to protect his head, catching the barrel. Soapy in trying to free himself, jerked the rifle back suddenly, which brought the muzzle against Reid's stomach. Reid continued to hold Soapy's rifle with one hand, but with his free hand he gently got hold of his revolver in his pocket and without taking it out, shot Soapy through the heart. Simultaneously Soapy pumped four shots into Reid's stomach. Soapy was killed instantly and Reid died of his wounds next day.

When Soapy's bodyguard saw him fall, they drew their revolvers and sprang forward for vengeance on the unarmed crowd. But at this point the second guard, Murphy, seized Soapy's repeater, aiming it at each of the leading men in the bodyguard one after the other. They then turned and ran, the crowd of citizens now following them like a bloodthirsty pack of wolves and capturing the gang. Some of them were hanged and others received heavy sentences.

Sybil clearly relished the drama of the story and Skagway's reputation as a wild west town. The shootout had only happened ten years before. She remarked that it could not have occurred in Dawson, where the North West Mounted Police were in charge.

Gold

In 1896, gold was discovered on the Klondike River by an American prospector named George Carmack, his Tagish[5] wife, her brother Skookum Jim, and their nephew Dawson Charlie. Just as in California fifty years before, the Klondike gold rush saw a tidal wave of prospectors flooding to this remote region of the Yukon. Between 1896 and 1899, an estimated 100,000 of them came from Seattle, San Francisco, from the East Coast and even from Europe. Some became wealthy but

---

5 The Tagish are a native American tribe of north west Canada (source Wikipedia).

the majority failed. They came with minimal equipment, trekking overland and by boat to get there and struggling to establish their individual claims. Dawson, on the confluence of the Yukon and Klondike rivers, grew from a hastily constructed town of wooden buildings in 1896 to around 30,000 by the summer of 1898.

The Klondike gold rush ended just as abruptly in 1899, when news came that gold had been discovered in Alaska, drawing away prospectors yet again towards the next Eldorado, leaving the field to the mining companies and their heavy machinery to continue to try to extract gold from the Yukon's soil.

Whitehorse

The Grey party travelled on to Whitehorse, aboard a special train. Sybil described the White Pass route over the mountains: 'Leaving Skagway the train begins almost at once a steady climb over wild and rugged mountains, and continues to climb for twenty miles until it reaches the summit where the boundary line divides Alaska from British Columbia.' She was told that the gradient to the summit was not as great as that on Kicking Horse Pass, but thought it infinitely grander and more impressive. 'The track has literally been hewn out of the side of a precipice with the rushing Skagway River hundreds of feet below. The line was started in April 1898 and reached Whitehorse in June 1900 – a distance of 110 miles. The men were working up to the summit all the winter; they were standing on glaciers and had to be roped. They must all have suffered terrible hardship.'

Until the line crossing the mountain was completed the crowds of prospectors bound for Dawson had previously to tramp across the mountains, over the White Pass and the Chilkoot Pass. The White Pass had earned the sinister name of Dead Horse Trail:

> A regular stream of men and horses ascended this pass in Indian file like a huge centipede. During the rush the narrow trail was blocked (standing room only) for the greater part of the 40 miles of its distance, so that neither man nor horse could go faster than the speed of the centipede that slowly wound its way over the pass. If a horse fell it generally meant death unless he could get up very quickly, which he seldom could as he was always very heavily laden.

Mr Graves told of how one morning he had seen the body of a horse which had fallen and been shot, lying across the path still warm; when he returned that evening, all that was left was his head on one side and his tail on the other, 'the traffic had ground him up.'

Sybil rode in the cab of the locomotive all the way up to the summit (Inspiration Point) from which the train descended to Bennett, the town on the other side of the mountains, now almost deserted, from which gold prospectors had set out in homemade boats to go up river to Dawson. 'Most of them had never even sawn wood before so their boats were flimsy to a degree, but very few lost their lives.'

They reached Whitehorse at 3pm and the whole town came out to meet them with a band beneath a beautiful triumphal arch. They inspected the town and were assigned two magnificent North West Mounted police troopers as their orderlies, 'great big tall good looking men'.

A special boat, the *Whitehorse*, was provided for their journey up river to Dawson. 'These riverboats are like huge houseboats and draw only two feet of water. They have six rudders and it is simply wonderful how they manage them. The river is very swift, averages about five knots, and twists and turns a good deal.' Often the channel was very narrow and the boat had to manoeuvre through the gaps. They stopped at Selkirk, third largest town of the Yukon, but found it: 'practically nothing but an Indian settlement with a big general store where prospectors and trappers fit out before their expeditions.' Earl Grey bought a pair of beaded Indian gloves for his wife. They tried to photograph some Indians who immediately vanished inside their houses.

They went on in a rather irritable and selfish mood: 'unsure whether we will like Dawson or Dawson us.' Sybil Brodrick suffered from acute toothache and Sybil Grey and her father were in low spirits: 'we had both either caught chills or been poisoned, the result being not conducive to play up to a lot of people who we have never seen before.' It was windy and Sybil commented: 'it is distinctly difficult to walk down ships' ladders with grace and dignity when your skirt is being blown over your head and your hat suddenly goes over one ear and then descends over your nose!'

Twelve miles from Dawson they were met by another boat, the *Lightning*, with about 80 to 100 people on board, again with a band playing. They were formally greeted by members of the Yukon Council, headed by Mr Henderson, the Commissioner, with an address read by Mr C B Burns, secretary to the council.

Dawson

They arrived at their destination: 'Dawson was gay with flowers and looked a very unpretentious little town nestling under a mountain and on the river. There was a triumphal arch on the wharf and heaps of bunting and a good many people, enough RNWMP [Mounties] in their red uniforms to make the scene look gay.' They were taken to Minto Park where another address was read to them by the Territorial Secretary, Mr Charles Macdonald, and they were presented with the text of the address in a huge album made of moose and caribou hide with long tassels and enclosed in a beautiful box. 'On the outside of the box was a description of what it was, done in poker work and in the centre a picture of a miner's pick, shovel and pan with some real gold nuggets on it. Inside were photographs of the Yukon and pressed flowers, quite beautifully done by Mrs Black wife one of the councillors.' (Martha Louise Black, an expert on local flora, and her husband George, were 'the first real Yukoners' to hold public office).

They stayed at Government House, the home of Mr and Mrs Henderson and their twelve-year-old daughter Gracie, who decamped to a hotel during their visit. While Sybil Brodrick visited the dentist, they were taken to see the town's hospital, run by an order of Catholic nuns. 'We were greeted as we drove up with a song of welcome sung from the balcony, the solo by a little boy and the chorus by some little girls very nicely dressed in white. Inside the nurses greeted us and some of the cream of Dawson society,' and they listened to more piano recitals and song.

Afterwards they visited the Carnegie Library, followed by dinner and a reception to which the whole town was invited:

A general notice had been put in the paper to say, 'all citizens are invited', so that we had the most delightful time, every sort of person coming. Old women and old men in their working clothes; tradespeople; the old timers; young boys all hopeful of making their fortunes; men who have already made theirs and others who have lost the game; but everybody cheerful and hopeful. Father and I stood at the door and shook hands, Father asking them each in turn, how long they had been in the country, what they were doing, and where they [had] come from.

There was a very good orchestra and refreshments. Each of the visitors were presented with a gift from the people of the Yukon made by the jewellers of Dawson: 'Father with a gold cigarette case the upper side covered with small squashed nuggets; Lord Harry with the same pattern as a matchbox; Sybil with a gold nugget and mastodon bracelet[6]; and self with a lovely gold nugget bracelet, with flat pearl shaped nuggets from Jack Wade Creek.'

Her father made a speech of thanks, but Sybil ducked the chance of doing the same: 'I missed my opportunity through not being able to make up my mind in time – a lesson for next time.' Sybil was just beginning to find her feet in public life. She met the aspiring young writer, Robert Service, who worked as a bank clerk. She had bought his debut book of poems, *Songs of a Sourdough* (a word for an old time prospector in Canada), famous for the poem *The Ballad of Dan McGrew*. Sybil admired his work, but she was doubtful when he told her that his next book, *Ballads of a Chechako* would be even better. Sybil wrote: 'I don't think a man is a good judge of his own work.'

King Solomon's Dome

The next day (13 August) they made an expedition to the Summit of King Solomon's Dome, some 30 miles from Dawson. They went in two cars, accompanied by Mr and Mrs Henderson and Gracie, Mr Congdon (a member of Parliament for the Yukon), Judge Craig and Major Wood. 'The road was fairly good but we were a good deal bumped about. Dawson is about 2,200 feet above sea level and the Dome is about 1,800 feet higher. We motored along Hunters Creek, past Last Chance which was immensely rich, Independence, Gold Bottom[7] et cetera, and then another couple of miles along the top of the ridge to the summit.' The journey took approximately three and half hours!

Here elaborate preparations had been made for them: 'a huge tent with luncheon, every kind of delicacy having been procured – they had to import cows to Dawson in order that we should have fresh cream and milk during our stay. There are also two small tents fitted out as dressing rooms – one for Father, one for S and self.'

It is one event for which we have a photograph – taken by a local photographer E. O. Ellingsen – showing the whole party on the Dome, standing in front of a large marquee, Sybil, Lord Harry and Earl Grey smiling, with little Gracie Henderson in

6 Mastodon ivory.
7 All famous sites of the Klondike gold rush.

The Greys visit the Solomon Dome at Dawson, Yukon (Yukon Archives)

between, while Sybil Brodrick scowls at the ground in pain from her toothache.

The two Sybils competed for men – Sybil Grey's diary jibed: 'Sybil sat by Dr Thompson to whom she quite lost her heart – she always manages to get hold of the nicest man and then sticks to him.' Sybil Brodrick replied in her own handwriting: 'Sybil Grey does the same, luckily there is always more than one nice man.'

After lunch they admired the view from the summit: 'From it one has the most wonderful all round view I have ever seen. One overlooks hilly undulating wild looking country as far as one can see, brought up by ranges of mountains on the horizon – the Ogilvie Range, the Rockies, etc. It was a glorious day when we were there and the sun was shining, but we could at the same time see half a dozen rain clouds, and the lights and shades were beautiful and the blue mountains wonderful.'

Sybil Grey asked whether she could stake a claim on the goldfield and it was arranged for her enthusiastically.

They were told that all the gold creeks radiated out from the Dome, which was the source of most of the Klondike gold finds. Gold was frequently found in association with quartz. Sybil learned quartz had been discovered within the Dome, 'now the question is whether it goes through any depth. They are tunnelling now at a depth of 800 feet and expect soon to hit upon the big vein if it exists. The theory is that the mother lode is probably there. On this depends the future prosperity of Dawson. If they fail to find quartz in the extent they expect to, Dawson is a thing of the past.'

On the way home they stopped and she walked half a mile from the road and staked her claim, proudly recording the coordinates. She wrote: 'my claim is in a direct lead to the Dome, so if that turns out rich, my claim will be of some value.' She paid $5 to register the claim, and was given a year in which to begin developing it – something she clearly never did.

After dinner, Earl Grey and Lord Harry were inducted into the Arctic Brotherhood – a secret society founded by the gold rush stampeders in 1899, to provide fraternal help and intellectual stimulus. The Dawson Lodge had 600 members: 'they presented Father with a beautiful address made of moose hide and about six feet long. They had a most convivial evening and got back after 1 a.m.'.

On 14 August they visited the four Dawson jewellers whose work was presented to them on arrival, Sybil buying presents – a gold pin for Evy and a bracelet as a wedding present for her friend Dorothy Onslow who married Edward Wood (later Lord Halifax)[8] in September.

They visited the great hydraulic engineering works above Bonanza Creek: 'where they have three "Giants" demolishing the hill.' After the first flood of individual miners had worked out Dawson's creeks, mechanisation was brought in to reclaim gold with much greater ease and in far greater quantities. Hydraulic diggers (the Giants) deposited the soil in troughs where the lighter waste was washed away, leaving the gold caught in pockets of the trough as it flowed downhill.

They then visited another of Dawson's mining marvels – the 'Ditch' running along the edge of the hill bringing water to the site for the digging machines. The Ditch was a channel 54 miles long bringing water from the Rocky Mountains. It had taken two years to build as work had to stop in the winter and the engineers had immense problems with unstable soil atop the glacier, which required them to dig deep down into the glacier to provide a foundation for a water channel.

Finally, they saw the 'Dredges' at work on Bonanza Creek. Formerly one of the richest creeks in the days of the gold rush, it was worked out from the point of view of individual miners but was still productive when worked by a dredge:

> The Dredge moves along the creek… it scoops up the earth in front of it in large buckets and empties them into the monster's stomach, the empty buckets returning in an unending circular motion for more earth and gold. Inside the monster there is machinery that washes and separates the gold from the waste, retaining the former and throwing out the latter by a shaft at the rear, so that it is all the time creeping slowly onward leaving a pile twenty foot high of waste and stones behind it. A terrible monster indeed.

They had a final dinner before departing. 'At eleven o'clock we all went on to the dance. At Dawson they always have a dance every Saturday. The band was quite good and the floor divine. I enjoyed it all very much. It was an excellent way of saying goodbye to our many friends.'

At midnight as they left the ballroom to go to their ship they found the street full of Arctic Brothers who had all come with torches to wish their new brothers God speed and escort them down to the wharf:

---

8 Lady Dorothy Onslow, Countess Halifax (1885-1976). Edward Wood, Lord Halifax, (1881-1959). They married in September 1909.

It was a very pretty sight – we slowly motored down to the wharf between two lines of Arctic Brothers. The wharf to our great astonishment was crowded and we felt really sad to say goodbye to all our friends. We stood on the top deck and waved our bouquets and they cheered and yelled 'Mush On'.[9] No people could have been kinder to us than they have been and we all four have enjoyed every moment of our time.

The party's return from Dawson to Vancouver was also full of incident and stories.

They journeyed for three and a half days by river back to Whitehorse. They visited isolated people en route, such as a Norwegian man named Hendrickson who lived in a cottage beside the river with his wife and two little children. 'Her cottage was a model of tidiness and care. Everything was soigné and showed good taste. She showed us some really lovely photographs that they'd taken.' Mr Hendrickson supplied wood to the steamers: 'he clears about $1000 a year after all living expenses – but it must be terribly lonely, miles away from any other human habitation, and after the boat ceases to pass in the Fall they hardly see anyone until the river opens again next year.'

They heard stories from Major Wood about the extreme rigours that people faced in the winter, particularly the dangers of snow blindness. 'He told us that three or four years ago he was snow blind. He was riding one day and after he been out for a long time he noticed that the snow took on a pink shade and then got a deeper pink. He knew at once that this meant he was going snow blind, so started to ride home; by the time he reached home he couldn't see at all and he was suffering agony.' He had to spend a fortnight in a totally darkened room until his eyesight recovered and his eyes grew accustomed to light again.

He was luckier than the Mounted Policeman they lost to snow blindness:

This poor man was sent on some mission and went snow blind, but he struggled manfully on. He fired his rifle several times and as he was groping about he found a wire fence. He got hold of this and walked alongside it, hoping to reach a hut. Unfortunately, although there was a hut within 300 yards of him he never found it, for the fence enclosed a circle with the hut in the centre. So he went round and round. They found him and his horse three days later, he was dead, the horse all right. On his breast was a piece of paper on which he had written, 'have gone snow blind, have tried to get through and do my duty but can go no further.'

Two stories stand out from the Greys' trip back down the coast – their two-day trip up the Nimkish River in Indian canoes, and the incident at Jervis Inlet where Earl Grey got lost in the forest at nightfall.

The Nimkish

Sybil related their trip up the Nimkish with vivid descriptions of their visit to an Indian settlement. The Greys arrived at Alert Bay and went ashore to see the totem poles: 'The totem poles are really wonderful here and each house has one in front

---

9 'Mush On' is a traditional command given to a dog team to start, probably from the French *marchons*

of it. It is really exactly the same as our (coats of) arms. The bear family marry into the salmon family, who in turn marry into the goblin family, so their totem pole consists of a bear, a salmon and a horrible grinning goblin.'

She described the houses: 'The middle of the roof is a foot higher than the rest so that the smoke from the fires can escape; also there are large cracks between the boards forming the sides of the house so that there is always plenty of fresh air, which is very lucky as otherwise they would die of tuberculosis. Each family make their own wood fire on the ground in the centre of their little patch and they lie round it with their belongings, food, pots and pans in a higglety-pigglety mess about them.'

The village was holding a Potlatch: 'All the Indians from the surrounding country having collected together to choose their chief for a year – the man who gave the most blankets and money away during the year being chosen. We found them all grouped together with their blue and red blankets thrown around them, sitting in the principal street and one of the principal men holding the staff of office and holding forth to them.'

The Greys arranged to hire two canoes with Indian guides to take them up the Nimkish River. And they admired a war canoe made out of the bole of a single tree – big enough to carry 50 or 60 men.

The party set out in their canoes the next day. Earl Grey and Sybil Brodrick in the first canoe, piloted by an Indian named Jerry; Lord Harry and Sybil Grey following in the second canoe. 'They are enormous and most comfortable boats. We had cushions and sat in the bottom of them with plenty of room for our legs. We each had a fishing rod, a rifle and a camera.' After paddling two miles across the bay they reached the mouth of the the Nimkish: 'It is the most lovely river, full of strong rapids and it is perfectly wonderful how the Indians manage to pole their canoes through them. One goes up one of these roaring rapids and turns the corner and comes upon an absolutely still looking pool.'

Coming round a bend in the river they suddenly encountered a bear:

> Lord Harry was sitting in front and as we turned the corner I suddenly saw him grasp his rifle, so looked quickly round and saw a black bear coming out of the bush at the river's edge a little way in front of us. He took to the water to swim the river and I had just shot at him and missed him, shooting too low, then Lord Harry did the same. His next shot hit him. All this time he was swimming towards us across the river. We finally killed him after shooting many times. Unfortunately I broke his jaw and most of his teeth – the shooting was atrocious, certainly on my part.

It was a good size black bear with big pads – weighing 240lbs., the length from the tip of his nose to his hind feet being six feet ten inches. They put him in their canoe and paddled down the river in triumph: 'both of us so pleased that we could hardly bear it.' At the mouth of the river they handed the bear over to the Indians to skin. The charge for the four Indian guides and two canoes for two half days was $22.50 and $3.00 for skinning the bear.

Jervis Inlet

Their second adventure took place at Jervis Inlet, on a remote part of the coast, surrounded by high mountains. They learned that a white man lived a mile down the Inlet. 'He turned out to be the most delightful American prospector, by name Johnstone. A fine big man six foot six, with a beautiful face and eyes – the eyes of a man well acquainted with the 'Silent Places' and life in the wilderness.' He would spend the summer away prospecting for about eight months, without seeing another human being. 'He has two fine sons of nineteen and seventeen that we saw – good looking, charming, well mannered lads, nature's gentlemen. He also has two other sons of twelve and four, and a daughter who we did not see.' The man offered to guide them the next day to the top of the mountain above the inlet, 5,500 feet high where they could hunt goat, deer and bear.

In a corner of her diary, Sybil noted his address: C. R. Johnstone, Slats Quarry, Deserted Bay, Jervis Inlet.

The trip up the mountain failed to come off because of an escapade that nearly finished off Earl Grey. That evening at 6pm the Earl took his dog Cabot out for a walk. The others had all spent the day climbing the hills and they rested, listening to two of the Quadra's sailors playing a guitar and a violin and singing Scottish airs and Negro spirituals. By 9pm they began to worry about the continued absence of his lordship. 'At 9.30 it had been pitch dark for an hour and there was no sign of him. I was afraid that he had sprained his ankle and was lying unable to move in the forest'; but he had the dog Cabot and a rifle with him. Two boats scoured the shore and they sent up mighty shrieks of the Quadra's steam whistle which echoed and re-echoed from the mountain tops. 'After that we listened intently and heard very far off the faint report of the crack of a rifle.'

By this time it was 10pm and Lord Harry set off in the third boat with extra coats and a brandy flask to search the shoreline. They spotted a fire lit on the shore some two miles away. It proved to be a fire made by the Indians, but the Earl had also spotted it and arrived there to meet them 'hot and absolutely played out.' The dog Cabot also turned up unhurt.

Earl Grey told them how he had had a frightful time coming down the mountain in the dark. He got about a thousand feet up the mountain when the light began to fade and he tried to find a quick way down. He lost the deer trail and got hung up in a ravine from which he couldn't get out. There was a lot of fallen timber and he picked his way down these logs at an angle of 45 degrees. At last he descended a 50 foot log in the dark. On reaching the end of the log he felt for the ground and instead encountered only empty space, dropped his stick and Cabot disappeared into the ravine. 'Well, he had no idea of whether the drop was six foot or thirty feet, but he didn't dare to try, so he had to laboriously climb up the log to the top again.' At length he made his way down the mountain. 'Finally after much wandering he reached the water's edge and was rescued, exhausted, bruised and with a new suit which he put on that day for the first time ruined.'

The modern map of Jervis Inlet shows a bay marked as 'Earls Cove' – clearly in memory of this adventure which was widely reported by the press when they returned to Vancouver.

Another event also marked the end of 1909. Earl Grey's finances could be chaotic and his Comptroller, Arthur Sladen, wrote to the Earl regretfully reporting the poor performance of a number of investments. As a result Sladen was replaced as Comptroller by a new man sent out from England. He was Earl Grey's banker in Newcastle, Lambert Middleton, aged 32. Sybil wrote to her father: 'I'm so glad that Mr Middleton has proved a success – I always believed he would be!'

Thirteen years later, in 1922, Sybil and Lambert were to marry.

9

Elections, a wedding, an engagement
and a bankruptcy

Above all, Sybil inherited from her father an interest in politics. The years 1909-10 saw Britain locked in a struggle for the future of the country and Sybil was captivated by the excitement of it all.

The Liberal Government which had taken power from the Conservative-Unionist coalition in 1906 was a radical reforming government. It introduced the first old-age pension (admittedly at a low starting rate of five shillings a week), and brought in the first scheme of Social Security unemployment benefit, with a measure of health protection. In many ways it was the swansong of the Liberal Party in government. Although it had a large majority in the House of Commons, opposition in the Lords was fierce and was able to block key aspects of the Liberal programme. A prime example was the proposal for Irish Home Rule, first advanced by Gladstone in 1886 and proposed again in 1893, and in 1912-14 when it was enacted but finally blocked by an Irish Unionist revolt.

The Liberal's success at home was not matched in the field of foreign policy. Sir Edward Grey,[1] as Foreign Secretary, ended Britain's 'splendid isolation' and helped build the Entente Cordiale with France – an alliance which was later extended also to include Russia. But he was less surefooted in his response to the perceived threat from Germany. He was a politician who made clear that he detested war, but he was ultimately unable to prevent the slide into conflict in 1914.

The People's Budget

Things came to a head with the passage of the 1909 budget, dubbed the People's Budget, led by the Chancellor of the Exchequer, the charismatic radical Welsh MP David Lloyd George. Brought up in poverty in South Wales, Lloyd George saw it as a 'war budget' – its purpose being 'to wage implacable warfare against poverty and squalidness.' The key measures in the budget were to raise both income tax

---

1 Sir Edward Grey, 1st Viscount Grey of Fallodon (1862-1933). A Liberal statesman, and cousin and close neighbour of Albert 4th Earl Grey. He was the longest serving foreign secretary of the twentieth century (1905-16). He is associated with trying and failing to prevent the First World War – saying on its outbreak 'The lamps are going out all over Europe. We shall not see them lit again in our time.' He was also a confirmed countryman, an expert on ornithology and on fly fishing and a published author on these subjects. When it looked as though Sir Edward was to have an earldom conferred on him as well on his leaving government, Albert 4th Earl Grey put his foot down, declaring: 'Two Earl Greys within five miles of each other will cause endless confusion.'

and death duties, and to bring in a new super tax of 16p in the pound levied on incomes above £5,000 a year. The most controversial proposal was a capital gains tax on the increase in value of undeveloped land.[2]

It was fiercely opposed by rich landowners, and in the City and the House of Lords. It became increasingly clear that if the budget was to be passed, the power of the Lords to veto legislation would have to be curtailed.

Both sides used increasingly colourful and barbed language. In October 1909, in Newcastle, the Grey's home territory, Lloyd George told an audience that 'a fully equipped Duke costs as much to keep as two dreadnoughts – they are just as great a terror and they last longer!' His audience could have been in no doubt that his target was the Duke of Northumberland, Lord Henry Percy, who lived in Alnwick Castle.

Lloyd George asked rhetorically if it could be right that the Lords: '500 men, ordinary men chosen accidentally from among the ranks of the unemployed,' should overrule the will and choices of millions of working people.

Writing to her father in Canada, Sybil Grey gave the Conservative and Unionist view of Lloyd George: 'They say that he knows absolutely nothing about finance and that the only financial training he had before becoming Chancellor of the Exchequer was handing round the collection plate in his village church in Wales!! – which office hardly gives sufficient training to conduct the finances of the greatest nation in the world.' She thought him 'a poisonous man… I hope his downfall will be great.'

Sybil was in the public gallery of the House of Lords to see the debate when the Lords rejected the People's Budget. 'It was extraordinarily interesting and I am quite delighted to have anyhow seen the end of that historic debate.' Conservative backwoodsmen peers had been drafted in. The result was a large majority against the Budget. 'The house was crammed to overflowing, as some newspapers said all the "wild peers" had come to town. I don't think they expected so large a majority but it caused no excitement. They had hundreds and hundreds of police outside the House as they expected a row, but there wasn't a soul and everything passed off quietly.'

Election

The rejection of the budget however triggered a General Election, the first of two in 1910. Sybil's brother Charlie, Lord Howick, stood as the Unionist candidate in Bradford Central, against the sitting Liberal MP, Sir George Scott Robertson.

Sybil threw herself into the fray: 'Nothing is so exciting as a general election.' Based in the Midland Hotel, Bradford, and at Temple Newsam, the Jacobean country house of her friends Edward and Dorothy Wood, Lord and Lady Halifax, near Leeds, she chronicled the election. Her cousin, Liberal Foreign Secretary, Sir Edward Grey, told her that 'there was never an election in which people have been thinking as hard as they are in this one.'

She wrote: 'Here the business black-coated men are nearly all against us, but

2 Sourced History Today, online November 2009, volume 59, issue 11.

the working people are to a great extent with us.' She was shocked at the lack of patriotism. At a political meeting, a well-known speaker, failing to get a hearing from his audience, demanded: 'What will appeal to you – patriotism?'

'A man got up instantly and replied, "I don't care the dirt in my fingernail for patriotism" and the entire audience got up and cheered.'

She was amused however at a mocking question addressed by a heckler to her brother: 'Will Lord Howick, if returned, support a measure to enact that the eldest daughters of Peer-Actress marriages have the hereditary right to "turns" in tights before the footlights, however malformed their legs, seeing that elder sons have the hereditary right to legislate however diminutive their brains?'

They were joined in the campaign by Comtesse Sophie de Franqueville, the re-markably feisty 58-year-old aunt of Charlie's wife Mabel Palmer. Born Lady Sophia Palmer and married to a French count of slightly dubious title, Madame de Fran-queville was a one-woman attack dog for the aristocracy. Out canvassing one day she passed a tailor's shop where the owner had dressed a tailor's dummy up as a peer in robes, with scandalous things about the peerage written underneath. She immediately confronted the tailor, who told her that 'the great day has come when all peers would be overthrown' and that there wasn't a single peer who in the past or present had ever done a stroke of work or ever had a single ounce of brains.

Madame de Franqueville answered: 'How very interesting because I am a very good example of the British peerage myself!' They argued heatedly for an hour, before she left with the parting shot: 'Well, you may continue to show that figure' (pointing at the tailor's dummy) 'but you know after what I've told you that it is a lie.' She then left him 'feeling ever so much better.'

They drafted in several speakers, among whom Arthur Grenfell stood out for his persuasiveness and clarity. 'He said he was a banker and a businessman and in no way a politician. As a banker he lent money to both Conservatives and Liberals, treating them equally.' He cast doubt on Lloyd George's competence in finance. 'If this wild man is returned to power, the City and the big City firms will not lend credits to English enterprises, having lost confidence, but would lend their credit abroad and how is that going to benefit English trade?' He went on to attack the new stamp duty citing his own experience of how it had deterred foreign companies from investing in public developments in Britain.

Sybil was critical of her brother Charlie's speech. 'He speaks fairly fluently and with little hesitation and it is almost always excellent matter. The criticism one might make would be that it is sometimes a little dull and that there isn't much fire or enthusiasm.' But the electorate liked the fact that he didn't dodge answering questions.

The excitement built up relentlessly. On the eve of the poll she wrote: 'I am too excited to write any more. We can none of us stop still. Charlie, Mabel and I drove around our thirteen committee rooms and polling stations this morning in an open carriage, covered all over with blue and union jacks. We are going to do exactly the same this afternoon. We may win by 20 or be beaten by 800; we haven't the faintest idea what will happen.'

In the event Charlie Grey failed to take the Bradford Central seat – and the sitting Liberal MP slightly increased his majority. Nationally, the election produced a hung parliament, with the Conservatives under Arthur Balfour and their Unionist allies gaining the largest number of votes cast, but the Liberals under H. H. Asquith narrowly winning the largest number of seats – with 274 to the Conservatives' 272. Asquith formed a government with the support of the Irish Parliamentary Party led by John Redmond.

Suffragettes

Sybil also touched on the suffragettes, one of the most divisive issues of the day on which she was otherwise silent. Her letter in early January 1910 said: 'The suffragettes have decided that they will abandon their peaceful methods and take up violent ones.' She heard that Mr Asquith, the Prime Minister, was now guarded by eleven policemen and that he was convinced that he would have vitriol thrown in his face before the end of the General Election. She added 'They know a lot of these women are practising in shooting galleries.'

In fact the suffragettes were very divided and only a small section of the movement took up violent action – which nevertheless included bombing and arson. Sybil was unsympathetic to the Suffragette cause and her letter made fun of a prominent society suffragette who had abandoned her hunger strike: 'They arranged that Lady Constance Lytton should sacrifice herself for the good of the cause and that she should die in prison. To this she agreed, but at the last moment in the most unaccountable manner she seemed to prefer to live an unheroic life instead of dying the glorious death of a martyr!'

But she did recognise that stronger minded suffragettes were quite prepared to die, and related the story of another 'first-class woman' who refused food and was suspected of having smuggled in poison to kill herself. She was released because the Home Office said: 'For God's sake let that woman out, we can't have a dead suffragette on our hands.'

Sybil was also surprised to learn that her cousin Lady Sybil Smith, the daughter of the reactionary Earl of Antrim, was a supporter of the movement: 'Sybil Smith has gone quite loony on the subject. So I suppose we shall find her leading processions. She has Mrs Pankhurst to stay with her at Rolls.' Rolls Park, near Chigwell, Essex, was the Smith's house outside London.[3]

Of course, not all women were sympathetic to the suffragettes, some feeling that they violated the norms of femininity, others perhaps unaware of how brutally they were force fed in prison. Violet Markham, a friend of Sybil and of Earl Grey, in some respects a social reformer, was a leading light in the Women's Anti-Suffrage League. Both Sybil Grey and her mother seem to have been curiously indifferent

---

3 Sybil Smith did not give up her activism for the suffragettes. In Hansard of 7 August 1913, Keir Hardie MP asked the Home Secretary about the release from prison after four days of a fourteen day sentence of 'Lady Sybil Smith, daughter of the Earl of Antrim and well known as a militant suffragette' and asked if the clemency given to her would be extended to other suffragette prisoners. (Hansard, Millbanksystems: Suffragist prisoners).

to what is now seen as the most significant women's movement of the time.

The political upheavals of 1910 did not stop there. A deadlocked parliament staggered on until later that year when a second election was called by the government. It resulted in an almost identical tied result. The Parliament Act that was passed the following year in 1911 was the Liberal Government's revenge on the House of Lords, heavily curtailing its power to veto House of Commons bills.

Arthur and Hilda's wedding

Aside from politics, the family life of the Greys continued to change. Hilda Lyttelton[4] was four years younger than Sybil – they had met at a shooting party at the Albemarles when Hilda was nineteen. Beautiful and vivacious she was one of the friends Sybil invited out to stay with the family in Ottawa, where she met Arthur Grenfell, widower of Sybil's older sister Vera, with his young children, 'V' (Little Vera), Reggie and Harry who needed looking after.

Hilda and Arthur were married in February 1909. Having been bailed out once before in 1902, by 1909 Arthur was once again in severe financial difficulties in New York, with debts that threatened the prospects of his business recovering. Hearing of this, the Lytteltons demanded that he agree to an expensive marriage settlement in favour of Hilda. Arthur's brother in law , Guy St Aubyn, wrote to Earl Grey: 'As you know, he suffers from megalomania, so it is not surprising that the Lytteltons should regard him as Croesus.'

Arthur certainly reinforced the image of being made of money when in 1910 he bought Roehampton House, a palatial Queen Anne house in south west London, which he proceeded to extend, even commissioning the famous architect Edwin Lutyens to build on a great ballroom. Later that year, Arthur held a lavish ball in Hilda's honour – with 140 to dinner, followed by dancing. Sybil described the occasion: 'The dinner was in the ballroom and the tables looked very pretty. Afterwards heaps of people came from London, we were about 300 altogether. We had Cassano's band and danced merrily till 4 a.m.. Hilda looked lovely in a silver and white brocade gown and made for the occasion with a great deal of pearl trimming on the bodice and her tiara looked beautiful.'

Perhaps his big marriage settlement and existing debts weakened Arthur's business; perhaps he was always incurably optimistic, but three years later, in 1913, Arthur was back in over his head. This time his business affairs collapsed when he tried to take over the Grand Trunk Railway[5] in Canada. He had taken out an unsustainable position through the purchase of securities which lost their value – and the New York Stock Exchange acted to protect its members, scuppering the deal. 'Grenfell soared too high', crowed the *New York Daily News*, reporting that 'Earl Grey

---

4 Hilda Lyttelton (1886-1972), daughter of Gen. Sir Neville Lyttelton. She was the second wife of Arthur Morton Grenfell. She was the mother of four daughters – Mary Grenfell (later Countess Waldegrave), Katharine Grenfell, Frances Grenfell (later Dame Frances Campbell-Preston), and Laura Grenfell (later married to Sir Bernard Ferguson).

5 The Grand Trunk Railway debacle was later used in the television drama *Downton Abbey* as the reason for the fictional Lord Grantham losing his fortune.

is believed to be among the heavy losers.' No-one could say that the Earl had not been warned.

The failure had big repercussions, not just for Earl Grey but many other investors. In 1914, Arthur lost his job and was declared bankrupt, and his investment bank Chaplin, Milne and Grenfell was suspended. Arthur had to sell Roehampton House, and Hilda the glittering tiara she had worn for the ball; but it wasn't the end of Arthur's business activities.

The Engagement that never was

Sybil's sisters and brother all married in their early twenties and it is puzzling why Sybil herself remained single until the age of 40. She was adventurous, self-confident and brave, and seems to have got on well with young men, but not to have felt it necessary to subordinate her own life and opinions to theirs – she could take or leave their attentions. There are some tantalising glimpses of friendships with young men that never blossomed into marriage.

She got on very well with her cousin Angus McDonnell. Angus was one year older than her. They remained close throughout their lives, but theirs was probably a platonic relationship, and Angus married another woman.

Another friend was Riversdale Grenfell, youngest brother of her brother in law Arthur Grenfell. 'Rivy' visited the Grey family in Canada and was one of those who saw Sybil off at Charing Cross Station on her round the world trip in January 1914. He was killed in France in September that year, near Mons, at the age of 34, but from her matter of fact reaction to the news of his death it is clear he remained just a good friend.

Finally, we have a tantalising glimpse of an engagement which never blossomed. In January 1909, Earl Grey wrote to his son Charlie referring to a 'sort of engagement' about which Sybil had reluctantly told her mother very late at night: 'She confessed that she had two days together with Lord E at Cliveden (the home of the Astors),' that he had been disappointed she had not been able to go and see a play with him the night before she sailed back to Canada, but that he had seen her off at the station with bunches of flowers and proposed to visit her in Ottawa. Sybil had told her mother that, although they had many of the same tastes and in her opinion were 'made for one another', she would 'not be unhappy if nothing came of it'. Her father thought that she was being wisely prudent and cautious, and not counting her chickens before they hatched.

'Lord E' might have remained anonymous had not Earl Grey added 'so we may hope to see her as hostess at Carberry next August.' Carberry Towers in East Lothian, was the country seat of Lord Sidney Herbert Elphinstone. Thirteen years older than Sybil, he finally married Lady Mary Bowes-Lyon, the sister of the Queen Mother, a year later in 1910.

Was Sybil indifferent to men? There is an extraordinary insight which Sybil herself shared with her sister Evy ten years later in 1919. Sybil had been to see a fortune teller in France – a 'palmist' – who told her: 'she had rarely seen any woman so unlike a woman and that the only really feminine instinct I had was the "Mother

Love" which was very strong in me.' The palmist said that Sybil was nearly entirely male, that she had been reincarnated as a man in seven previous lives and had fought as a soldier. She added: 'I see quite a number of men round you, but you always let them fade away, you never can keep up your real interest in them. Men like you very much at first, until they find you out.' Sybil retorted: 'Find me out in what?' and the palmist replied: 'You know men instinctively so well having been a man so long that you are not taken in by them and you never play up to them and flatter them – when they find this out they cease to be interested in you, although they remain very good friends.'

Disconcertingly the palmist told Sybil: 'You have never really been in love and you never will. You will always make a mess of anything of this kind.' She doubted whether Sybil would marry (though accurately predicting two children if she did). She said that Sybil had recently thought more about matrimony than she once used to, but that was because she wanted a child. 'If you marry and had a child, the moment it was here you would cease to take any further interest in your husband.' She predicted that: 'You will always be happy, married or unmarried, and you will always keep your friends of which you have many.'

It is very likely that Sybil held this view of herself, and it might explain her apparent standoffishness. It seems to have been the result of a strong character that would not simply play the conventional game of seeking security in marriage. In that sense she was perhaps too 'modern' for many men of her time who looked for a more compliant and less independent woman. It was only much later, at the age of 40, with the biological clock ticking, that Sybil and Lambert Middleton decided to wed.

Sybil of course also had many close friendships with women. She remained life-long friends with Dorothy Onslow, wife of the 1st Earl of Halifax and with Aileen Roberts,[6] daughter of Field Marshal Lord Roberts, some twelve years older than her. When in difficulties in Petrograd, Sybil wrote that she wished that Aileen was there to advise her.

There were also younger women, like Olga Poutiatine, the young Russian countess who accompanied Sybil to Petrograd as translator. Six years younger than Sybil, Olga clearly hero worshipped Sybil and had a pet name for her – 'Seraia' (Russian for Grey).

There were other close friends throughout her life – Violet Markham (later Violet Carruthers) whom Sybil visited in Cologne after World War I, and Jeanne Malcolm who suffered from a number of the nervous conditions and who spent a whole month together with Sybil in Nancy, France, visiting the healer, Emile Coué. There were friends from her home in Northumberland – such as Zella Leather-Culley. and there was Elsie Reford, her friend and mentor at Grand Metis in Canada. Older women such as Aileen Roberts and Elsie Reford perhaps helped fill the gap left in Sybil's life by her elder sister, Vera.

There is no suggestion of an affair with any of these women, just as there is no

---

6 Countess Aileen Roberts (1870-1944). She succeeded to the title of her father, Field Marshal Frederick Roberts, 1st Earl Roberts VC, in 1914. She was one of Sybil's oldest and closest friends.

evidence for any relationship with men until she finally decided to marry at the age of 40. Sybil certainly kept her feelings to herself and this reticence and independence meant that she was not attracted to a conventional dependent relationship with a man until late in life.

However, by 1908, it certainly seems that her family were becoming restive about Sybil's unmarried state. Her friend Violet Markham wrote to Earl Grey, saying that she had dreamt that she was in a great English country house and 'Sybil in yellow satin and pearls was somehow the gracious ruling spirit of it.' She went on 'I should like to see Sybil as I saw her in my dream – a gracious and beautiful English great lady, filling a position of that kind as she would fill it, in a way to make her of true service to her country and generation. That this is her real niche I have no doubt at all.'

It seems however that Sybil did not share Violet's vision of her future, and that she saw her destiny in a different form, which was to be realised in her service to her country in Russia and France during and immediately after the First World War.

10

Interlude: Leaving Canada; visiting Africa

The years between the close of the Edwardian era and World War I were marked by political deadlock at home as the Conservative and Unionist opposition blocked the Asquith government's reforms in the Lords. Abroad, the chess board of international relations became ever more complex and fraught with menace as relations between the big powers deteriorated, particularly between Britain, France and Russia on the one hand and Germany and Austria-Hungary on the other. It was a time also of historic tragedies including the sinking of the *Titanic* in 1912, the year after the Greys returned to England. Had they still been living in North America, who knows if some of them or their friends might not have been tempted to journey out on the famous liner's maiden voyage to New York? There was also the heroic but doomed attempt by Robert Falcon Scott to reach the South Pole first in 1912 – his whole party dying on the return journey after having been beaten to the Pole by Amundsen. There was the death of the iconic suffragette leader, Emily Davison, throwing herself in protest under the King's horse at the Derby in 1913.

Leaving Canada

1911 was the last year the Greys spent in Ottawa. Earl Grey's term as Governor General had been due to finish in 1910, but his successor, the Duke of Connaught was not yet ready to move to Canada, and so Grey agreed to stay on an extra year. For Sybil it continued to present a chance to travel to new places. She accompanied her father and Lord Percy for a 'week's frisk' in January 1911 to New York, where they stayed overnight with the former president Theodore Roosevelt at his house Sagamore Hills at Oyster Bay. Sybil observed Roosevelt: 'It was extremely interesting, he always fascinates me. He has such vitality, energy, enthusiasm and such an alert brain.' She would also have shared Roosevelt's interest in the wild places in America, where the former president had hunted and shot game. She was dismissive of political critics of the former President who saw him as finished: 'I don't believe it for a single second, that sort of man doesn't get snowed under by his first reverse.'

The issue of the Day in Washington and in Ottawa was that of 'Reciprocity' between the United States and Canada – an attempt to broker a kind of free trade agreement between the two countries. It was promoted energetically by Canadian Prime Minister Laurier but seems to have been voted down by the Conservatives in Canada. Sybil was very much against it – 'I loathe it'– probably reflecting the political views of her father and brother, both of whom had grown suspicious of free trade (an old Liberal tenet) and tended to support the protectionist alternative, 'Tariff Reform'. These issues have echoes even today.

On 9 October 1911, Sybil wrote to her great aunt Harriet Loyd-Lindsay (whose money had made it possible for Earl Grey to take on the role Governor General), 'This is our last day in Ottawa.' They must have spent their final months saying goodbye to their many friends and to the great and good throughout Canada. In fact the process of official farewell had started as early as 4 May that year, when Earl Grey was presented with an address by the Senate and House of Commons of Canada, with a speech by the Prime Minister Sir Wilfred Laurier to Grey expressing 'our high appreciation of the great services he has rendered to this country.'

Canada remained a reference point for Sybil Grey for the rest of her life. Journeying in Russia in World War I, she was continually reminded of Canada – she thought of Rockliffe (the forested area around Rideau Hall) when riding in a sleigh through the royal park at Tsarskoe Selo outside St Petersburg, and she thought of Ottawa when she visited Kiev and saw the great monastery – the Pecherska Lavra – perched on a bluff above the Dneiper river, just as Parliament dominated the skyline above the River Ottawa. She carried a picture of Canada in her heart – of a land of opportunity for all who were prepared to work hard to get on, a land with wide open spaces and trackless wildernesses, of the fishing on the wonderful St Lawrence at Grand Metis and on the remote island of Anticosti; and of the Rockies and prairies which she loved. Canada had been the place where she really came of age and it widened her horizons literally and metaphorically. She loved the country.

It was also the place where she had known great sorrow – where her sister Vera had died. But for Sybil it was always a place of optimism and limitless possibilities.

Visit to Africa 1912
In July 1912, Earl Grey made his final visit to Africa to unveil a memorial to Cecil Rhodes, his friend and mentor. Rhodes had died in 1902 in England and was ultimately buried in the Matopos Hills in Rhodesia, but the memorial was set up on Table Mountain above Cape Town. Earl Grey was accompanied by his wife Alice and by Sybil and Evy. Together they visited Rhodesia and made an excursion to Victoria Falls and to a 'shooting camp' nearby. They also visited Beira (in modern Mozambique) and Sybil made an unforgettable trip north into the Congo. It was here that she herself experienced big game hunting – not just as a spectator as most women at that time would have confined themselves to doing, but actually stalking and shooting eland and other big game out in the bush in the company of the menfolk, with native trackers.

The trip may have been paid for by Sybil's generous great aunt Harriet Loyd-Lindsay (all the family wrote letters to her with accounts of the visit). For Earl Grey and his wife it must have brought back bittersweet memories of their visit to Rhodesia with their elder daughter Vera some sixteen years earlier.

They gathered for the unveiling of the memorial on Table Mountain, high above

Cape Town. Sybil wrote: 'We had a perfect day for the unveiling and a great crowd assembled.' Her father spoke for about half an hour: 'It sounded better than it read, because the wonderful surroundings and the atmosphere that pervaded the whole place added so much… the monument itself is really very fine and commands a magnificent and extensive view of the valley beneath, and there in the distance on the horizon is the beautiful mountain range of the Hottentot Hollands.'

They were given 'two most comfortable railway cars' by the Union government to travel on to Bulawayo in Rhodesia and the Victoria Falls where they viewed 'a vista of glorious rainbows pierced by the sun's rays falling on the masses of spray rising and falling up the chasm.' As always, Sybil was interested in the modernity and progress she saw in the country, although inevitably she saw it through a very European prism:

> It is really most remarkable how far advanced Rhodesia is, when you come to think that 20 years ago Lobengula sat under his tree in Bulawayo beheading his wives, and that there wasn't practically one white man in the country; and now in Southern Rhodesia there are over 2,000 farms and in Northern Rhodesia about 180. Quite good shops in all the towns, all these small towns have their tennis courts, golf courses, polo grounds etc, and the farms look prosperous and the people seem to be getting on and very optimistic as to the future of the country. Yes, I think it is wonderful how much headway they have made in these twenty years considering that they have had to face rebellion, rinderpest, malaria, blackwater fever, wild animals, etc. Fifty years hence it will be a great country, I should think.

Lobengula Khumalo was the last king of the Ndebele (Matabele) people, who resisted the British and died during the First Matabele War.

Earl Grey and Sybil, accompanied by two other men – Mr Dove and Captain Pennant – went on to Northern Rhodesia, just north of the Kafue River. They visited farms belonging to big landowners in Britain:

> They are all 10,000 acre farms, and three years ago no white man had ventured farming so far north. It is still a question as to whether it is a white man's country there or not. I should think, given all we have seen and heard, that it was. It is all absolute pioneer work there, and therefore it is very valuable having rich men like the Duke of Westminster and Lord Wolverton ready to spend money and make experiments there. They are growing mealies, and they are experimenting with tobacco and cotton and oranges and lemons – everything appears to be doing well very well with the exception of cotton and that is owing, largely I believe, to their having no cotton expert to show them how to grow it.

Sybil, her father and the two men then made a 'rush visit' to Elisabethville in the Belgian Congo, where they were duly impressed again with the signs of European civilisation being established in the dense primary forest.

Sybil said: 'Although two years ago they hadn't cut a single tree down there or put up a hut, they now have quite a nice and attractive town of about 1,000 whites – beautifully laid out and arranged and marvellously clean.' The Belgian Government had spent £250,000 developing the town and had established a gigantic Marconi installation there. 'They had succeeded the day before we arrived in sending and receiving a message from a plane 1,000 miles north.' The governor's chauffeur, Lescaut, was a 'great aereoplaneist' who was planning to make a pioneering flight 1,500 miles from Elisabethville to Boma on the coast. Sybil mused: 'How flabbergasted and bewildered the natives of Central Africa will be when they see this gigantic bird flying over them making a huge buzzing sound!'

In the Congo they witnessed an impressive parade by 400 native troops officered by Belgians. Sybil commented: 'Such smart men who went through their drill like clockwork – they told us that a great number of the men had been actual cannibals, they were Askaris a very fierce fighting tribe, but made excellent soldiers and obeyed their white officers well, but if a civilian was foolish enough to give them an order he ran a grave risk of being instantly made into soup!'

Above all, Sybil enjoyed the life in the shooting camp where she and her father and the two men lived near Victoria Falls. Her mother and her sister, Evy, showed no interest in the wildlife, or in hunting the game. In contrast Sybil spent every day accompanying the men tracking and shooting game in the dense bush. She wrote to her brother Charlie in England:

> On the way back to join the horses we came across a red buck. I took a shot head-on, and must have hit the fellow in the chest, for we saw he was hard hit and he went off at a slow canter and stopped. I ran like a horse, got very hot and of course when I got near enough to shoot missed the brute. Then he disappeared out of sight through some bushes, more breathless running and then we saw the doe canter past us but as she was not followed by her Lord and Master we knew he was near, and we suddenly came on him lying down as I thought dead, but when we were within ten yards and he jumped up and bounded away but stopped fairly soon and I got him through the heart and so finished him.

She described how her sister Evy spent time in camp writing innumerable letters: 'It was really very funny the day we rode into camp seeing a black boy marching ahead of us carrying in one hand, as a waiter carries plates, Evy's blue leather Asprey writing case and in the other hand a spear.'

Earl Grey and his family finally went on to Beira before going back to Cape Town and travelling home by sea. Africa appealed to Sybil's love of the wild, and she revisited it much later in her life, but she never formed the close and abiding connection that her father, his cousin George Grey and others in the family had for it, including the Grenfells – Arthur Grenfell's son Harry later worked in the Zambian copper mining industry. But, as well as commenting on the potential development of Rhodesia she brought a sensitive and personal dimension to her description of its people, describing a 'jolly little girl of seven' whom they came on when visiting a convent. The girl, who may have been African or of mixed race, had 'very light brown eyes and a fuzzy little fair head' and was practising the piano. 'We asked her where she came from – "From crocodile valley farm," came the answer. We then asked her if she saw crocodiles there. "Oh yes," she said, "lots and lots of them," they might have been rabbits from the way she spoke.'

*Sybil's sketch of Evy's writing case being carried through the jungle,
on Government House writing paper (Howick Hall Trustees)*

Evy's wedding

The Greys returned to England in October in time for Evy's wedding to Lawrence Evelyn ('Jonah') Jones[1] on 23 November 1912.

'Jonah' came from a family of landed baronets in Norfolk whose home was Cranmer Hall. His great great grandfather, Sir John Jones, had fought with Wellesley in the Peninsular War. The Jones family, like many others, had money problems in running Cranmer and his father leased the hall out and took his young family overseas, renting a villa on the shores of Lake Geneva. Jonah, a boy at the time, exulted in the new horizons that it opened up, commenting, 'if this was life "abroad", then abroad was the place to be.'

Jonah was a tall man, 6 feet 4 inches in height, and it became a standing joke in World War I when he was placed in charge of the 'Bantams' (the Army recruits below regulation height.) He commanded a training school on machine gunnery, before being badly wounded at the front, captured and spending the rest of the war as a prisoner of war. After the war, he became a banker and then a successful writer,

---

1 Lawrence Evelyn 'Jonah' Jones (1885-1969). He was the second son of Sir Lawrence John Jones and Evelyn Bevan, and was one of five children – his elder brother Willoughby died aged only fourteen.

publishing several volumes of his memoirs – including *Victorian Boyhood*, *Edwardian Youth* and *Georgian Afternoon*. He and Evy would have family of five children – all girls – two of whom sadly died young.

Another wedding, on 12 July 1912, which Sybil and her family were not able to attend as they were already in Africa, was that of Sybil's uncle, Sir George Holford. It was a magnificent affair. Sir George's bride, Susannah Menzies (née West Wilson), was the recent widow of John Graham Menzies who had combined to drink and gamble himself into an early grave. The wedding took place at the Chapel Royal, attended by the King, the Queen, the dowager Queen and Princess Victoria. NCOs from Holford's regiment, the Life Guards, lined the aisles and the bride was escorted to the altar by her two adult sons, Stewart and Keith Graham Menzies. Stewart Menzies[2] was to play a very significant future role in the fortunes of the nation – from 1915 onwards, when he joined General Haig's staff, he was an influential intelligence officer, rising in due course to become 'C', head of the Secret Intelligence Service, MI6, from 1939 until 1952. His mother, now Lady Susannah Holford, known affectionately as 'Tottie', was an important member of the family. Reclusive and secretive, Stewart Menzies's influence was no doubt felt behind the scenes.

---

2 Stewart Graham Menzies (1890-1968), son of John Graham Menzies and Susannah West Wilson whose family owned the Wilson shipping line. He became part of Sybil's family when his mother married Sybil's uncle.

11

Round the World

In January 1914, Earl Grey, his wife Alice, Sybil and Fernande Boutet (Alice's French lady's maid and companion) set out on a four-month round the world tour. It took them across the Mediterranean, through the Suez Canal to Ceylon, and on to Australia, Tasmania and New Zealand. They then returned across the Pacific by way of Fiji and Hawaii, docking at San Francisco before crossing the United States and returning home on the German ship *Vaterland.*

It is noteworthy that once they had reached Port Said on the Suez Canal (then administered by Britain) they never left the territories of the British Empire until they reached Honolulu in the United States. They were seen off from Charing Cross Station on 7 January by more than a dozen members of their friends and family and departed for France. At the French port of Toulouse they embarked on the liner that would take them to Australia – the *Otranto.*

The whole trip as far as the western seaboard of America is recorded in a linen bound diary kept by Countess Alice, in which she gave vivid descriptions of the places they visited. Being the daughter of Robert Stayner Holford, she had an extensive knowledge of plants and their Latin names and, and was shown round many of the most beautiful and exotic botanical gardens in Australasia, sending gifts of seeds home to her brother George at Westonbirt. She also had a painterly eye for detail, describing the hues and colours of what she saw, together with little pen and ink sketches of people, places and plants.

On the way out they visited Naples, taking the opportunity of seeing the ruins of Pompeii which impressed Alice greatly – 'I was amazed at the exceeding beauty and dignity and grandeur of much that we saw.'

They visited Port Said on the Suez Canal, where they were met by their friends Sybil Graham (née Brodrick) who had accompanied Sybil to the Yukon and her husband Ronald, who were now stationed in colonial Egypt.

They reached Ceylon, where Alice gave a vivid description of their first exotic view of the island on their way to Kandy: 'In a few minutes we were bowling along through the native streets thronged with people of all shades of colour (white excepted) – the real East full of variety and brilliant colour, past native shops whose dark interiors framed wonderfully picturesque groups of people, at all sorts of occupations, selling fruit and goods of all kinds, occupied with cooking, forging metal, dressing and plaiting their hair and intent on all sorts of business, or merely sitting on their heels and gossiping.'

They then sailed for Australia. They were part of the Captain's table and a social circle gathered around them for the trip – a collection of people who continued to be associated with them throughout their journey round Australia – 'the Hon. Tell' (The Honourable Percy Thelluson, a slightly pompous 40 year old who knew Australia well), Major Ashmore, Mr and Mrs Strang, Miss Ganesco, the Streatfields, Capt. Baynham (the captain of the *Otranto*), and Capt. Anderson. The Greys were particularly interested in 'the child' – Alex Ganesco, a young half Romanian girl who was on her way out to marry a man in Australia. Alice observed 'her gradual sense that she was doing a wild and foolish thing coming out alone like this to be married in Australia to a man she has not seen for three years and to whom she has engaged herself by cable.'

The trip was at least partly a political one for Earl Grey – he spoke at public meetings in Australia about his political causes, principally proportional representation, the Empire, and his personal project to create a 'Dominion House' (a sort of mega-embassy where all the great dominions – Australia, New Zealand, Canada and South Africa – would set out their wares and attractions). The Greys received lavish hospitality from British governors, consuls and officials wherever they stopped. Earl Grey was after all a former governor general and cousin of Sir Edward Grey, the British Foreign Secretary.

On their arrival in Freemantle, on 3 February, nearly a month after they set out, Albert Grey immediately went into the role of visiting politician, answering 'Marconi's' (shipboard telegrams) and receiving reporters. He was invited to lunch by the Governor of Western Australia and by the Million Club of Perth. During these political lunches, Alice and Sybil were taken to see public parks and the botanical gardens at most of the cities they visited in Australia – Perth, Adelaide, Melbourne, etc.

Alice described and sketched the Government Houses they visited in Melbourne and elsewhere – her experienced eye as a wife of a former governor general constantly noting the features of public buildings – their advantages and defects. At Melbourne, Alice went to see the Queen Victoria Hospital and they went to the Melbourne races where a horse named Earl Grey failed to win. They met a great variety of people – they visited the cottage of Dame Nellie Melba, a famous Australian born opera singer in the country near Melbourne. Later on their way back through Australia they dined with Maud Jefferies, an American actress – the Greys were very interested in and taken with the arts and creative people. They also visited people out in the Australian countryside – for instance the house of Mr Molesworth Green 'a very wonderful old man, 88, beautifully turned out and quite upright in his carriage, does not need spectacles to read with, rides young horses and in the evening he reads to his family for two to three hours every evening' – obviously a very old fashioned patriarch.

Alice admired strong, independent often self-made characters – for example a Mr Triggs whom they later met at Canberra (the proposed site of the new capital). He was an Australian millionaire, born near Birmingham, who had emigrated at the age of 20, borrowing money for the passage, arriving with nothing and setting up as a sheep farmer. He now owned half a million sheep, despite having had to overcome setbacks such as drought which had cost him £60,000 a few years before. He had paid for the education in Britain of his own brother, who had now married the daughter of a baronet.

They repacked their luggage before travelling on to Tasmania. It shows what a huge amount of baggage they took with them. In Australia they left behind six trunks, several book boxes, hat boxes, an umbrella case, and golf sticks to be collected on their return. They took with them four trunks, fishing rods, a gun case, the medicine basket, and deck chairs. And they sent ahead yet more deck chairs, camp stools and a card table.

They visited Tasmania, a place dotted with West Country names such as Launceston and the Tamar. They were taken to see the Huon Timber Company with its logging operation, and a jam factory founded by Mr Jones, 'an entirely self-made man having started life as a boy carrying tins in a jam factory.'

They went on to visit New Zealand, travelling by the Governor's car to Dunedin. Alice described countryside – 'rather like the Northumberland country round Learmouth.' Dunedin was 'a thoroughly Scottish town inhabited by people who are Scottish and proud of it.'

Sybil made two separate journeys, independent from her parents – one in New Zealand to a remote fishing camp, and later when they were back in Australia she travelled from Sydney to Melbourne, a distance of about 1,600 km round-trip, for her friend Alex Ganesco's wedding.

In Dunedin, Alice visited an exemplary kindergarten and the Karitane Hospital, a maternity hospital. The free kindergarten provides a fascinating view of nursery education for three to six year olds at the time. The teacher, a Miss Darling, led the children in progressive activities with pupils learning to play and observe – singing, dancing and storytelling, which one might expect in schools today – but there was also a detailed lesson on house work including sweeping, brushing, washing and ironing.

The Karitane Hospital was a model hospital set up to improve care of babies by New Zealand mothers – focusing on regular breastfeeding and hygiene – and on training nurses to deliver this programme. The nurses were 'Plunket Nurses', called after the wife of a former governor general. Karitane was the personal project of Dr Truby King and his approaches had resulted in a huge fall in infant mortality in New Zealand.

They visited Wellington and its museum of Maori artefacts, including jade war clubs, as well as meeting Maori people. Alice described them very sympathetically:

Some of the Maoris are extremely good-looking; two women guides, twin sisters called Georgiana and Eileen, are very pretty notwithstanding that like most Maori women they are tattooed on the lips and chins. They have the most charming and gentle expressions, and a most gentle and melodious and refined way of speaking. Their English is absolutely pure without any accent and they express themselves remarkably well. The Maoris are susceptible to a high amount of education and assimilate culture very easily. They have a great sense of melody and rhythm, are poetical and many of the men are very eloquent as speakers.

She noted 'there seems to be little if any stigma attached to intermarriage between a white person and a Maori.'

They visited Geyser Valley near Rotorua and Wai Pa Prison, a model prison on the Green Lake, where 'each man has his own little wooden hut' and the prison houses fronting the lake had beautiful views.

They went from Taupo up the coast to a remote fishing camp at Waihora Bay. There, Sybil and the younger members of the party had already been fishing for about a week, sleeping under canvas. They lined up on the shore to welcome Alice and Albert, and Alice was shocked at their scanty camp attire – 'Dorothy and 'the child' in extraordinarily short petticoats, more convenient than pretty, and with hair down their backs tied only with a ribbon.'

They slept in eight tents all in a row. The following day Alice watched Sybil fishing while Albert returned to Taupo where he planned to write in peace. Sybil, who adored wild places and fishing, was in her element, and was very loathe to leave the camp even when the weather turned against them. Two days later there was a relentless downpour – 'it pelted all night long'. In the middle of the night Alice went out in the dark to Albert's deserted tent to retrieve his bedding, but she was in for a shock: 'I was terrified as I entered the dark tent by a sort of loud grunting bark, while some big object with shiny eyes heaved itself up by the tent pole. I fled in a hurry to call for help.' They found that it was a wild sow and her thirteen piglets which had been running about the camp which had taken over Albert's abandoned tent.

Next day the downpour continued without ceasing, while Sybil insisted on going on fishing. At length she returned at 1 p.m. having broken her rod, by which time Albert had sent a government launch to take them off, and they left, abandoning their tents to the pigs.

Arriving back in Taupo they were still dressed in their fishing clothes and there was an awkward moment going into dinner improperly dressed – 'Dorothy in her fishing skirt, so we had to cover her with Sybil's Ulster before taking her into the supper room.' Formality was still very important even in the remoter parts of New Zealand!

They went on to visit the geysers at Wairaki. Although the views were beautiful, Alice found the geysers and the hot steep walk up to them tiresome: 'Hot water and the boiling steam given out by the geysers and the fumes of sulphur make it very oppressive.' She described it as 'a very Hell's Gate, everywhere you see cauldrons of bubbling boiling water, some blowing off steam at stated intervals.' If you left the path you risked 'finding your foot going through the crust of the earth and being badly scalded... How I longed to get away.'

After dinner they saw Maori dancers: 'one of the dances was especially beautiful when all the women acted as if they were rowing a canoe, standing in a long row, playing the 'poi' (a sort of whirling balls on strings) and swaying altogether in a wonderful rhythm.' Alice added perceptively: 'Maori games and dances will die out, unless kept up in some way such as in this performance.'

Later they visited a museum to look at Maori carvings and relics: 'a magnificent war canoe was over eighty feet long and seven foot in the beam and beautifully carved and coloured red.'

Back in Australia, they watched a huge parade of cadets who were inspected by Sir Ian Hamilton, the British forces overseas inspector with whom they had travelled out on the *Otranto*: '25,827 men and lads divided into 23 battalions comprising six brigades, nearly all drawn from the population of Sydney... they were a body of young fellows to be proud of. They went by the saluting post at a quick march, eight to a hundred men marching abreast with lively tunes.'

They were amused to observe an Australian wedding party which took place close to their table at the hotel. Their remarks were certainly patronising as they struggled to place these ordinary Australians on a social scale: 'The bride's father had not an H at his command to our great surprise, but made a facetious speech, the bridegroom of course spoke and to our great dismay with the most horrible Cockney accent.' Alice added of the women: 'We could not quite class the people, they were rather above shop people, but with no pretence to belonging to a sort we would call society, but were quite prettily dressed.' The older Greys were evidently bemused at encountering the much more egalitarian nature of Australian society.

They discussed prospects for agriculture with a number of Australian farmers. Incisively, Sybil asked Mr Kempster, a visitor from Rhodesia, 'where he would settle if he was given the power to choose and a thousand pounds to start with.' He replied that he would come to Australia, buy 300 acres of land and grow citrus fruit and grapes – 'he felt certain he would make his pile that way and be able to return to live in England.'

Albert Grey swung into political mode, addressing a big meeting at the Sydney Town Hall on proportional representation, one of his great political crusades. It was reported in the *Sydney Daily Telegraph*. He won over his audience, telling them that he would give them a 'dry and scientific lecture' on PR and then delighting them with a barnstorming speech punctuated by frequent laughter and applause. Speaking in favour of the single transferable vote system, he explained the way the first past the post system disenfranchised significant minorities, using an amusing analogy: 'Suppose a man went to church to marry the woman he loved, and the Minister told him he had to choose one of the ladies (one with a hump and the other with a squint) selected for him by the two great party machines.' (Laughter.) 'Gentlemen,' said Earl Grey, 'you think that example laughable, but it is absolutely correct.' He told them they were slaves of the political system and must emancipate themselves.

He ended on a good radical note by attacking corruption in American politics: 'In America the party system is not government of the people, by the people, for the people. It is government of the people, by the rascals, for the rich. (Applause).'

Alice Grey also gave an interview in which she praised the Plunket Nurses, and spoke of the way fewer young women now wanted to go into domestic service. She said that electricity and labour saving devices were partly helping to solve the problem – she could now use an electric stove to make tea or hot water in her bedroom rather than ringing for a servant to do it.

As Sybil set off on a train alone from Sydney to Melbourne to attend Alex Ganesco's wedding, Alice, Albert and Fernande travelled by special train into the Blue Mountains, to Mount Victoria and the Jenolan Caves. The caves, which were originally discovered and inhabited by an escaped convict, were accessed through narrow irregular passages which broadened out into huge caverns sometimes nearly 200 feet high lit with electric light and with wonderful stalactites and stalagmites.

At the last minute they changed their plans about how to travel home. They had been planning to go across south-east Asia via Korea, up to Harbin in north-east China, and then to board the newly constructed Trans-Siberian Railway to come home via Moscow. They changed their plans because Arthur Grenfell sent a cable saying he wanted to meet them to discuss oil interests in San Francisco, so they instead decided to cross the Pacific to the West Coast of America.

After a 'hot and muggy' voyage, they arrived in Fiji at the tiny capital of Suva in mid-April. At the quayside, they observed the brightly coloured motley crowd on the pier below. 'Europeans all dressed in spotless white ducks, Fiji natives of splendid physique and beautiful shiny brown skin with enormous heads of fuzzy upstanding hair like a brush' – Alice drew a wonderful sketch of a Fijian head, which half obliterates the diary text.

The pier was lined with natives selling all kinds of articles: 'big shells, white coral in fantastic shapes, plaited palm leaf baskets, filled with green but quite ripe and deliciously sweet oranges.'

Their next stop was Honolulu in Hawaii, where they were as usual ranged into two lines facing one another and were inspected on deck at 6 a.m. by a doctor – a health measure in all the ports they visited. They went to the Manoa Hotel, about two and a half miles out of town. Built directly on the shore: 'a big wooden structure with open galleries, all painted cream and the ornamental woodwork white,' it had a green grass courtyard and an arbour from which, 'you look out over a sea vividly blue, rolling gently in and washing against a strip of sand a few feet below one.'

Surfing was the great attraction in Hawaii. Alice wrote: 'it is a wonderfully pretty sight.' They all tried it out – 'Sybil simply revelled in it

The promotional brochure on Honolulu (Boyd family collection).

and said she'd never enjoyed anything more.'

They went out in a surf canoe paddled by three islanders. The next day they were given personal instruction (each had a experienced surfer with them who showed them how to use their surfboards). 'One of our men showed off by coming in on the board, standing on his head.'

As important visitors, they were taken round military installations on the island by the American Governor, Eugene Pinkham. They saw Pearl Bay 'a splendid natural harbour' which was just being converted into the great naval dockyard of Pearl Harbour.

They also visited a Japanese club for dinner, complete with Geisha girls singing and dancing. Alice gave them artificial silk flowers to put in their hair, and the geishas were thrilled when Earl Grey showed them his cufflinks which he had been given by one of the Emperor's chief ministers, Prince Fushimi, with the Japanese and English flags enamelled on them.

Photographs of surfers possibly taken by Sybil Grey (Boyd family collection).

On their last day in Hawaii they went to a big public school and witnessed the opening ceremony, where each week the pupils formed up in ranks before the American Stars & Stripes and the old Hawaiian flag, and recited poetry and praised the flags and what they stood for.

As they left Hawaii, they were garlanded with 'leis' – wreaths of flowers that one's friends placed round one's neck before parting on the quayside: 'Mrs Cooper gave me a lovely lei of begonia venusta, one of lovely pink carnations and one of frangipani from Mrs Swanzy… while Sybil had also another three, and Albert two. Fernande had two and everyone on the ship was covered with lovely leis. A Hawaiian band played and altogether it was a very gay scene.' Passengers on the ship and their well-wishers on the quay were given opposite ends of multi-coloured paper streamers to hold, making a rainbow of bright colours, until the ship steamed out and broke the fragile link between them.

On May 5 they arrived in San Francisco almost four months after they set out. They were met by Evy and Jonah and by several American businessmen who were interested in Arthur Grenfell's putative oil business.

They were invited to the PPIE (The Panama Pacific International Exposition), a huge world trade fair with specially constructed pavilions, that dominated San

Sybil, Evy, Alice on Vaterland, 'three great ladies' (Library of Congress).

Francisco for the next year.

Earl Grey and Jonah then set off for business meetings about oil in Los Angeles, while Alice and Sybil and Evy were taken to see the Yosemite Valley and its towering cliff face El Capitan.

The diary of the round the world trip ends at this point. Afterwards they must all have met up once again and travelled across America to the East Coast, presumably to New York from where they made their way home on the German ship the *Vaterland*. There is a striking photograph showing Sybil, Alice and Evy seated together on the deck – three great English ladies taking their ease, in the final months before the outbreak of the First World War.

PART II

Howick Hall Hospital (Howick Hall Trustees)

12

The coming of war

Why did Europe, that had known peace and prosperity for nearly half a century, suddenly lurch into the worst war in its history, particularly when many of the crowned heads of pre-war Europe were closely related to each other? With the exception of the localised Balkan Wars of 1912-13, there had not been a major European conflict since the Franco-Prussian War of 1870-71, over 40 years before. The causes of the Great War were complex and stretched back several decades, and lay in inherent conflicts of interest and distrust between the major European powers. These included the rise of new powers in Europe such as Germany and Italy. The German Empire sought to expand its influence and unwisely did so by building a High Seas Fleet with the express purpose of rivalling the Royal Navy and Britain's dominion of the seas. This led to a naval arms race between Britain and Germany that lasted from 1899 until the outbreak of war.

Similar arms races on land led to development of huge armies (particularly in Russia and Germany) armed with ever more powerful artillery and modern weapons such as the machine gun. Complex systems of alliances had been designed to guard against surprise attack, but when it came to it these actually locked countries into a potential collision course – the Anglo-French Entente Cordiale and the Anglo-Russian alliance forming up against the alliance of the Central Powers (Germany, Austria-Hungary). The personal role of key people was also important, particularly the unpredictable Kaiser (whose bravado and apparent inferiority complex resulted in dangerous brinkmanship) and the largely unaccountable Austro-Hungarian and Russian emperors. In almost all countries, the power of decision-making on war and peace lay in a very few not very reliable hands.

There were underlying tensions: between Austria and Serbia (which Austria considered a part of its Empire); between Germany and France; there was mutual distrust between Austria-Hungary and Russia, and between Germany and Russia; and there was increasing competition between Britain and Germany, with Britain resenting and fearing the rise of German sea-power and Germany feeling thwarted and encircled. The decade of build up to the outbreak of the Great War saw incidents where the status quo was challenged by Germany – for example the two Moroccan incidents – without actually leading to war. There was no really effective forum where grievances and conflicts could be addressed, nor anything approaching the modern world's almost instantaneous shared information and rapid international diplomatic initiatives.

The various powers prepared military plans in the event of war, with general staffs in Germany and elsewhere theorising that a limited, rapidly fought war could be won. No-one seemed to have fully anticipated the huge extent of a European conflict fought with modern weapons, leading to gridlock in fixed lines of trenches and the catastrophic extent of the casualties that resulted. Ultimately military brinkmanship won out over statesmanship and diplomacy. It was a different time with different attitudes, when imperialism and war were accepted by European powers as a means of settling disputes and controlling colonial peoples. In Britain there had also grown up a dangerous expectation that she would win such wars (despite the close calls experienced in South Africa against the Zulus and the Boers, in the Sudan against the Mahdi, and earlier on in India during the Mutiny).

Sir Edward Grey

The role of Sybil's cousin, Sir Edward Grey, Foreign Secretary from 1905 to 1916, was important. Sir Edward was an odd mixture of a successful politician (the longest serving Foreign Secretary of the twentieth century) and a very private reclusive character – an English country gentleman with a passion for fly fishing and for birds (and an admired authority who wrote successful books on both subjects, *Fly Fishing* and *The Charm of Birds*). He was in modern parlance perhaps 'too hands off' – given to leaving the Foreign Office on a Friday night and travelling by train to the Itchen Valley where he stayed the weekend in a lean-to shack of his own construction to fish and to be close to wild birds.

He never really travelled abroad – when not in London he preferred the comfort and seclusion of his country seat at Fallodon in Northumberland, a mere six miles from his Grey cousins at Howick, where Sybil certainly fished with him. He tended to rely on caution and calculation, without possessing the steel and decisiveness to deal with opponents such as the German Kaiser and his ruthless pursuit of German self-interest. He steered Britain away from the former policy of 'splendid isolation' towards more involvement with the European powers, developing the Entente Cordiale with France and the alliance with Russia. He sought to manage and contain conflict with Germany despite not really trusting her, at one stage even seeking to develop an understanding with Germany, only to be rebuffed by the Kaiser. He genuinely hated war but failed to prevent it.

In retirement he became a reclusive figure devoted to the natural world – a famous photograph shows him seated on a garden bench, with wild birds perched on his deerstalker hat and eating out of his hand. He has been criticised for not making Britain's commitment to defend France and Belgium clearer to Germany in advance, but he and the British government were men of their word and stuck by their treaty obligations to Belgium when Germany invaded the country, acting in defence of British interests as they saw it.

War

War began in August 1914, after the assassination of Archduke Franz Ferdinand, heir to the Austro-Hungarian Empire by Serbian nationalists in June 1914, tipping the opposing alliances into pre-ordained battle lines. Britain only became involved when the German Army marched into Belgium which was protected by treaty guarantees signed by Britain, France and many European powers including Germany herself. What had begun as an essentially eastern European war became a truly global conflict with the involvement of the British Empire.

Antagonism to Germany had built up in Britain over the years (reflected in spy stories such as John Buchan's *The Thirty-Nine Steps* and Ernest Childers's *The Riddle of the Sands*) and when war came many welcomed it. Although they had visited the country, Sybil and her family were firmly in the Conservative and Unionist camp opposed to Germany, and they saw the war in patriotic terms.

There is a fascinating vignette of Sybil's participation in a select private meeting on 1 August, two days before Germany declared war on France, at which the guests all declared themselves against the British Government's indecision and weakness, and committed themselves to press for robust confrontation with Germany. The account was written by Leopold Maxse, editor of the conservative *National Review*.[1] He was invited to a specially convened breakfast meeting by Gen. Henry Wilson, Director of Military Operations at the War Office, at his home. 'The party consisted, besides our host and hostess, of Lady Sybil Grey, Lady Aileen Roberts, L. S. Amery MP and myself. At first we were speechless. We simply hung our heads. England was to look on while Germany attacked France.'

Maxse says that one of the party suggested bringing in the Unionist Opposition to discuss the European crisis with the Government. 'There was no time to lose, we there and then constituted ourselves into an informal 'Pogrom' as it was called, under the inspiration of the General... We felt this to be a decisive moment in the history of the world, threatening a tragedy that would for all time make English men and English women ashamed of themselves, while there was a real risk of Europe being blotted out. It was very late, but not yet too late. As Ministers were wobbling the wrong way they might wobble the right way under sufficient pressure.' The unfortunately named 'Pogrom' broke up so that each of its members could go and seek to build pressure for Britain to resist German aggression.

On the outbreak of hostilities Sybil lost no time in volunteering to do her bit. She was the first woman in Northumberland to volunteer as a Voluntary Aid Detachment nurse who acted as supporters and assistants to professionally trained nurses. And she enrolled for some unofficial training at the Newcastle Royal Infirmary, training alongside nurses who were gaining their first experience.

She shared a room at the Imperial Hotel with Nurse Chipman, another woman who was also training as a Voluntary Aid Detachment nurse. 'Chip' became a close friend. Sybil wrote to her mother: 'We have had a most interesting day and have both thoroughly enjoyed it. Nurse Chipman and I made excellent buttered eggs in

---

1 Maxse's article 'A Fateful Breakfast' was published in the *National Review* 1 August 1918. Lady Sybil Grey kept a copy of it with her papers. It was a very odd meeting indeed – an influential general, two society ladies, an MP and a journalist – and its outcome if any is unknown. Aileen Roberts was presumably there because her father was Field Marshal Lord Roberts, and Sybil because of her relationship both to the Foreign Secretary, Sir Edward Grey, and to the Unionists. It sounds like a clumsy attempt by General Wilson to pressurise the Government by involving the Opposition. It was important enough in Maxse's mind for him to publish a report of it four years later.

our little dish, and we talked over our experiences like two old hospital cronies.' For the first time in her life, Sybil had shared a demanding day learning about nursing with other young women without being accorded any special privileges, and she was elated.

She continued: 'Now to recount Nurse Grey's first day at the hospital. We all arrived there feeling rather sick with fear. The matron came out and told us what wards to go to, each to a separate ward. My ward is No. 6, Men's Surgical Ward. It has 30 beds but only 20 patients for the moment. I was taken up to my ward by a nurse and handed over to the sister in charge of the ward. The sisters, staff nurses, nurses and probationers have all received orders to show us as much as possible.'

She found that the sight of wounds did not put her off: 'One poor boy, such a nice boy, a miner aged 22, married four years, had an awfully bad septic knee. The knee and for about eight inches above looked like a raw bit of mutton... Then we did a man who had had his eye completely taken out. There was nothing but a raw red hole. I thought I should mind seeing those sorts of things but I didn't in the very least.'

She witnessed a variety of operations in the operating theatre – 'a very bad appendicitis which took over an hour; a hernia case; an operation on the hand, one of the worst compound fractures they have ever had, both bones broken and through the flesh of the wrist.' The patient was sent down to their ward where she was allowed to dress him, take his pulse and temperature and fill in the readings on his chart – 'Alone I did it!' She had been nervous at the prospect of seeing operations, 'but the moment I saw the knife in the flesh and the surgeon pull it apart I thought, why it is exactly like the gaff in the salmon, and that

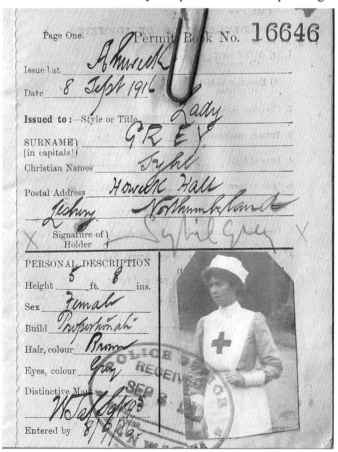

Sybil's War Office passbook photograph
(Boyd family collection).

ended my feelings of nervousness.'

With her cut glass accent and lack of nursing knowledge she stuck out. She wrote to her mother: 'I am looked upon in the ward by sister, staff nurses, nurses and even probationers as a huge joke. Why, I can't imagine and now almost whenever I open my mouth they rock with merriment. I think it is my unprofessional jargon. However they are goodness itself to me and they are only too anxious that I should not overdo myself.'

At the end of some three weeks, she and her companions passed out as VADs with some rudimentary experience of wounds, surgery and nursing care. After leaving the infirmary she went to work as a VAD in Howick Hall Convalescent Hospital for officers, the hospital opened at her family home, of which she ultimately became commandant.

Recently a fascinating photograph album has been rediscovered at Howick Hall, containing a rich collection of photographs of patients and staff at the hospital, and with copious letters from grateful former patients (and sometimes from their parents), Christmas cards and even some poems of thanks. A number are in French (from Belgian or French patients). Many are addressed to Lady Sybil Grey, and they express gratitude to her and to the staff for their care and treatment, and the enjoyment and peace they found in what for them was such a novel environment. Most of the letters in 1915 are from privates or from non-commissioned officers, which makes one wonder at what stage the hospital became one specially for officers.

It is obvious that Sybil and Howick Hospital made a point of sending their

Howick Hall Hospital, with Lady Aileen Roberts and Lady Sybil seated in the centre. The soldier on the right is Belgian. (Howick Hall Trustees)

photographs to the patients (many requested further copies). Many of them posed formally for their photographs, but there are also pictures of them in the ward, with the staff, relaxing in the grounds, playing tennis or croquet and picnicking. Some posed in groups with Sybil, her mother Countess Alice and sister-in-law Lady Mabel Grey, or with Sybil's friends Aileen Roberts, Zella Leather-Culley and Miss Chipman, also in nurses' uniforms.

It was obviously a radically different experience from most other hospitals they could have gone to – some complained that they had afterwards been sent on to the more spartan Armstrong College Hospital in Newcastle.

A few letters included poems, such as the one beginning:

> *There's a little place called Howick Hall*
> *Where soldiers go for a rest*
> *While trying to give of their best.*

It went on:

> *It's kindly lent by Earl Grey*
> *And it seems there's nothing to pay*
> *With Lady Sybil in charge*
> *We'll soon be at large*
> *And the Germans will remember the day.*

> *Lady Sybil she's a brick*
> *And she attends to all the sick*
> *And her smile on you never fails*
> *If she's short of a job she'll turn the door knob*
> *And say I'll be back in a minute and cut your toe nails!*

Many of them were going back to the front after a few days 'furlough'. The most poignant read:

Dear Lady Sybil,
   I am well again thanks to you and sister and I leave for the Dardanelles to finish my duty off, hoping this finds you all well to carry on with your good work. Good Bye until we meet again,
         Capt. J Bryan, 3rd Border Regt.

It is not known whether he survived Gallipoli.

Finally, there is a telegram from Sybil herself in Petrograd, late in 1915 wishing: 'Good luck to the staff and patients on the anniversary of the [Howick] Hospital opening.'[2]

Earl Grey also pitched in to do his bit. At the end of August 1914 he addressed a recruitment rally of miners at Blyth, urging them to join the newly formed Miners' Battalion of the Northumberland Fusiliers, telling them: 'if you don't take this opportunity you will go to your graves feeling that you have not played the game.' The *Newcastle Chronicle* reported: 'The large crowd, with band, sang the national

---

2 From the World War One photograph album belonging to Howick Hall, digitised by Northumerland Archives.

anthem, with Earl Grey as conductor, and afterwards rousing cheers were sent up for the success of Allied arms, and especially for the plucky little Belgians. The meeting ended with another round of cheers for Earl Grey.'

Believing as many did that the war would be won by Christmas, Earl Grey perhaps was not to know that so many of them would indeed be going to their graves.

The menfolk of the family also volunteered to join the Army – Sybil's brother Charlie Grey joined the Northumberland Fusiliers (the 'Fighting Fifth'), Arthur Grenfell joined the Royal Berkshire Hussars and Jonah Jones joined the Bed-

Charlie Grey in uniform (Boyd family collection).

fordshire Yeomanry, later in command of training the army in the use of machine guns, before being badly wounded, captured and spending the rest of the war in a prisoner of war camp.

Many paid a far greater price. The Grenfell family in particular suffered terribly. Already three of Arthur Grenfell's elder brothers had died serving in the army (two of them killed in action) in the wars in Sudan and in Rhodesia at the turn of the century. His two youngest brothers – the twins Francis and Riversdale ('Rivy') Grenfell now suffered the same fate. Born in 1880, two years older than Sybil, the twins looked almost identical and were very close and were champion polo players. After leaving Eton they pursued separate careers, Francis joining the Seaforth Highlanders and Rivy attempting to forge a career in business. Rivy then trained with the Bucks Hussars and at the outbreak of war went out with his brother to join the 9th Lancers as part of the British Expeditionary Force, (the 'Old Contemptibles'), a small professional army which was too small to hold back the much greater German forces.

Rivy was the first to die, killed at the battle of Aisne during the retreat from the Marne on 14 September 1914, barely a month after the war began. Francis was wounded at Mons while attacking German machine guns, winning a Victoria Cross for his action. He was deeply affected by the death of his brother. He returned to France and was killed in the 2nd battle of Ypres at Hooge on 24 May, 1915. (Before I knew this, I visited Hooge where a huge mine was detonated, leaving a great crater filled with green grey water to this day).

Their two Grenfell cousins, Julian and William ('Billy') Grenfell also died early in the war. Julian Grenfell, a friend of Stewart Menzies and Patrick Shaw-Stewart at Eton, was a bully – known as 'Rough man' or 'Roughers' he went on to Balliol College, Oxford, where he wielded a huge Australian stock whip to intimidate those he did not like. He joined the army as a regular soldier, serving in India and South Africa in 1911.

He wrote home from Flanders in November 1914: 'I adore war. It is like a big picnic, but without the objectivelessness of a picnic. I have never felt so well or so happy.' He enjoyed stalking German sentries in no-man's land, recording his kills in a game book – '105 partridges, 2 Pomeranians.' As well as this ferocious side, he was an admired poet with a lyrical gift for verse – his poem *Into Battle* was published in *The Times* the day after his death. The *Dictionary of National Biography* summed up these inconsistent sides of his character as 'combining aesthetic sensibilities with primitive instincts in a manner alien, even alarming to, later generations.' He died on 26 May of head wounds in hospital at Boulogne.

His younger brother Billy Grenfell was killed on 30 July, barely two months later, at Ypres.

The effect on Sybil and her family of the death of so many young men she knew well must have been profound. I had toyed with the notion that Rivy Grenfell, whom she knew very well, had perhaps been a lost love of hers. Her response on reading of his death in the newspapers on 20 September 1914, while she was training at the Newcastle Infirmary, served to scotch that idea. She wrote to her mother: 'I see Rivy's name is in the papers today among the killed, poor old boy, but I am sure it is the death he would have chosen.' Sad and stoical, but certainly not bereft.

Sybil's other cousins also signed up: the Benson brothers, Guy, Rex and Con, all served at the front, and Sybil's cousin by marriage, Stewart Menzies, was serving with the 2nd Life Guards. He also fought early in the war, before being badly wounded and gassed at near Hooge.

Angus McDonnell returned from Canada heading a contingent of engineers and lumberjacks, tasked with building railways to serve the Western Front. Extraordinarily, David Lindsay, 27th Earl of Crawford, enlisted as a private in the Royal Army Medical Corps, serving as a medical orderly in casualty clearing stations in France, before returning to join the Cabinet.

Many of them were to end up in the army intelligence corps, including her brother Charlie, Rex Benson and most notably Stewart Menzies, who on being invalided out of front line fighting, joined Field Marshall Haig's intelligence staff, and ultimately went on to join and lead MI6.

13

Arrival in Russia: Petrograd

At the start of the book, we left Sybil and her companions arriving at St Petersburg, on 12 October 1915, after a week's journey across the North Sea and overland through Scandinavia and Finland.

The country they had arrived in was extraordinary. Russia was cold and alien, with a difficult language, an unfamiliar alphabet, an antique dating system and even an archaic temperature scale – degrees Reamur (R°). Despite superficial similarities with Britain – the Emperor, Nicholas II, was a cousin of King George V – the country was far removed from Britain politically and socially, like a step back in time to an earlier Europe. The Russian Emperor was an autocrat, the only source of authority, the Russian parliament (the Duma) being simply a rubberstamp for the Tsar and his appointed ministers. A gilded court surrounded the Tsar, cocooned from the modern world. The political system rather resembled the England of Charles I in the 1640s or the France of Louis XVI in the 1780s, both countries on the brink of their own revolutions.

Socially Russia was even more remote from Britain. The serfs had only been freed 50 years before and more than four fifths of the population were still peasants, living in an almost feudal relationship with great landowners. There were the beginnings of modern industry but Russia lagged far behind western Europe. Tsar Alexander II – the 'Liberator Tsar' who had freed the serfs and instituted some degree of representation at national level through the Duma and at local level through Zemstvos (community councils) – had been murdered by young revolutionaries. His son, Alexander III and grandson, Nicholas II, had recoiled from his reforms and social and political progress was effectively stymied. The regime had just ostentatiously celebrated 300 years of Romanov rule in 1903, and on the surface looked as if it would continue for ever. It was not to be!

Already revolution had broken out in 1905 only to be crushed – the famous incidents of the mutiny on the battleship *Potemkin* at Odessa and the shooting of peaceful demonstrators on 'Bloody Sunday' at St Petersburg. Since then, reactionary repression had been followed by limited attempts to encourage progress through the Duma. With the outbreak of war in 1914 the country formed up patriotically in defence of the Tsar and the motherland. But as the great losses mounted at the front and as the regime became ever more inept, and as food shortages became routine and refugees flooded into the cities, the pressure built up once more towards revolutionary change.

Sybil and her party arrived in the coldest winter since 1812. The country had

The Anglo-Russian Hospital in Petrograd's Dmitri Palace, 1916, now known as the Beloselsky Belozersky Palace (Boyd family collection).

already suffered huge losses on the battlefields of the Eastern front, where Russian soldiers, who often had no rifles, huddled in inadequate trenches in the driving snow and biting frost. St Petersburg (renamed Petrograd to exorcise its German sounding name) was full to overflowing with soldiers and with Russian refugees – half a million of them – whose homes had been burnt by the Russian army as it retreated in the face of the German advance. Sybil and her colleagues heard that there were hundreds of hospitals in Petrograd alone, often voluntary hospitals housed in great palaces and run by patriotic noble families.

On the first morning, 13 October 1915, she visited the British Embassy for lunch, accompanied by Sir John Hanbury-Williams, a former aide to her father in Canada who was now British military attaché to the Tsar. The British expatriate community (the 'British colony') was riven with rivalries and petty jealousies. Lady Georgina, wife of the Ambassador, Sir George Buchanan,[1] had boundless energy which she channelled into running a hospital and into care for refugee children and mothers, but was resented for being autocratic and for seeming to take credit for all the efforts of the wider British community. Sybil was warned not to let 'Lady GB' take over the Anglo-Russian Hospital.

Sybil was initially unimpressed with the Embassy – 'There was a wet blanket feeling over the whole show. Sir George is a weary looking tired lifeless sort of person, who gives one the impression of being too tired to really care much what happens. Lady Georgina I was not attracted to.' This atmosphere of wary distance was to change slowly as she got to know and admire the Buchanans, who became

---

1 Sir George Buchanan (1854-1924), British Ambassador to Russia (1910-18).

good friends.

Walking back through the streets to their hotel they saw soldiers everywhere drilling in every street and square:

> There are 500,000 soldiers in Petrograd and another 150,000 coming next week. This is the Second Reserve, men who were called up about a month ago. The last time that the second reserve men were called up was in 1812. They have called up six classes of them, ages 20 to 26. They are all men who are usually exempt from military service, only sons, etc. Nearly all I saw in the streets have uniforms and some have rifles, very few dressed as civilians.

Sybil and her colleagues were nonplussed by the apparent lack of preparation for their arrival. She confided to her mother, 'I really don't know quite what to tell you, for none of us ourselves know quite what we think and what we don't think. Nothing really had been arranged for us here and I don't know and cannot really find out whether we had been offered the Russian Red Cross or not. There is one thing that there seems to be no doubt about and that is the political importance of it [the Anglo-Russian Hospital].'

Sybil set about finding a home for the Anglo-Russian Hospital. Only one of the buildings she was shown was the right size and location – the Palace of Grand Duke Dmitri Pavlovich, a young and rather dissolute first cousin of the Tsar. A large ornate pink building, lined with caryatid statues, it stood on Petrograd's grandest avenue, the Nevsky Prospekt, overlooking the Fontanka Canal. It was here just over a year later that soldiers would fire into a crowd of protesters, sparking the revolution.

They were offered one floor of the palace, which was big enough to house nearly 200 beds, but which could not accommodate the doctors and nurses. It also required major building works to make it fit for a hospital. Sybil was a realist and fought to

Nevsky Prospekt, Petrograd (John Massey Stewart at Mary Evans Picture Library).

get the palace accepted:

> A great difficulty is to make Dr Fleming understand that we cannot get an ideal place in which to make the perfect hospital, and that it is no use refusing a place because it is not that, when there is nothing better to offer. We came here fourteen months after the war started and find 600 hospitals in town, so we naturally cannot expect to find a perfect house left. We shall have to take what is offered to us if it can be made suitable and show what we can do. Beggars cannot be choosers, and this is War not Peace.

She initially expected the building conversion to take about 'a month to six weeks and that it will cost well over £1,000, nearer two.' She feared that 'this will be a long wait and rather trying for the engaged staff. Quartering the staff is another great problem and one of the greatest problems of all, the language.' In fact it took nearly three months to convert the building before the hospital could open, at a final cost of £2,946-17s-7d (over £200,000 in today's money).

But despite the difficulties she was upbeat:

> This sounds a gloomy letter to start with but it isn't really and we shall get through a shake down, but I think we shall have difficult water to steer through. It is so difficult to find out anything definite from anybody in this place; what the military hospitals are, what the Red Cross is, who controls what, and whether one is really needed. I personally think good hospitals are, for they are very short of good doctors and good nurses and equipment. But at the present moment there are fifteen military hospitals of 200 beds each in Petrograd with their equipment waiting to be housed.

She was helped by a team from the Russian Red Cross headed by Mr Poluvstov, a rich and engaging man of about 48, on his second marriage, a real problem solver and a fixer. He was supported by Colonel Fénoult, a 40 year old cheerful and obliging soldier from the Imperial Guards seconded to help them, and aided finally by Dmitri Ivanovitch, a shy young aide de camp, aged 24, 'the baby – handsome and faithful like a dog.'

Together they set about transforming the palace into a hospital. Like most Russian palaces it had no proper piped water or sewage system, which had to be installed. The great ballrooms and reception rooms had to be subdivided and turned into wards, dressing rooms (where wounds were bandaged), an operating theatre, a laboratory, X-ray department, offices, dispensary, store rooms and kitchen. A small mortuary was also added.

Sybil was impressed with the inventive use of a material called Arborite (large panels of matchwood stuck together like plywood and painted white) which were used to subdivide rooms and to hide the valuable paintings that hung on the walls – turning the palace into a gleaming white clinical interior.

She and Dr Fleming took the plans back to the hotel and worked until 2 a.m., trying to squeeze all the beds in. 'We finished by deciding we could get no more than 150 to 160 beds into the palace if it was to be done in any way like an English hospital. We sat gloomily looking at each other and went off to bed feeling rather depressed.' The next day they consulted Mr Poluvstov and agreed to buy 200 beds and fit in as many as they could.

One of Sybil's strengths was her ability to sensitively handle people, even those she didn't agree with. She was visited by Lady Georgina Buchanan whom she had been warned would try to interfere with the Anglo-Russian Hospital. Sybil wrote:

> What am dreading is when she says, 'I should like to come on your Committee for I could help you so much with all my knowledge of Russia, you who are so new and who are getting into the hands of the wrong people.' How to politely refuse? I shall fend it off as long as possible and try to be as friendly as possible.

The interview went well and Lady Georgina did not push her luck:

> I told her frankly what we were doing and she didn't say she thought it all wrong, but we kept off dangerous ground and I talked of it naturally as if it was our show and that she was an interested well-wisher. I got on to her own things as much as possible and how much I admired the immense amount of work that she does (I do honestly admire a lot she does).

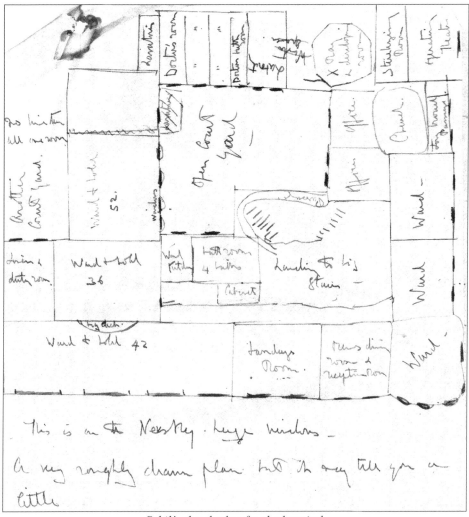

Sybil's sketch plan for the hospital

Over time their relationship blossomed from one of distrust into mutual admiration and friendship, and when Sybil left Russia a year and a half later, Lady Buchanan lamented the loss of her good advice and judgement.

The Empress

From the start, the Anglo-Russian Hospital was backed at the highest level in both England and Russia. The Tsarina was a patron who had thanked the Anglo-Russian Hospital's Committee in London for the 'beautiful gift' of the hospital they were sending out. The hospital was based in Grand Duke Dmitri's palace, formerly owned by the Tsarina's sister, so it was natural that the Tsarina should have a keen interest in it.

On 20 October, Sybil and Ian Malcolm were summoned to meet the Tsarina, Empress Alexandra Feodorovna, at her palace at Tsarskoe Selo outside Petrograd.[2] Such a personal interview was a privilege granted to very few foreigners. After being conducted down miles of corridors, Sybil was shown into the Tsarina's personal sitting room, guarded by a magnificent black servant. She was struck by the Empress's appearance:

> She got up and came to meet me, dressed as a Nurse. It suited her extraordinarily well and she looked very, very handsome, but utterly different to what I expected. I expected a cold tragic face with all life gone out of it. Instead it was a beautiful face full of sympathy and charm, such a charming smile, beautiful English and very, very easy to get on with, so much so that it was extraordinarily difficult to remember who she was. But somehow one came away with a heavy heart and thanking God one wasn't an Empress, especially this one. There was an atmosphere about her which cried out for sympathy, I have never felt it so strong with anyone. I daresay she has made many mistakes and done many silly things, but what that woman must have suffered! It is extraordinary how much she is hated here. You will be glad to hear that I have quite made up my mind not to marry an Emperor!

The Tsarina was hated chiefly because she was born German, despite going out of her way to stress her patriotic duty to Russia, heading up her own hospital at the Winter Palace, and ostracising pro-German relatives. She was also distrusted for her reactionary influence on her husband, favouring incompetent ministers, but above all for her devotion to the extraordinary libertine and self-proclaimed 'holy man' Grigori Rasputin, the so-called 'mad monk', who exerted an incredible influence over her due to his claim to be able to cure her haemophiliac son, the Tsarevich.

Sybil and Ian Malcolm also paid a visit to the Dowager Empress, Maria Feodorovna, mother of the Tsar. Sybil wrote to her own mother:

> The old Dowager Empress was very nice to us yesterday and was also guarded by a coal black gentleman. It seems the fashion for Empresses. She sent many messages to my delightful Father who is doing such good work in starting garden cities. She will never forget the most interesting morning she spent with him at Hampstead.

---

2 The Imperial family lived at the Alexander Palace, one of several at Tsarkoe Selo. It was smaller and more comfortable than the colossal Catherine Palace.

Earl Grey, a keen advocate of Garden Cities, had obviously shown the former Empress round Hampstead Garden Suburb, established in 1906 on 243 acres of land purchased from Eton College.

On October 29, Sybil returned to Tsarskoe Selo, to have lunch with Baronesse Sophie de Buxhoeveden, a lady in waiting to and friend of the Tsarina (later to become her biographer after the Revolution). She was shown round the huge palace built by Catherine the Great, and found it an extraordinary melange:

> The Palace is the most gorgeous and hideous thing I have seen for a long time – miles of rooms, many of them with really beautifully painted ceilings but the rest of the rooms garish colours and tons and tons of gilding. There is one room where the walls are all made of amber! with carved panelling of amber on the amber walls, and this is mixed with much gilding.'[3]

Sybil had been brought up in houses like Dorchester House dedicated to the tasteful display of great art, so the palace jarred with her aesthetic sensibility:

> One room of pictures, the whole wall being covered with them: they fit right against each other like a jigsaw puzzle. There isn't an inch of wall anywhere – big pictures, little pictures and all kinds, some lovely ones, some horrid, etc. But it is very difficult to admire the beautiful ones because they probably have a poor picture of another period next to them.

But she did admire some of the rooms, such as the Chinese room:

> The whole room was done with Chinese lacquer like those beautiful old screens, and in the centre a beautiful red Chinese Vase, presented to the Romanoffs by China on their having reigned 300 years. Then the big ballroom, which was one mass of gilding, but a very fine room, had an extraordinary peculiarity, for it had the most astonishing echo. If you clapped your hands the noise of the echo rolled round and round like thunder for several seconds.

Sybil began to get to know the city, which was magnificent. Founded by Peter the Great in the early 1700s as Russia's window on the West, reluctant Russian courtiers and merchants had been ordered to build a new city here graced by palaces and a system of canals sometimes called the 'Venice of the North'. She found herself coming to admire this strange, beautiful city which only had six hours of daylight a day in the depth of winter, and was ferociously cold, with the gleaming gilded roofs of the Admiralty building, the Peter and Paul Fortress, and the dome of St Isaac's Cathedral – and of course with the splendour of the gigantic Winter Palace on the banks of the Neva.

The streets were crowded with people walking through the snow, the buildings and trees brilliant with their coating of snow, and the tramcars winding their way along metal tracks. The shops and all the signage was of course in Cyrillic, making it difficult for new visitors to make out the street names. Sybil felt helpless – she couldn't even instruct a taxi where to go.

---

3 The Amber Room was subsequently looted by the Nazis in World War II and taken to Konigsberg in East Prussia, never to be seen again.

She wrote to her mother:

The accounts we heard of the Petrograd climate are quite correct. It is beastly although we have had very little frost as yet in the day, it is a penetrating cold that goes through one and it is very difficult to avoid catching cold. The days are mostly very dark too. In about four weeks, at the darkest time, we shall have electric light till 11 in the morning and light it again at 2.30.

Culture and Society

Although in many ways Russia was so backward in the social and political spheres, in the arts it was at the forefront of great culture which it exported to the world. In music, it was the home of Stravinsky whose *Rite of Spring* had premiered in Paris in 1910, and of Rachmaninov and of the young Prokofiev whose first opera was performed in 1911. In the world of ballet, the great art form of Russia, the impresario Diaghilev had dominated St Petersburg before leaving for Paris to found the *Ballet Russes* with which he toured the world, with dancers like the young Nijinski. In literature and theatre, it was the land of Tolstoy and Chekhov, both dead by 1915 but towering figures. In the field of painting, Kandinsky who was credited with bringing in the first abstract art, returned to Russia in 1914 at the start of World War I after living in Germany for many years. And in opera, the singer Chaliapin, whom Sybil saw perform in St Petersburg, had toured the West, wowing audiences in New York, Paris and London.

Young, intelligent, amusing and good company, Sybil was in great demand. She was invited out almost every night – to the theatre, to the opera and the ballet which was the soul of Petrograd, to concerts and to dinners, which were invariably followed by gambling on games of cards such as bridge or bezique far into the night. She lunched regularly with Sergei Sazonov, the Russian Foreign Minister, and his wife. Sazonov was drawn to this attractive and lively young British woman, and he was no doubt also keenly aware that her cousin Sir Edward Grey was his opposite number, Britain's Foreign Secretary. She attended great functions – the opening of the Winter Palace Hospital set up by the Empress; the St George's Day ceremony where 16,000 war heroes were feasted and presented with their medals in the People's Palace; the reception of the gravely wounded Russian prisoners of war, 'the grand blessés', exchanged for German prisoners and returning home to an emotional welcome, often mere shadows of their former selves.

Her letters were full of humour. She described a hilarious episode when she was invited to dinner by Grand Duchess Vladimir, a grand old lady with a taste for indecent jigsaw puzzles. Sybil set out in a horse-drawn sleigh, but halfway there the horse which was old and sickly lay down in the snow and refused to move, forcing Sybil to 'take to my ten toes' and run through the snowy streets in her grey fur coat. To make matters worse she had been given the wrong address and couldn't speak Russian but eventually luckily recognised the house, arriving breathless, late for dinner and 'making the most of my excuses which were jolly good.'

Grand occasions

Early on Sybil and Ian Malcolm were invited to the opening of the Winter Palace Hospital. The Tsarina had turned over part of the huge palace to a hospital. Like everything to do with the Winter Palace it was planned on a gigantic scale – with 800-1,000 beds for patients. Sybil wrote:

> It is all too beautifully arranged but the wards are really too big, one hall has 200 beds in it – a big white marble room with a certain amount of gold. All the floors are covered with linoleum and the beds are all white enamel with white coverlets, and are frightfully close together, they are less than two foot apart, in rows down the room back to back, and between each bed a white enamel and glass table. It is all done regardless of expense, £10,000 having been spent on the alterations alone.

People were already criticising the expense, but Sybil felt that anything the Tsarina did would have been criticised.

Sybil and Ian Malcolm were the only foreigners invited to the opening ceremony of the Winter Palace Hospital: 'Nobody but Russians of the Court, Government and High officials, all in gorgeous uniforms and strung all over with medals and orders like a Christmas tree.'

Sybil described the magnificent opening ceremony:

> The 50 nurses were all drawn up at one side and the Red Cross orderlies; and all the Court officials and Ian and self on the other; we were introduced to crowds of celebrities whose names I didn't catch. Near the altar at the end of the room were eight priests in brilliant green and gold vestments, and standing to one side of these the Imperial Choir in claret red and gold. At 3 o'clock the two Empresses and the four young Grand Duchesses came in, the Dowager taking precedence, the four girls were all dressed exactly alike, dresses, hats and boas, very nicely dressed. Then the service started with the marvellous deep and gigantic voice of the Deacon. I have never heard anything the least like it, it is too wonderful, how do they get it, but they go on from father to son and have special training for the development of this overpowering voice.
>
> After 40 minutes of prayers, at which we all stood first on one leg and then the other, the service proper finished but the Priests came and sprinkled us all with Holy Water and then a Procession started throughout the hospital, the choir and five of the Priests walking in front down the centre aisle of each room chanting prayers and *Te Deums*, and the other three Priests with assistants walking down the centre and side aisles sprinkling Holy Water on all the beds. Young nurses stood at attention one between about every five beds down the centre aisles looking awfully nice in their grey dresses with the white head dress, and we all followed.

Half way round the Tsarina spotted Sybil and came across to speak to her, with her daughters, the Grand Duchesses Olga, Tatiana, Maria and Anastasia.

> I was then introduced to all four daughters so I had a good look at them, the eldest three nice looking but none beautiful, or even very pretty, and the youngest of fourteen, ugly. This interlude stopped the whole procession which made me feel rather shy and then the old Dowager Mother who had gone on ahead turned round impatiently to see what the delay was, and thought that she had better not be left out of all the good things so came back to allow me the pleasure of kissing her royal hand.

Sybil visited a number of other hospitals, some of which inspired her, some of which almost made her weep. She was keenest on one run by Madame Sazonov, which had a different atmosphere to any other in Petrograd:

It is the only hospital I have seen where the men, every single one of them, smiled and looked happy. They always look patient in all the hospitals but they generally have such a dreary dull look. Here they were alive and smiling. The moment she entered a room every man's face lit up and grinned with pleasure.

Sybil resolved: 'I must try and get that atmosphere into our hospital, now that I see that Russians can be made to look like that.'

She also visited the 'the saddest place'– the big central hospital where soldiers who had lost limbs were sent for assessment to decide how soon they should be given artificial limbs:

Somehow when you saw these legless men by the fifties it did make your heart ache for all this wrecked humanity. Far the saddest sight though were the men with absolutely no legs at all, just trunks, great big men cut off in the middle, if they were standing on the ground they came up to one's elbow. I saw one great big huge young fellow aged about 21, such a nice looking boy, being carried into the room to be inspected, he hadn't a couple of inches of leg and only one hand. They have already at this Petrograd hospital fitted 8,000 men up with artificial limbs and 1,000s are waiting, and this is only Petrograd.

She was pleased to note however that they were looked after financially: 'They all get fairly good pensions starting from 20 roubles a month. Then they all are given the St George's Medal one of the 4 grades of it. It carries with it an extra pension of the lowest grade 12 roubles a year and the highest grade 36 roubles. The St George's Cross also in 4 grades starts its pension at 28 roubles and goes up to 120 roubles a year; all that is really very good I think.'

As a point of comparison, Sybil herself paid 25 roubles per month to the woman who cooked and washed for her at the Anglo-Russian Hospital. She also went to see the return of severely wounded Russian soldiers, exchanged for German prisoners:

This morning I went to see the Russian *Grand Blessés* arrive – 211 cases. It really was a most moving and touching sight. At the station they arrive at is a long wooden building painted white inside. Here is prepared a feast for them, tables seating about a dozen per table down each side and then the stretcher cases on the floor in the centre with a low stool table between them for their food, à la Japanese. They are given a very good meal and every man has a couple of flowers by his plate and a packet of cigarettes, and wine to drink. At the end of the room a table was arranged as an altar and the priests were there and then a band and a choir.

As at the hospital for limbless soldiers, she was struck by a sense of waste:

Some of the men looked very ill, terribly white and bloodless and some very thin. Very few were smiling. They are too emotive for that. The National Anthem was first played when they were all seated and the men cheered all the time, it isn't a 'hurrah' but a continuous cheer with no break in it. Then an old Dodderer of the Red Cross made them a speech, then a short service took place. A large number of them were crying, nurses as well. There was a most pathetic sight of a man who had lost both his eyes, sobbing his heart out.

Refugees

They were told of the ghastly refugee problem, caused mainly by the Russian Army's scorched earth policy, burning Russian villages as they retreated leaving nothing to the Germans, and forcing the villagers to leave their homes and take to the roads in the depths of winter:

> Sir George Buchanan told us that the refugee problem was quite appalling. Nobody had ever seen anything to touch it – 3,000,000 people suddenly swept from their homes with absolutely nothing in the world; their houses burnt and nothing prepared in the way of organisation for feeding them; starvation and death from fatigue staring them in the face. Thousands upon thousands died in the woods and at night could be heard howling like wild animals from hunger and madness. It is a horrible picture.

She described the plight of the refugees living in Petrograd:

> They live in huge barns all huddled together in mud and filth; babies dying of pneumonia, women having children, scarlet fever and measles quite prevalent. It really is heart rending and these are the most fortunate of the refugees. 1000s upon 1000s are dying on the roads. They tell me that even in peacetime life is held very cheap in Russia, it certainly is in War time.

On 14 October, they were taken by Lady Georgina Buchanan to see some of the refugees and then to see her own hospital:

> She first of all took us to see some of the refugees living in sheds, all crowded like sardines, the filth and smell was terrible. It is really rather good of her, she goes and takes the babies and children and washes them and clothes them in new and clean clothes. Lady G and one of the Grand Duchesses have started a home for lost babies. In the flight of these poor refugees, the children often get separated from their mothers. The mother gets out of the train to buy some food, and the train goes on without her and she has no idea where it is going to. How tragic it all is. After seeing some of these poor people we went on to the English Colony Hospital, a dear little hospital very well arranged of 80 beds, a little overcrowded but then Lady G said it was only meant for 50.

They became aware also of the brutal side of the Russian army. Sybil was told a story by a Russian surgeon about an incident involving refugees on a road near the front where he was serving:

> One dark night many of them had fallen down on the road from sheer exhaustion unable to go further, all huddled up one against the other when several heavy batteries of Russian artillery came galloping along, they went straight over them killing a large number and wounding and crushing many more, he did what he could to repair some of the damage on those poor, hunted, homeless people, but he could do little. I believe when the history of the war is written, the most pathetic chapter will be about the Russian Refugees.

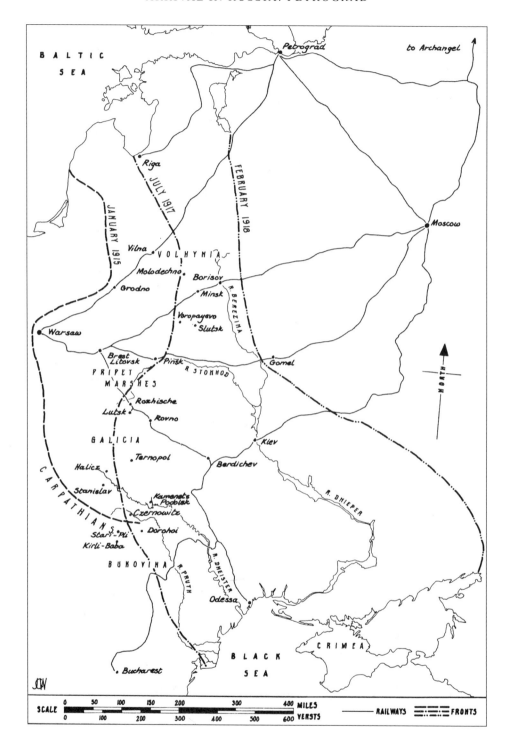

Map of the Eastern Front, 1915-18 (from 'The Forgotten Hospital' by Michael Harmer, with acknowledgements to William Harmer.)

Sybil wrote to her parents: 'As you know, Russians although they are supposed to be such kind-hearted people can be amazingly callous and brutal.' She related a shocking story told her by a visiting British military attaché, George Lloyd, who had heard it direct from a Russian general. The Russians had taken 5,000 Germans prisoner near the shores of a small lake and had to convey them to the other side, with only a very few little boats to hand. Sybil told what happened next in spare and chilling words:

> They hadn't enough boats to do it quickly and what boats they had were small, so in order to avoid giving themselves too much trouble, they turned their machine guns on the 5,000 prisoners reducing their number to 2,000, these could be more easily dealt with and would take less time to transfer across the lake than the larger number.

The British military delegation were so shocked by the story that George Lloyd was sent back to check that he had not misunderstood. Lloyd tried to suggest to the Russian general that there must have been some accident and asked, 'Did I understand you to say that you lost some boats and prisoners when you were transferring them across?' But the Russian swept the suggestion aside: 'Non, mon cher, we had no accidents – we killed them first because there were too many of them. What does it matter, it is war.'

Sybil added to her parents: 'A nasty story isn't it. Not one for our side to publish.'

Staff arrive

Sybil and her colleagues had been a small advance party sent out to establish the hospital. Now the main body of the doctors and nurses arrived – over 30 of them, each unprepared for the cold and having to adapt to an existence where they had no patients to treat as the hospital was not yet ready or equipped. They arrived at the 'unspeakable hour' of four in the morning, as their train had been delayed. Sybil had been able to arrange temporary accommodation for them in a dormitory for poor gentlewomen. They were later moved into 'the club' – a former merchants' club converted to house the Anglo-Russian Hospital staff, about eight minutes' walk from the hospital on Vladimirsky Street. The nurses in particular insisted on keeping the windows of their bedrooms open at night:

> They will not listen to reason and understand that it is a cold country and a vile climate. They say we cannot possibly sleep without our windows being wide open. Consequence, the club is freezing and they, many of them, have severe colds and are now beginning, thank goodness, to say, "Well, I suppose it is true, but who would have believed it?"

One nurse in particular fell ill with a mystery illness and ended up being treated in a Russian hospital. The nurse was diagnosed as suffering from nerves and acted like a child, hiding her head when Russian nurses approached. Sybil commented: 'So far the Anglo-Russian Hospital instead of nursing the wounded is having one of its own staff suffering from nerves being nursed in a Russian hospital – the staff think it bitter.'

Sybil had to pour oil on troubled waters and keep tempers from fraying, among a large staff marooned in an unfamiliar environment with nothing to do. So she set them all to learn to Russian, studying at the local Berlitz school.

Loss of the Stores

More problematically, as the palace was slowly transformed into a hospital, they found out that the carefully selected stores and equipment which they had sent out by ship from England had been delayed. They received inconsistent and contradictory accounts – first that the ship, the *Abaris*, had been damaged and had had to turn back to England, but at the same time that a ship of that name had already arrived in Russia. It finally transpired that there had been an almost farcical mix up of two different ships – the *Abaris* and the *Arabys* – both sailing to the by now ice-locked Russian port of Archangel. They resigned themselves to the fact that the stores could not be landed before spring, forcing them to buy replacement equipment from whatever was available locally.

St George's Day

One of the great celebrations in the run up to Christmas in Russia is St George's Day (or St Yuri's Day), apparently celebrated twice a year in December and in May. Sybil was invited to witness the ceremony in the People's Palace, 'a gigantic building with an immense sort of opera house holding 4,000 or 5,000. There Chaliapin and people of his calibre perform at stated intervals in all the best Russian operas. No seats are more than 1/-, they vary from 1/- to 3d, and in that way the best of Russian opera and drama is played to the people at popular prices. Excellent idea, one I am sure that Father will thoroughly approve of. Wholesome amusement by the best artists at prices that the very poor can pay.'

On this particular day, the People's Palace was full of all the soldiers in or near Petrograd who had won either the St George's Cross or the St George's medal:

> The cross is only given for bravery – there were 16,000 (sixteen thousand) of them! And they were all given a meal at once. I have never seen such a wonderful sight or anything so well organised. We walked through hall after hall, all densely packed with soldiers all with cross or medals sitting at long tables. The entire building was decorated with the St George's ribbon, orange and black stripes. Sixteen thousand men being fed, four and a half kilometres of tables, all with beautiful white table clothes on. 8,000 chickens and I forget how many tons of other meats! Each man had a bottle of red wine to himself and a bottle of wine made out of some preparation of honey – fairly potent I am told. The first wine that most of these men had touched since the beginning of the war. We will leave till later the results of such lavishness. Finally after much walking we came into the big opera place that I spoke of before. It really was a most wonderful and impressive sight. You must imagine a huge opera house all pure white, no decorations in mouldings or gilt or colour. Three tiers of galleries, big deep galleries with plain white pillars. The floor of the house gradually heightened from the stage to just below the first gallery. Round the galleries the orange and black ribbon of St George, with two or three foot sized crosses or stars of the order.
>
> After the service two of the Cossacks of the Emperor's body guard blew on their

silver trumpets and the food was brought in. A procession of servants marched in carrying huge silver trays on their heads piled up with various meats. It reminded one of Fairy Tales and Kings' feasts. After the first course, twelve silver trumpets each about seven foot long, blew a mighty blast from the centre of the top gallery. Prince Oldenburg then called for the Emperor's health. Every soldier rose, and three bands played the Russian National Anthem accompanied by the twelve silver trumpets glittering in the light. One's eyes seemed to focus on those glittering trumpets in the centre of all this white and orange and black with the sea of faces looking towards one. Every man having his little ribbon, or ribbons of orange and black on his heart and many with white arm slings or bandaged heads or on crutches. That glorious anthem pealed forth to the accompaniment of the cheering of 16,000 soldiers, of course we only heard the 5,000 in the centre theatre but as it died down you heard them in the far distance. As I told you it is a continuous cheer which lasts the whole time the anthem is being played (and it is much longer than *God Save the King*) it has the same effect as the continuous roll of drums, gives you shivers down your spine and makes you feel like crying.

She wryly noted, 'It is curious how the Russians can organise a thing like this and make such hopeless fiascos over the things that really matter. I must say they made a mistake in the amount of wine they gave for I believe 1,000s were drunk late in the afternoon.' They were tempted to be critical only to find their own perceptions challenged:

Miss Robertson (the matron) and I noticed a young nurse very rouged with most suspicious looking golden locks curled saucily on her cheeks peeping out of her nurse's white veil – (worn like a nun like all the nurses wear here). She wore three golden St George Medals. Stepped straight off the Gaiety stage but very pretty in spite of rouge and hair dye. We passed some rather scathing remarks upon her until we heard that during a very hot engagement she had saved the Colours of the Regiment from the Germans. After that we looked at her rouge and hair with a far more lenient eye.

And they themselves were looked at askance: 'There was one old veteran officer there, an old Crimea warrior aged 92. He didn't look more than 80 and wore a black silk skull cap on his venerable head. I thought he looked at Ian and Doctor Fleming in their uniforms with an eye of loathing as he passed us, he must have been remembering Sebastopol.'

Christmas in Petrograd
Christmas Eve approached and Sybil and the staff were interested to find out how Christmas was celebrated in Russia. In fact, they celebrated two Christmases and two New Years, the first according to the British calendar and the second according to the Russian calendar thirteen days later.

On Christmas Eve, 24 December (British date), she wrote to her mother:

It is Xmas Eve so I write to you. I have had an exhausting day, although I have not been out. First I have a cold that I was nursing. Secondly it is absolutely beastly out today, 25 degrees Reamur, which means between 20 and 30 below zero – much too cold. Thirdly I have been wrestling with accounts all day and have finally balanced them fairly correctly, only three roubles out in a sum of 43,778 roubles. A real feat I consider it when there are at least six different people that come for money and have different accounts, besides men coming in for bills to be paid and as they don't like to be paid by cheque in this country one has to draw the money oneself and dole it out. My despatch box comes in awfully useful and keeps it all. Doctor Fleming is not good at accounts, that is why I do it.

She commented:

Horribly cold country this is, the poor men in the trenches, I don't know how they survive. I started at breakfast time by strongly insisting on my fire being lit at once. They generally light it, let the half dozen logs burn and then go away. Today I was quite firm and made them bring up more wood and kept it alight till 4.30 p.m., by this means raising the temperature of my sitting room from 52 which it was when I breakfasted to 58, the warmest it has been for about three weeks. The wood is very scarce and very often the hotel runs out of wood for the day. However I am getting quite used to it now and awfully lucky to have an open fireplace in my room.

The next day, they held a Christmas party in the club, for the Anglo-Russian Hospital staff and some Russian friends. 'It was quite a success and four excellent musicians came in and played for us. Then we all sang *Auld Lang Syne*, and the Russians thought it most strange, I think. It lasted from seven to one. We ate turkey but no plum pudding.'

In Petrograd, as the year came to an end, Sybil turned her thoughts on the coming year:

What will 1916 bring to Europe, I wonder? Victory for us it must. I can't believe that the Germans will be able to keep up their strength and we must be getting stronger if only we all stick to it. They tell me here that in March Russia will have 3,500,000 fresh troops absolutely ready to take the Field and jolly good troops too. That ought to help to put fear into the hearts of the Germans.

And she considered Russia and its possible future:

It is very interesting here, but rather difficult to write about. I suppose it is quite safe. There seems to be a universal feeling in all classes of society, as far as I can make out that Russia must have a Revolution either before the end of the war or more likely after it. What sort of revolution it will be is a question. If Germany is smashed I think the chances of real big revolution are much less; if she is not smashed and the terms of Peace do not satisfy Russia, then there is certain to be real trouble. What interests me is that nearly all the society Russians that I have seen who have spoken of it, all hope for it. I was talking to a young couple last night. They said if we have no revolution Russia is lost, hopelessly lost. They said that up to two years ago… [the Imperial Family] was never criticised by Society. A year ago everybody criticised but said nothing. Now they all talk about it. This young couple say that if there is no revolution it means the end of Russia because it means that she isn't big enough to do it, that she is still asleep; doesn't care enough; hasn't any real patriotism; hasn't the character for it; that's why we want it, etc, etc., and I expect if there is one all these people will be the first people to go.

14

News from home

The First World War changed Britain profoundly. It marked the end of the Edwardian era, with its nineteenth century political parties (Liberal and Conservative), often dominated by the House of Lords and an aristocracy and landed class owning huge estates; and it ended the easy presumption that Britain was the unchallenged ruler of the waves and supreme world power.

It brought the shock of early military reverses in Belgium, and an increasingly terrible toll of young lives lost at the front; it brought air bombardment of England by Zeppelins; and it triggered huge social change as increasingly women stepped forward to take the place and the jobs vacated by men who departed for the front.

Servants became hard to retain and harder still to recruit. As the German Navy began an unprecedented U-boat campaign designed to starve Britain into surrender by indiscriminate sinking of British and neutral shipping, the population of Britain experienced shortages and scarcity of foodstuffs and basic necessities, and rationing was brought in. Services such as the postal service became less frequent – one delivery and collection a day in place of the previous morning and afternoon post.

The most important of all these were the social changes around the role and image of women – no longer in the position of being meekly dependent on men as the family's only wage earners, but stepping forward to take on new roles – office workers, bus drivers, agricultural workers, the 'canary girls' working with dangerous chemicals in the munition factories – all learning new trades and earning their own money. For those like the Greys, seeking to upkeep and maintain large houses, the war posed very real problems – already scarce resources were being stretched further still.

Countess Alice kept Sybil up to date by sending an almost daily digest of news about the war and the country, gossip and stories about the family, society and politics, jokes, and clippings from the newspapers. Then she would wait for three weeks or more for Sybil's reply to come from far away Russia. Alice's stories included developments at the hospital she ran with her daughter-in-law Lady Mabel Grey at Howick Hall, and also how the menfolk of the family were faring – her son Charlie Grey and her sons-in-law Arthur Grenfell and Lawrence 'Jonah' Jones, in their respective regiments.

We have a charming picture of Alice and Earl Grey receiving Sybil's letters in the early morning, which are brought up to Alice's bedroom:

> The letters come in with my morning cup of coffee at 8 o'clock, and the moment I see them I always grab them greedily to see if there is one from you. When I see there is,

I call out to your father 'A letter from Sybil', and back comes the answer, 'I am coming in to hear it', and then I have to squeeze myself against the wall in my bed and make room for him, and he comes and wriggles down into the bed with all my little pillows comfortably arranged behind him, and drinks some of my coffee, and is deliciously comfy and warm and happy listening to your letter and making affective remarks full of admiration and delight as it goes on. Can you see the old birds gloating over this precious letter?

The public mood at the start of the war was fervently patriotic and frankly jingoistic. Alice's early letters include anger at the barbaric actions of the enemy – particularly at the execution 'which has so shocked the world' of the British nurse Edith Cavell for aiding British servicemen to escape from Belgium. She sent gleeful stories, such as that of the British airman who was captured with his aircraft, and forced by his German captors to fly back over the British lines so that they could observe them. The pilot however had other ideas, and strapping himself in tightly, looped the loop, tipping his unsuspecting 'passengers' out in mid-air to fall to their deaths. It was probably an apocryphal tale, but Alice and Sybil both enjoyed it – Sybil replying 'What fun it must have been. I do hope it is true.'

Only a matter of five months later, however, when the terrible death toll only showed signs of increasing, Alice wrote to Sybil with another story of German airmen, this time the crew of a Zeppelin which was shot down over northern France. She related a harrowing eyewitness account of the Zeppelin's end, as the huge gas balloon above the crew's compartment caught fire and burned, with the cries of the airmen as they ran up and down in their flying coffin trying desperately to escape, some by hanging onto ropes from below the zeppelin, until the burning envelope sank down and engulfed them. Alice wrote 'it must have been a terrible sight.' No more crowing laughter at the deaths of enemy combatants!

There was a litany of early battles – the battles of Mons and of the Aisne which killed Rivy Grenfell in September 1914, and the first battles around the doomed town of Ypres, where Francis Grenfell died in 1915, winning the Victoria Cross. Later while Sybil was in Petrograd she learned of other battles which tested the Allied strength – the failure of the expedition to capture the Dardanelles and knock Turkey out of the war; the terrible grinding attrition of Verdun, with the French defenders doggedly denying passage to the Germans; the catastrophe for British arms at Kut el Amara in Mesopotamia, which killed one of Sybil's relatives, The Hon. Robert 'Bobby' Palmer; and the great naval engagement at Jutland in May 1916, the only occasion when the British Navy and the German High Seas Fleet confronted each other face-to-face.

Howick

Of course Alice wanted to give her daughter a picture of life at home. One of Alice's first and most entertaining letters describes the Christmas party at Howick, given for the officer patients convalescing at the hospital. She told Sybil of her plans:

I think I told you we are having a Christmas tree in the staircase hall on New Year's Day, for the 32 soldiers, about twenty nurses, seventeen schoolchildren, mothers with an extra seventeen little tiny ones including babies, servants in the house and ourselves, Mrs Anster and three children and Mrs Francis and three children. Altogether I suppose about 140. We are teaching the soldiers some of the carols to sing on the occasion and Jonah is to be Father Christmas.

On Christmas Eve, Alice filled the men's stockings with presents to hang on their beds:

Nurse and I prepared all the men's stockings, and laid them in order with the name pinned to the outside of the stocking and also a Xmas card. Inside we put in orange, a Canadian apple, a charming little square packet of the best toffee, a little calendar, a pencil and for the pipe men a quarter of a pound of tobacco and for the cigarette men two packets of Player's Navy Cut in each stocking.

Early on Christmas morning she and her husband's secretary set off in disguise to deliver the presents:

Gilly and I were called at a quarter to six on a pouring wet morning. I put on my fishing boots over my stockings and over my blue dressing gown a very long thick white flannel bath cloak I have, gathered very fully at the neck with a very big peaked hood. I dressed Gilly in my Bermuda white blanket coat and on her head a big knitted woollen scarf which also makes a peaked hood, so we were beautifully disguised and very Xmasy like this creeping along in dead silence.

I carried my little electric lantern – first of all we loaded ourselves with a tray that had on it all the stockings for the two upstairs wards, and this Gilly carried, while I had thirteen glorious big lovely shaded balloons all with strings attached. We let ourselves out of the front door, so as not to pass through the downstairs ward. The whole gravel space was filled with pools of water, so I carried a big umbrella over the balloons and shaded them from the falling rain, and was very glad of my high waterproof boots.

Once in the wards with the sleeping patients, they hung a stocking on each bed:

We tied on the stockings and fastened the balloons at the foot of each bed by loose tie; there were sighings and mutterings from the sleepers, but no one showed signs at any rate of being awake and we escaped from that ward and went and did ditto in Ward No. 2. Even if awake no one could possibly see anything but two closely enveloped figures with high pointed hoods falling over their faces.

The Christmas festivities were a great success and culminated in a dance held in the men's ward that afternoon and evening:

The crowning event of the day was a dance if you please, beginning immediately after tea (which is about 4 o'clock) till 9.30. The beds were all arranged round the room alongside the wall so touching each other all round and giving us plenty of seats, the big tables were removed only leaving the piano, and the flooring (linoleum) was plentifully sugared all over with boracic powder sprinkled from a sprinkler, in place of French chalk. It proved itself most effective making a good slipping surface, very sanitary and easily washed off next day.

The whole Grey family, their servants and of course the patients took part:

No outsiders were invited merely all the household, so Charles and Jones were the only two men beside the soldiers. We all went in, your father too and Molly and Nisset[1] who were to dine with us and sit up late as it was Xmas Day. The two children danced wildly until 8 o'clock when we took them away to dinner. Gilly also danced and Sister, and Mrs Steele alternatively danced with tremendous spring and vigour and played every dance tune you could think of on the piano for the others to dance to, all by ear, she was beyond price last night I assure you. One of the men also plays quite decently and now and again played a valse and relieved Mrs Steele at the piano, besides accompanying some of the others when they sang some songs. Gaunt favoured them with a song or two and almost for the first time appeared with his usual comic grin but a well washed face and collar. I thought Jessie the belle of the dance, with pretty puffed hair she really looked awfully well.

They sang *Auld Lang Syne* and joined hands, and cheers were given for everyone and then Mabel came and sat in my sitting room just before I was ready for bed and told me how after everyone had been cheered, Xmas dinner and all, a nice Scotsman named Brenner came forward and said he would ask for cheers for "an absent friend, Lady Sybil Grey" – wasn't that delightful, and will show you that your reputation and memory still live and are handed down to the men.

Alice also relayed wartime 'good housekeeping' advice which was being handed out through public lectures in England – for example on making a 'Hay Box Cooker'. This was a box packed with insulation which retained heat, into which partially cooked food was placed to finish cooking. Hearing about it from the cooking lecturer Alice resolved to make one:

So I chose an old packing case over at the stables, got Urquhart to make me a hinged lid for it with a fastening, and all this evening Mrs Dodson and I have been lining it with about 20 thicknesses of newspaper, over that we have tacked some woollen material, fastening it on with nails, and now it is ready to have the hay packed tightly into it.

She explained how it worked:

You take your casserole, cook in it whatever you wish to consume either next morning – porridge, stew, fish or whatnot; you start cooking it on the fire or stove, bring it to the boil or if it is a stew near the boil, then you take it quickly off the fire, wrap a bit of stuff or newspaper round the casserole, and plunge it into the hay, scraping a hole for it until you have submerged it and tightly packed the hay all round it – a sort of little mattress made of hay goes over the top to keep all air out – and then you shut the lid

---

1 Lady Mary (Molly) Grey (1907-2002) and Lady Elizabeth (Nisset) Grey (1908-41), young daughters of Charlie Grey, Lord Howick, and his wife Lady Mabel Grey (née Palmer).

firmly down, and allow the process of cooking to go on slowly in the box. The results are said to be delicious, all the juices are kept in, and the slowness of the cooking brings out all the flavour and makes it beautifully tender. It saves fuel because you can let your fire out sooner, it also saves time – you can put your porridge in at night time and next morning you will find it admirably cooked.

Next day she got her grandchildren, Molly and Nisset (Elizabeth) aged eight and seven, to help pack the hay in by getting into the box and energetically jumping up and down. They then proudly carried the hay box into the kitchen to put it through its paces. Next morning the servants' porridge was perfect, but the jacket potatoes were not properly cooked and the tapioca was stodgy.

News from the front
Charlie Grey, Sybil's brother, had steadfastly avoided telling his mother about the conditions at the front. Now that he had moved from front-line service to an intelligence role at Divisional HQ, Alice, his sister Evy and his wife Mabel Grey succeeded, 'after an hour's searching probing', in getting him to describe his working day:

His Divisional HQ is about three miles from Ypres and he lives billeted in a little cottage, all ground floor. He has a tiny room with one little window and gets into it through the kitchen up three little wooden steps. It contains a wooden bedstead, a mattress and two sheets, and he sleeps in his bag, with I think he said two waterproof sheets spread over him to keep him warm, the rest of the furniture in the room consists of a couple of boxes that are arranged as a cupboard for his clothes, and of a wooden tub that he uses for his bath; his servant sleeps in the kitchen and the man and his wife proprietors of the cottage sleep in a room beyond the kitchen. They are on Belgian not French soil, and these peasants are Belgians and do not speak French.

He is called I think about 7.30 and when dressed walks a couple of miles to the village (Headquarters); he tries to time his arrival at the moment when the General, his ADC and the 1stGSO are just off in the General's car to the trenches, only a couple of miles away, the general visits every day. C then eats his breakfast peacefully and reads his newspaper, before beginning his office work about 9.00. He is doing this all the morning, then about 1.30 the general gets back to luncheon; every alternate day Charlie and the GSO2 have the use of the other motor – the days Charlie has in, he starts about 11.30 after some office work and is out until about 4.30.

She described his duties:

His job is to be cognisant, not of what goes on in our trenches, which occupy (for that Division) about two miles of frontage, but to know all about the German lines opposite, all the reports from the six different battalions and the engineers attached coming to him as to the German lines, and if anything has been noticed, such as a bit of earthwork being thrown up here, or some sandbags being built up there, then he has to go and enquire and see and find out what it all means, and if there is anything to worry about it; also they get photographs taken from aeroplanes of the line opposite to their own lines and have to study these photos with magnifying glasses comparing them with photos of the same section taken a week or two back, so that they may see if any new work has been done and in what direction, and what it may lead to. Later in the day, news comes in from the different battalions that has to be summarised, etc., and that is the sort of work he does.

Alice was obviously very relieved that her son was now in a much less dangerous situation than in the front-line trenches of the Ypres Salient – a killing zone.

> He says it is more interesting than being just with your regiment as company officer, besides naturally being a much more comfortable life. Once a week he goes some little distance and sits in a tub in a row of six for officers, and has hot water poured on him from overhead and comes away feeling very clean and comfy. He likes his General I think, they are a mess of ten – and seems to get on very well although he doesn't seem to find any of them thrillingly interesting. He never looked better in his life, he is not fat so to speak but well covered and solid-looking.

The account given by Charlie Grey seems to be of a comparatively easy life, and certainly a much less dangerous existence than that he had faced as an officer in the firing line.

Humour

Alice always had a strong and self-deprecating sense of humour. It comes out in her story of an auction held at Alnwick to raise money on behalf of the Red Cross. Pressed for time, Alice donated what she thought was an ugly old set of a glass decanter and goblets from Howick which she never used. When she took her seat at the auction, she was in for a shock:

> I went in and got a foremost seat, just under the auctioneer's table in a crowded hall. Then said Mr. Henderson, the auctioneer – "These I consider the gem of the auction" or some such words – "they have the Grey crest on them and are a presentation gift." I sat up feeling very uncomfortable, not having known anything about them being a presentation gift, and considering on what occasion they had been presented to the family. The auctioneer then turned up the decanter shaped vase and read out from a letter engraved flat on the bottom "Presented by Queen Victoria in 18.." I was horrified and did not know what I ought to do, buy them in or what. Then the bidding began and I hastily communicated to my two neighbours that not having realised they had been a gift of the Queen's and did not know what Albert would say at their having been put up for auction. I heard Mrs Scholefield bidding behind me, and turned round and whispered to her the state of the case, and that should Albert be annoyed, she must allow me to buy them back from her. She said she would and bought them for £17-0-0. As Mrs Allford said to console me, after all it was going for a very honourable purpose so there was nothing to mind in having sent them to be auctioned. Your father was immensely amused when I got home at finding what we had done, but said of course Mrs Scholefield must keep them – and so there it is – anyway our things brought the Red Cross Fund £26-0-0 and as I had to buy a little and spent £5 they made £31 by us.

Money troubles

She also wrote to Sybil about the parlous state of the Grey family finances. Although they owned a great deal of land (17,500 acres at Earl Grey's death in 1917), the Greys were never very rich by comparison to their peers and other families. Indeed their estates were encumbered by very high debts – including loans and mortgages these amounted in early 1900s to about £250,000 – the equivalent today of perhaps £20,000,000. The Durham University Archive comments that Earl Grey lived in constant daily terror of interest rates rising by half a per cent. And indeed the matter of money and the need to economise came up repeatedly in Alice's letters, as she struggled to make savings in the running of a big house, and worried about the effect that the finances were having on her husband's health. They realised that the family needed to get rid of the expensive lease on the London house in South Street, and they took advice on what hope they might have of renting out Howick Hall itself.

She finally wrote to tell Sybil of the 'great decision' that she and Albert had taken one evening, at her prompting, to close Howick Hall and to move to two converted cottages at Peep o' Sea on the Howick estate: 'We are going to shut up this house, if we cannot let it, which we shall try our very best to do, and we are going to settle ourselves in the Peep o' Sea cottages.' She had already told her daughter Evy, 'She was delighted at the idea and strongly applauded it, seeing how difficult and anxious a thing it is to try and cut down things in a big house like this. It is a constant effort to keep things down and to try to do with less servants, and I am always being defeated and told it is impossible.' Albert Grey, she knew had been 'worrying over the future and what would happen if the people who hold the mortgage asked us to pay off still more yearly than the £2,000 that we have had to pay off extra in the last two or three years,' (the equivalent of about £160,000 in today's money).

Her daughter-in-law, Hilda Grenfell, also had to raise money to help pay for the debts incurred in 1914 when her husband Arthur Grenfell caused the suspension of the private bank Chaplin, Milne & Grenfell over the failure of his speculation to acquire the Grand Trunk Railway Company of Canada. Hilda raised £2,000 by selling her tiara, 'It is a relief as it will enable her to pay off all the lost money minus £300.'

Alice rapidly sketched out her own plan for conversion of the two Peep o' Sea cottages, to which they planned to move with a very diminished staff: 'We should just have one housemaid, one kitchen maid and my maid whoever she is who will have to help in the housework or perhaps lay the table; it would be like going up to Scotland for a while every year and perhaps the servants would not mind doing work a little out of their normal circumscribed spheres.' She added: 'Any way we shall have to attempt it and take our own beds from here, and what pretty bits of furniture can be spared to make it homey and pretty, and if we like it and spend a little money on it, it should do us quite well, the only sadness is that we should have no spare rooms for Evy and the baby or Vera or anyone, but then we must cut our costs according to our cloth mustn't we, and this war is going to revolutionise living for many of us in England if it goes on for another year or more.'

They ran into trouble when they suggested it to their son Charlie who immediately pooh poohed their plan. But Alice didn't forget the idea, and about four years later, after her husband's death, she was indeed installed in the Peep o' Sea cottages.

Now, in February 1916, she wrote prophetically to Sybil: 'I wonder if we shall ever live again the same way as before the war, I doubt it, we shall all have to live carefully for years to come I expect, and by then things will have altered, and the upper classes will perhaps no longer own land and have big houses and properties, so that our present life will alter in character.'

In March, Alice wrote to Sybil from their house at 22 South Street. She had persuaded her husband to have drawn up for them:

> a really complete statement of our present financial position, exactly what we can count on having to spend a year, after all charges are made on mortgages, and a moderate but adequate sum put aside by the agents for upkeep of premises including Howick and its surroundings, also after taxes and rates are paid for Howick – in fact money that we can count on just for our own selves and servants and for whatever house we may settle to live in. For we must at once set about getting rid of the remainder of this lease and finding a smaller house in a much less expensive part of London. I am afraid as the lease is only for another twelve years we shall get but little for it, but we shall be saving, the large sum that it runs us into every year for rent and taxes.

She relied on Robert Benson, her brother in law, a banker: 'Robin is rather shrewd over these things and I am going to see him tonight over the best way to try and get rid of the lease to the best advantage.'

After their abortive decision to move into the Peep o'Sea cottages, Alice nevertheless started to cut back on staff at Howick. Mrs Dodson, the housekeeper, decided to leave quite peremptorily. 'It was a considerable shock to me to find on my arrival last night, that Mrs Dodson could not stay beyond tomorrow morning leaving me just one day in which to ask her about things and get answers to my questions; she has accepted a post as assistant mistress to a large girls school in Wantage, and they require her services next Saturday, she accepted it at once.' Mrs Ross, the cook, went reluctantly, 'very sad at leaving Howick.' The Greys also decided to mothball their motorcar and their chauffeur, May, took a job with Alice's sister, Evelyn Benson.

Alice was told by a neighbour in the little fishing village of Craster, a few miles away, about the government's preparations for home defence against the imminent threat of German invasion:

> I asked Mrs Craster if she was preparing for the invasion that we are all told to look for before long. She had sent away the twins she told me, so no longer felt nervous. She said that every cottage in Craster has received its orders, and every soul knows exactly where they are to go immediately they are warned. They have been told which cart they are to get into, where it will be, and who will be its driver; each driver knows what cart and horses he is to take, the names of the people who are to go in it, so there ought to be no panic or delay in getting away if the Huns do come to this bit of coast. All these arrangements Tom Craster has made for Craster and its surrounding hamlets. Mansfield[2] is supposed to plan out the same arrangements for Howick and I shall make it my business to see if he has done this and given the necessary instructions to all the cottagers.

---

2 The Howick estate manager.

Earl Grey's illness

Through these tumultuous years, Countess Alice was concerned with what was happening to Sybil, far away in Russia, and with her family, especially her grandchildren, and above all the health of her husband Albert. Alice's letters detailed her endless and ultimately fruitless search for a cure for Albert's ill health. She sought out a host of opinions and doctors – ranging from their family doctor, Dr Waterson at home in Northumberland, to distinguished doctors in London, Dr Fripp of Guy's Hospital, and trusted practitioners such as 'Byles Mori' who dispensed homeopathic remedies and 'packs' to treat Alice herself for attacks of hives and Dr B.O. (Dr Beckett Overy, who later became Winston Churchill's personal physician). One suspects that she was not terribly well served in the advice she sought about Albert's condition, and was too easily brushed off with diagnoses of some kind of gastric disorder, acidity and indigestion, whereas it seems likely that Albert Grey was suffering from a much more serious condition, probably the cancer that ultimately killed him in 1917.

Alice wrote continually to Sybil about Albert, giving his weight, how he was feeling – on good days he was energetic and interested, reading in his study or his garden 'shelter' and meeting people, on bad days he felt 'seedy and slack'. She tried as far as possible to limit the amount of work he still tried to do, meeting people, giving talks on his various political interests, etc., and in particular she sought to prevent him going down to London which she thought tired him out. She also believed that worry about the family financial situation was affecting his health.

Interestingly, despite her committed patriotism and opposition to Germany, she wrote at one point to Sybil that, 'If there was no war, I think the right thing would be to go to Germany to one of their doctors, who seem to study this kind of illness.'

Throughout these years, Albert Grey continued to waste away, until the point in spring 1917 when his 'poor legs look like sticks' and he resembled a 'beautiful Dodge'. When in 1917 he finally received a clear and unambiguous diagnosis that his condition was terminal, almost the first thing Albert did was to commission his own political testament, in the shape of a memoir about his political concerns written by the journalist and biographer Harold Begbie.

Meanwhile family life continued at Howick Hall. We have a series of pictures of the Greys with their grandchildren. Early in 1916, Alice describes Earl Grey at home with his young grandchildren Mary (Molly) and Elizabeth (Nisset), Charlie Grey's daughters:

> I wish you could see your Dad at this moment – he is lying on the big sofa by the fire in the dining room with Molly cuddled against him with his arm round her, and her head tucked into his neck, while he is reading aloud to her some stories of Algernon Blackwood's.
>
> Nisset is also listening but as usual is manipulating a 'Berlin'[3], the two children are never tired of getting to Berlin and back, it is too extraordinary it never palls.

3 The 'Silver Bullet' or the 'Road to Berlin': a handheld dexterity game. Manufactured in 1914 by the British firm R.F.&S. (source Project B).

Nisset was playing a hand held game of dexterity called 'the Silver Bullet' or the 'Road to Berlin', which involved rolling a ball bearing along an obstacle path, the 'Route to Berlin', with holes into which the ball might roll if one made a mistake. It was manufactured in 1914 and sold very well.

On a later occasion, they had Evy and Jonah's daughter, Nancy, to stay:

I find it very difficult to write for Nancy is in the room playing on the floor at building houses with cards. Arthur is helping her and Evy is looking on adoringly, Albert is attending to the gramophone, and the song that is ringing through the room is Harry Lauder[4] explaining why he will never wear his trewsers anymore.

Harry Lauder was a Scottish entertainer, described by Sir Winston Churchill as 'Scotland's greatest ever ambassador!' He began working in the mines, and became a professional singer of comic songs and songs of Scotland (generally dressed in kilt and sporran, not trousers!) and starred in the first ever Royal Command Variety performance in front of King George V. In World War I he raised funds for war charities and entertained the troops at the front. His only son, John, was killed in action in December 1916, and Lauder wrote the song 'Keep Right on to the End of the Road' in his memory.

Alice also related some of the tragedies that had befallen local families that had lost men in the war. On 29 April 1916, she wrote: 'Poor Mrs Scott has now lost three brothers in the War, a fourth is out in France fighting, the fifth and eldest is commanding somewhere in England and not qualified medically to go overseas but the sixth is just going! You can imagine the poor mother is feeling his departure very much as he is her favourite and she dreaded having to make the sacrifice of any more sons.'

---

4 Sir Henry Lauder (1870-1950).

15
Getting ready

Petrograd

Meanwhile in Petrograd, Sybil was taken up with the final stages of converting the palace into a hospital. The longer she stayed in Petrograd the more she admired parts of the city: 'St Isaac's Cathedral next door to the hotel here is most beautiful – several times lately it has been completely covered with snow, quite beautiful especially one moonlight night; the whole cathedral, pillars and all looked as though it was built of white alabaster and the bronze statues and capitals of the pillars stood out black against the white, the whole thing surmounted with a gold dome. Then there are two lovely slender graceful gold spires that catch every glint of sunshine that we ever get. Then all the quays down the river are lovely and the Winter Palace, etc. – many beautiful bits that grow tremendously on one.'

She was taken on a sleigh ride in the park at Tsarskoe Selo by one of the Empress's ladies, and for a moment she felt she was in Canada again:

> How it reminded me of Ottawa – deep snow and park and pines and firs so like Rockliffe – only much bigger and no river. I really felt almost as if I was back there. I also saw the Tsar but not to speak to, he was just leaving the door just as we started in the sleigh and the Tsarevitch as well. He is a far finer looking man than cousin G [King George V]. We slowed down a little in our sleigh to let him pass in the motor and I was awfully amused to see that his three daughters were sitting on the comfortable backseat of the motor and the Tsar of all the Russias on the little chair up in front.

She adds, 'he was driving up to a place outside where there was a crowd of people waiting to see him. True politeness.'

She gave a vivid picture of everyday life, writing from her bedroom in the hotel:

> A man in a red blouse is trying to coax my fire to be pleasant and burn, it takes a lot of coaxing as the wood is so wet, and as the room has descended to the comfortable temperature of 53 again it is a matter of considerable interest to me whether he succeeds or not… Hurrah the fire has started to burn. Talking of fires we had a narrow escape the other night, for at 2 a.m. the house next door to the Club caught fire and the firemen came into the Club and there was a great to do. If the Club had burnt down that would have been the last straw, I think the staff in a body would have resigned.

She had a reasonable working relationship with Dr Fleming. She described their regular meeting to go through the accounts – a task they both heartily disliked: 'I am sitting in front of a fire writing on my lap with an evening of accounts in front of me with Dr Fleming – ugh! how I hate it! He is awfully bad at figures too and I shouldn't be a bit surprised if I quarrelled with him tonight.'

She talked about Dr Fleming: 'He can be very trying at times but he doesn't mean to be so I forgive him. He and Matron don't really hit it off at all well, but luckily I am able to smooth things over a good deal. He is much too much of an autocrat in the way he tries to do things and I quite see the way he says things is most irritating at times. He is very forgetful and he says one thing one day and the next repudiates it in a most annoying manner, with a tone of voice "what the devil do mean by doing that" until you point out to him that it was his own wish.' She adds 'I notice that matrons do not like being ordered about in what they consider their department, anyhow not in an autocratic way. However I think I can keep the peace.'

Sybil and he basically got on well:

> except that he drives me wild by perpetually coming into my room about every sort of foolish question. If you are trying to write or do anything it is maddening and I feel inclined to say, "now think of everything you want to say and don't come near my room for the next hour." I am very rude to him at times especially when he will come in and walk up and down my room whilst I am eating breakfast. Now I have told him that I will not discuss anything before breakfast, and if he comes in I send him out again.

Within weeks Sybil had to demote Dr Fleming due to what was effectively a mutiny by the other senior doctors who found working under him intolerable. When this happened he proved surprisingly adaptable, agreeing to work under others and continuing to serve the Anglo-Russian Hospital.

One morning, she and Dr Fleming were summoned to meet the Grand Duchess Sergei (born Princess Elizabeth of Hesse, the sister of the Tsarina). As the former owner of the Dmitri Palace, the Grand Duchess wanted to see over their hospital which was nearly ready to open. It was 8.15 a.m. on a freezing cold morning and they drove there in a cab, grumbling:

> It was 24 below zero Fahrenheit and there was a wind blowing, it was beastly and Dr Fleming kept assuring me that if we didn't arrive soon he would become an anarchist. I must say 8.15 on a cold winter's morning is a little early to see over an empty hospital.'

They assumed that the Grand Duchess must have stayed overnight at the palace, 'but not a bit of it, she had come this morning from Tsarskoe by train, having already been at the palace for half an hour when we arrived, had had breakfast and had had two interviews! I suppose she is used to getting up at 4 a.m. to say her prayers.

The Grand Duchess was famous in Russia for her piety having started her own religious community which visited the sick. However, being German, she was now very unpopular in Moscow and was derisively called the 'German Madonna'. Sybil and Dr Fleming however found her charming and appreciative of the hospital and she offered to arrange for Sybil and the Matron to have living quarters in the palace. After the Revolution the Grand Duchess was murdered like her sister and much later (in 1981) was canonised as a saint of the Orthodox Church.

Another person with whom Sybil had a lot to do and with whom she got on very well was Mr Poluvtsov, one of the heads of the regional Russian Red Cross. (It appears that the anglicised spelling of his name was perhaps 'Polontzev', the name which is inscribed on the ikon which he and others presented to the Anglo-Russian Hospital).

She described him as 'a delightful person in the way of being very clever and amusing', and later 'he is an engaging rascal and I have a very weak spot for him.' He appears also to have been very attractive to women while being quite unscrupulous in his treatment of them:

> he treated his first wife too disgracefully for words I believe and she divorced him. He then went to Persia where he lived for five years in paradise he tells me – gorgeous country, built himself a palace there, lived in marble halls with gardens full of exotic flowers and I haven't the least doubt had a harem. Came back and met a charming and pretty girl in the provinces, married her, took her to Paris and stayed there for two years while she was having the finishing touches put to her education, and then brought her back to Petrograd the chicest and smartest of products.

Sybil's affection and admiration for him come across very clearly.

Just now, however, he had upset her by foisting an aristocratic friend of his, Princess Marcia Shakhovsky, on the Anglo-Russian Hospital:

> He is in my black books just at present – he has done a most tiresome thing. I had been up to the office one day to see him about something and he said just as I was leaving, "I am most anxious for you to meet a friend of mine, Princess S. She lives quite close to your hospital. I thought she might possibly be of use to you when I am away, as I have to be in January for six weeks. If you can't get the people at the Rayon to do what you want, appeal to her and as she knows everybody and as she is a woman of character she'll get it done for you."

The Rayon was the regional office of the Red Cross. Sybil wrote: 'I was in a hurry so I said alright, thought it over and decided that it might lead to difficulties and besides which I thought I could manage the Rayon alright even when he was away, and decided to say so.' But at dinner the following night Poluvtsov told Princess S in front of Sybil, 'Well we must give you some sort of official position so that you can help Lady Sybil if she needs it while I'm away.' Sybil commented, 'it was done and I could only say it was most kind and that if we got into real difficulties I would go and ask her for help.'

Sybil summed up Princess Shakhovsky:

> She is a very clever and determined woman of about 50 with a hard face and the corners of her mouth turn down. I have found out that she has the devil's own temper and she beats her children (she has five girls) – the second ran away three years ago was eventually found in a pub, the whole of Petrograd knew it and it was a scandal. At the same time she is very clever and has a will of iron. She has lots of friends and lots of enemies in Petrograd.

The situation developed into a long-running conflict between the two women, managed politely but with a clash of wills on each side, which Princess S gradually won despite Sybil's opposition. The first surprise came when Col Fenoult told Sybil that Princess S had been coming to the hospital every morning to ask what needed to be done. Horrified Sybil met Princess S for lunch, 'She said she so much hoped to be of use, talking Russian, scolding the servants etc.' Sybil replied that they wouldn't need to bother her with that because they already had someone to look after the servants and sanitars and order all the stores.

Sybil confided her worries to Poluvtsov who brushed her fears aside, and the problem continued. Next, Sybil came on Princess S while she was showing two of the embassy men over the hospital, and she vividly describes their verbal confrontation:

"Why haven't I seen you these days, I have come to see what I can do, now I am officially asked to help you I must work all the time. What are we going to do this afternoon?"

I replied: There is nothing to do here this afternoon Princess, I am only showing these two gentlemen the hospital, and the workmen are hard at work on the floors, everything else is finished.

"Oh I see I am not wanted, *Je suis le cheveux dans la soupe*," etc. Corners of the mouth a little more down than usual. On her high horse at once. "You will lunch with me? when, Monday? And what are we going to do all day long?"

I told her that I would telephone but that I was afraid I was lunching out on Monday and had already made engagements to go and look at certain things with our head doctor.

"Oh I see I am a bore and not wanted," with pursed up lips.

Sybil fumed: 'An intolerable woman. We shall have nothing but rows if she comes in. But she is a formidable woman and how are we to tackle her? These are the times that I so wish Aileen or somebody like that was out with me.' Sybil yearned for the advice and support of her best friend back in England.

The war
Fighting on a front that stretched from the Baltic to the Black Sea, much longer than the Western Front, the war in the east was more fluid and less prone to become bogged down in trench warfare, often seeing breakthroughs followed by spectacular reverses.

At the start of the war in 1914, Russia had launched two offensives – the first in the north east into German held East Prussia, taking Konigsberg (now Kaliningrad) on the Baltic, and the second invading the Austro-Hungarian province of Galicia in the south west. The Germans had struck back swiftly in East Prussia, decisively defeating the Russian armies at the battle of Tannenberg in August 1914. The Russians succeeded in taking almost all of Galicia, leading the Germans to move considerable forces to the east to counter this.

In May 1915, the German campaign proved successful in Galicia, and to the north the Russians were expelled from Russian Poland. At the end of the year, the Russians had been pushed back on both fronts and the German advance was halted on a line stretching from Riga in the Baltic to Ternopil in the present day Ukraine.

Petrograd was far from the southern front where much of the fighting was taking place and it was difficult to get a clear picture of what was happening. At the start of 1916, Sybil wrote: 'Everything is shrouded in mystery as to what is happening in the south. On one hand one hears that the Russians have lost very heavily and on the other that it is all a lie and that they are advancing splendidly and have lost comparatively few men. So what is one to believe?'

She was told by Sir John Hanbury-Williams about growing distrust of and hostility towards England among some Russians, angry at the British failure in the Dardanelles and unaware of the Allied efforts on the Western Front. Sybil thought that a British propaganda campaign should be mounted in Russia, using films of the British forces in action. Drawing on her own personal interest in cinema she suggested what such films should show:

> There is a scheme afoot of getting the Government at home to send out a number of films with a good lecturer to go round Russia, showing and educating the people on what England is doing and has done. I believe it would be a first rate plan. The films should be very carefully selected. You want to show them Kitchener's army recruiting – next picture those same men at work, then the next is the trenches in France, the Navy, etc. Map of the World, showing how our Navy is guarding commerce and how without that Russia as well as other countries would be in difficulties. Another map showing how the German ships were before the war, then one now with no German ships anywhere except bottled up, etc. Something, well got up on these lines.

Sybil sympathised with the Russians:

> Russia has not got over the fact that long before she was ready she had to alter all her own plans of campaign to move forward, in the early days of the War in order to help to save Paris. By this she sacrificed well over 100,000 men in order to help the Allies in the west, and when she in turn wanted help last spring when we said we would advance, we did nothing of the sort but folded our arms, watched the Russians retreat and did nothing. They don't realise our difficulties and I quite understand them not understanding. So the more the people are educated on what we have done and are doing the better, and of how determined we are to go on to the bitter end.

Anti-German feeling was understandably running very high in Russia and she told the story of a pro-German Russian Princess Wassildikof, who had fallen in love with an Austrian.

> She belongs to a very good family here. She left Russia and bought estates in Austria. She was there at the beginning of the war and instead of returning to Russia she remained in Austria. The other day she returned and she asked for an audience with the Tsar, Tsarina, Grand Duchess Wladimir, etc. All absolutely refused to see her. She brought with her letters from the High and Mighty in Germany, even William himself I believe, and one of her pretty little stories was that she knew on the highest and best authority that the English had already negotiated with Germany to make a secret and separate peace. The Russians are simply mad with her and believe none of her stories. Her rooms were searched by the police and she has been sent into enforced retirement somewhere in the depths of the country.

Sybil told her parents that fines of 3,000 roubles had been brought in for speaking German in the street and for speaking any language but Russian on the telephone, 'luckily I have a permit to talk English.'

She dined with Sir John Hanbury-Williams who had been inspecting munitions factories. She got on well with him and clearly valued the friendship with a man almost old enough to be her father. 'He was most interesting at dinner and told me many interesting things. He said, I tell you all these secrets because there is nobody else in Russia I can tell them to. So the man flatters the woman!'

The cold was intense:

> All Russians tell one such a winter has not been known for 50 years or more. Apparently in all the big wars of the nineteenth century the same strange thing has happened, quite abnormal cold. But I suppose it hits the Germans harder than it does the Russians, although even the Russians, poor people, are being frost bitten in the thousands. One feels the cold more I think because even people like us rarely get our rooms above 50, so what must the poor people do. It must be truly appalling.

She was critical of the Russian lack of organisation: 'The authorities have stopped all traffic to and from Moscow for seven days, in order to bring up provisions and fuel. If they really organised it well they ought to be able to bring up quite a lot in a week.' She dined with Sazonov who thought it 'the most bitter and humiliating thing to think of the state in which Petrograd found itself, practically without fuel and without certain provisions, especially when everything of this sort was there to hand, and a little organisation and thought would have prevented a shortage of anything, if only it had been done before the winter set in. It really is a scandal, the guilty general really ought to be hung!'

Sazonov predicted that no lessons would be learnt: 'Nothing will be done; everybody is horrified and scandalised, the summer will come and all the necessities of life will pour into Petrograd quite easily and people will forget, and just as likely do nothing and find themselves in the same impasse next winter!'

The problems of poor food storage and transport, of course, had existed almost as long as Russia – and continue to plague the country to this day.

16

The Hospital in the Palace

By 23 January, the hospital was ready: 'The hospital is now beginning to look like a hospital and will really look beautiful I think. It is a palace, but it at the same time has the appearance of a hospital. I think it will make a very good impression.' Mr Poluvtsov, Colonel Fenoult, Dimitri, Doctor Fleming and Sybil had their photographs taken together by the best photographer in St Petersburg. Just as the opening date approached however Sybil learned that her 'trio' of Russian helpers was being broken up:

> I am miserable to tell you that Mr Polovtsoff leaves the Red Cross for good the day after tomorrow, Sazonov has persuaded him to return to the Foreign Office. I am absolutely in tears about it, just as we are starting too. If you ever have any difficulty or trouble go to Polovtsoff and things will in all probability be satisfactorily arranged, and above all he is a gentleman. Now the man who takes his place is a novice at the work and only talks Russian! Then Dimitri Ivanovitch also goes, he is joining the Navy – we are being given another young man, quite nice but shy, a Prince Radziwill.[1] Colonel Fenoult I am glad to say remains on simply to help look after us. But it is sad our happy party being broken up.

She wrote to her mother: 'Do you know it is nearly four months since I left you all and the hospital is only just opening. I think and hope it will be a great success only for the moment there are practically so few wounded here. They say in the Spring when the fighting starts round Riga that this place will be full.' Without work the Anglo-Russian Hospital nurses were 'childish and unreasonable', and there was friction between Dr Fleming and the Matron, Sister Irvine Robertson: 'instead of improving I think it is doing the opposite. I think perhaps when we are running there will be less friction. They don't understand each other and don't see each other's good points.'

Her mother had sent her a set of new clothes, and although due to move in a couple of days to the converted palace, she couldn't resist unpacking them: 'After all my curiosity was too great and last night I had to unpack them and try them on. Both the evening and day dress are perfect, not a hook to change. I simply don't know how you managed to be so clever. I think they are both lovely especially the day dress. Thank you, thank you, thank you.'

On 27 January she wrote with the news that the hospital was to open on Sunday 31 January, at 2.30 p.m. She told her mother of a wonderful good luck present they

---

1 Radziwill is a Polish Lithuanian noble family.

had been given:

The day before yesterday, Mr Polovtsoff came to see how the hospital looked before leaving Petrograd. I was rather surprised to see Prince Obelensky, Count Pouchkine [Pushkin] and all those boys come too, and then Polovtsoff carried in a lovely old ikon, of a warrior saint, date of ikon about 1720, size about eighteen inches broad and two foot high. A really lovely one. It was a present from them all to the committee, for us to have in the hospital to bless it and bring us good luck. On the back was a big silver plate, with the date, in Russian 'To the Committee of the Anglo Russian Hospital from their Russian friends' and then all their names in their own handwriting. In presenting it to me, Polovtsoff said – It was for the hospital during the war and they hoped I would take it home with me afterwards as a souvenir. You bet I will.

The holy Ikon given to the Anglo-Russian Hosptial
(British Red Cross Museum and Archives)

The opening finally took place on 1 February.:

> The opening was a great success and everybody seemed pleased. The staff too were delighted in the way that it went off. The Empress, most gracious. She gave us a great deal of work by suddenly announcing at 6 p.m. Friday night that she felt well enough to come to the opening so would we put it off from Sunday till Tuesday. But I am very glad she came. The palace really looked quite charming. These large finely proportioned white rooms with the white beds and a little ikon tied on the back of each, white enamel lockers and a white stool for each bed. Then we bought some pots of bright coloured tulips and to relieve the dead white and Mr Polovtsoff lent us cart loads of Palms. So the place looked a picture. Such a scurry and hurry. I find I can get a couple of photos off to you tonight so I am doing so.

The opening ceremony was actually carried out by the Dowager Empress, with the Empress also in attendance. Three months later, the Tsarina and her daughters once again visited the hospital. Photographs show the visitors and the staff of the Anglo-Russian Hospital grouped in one of the biggest wards. The Tsarina is seated between Lady Muriel Paget and Lady Sybil and flanked by the Grand Duchess Olga, Maria, Tatiana and Anastasia, and by Lady Georgina Buchanan and Sir George Buchanan, with the English doctors and nurses, and Russian nurses and sanitars. The young Grand Duchesses were all identically dressed in ermine hats and stoles, looking out

The Imperial family attending the Anglo-Russian Hospital in May 1916 (Leeds University Library, Special Collections, Leeds Russian Archive MS 781/6)

curiously at an outside world that they were very seldom given the chance to visit. Two years later the Grand Duchesses and their mother, father and brother would be dead, their bloodied corpses shot and bayonetted and flung down an abandoned mine shaft in the Urals.

A working hospital

Now the Anglo-Russian Hospital was open and patients began to arrive.

On 11 February, the first 50 patients were promised. In the event only a few turned up, but Sybil was relieved as they weren't really ready to receive them. 'At 9 p.m. we got fourteen men instead of the promised 50. Eleven medical cases and three wounded but only slightly. One of the sick men very ill. The arrangements went fairly well but it is just as well that 50 didn't come.'

The first real flood of patients arrived five days later with very little warning but the Anglo-Russian Hospital coped. On 16 February she wrote : 'Had early lunch. Got back to hospital at 1.45 to hear they had just telephoned to say they were sending 50 men! I telephoned trying to stop it as we didn't really want any today certainly not 50. But I was too late and they started pouring in.'

Her job was to take the patients' property for safekeeping: 'My business is to collect their money from them and give them a receipt – very good for the practice of Russian. 49 came, about 20 stretcher cases, some of the men very badly when wounded and about 30 I should think sick not wounded.'

Sybil described their youngest patient – 'the Baby'. 'Our youngest patient is fifteen years old but doesn't look more than twelve at the outside. Poor little fellow he has both hands badly wounded. They were wounded by a hand grenade I believe. Half the left hand is gone and I'm afraid the rest may have to be amputated – the right hand they say will be saved. Curiously enough he is in a bed next to a Tartar and they have been companions for seven months. The boy has no father or mother and his elder brother forced him to the war. Cruel.'

One day a boy Cossack arrived out of the blue, much to the delighted amusement of Sybil and the staff:

I wish you could have seen a small Cossack that came into the hospital the other day. He just walked in because he said he wanted a meal. He was aged twelve and a great deal smaller than our wounded boy. Ever so much smaller than Harry.[2] He had his little top boots on, his great coat down to the ground, his little sword and his Cossack whip hanging by his side and his small haversack on his back, and rather a big soldier's cap. You never saw anything so absurd or delicious. He swaggered into the wards and was at once surrounded by the soldiers who asked to hear the news. He sat on one of the beds and hit his leg with his whip and talked just like a little old man. He was going to Dvinsk with his regiment and father that night. I wonder why they allow these babies in the firing line.

A photograph shows the young Cossack posing cockily on the edge of a bed, completely taking up the attention of everyone in the ward.

---

2 Sybil's eleven year old nephew, Harry Grenfell (born 1905), son of her elder sister Vera.

The waiting had tested everyone's patience. Sybil wrote:

> Well, at last we are really starting. This waiting has been rather trying. There has been a good deal of unrest in the air lately. I hear all sides of these stories and try to oil the machine as much as possible – but it isn't always easy. I don't feel I am half as successful as many another would be at it. I am not a bit certain that Muriel wouldn't have done it far better. I think she would.

In the next few days there was a flurry of activity and entries in Sybil's diary got terse: 'Dr Fleming departed for the front. Problems in the bandage room were sorted out by Matron. All the dressing done in half the time, but Sister Whitehouse black as thunder. Sister Hayes also behaving like a silly little goose, they are a difficult team to run.' Sybil had a long talk to Dr Flavelle about X-Ray – he was most indignant at the London Committee having completely changed his orders. The next batch of 20 patients arrived with a mere 30 minutes' notice and they had to rush to make them received.

There were always a mass of details to sort out – the drain in the nurses' accommodation, the water in the bandage room wasn't hot, too few staff in the kitchen, too few sanitars (Russian orderlies). Their consumptive patient died: 'I am glad that the end has come. He came in with bad pneumonia being already very far gone in consumption. He was so patient and good.'

'The men are all trying to learn English and have English and Russian manuals to help them.' As part of their recuperation, the Anglo-Russian Hospital offered the patients English lessons and occupational therapy.

'Four operations today all successful. Our first quite big bit of shrapnel taken out of a man's arm.'

She heard that the Turkish fortress of Erzurum had fallen to the Russian Army. She also got news from England – that Zeppelins 'have been very busy'; that Bobby Palmer [Mabel Grey's brother] was said to be wounded and his mother Lady Selborne had gone out to India to look for him; 'also that Arthur Grenfell was nearly killed by a shell, he was concussed and one ear badly damaged, and the man next to him killed.' In fact Bobby Palmer was already dead, killed in a battle in Mesopotamia, but his family would not find out his fate for another four months, and his mother, a redoubtable woman, travelled out to Egypt and on to India vainly searching for him among the British wounded that had been evacuated from Mesopotamia.

Sybil met Hugh Walpole, the novelist, who worked with the Red Cross in Russia. 'I liked him very much. I think he will be a great help when we start the field hospital.'

Despite the hectic pace she took time to commission a child-size Cossack uniform for her niece Nancy, to be made by the Military Tailors of the Cossacks of the Imperial Guard. 'It will be exact in every detail, boots and all and she ought to look the greatest darling that ever was in it.'

The staccato diary entries continued:

Saturday, Feb 19

Red Cross Fire Inspectors came round and inspected the hospital. They made several

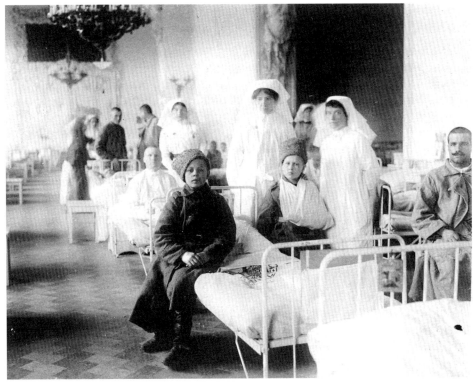

The young Cossack and boy patient (British Red Cross Museum and Archives)

suggestions, all of which we are carrying out. Three operations today.

Went to the Mariinsky Theatre with Paléologue.[3] The Lindleys and Monsieur Basily also there. A short opera and a number of most attractive Russian dances.

Sunday, Feb 20

Snowing hard. Mr. Andrews to do accounts. After lunch the Grand Duchess Marie Pavlovna, Dmitri Pavlovitch's sister, came to see the hospital. She was dressed in Sister's clothes. She has a hospital of 400 at Psoff [near Riga]. Everything is beginning to go smoother now.

Dined with Princess Yusupov – Princess Shakovsky took me in her motor. About ten people there. Nice couple. House like a museum full of collections of all sorts – one of the richest families in Russia. Her eldest son killed in a duel and the second married to G. D. Xenia's daughter.

The Yusupovs had been in Berlin when war was declared and had been detained: 'The young Princess Yusupov telephoned to her cousin the Crown Princess, who said at once that she would get them leave to go. Three hours later she rang up to say the Emperor wouldn't hear of it. They got leave later and left with the Russian Ambassador and were spat at and things thrown at them. The Emperor didn't find out until too late that they had gone down and when he tried to stop them they were already over the frontier.'

---

3 Maurice Paléologue (1859-1944), French Ambassador to Russia in the First World War.

The Yusupovs were of course Prince Felix Yusupov and his wife Irina, who play a key part in the story when we come to the assassination of Rasputin.

Monday, Feb 21
Hospital all morning. Lunched at Sazonovs – Mr. Bruce, Mr. Basily and three Russians there. Sazonov said he thought there might be rows at the opening of the Duma tomorrow, anyhow expects to be treated with the greatest coldness. After lunch went to see Mr. Tichlson at the bank and Mr. Wyatt – arranged with the latter that they should write the books up every week. Also went to arrange about classes for soldiers. Went to Rayon at 5 and saw Colonel Fenoult and Col Koutchenzoff about laundry and Dr. Bellasvodskoi [an incompetent woman doctor]. Dined home and did accounts.

Tuesday, Feb 22
Hospital all morning. Quarrel between Mr Flavell and Mr.Bott – with some difficulty smoothed over and a compromise arrived at. How tiresome they all are. Matron very bad with rheumatism. Mr. Shalonsky came and we arranged that the only class that we have room for was leatherwork. Have arranged for it to start in a few days.

The problem with Dr Fleming's leadership of the medical team came to a head when the rest of the Anglo-Russian Hospital's doctors as a body complained to Sybil of his autocratic management. Sybil said obliquely: 'Had a long talk with Dr. Fleming. I think things will smooth over if he is careful. There are wheels within wheels.' The problem nevertheless resulted in Sybil having to demote Dr Fleming from his leadership position, and his going off to the front to assess the need for a field hospital.

Sybil herself moved into the palace and was given a suite of rooms:

The sitting room is a large and pretty room. The walls of very pretty panelled wood, painted white; parquet floor, with an Indian carpet in the middle; the chairs and curtains and sofa covered with a white and blue chintz, pretty and restful. Very nice writing table and lounge and all charming. Out of the sitting room is a very nice bedroom with a dark Oxford blue carpet, comfortable bed and white walls. In the passage outside plenty of cupboards, two or three empty bedrooms and then a bathroom. My windows look out onto a courtyard of the palace. I get up at about 7.30 to 8, have my bath, breakfast in my sitting room, do odd jobs and then go into the hospital at about 9 to 9.30. When people come to see the hospital, if I want to talk to them I simply take them down to my sitting room.

She reassured her mother that she was being well looked after by the wife of one of the palace servants 'who is going to look after me entirely, bring me my breakfast, buy it, make the coffee, mend my clothes, etc. I shall pay her 25 roubles a month.'

She later said: 'My little maid is excellent and most attentive. When she and her husband think I don't understand they just shout louder and louder, until in desperation to save my ear drums I say "Ja ponimaou" which means "I understand", whether I do or not.'

Visiting St Petersburg a hundred years later, I was amazed by how the city has survived the tribulations that history has thrown at it – revolution, over 70 years of communism, two world wars and the appalling 900 day siege in 1941-43 when it

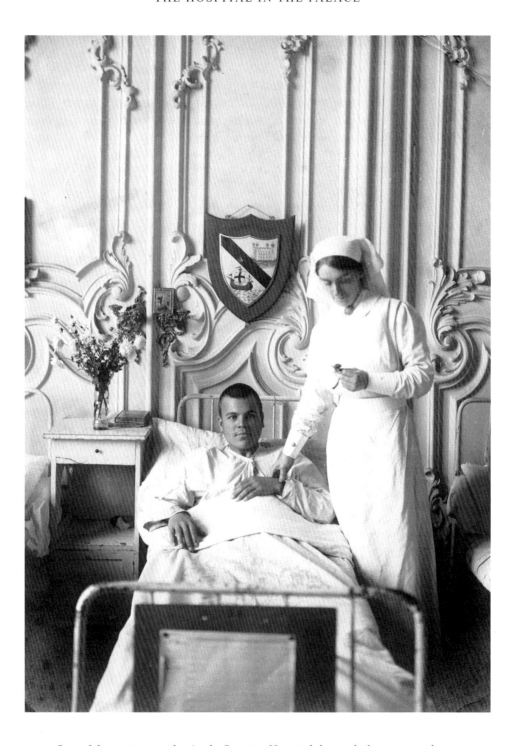

One of the patients at the Anglo-Russian Hospital, beneath the municipal arms
of Stepney. (British Red Cross Museum and Archives)

was pounded by the German Army. So many of the eighteenth and nineteenth century buildings have survived that it is easy to envisage what it must have looked like a century ago. The places I have come closest to feeling Sybil's 'presence' are along the magnificent Nevsky Prospekt, still bustling with crowds hurrying past the buildings that she must have known, and in a back corner of the Dimitry Palace (now called the Beloselsky-Belozersky Palace), looking out onto the internal courtyard, where Sybil's private rooms were situated.

The Duma

Sybil was lucky enough to witness many unique historical occasions. On 22 February, she was given a ticket to the formal opening of the Duma, the Russian Parliament, which she eagerly accepted. It was the only time that Tsar Nicholas II attended:

> I arrived a little late unfortunately and the crowd was great. I couldn't get into the gallery overlooking the big hall and Duma chamber but was able to see a little though a side piece of glass. It was a most historic occasion as the Emperor for the first time in his life set foot in the Duma. Nobody knew that he intended coming until 10 o'clock and the opening was at 2. There was great enthusiasm. It was a masterstroke, as it was not only a sort of official recognition of the Duma, but it shut up the mouths of the members who had intended to make themselves very disagreeable. They held the ceremony to bless the opening first in the big hall. Gorgeous singing, a very high hall and it therefore sounded quite lovely. Then the Emperor made a speech. He said how delighted he was to be amongst his people of the Duma, how we should send every available man if we were to end this war victoriously, and how Russia must go on to the end – and then called for three cheers for the Duma. He then walked into the Duma itself and walked all round it amidst a burst of applause. I saw him well as he walked out again looking very pleased. His being there has completely taken people's breath away and is looked upon as a most masterly move: especially coming alone, without the Heir Apparent. Instead of rather a hostile house it changed it into an enthusiastic attitude.

She added to her mother: 'They clap their hands tremendously, quite unlike the House of Commons. I wish I had been able to see better, but the crowd was fearful. I was very lucky to be there at all.'

Unfortunately, the Tsar never repeated this bold stroke, something which both Sybil and Ambassador Buchanan both urgently advocated a year later as Russia spiralled towards revolution.

On 24 February she dined at the Embassy with Sir John Hanbury-Williams. They played planchette, the spiritualist game of 'table turning'. It predicted a huge naval battle on Sunday 16 April, in which Germany would lose 24 battleships while Britain's Fleet would only lose eight. Sybil commented, 'We will now see if it comes true.' A month and a half after the forecast date, on 31 May-1 June, the Battle of Jutland, the greatest naval engagement of the war, resulted in a costly draw, with the British fleet losing more ships than the Germans and twice as many men. It may of course have been relatively easy for someone present (perhaps even Sir John himself) to tilt the planchette table to 'predict' the clash of the two largest fleets on Earth.

The position with Princess S became in Sybil's words 'impossible'.

> She is trying in many small ways to interfere and then tells everyone outside that she is here every day all day and has to attend to everything and that without her the hospital would be a failure. She tried today to question an order of the Matron in the wards to one of the sanitars – told him in Russian that it wasn't necessary to do what the Matron said he was to do. It ended in a victory for the Matron – and the Princess walked away and a huff. She afterwards came and said to her with a forced laugh, "I was told you were a terrible woman and I now know you are."

Dr Fleming returned from the front having visited the Russian 8th Army at Rovno, where he had met all the organisations and staff involved: 'He was cordially invited to take our field hospital there in the spring. He is looking very well, but is delighted to be back.'

Society
Sybil recorded her sometimes conflicting impressions of Tsarist society. She was hugely impressed by the energy and dedication of some of the best of the aristocratic ladies, who worked tirelessly, often in hospitals that they help to set up and run.

Of Mrs Sazonov, wife of the Foreign Minister, she said: 'She told me that she got up every morning at six and goes to bed about one and works steadily the whole time except mealtimes. It is really most remarkable but most of these Russian women seem to work like this.'

But she had a quite contrary view of some of the young men from well born families who were assigned to work with the Anglo-Russian Hospital. In particular she was exasperated and slightly mystified by Alexei Homiakov, young scion of a good family, who'd spent a couple of years at Cambridge, and who was later allocated to head up administration of their field hospital in Kiev. She described him:

> Every nurse and doctor who has ever had anything to do with him says he is absolutely hopeless. He says he will do a thing but rarely does it and if you depended entirely on him you would be completely lost. Here we find ourselves saddled with this boy, a dreamer and philosopher and utterly unbusinesslike but whose father is the head of the Red Cross down in our parts. So one has to be very careful not to offend Papa by saying his son is hopeless.[4]

Scathingly Sybil summmed up the young Russian aristocrat, born to wealth and leisure:

> With all the laziness of the young Russian nobleman, interested in art, philosophy and religion. With inexpressibly sad and dreamy eyes, utterly bored with life, with the wish to be a monk, if it wasn't that he was shortly to be married, a thing too that bores him inexpressibly. He likes going to bed at 5 a.m. at the earliest, and to get up at 1 p.m. He will sit for hours in a chair drinking tea, smoking innumerable cigarettes and dreamily

---

4 He may have been the son of Nikolay Alekseevich Khomyakov, who was speaker of the third Duma (1907-10) and who later worked with the Red Cross in Denikin's White Russian forces in the Russian Civil War before emigrating to Yugoslavia. It is not clear whether his son was also involved in the Civil War.

looking into space, but with an odd charm and attraction as long as you don't have to do business with him. Very intelligent but so bored with life at 25 that nothing is worth while.

She was also critical of the views of Grand Duchess Victoria (wife of the Grand Duke Cyril) – who contemptuously referred to the ordinary people of Russia: 'G.D. Victoria, hard featured woman accustomed to getting her own way I should think. She said when talking about what would happen after the war, "Oh, there won't be any disturbance here, the way to treat these people is to crush them," or words to that effect – foolish woman.'

But she was drawn to many of the people with whom she worked and as always she was intrigued by their wide variety of characters. Sybil's mother, Alice, had seen a photograph of the staff of the Anglo-Russian Hospital and had inquired who the woman with the face like a Madonna was. Sybil had written back that it was 'a Miss Danzas', daughter of a good family that had fallen on hard times:

> She is a most delightful woman; aged about 38 but looks much older: belongs to a very good family that has lost all its money. She is Matron of an Officers' Hospital here but comes to us every day from 12 to 4 to help us with our Red Cross papers that have all to be written in Russian. She has had a most tragic life and is one of the saddest people at heart that I have ever met. But she is charming, talks English as well as you or I and the whole hospital is attached to her. Everybody is feeling slightly ruffled and annoyed and then she arrives and looks so calm and serene that she brings in an atmosphere of peace to the whole place.

And she had great admiration for the stoicism and patience of the ordinary Russian soldiers who soon filled the wards of the Anglo-Russian Hospital. 'These wounded men are too wonderfully patient for words, they rarely if every complain and are so full of gratitude for any little thing done.'

The Anglo-Russian Hospital took its responsibility to them very seriously and even ran English language lessons for the patients: 'they are all learning English and have very good pronunciation. We have got a number of paper books of Russian and English with the English written in Russian the way it should be pronounced.' One day Sybil was taking a Russian lady round the hospital who had just been talking to one of the men in Russian and was going on, when the patient said in English, 'Goodbye, I am very pleased to have met you.' Sybil was delighted.

Entertainment

There was a rich variety of entertainment in the Russian capital, from going to the opera and the theatre, to gambling at bridge and piquet, to concerts and dinner parties. Gambling was particularly common, with Sybil's appointments diary for 1916 regularly listing her night's winnings or losses!

She heard the Russian national instrument – the balalaika. On 2 March the Dowager Empress sent the Imperial Guard Band of the Balalaikas to give an afternoon concert at the hospital. 'We had it in A. Ward and brought as many beds in as we could get. About 30 men came to play the balalaikas and another 20 or 30 to sing choruses, then two of the soldiers danced quite admirably. They were all

*The Anglo-Russian Hospital staff, photograph taken around April 1916. The front row,
left to right, unknown, Dr Harmer, unknown, Lady Sybil Grey, the Matron, unknown and
Dr Andrew Fleming. Included in the second row are Dr. Mark Gardner,
Assistant Matron Miss Bates and Dr Gould May.
(Leeds University Library, Special Collections, Leeds Russian Archive MS 781/6)*

extremely good and it was a great success.'

A fortnight later she attended another performance by an orchestra led by W. W.
Andreeff which had triumphantly toured London and New York in 1910. Andreeff
was promoting the adoption of the balalaika and had adapted the basic instrument
to cover a wide musical range:

> Last night I went to the Obelenskys to hear Andreeff and his remarkable Balalaika band.
> He only plays in Petrograd about three times in the winter and never in a private house.
> He lectured first on the instrument, its origin and why he had taken it up and improved
> it, etc. How it was the national instrument of Russia and cheap enough for any to buy
> and how it should be encouraged, etc, many of the professors being against it. After
> the lecture they played a dozen things – an orchestra of about 50 men. The balaliaka
> consists of a wooden instrument which looks like a mandolin. It has only three strings
> and you play with your fingers. Andreeff has taken the old instrument and improved it
> and made many different sizes and shapes of the same thing, but no instrument has
> more than three strings. You can play every kind of music and it really is most won-
> derful, it is exactly like an orchestra of violins. Of course he is a genius and his or-
> chestra is quite splendid, but it shows what can be accomplished by these simple
> instruments.

Afterwards a Russian woman sang peasant songs. 'She is a peasant who was discovered in some village, she has a talent for singing these national songs above the
ordinary and now she is very well known. It was very interesting. A deep nasal

rather harsh voice, it was more like the singing of natives than anything I have ever heard. The people there told me it represented exactly the singing of the peasant people. I could hardly tell them that I had seldom heard anything more native – but the soldiers singing doesn't remind me in the very least of this. There is no doubt that the Russians are not Europeans.'

Sybil was presumably reminded of native African or even native Canadian Indian singing. She also described a less elevated but also very popular and 'traditional' form of entertainment – a visit to the Gypsies (or Cyganes) who lived on the islands outside Petrograd. Popular with sections of the well-off, this excursion took place very late in the evening and sometimes lasted all night and until next morning. It involved the gypsies singing and a greeting ceremony for the guests. It was important to bring with one a large quantity of alcohol – preferably champagne – which formed part of the welcome ceremony.

She went with a party, including Dr Fleming, to witness a gypsy hospitality ceremony:

> The other night I went out to hear the Cyganes (the Russian Gypsies). It is interesting as a peep into Russian customs and life – a thing to be done once but not twice.
>
> You start at midnight, fifteen of us went. Four were English – Doctor Fleming, two of the Embassy men and myself. You motor out to a house on the islands where the gypsies live; you enter a small dirty house lit by oil lamps and candles; you all sit in a small poorly furnished and dirty room about the size of your sitting room at Howick, only with a much lower ceiling; we fifteen sit one side and the Cyganes all sit opposite, about 40 of them, men and women. The women are uglier than the others; some dressed in Paris blouses and some in bright red and green sort of gypsy clothes.
>
> The one essential thing that one has to have according to the Russians is champagne. Well it is so difficult to get drinks in Petrograd that the first night that we were to go it was put off at a quarter to 12 because the party had only been able to secure one bottle of champagne. So we went the next night instead – they had collected eighteen bottles of champagne and one of whisky and one of brandy. So armed with all this intoxicant for fifteen people we sallied forth.

Sybil left a vivid if rather contemptuous description of the ceremony:

> You sit in this stuffy dirty little room and smoke and drink and listen to what I should call Kaffir singing until any hour you like. A very short fat little man with a most comic face opens the bottles of champagne and comes and pours it out. He made me laugh every time he came in.

A guest's name would be called out and the gypsies chanted it while a glass of champagne was offered to the guest – which they were expected to down in one go:

> There is a drinking song that the Cyganes sing and play and one of the guests' names is coupled with it. They start this and at the same time one of the men guests come up to you with a small tumbler full of champagne and offers it to you on a plate first making a low obeisance to the floor in front of you. You have to get up and take it and drink it off without stopping, whilst the whole company stand up. Until you finish it the song goes on, and the people remain standing. I had no idea of this when they started by

me. Well half an hour after my first glass the second was brought to me by a Russian and I said, "No, I simply can't" but everybody was standing and he said you have got to. It was no use arguing so it had to be done, but I then said firmly to Colonel Fenoult who was there that they were not to bring me another and that I wouldn't drink it for the Czar himself. I had been totally unprepared for the second glass as I thought once the rite was performed it was over for the evening.

On the third occasion that Sybil's name was called she got Dr Fleming to intervene.

A little later in the evening I by chance heard one of the men giving my name again to the Cyganes, so I got hold of Doctor Fleming who was near and said stop them presenting it. So he jumped up and took the glass out of the man's hand and gallantly bowed to the earth and presented it to another lady! So your daughter was saved a tiresome argument.

She found the drinking ceremony distasteful and, probably rightly, thought that the gypsies were trying to get their female guests drunk, herself included.

Seriously it is a disgusting game. There were five other women there besides myself and I consider that the men set out deliberately to make the women drunk, what is there amusing or funny in it. None of them, the women, were sober in the end. One was as drunk as could be, stupidly so, not noisily so I am glad to say, but she had seven glasses of champagne. There was one young girl, a very nice girl who had never been there before, who had had much too much and who went outside and was ill I should think. Doctor Fleming said to me, "get hold of that girl if you can and make her lie down, in a small room that was there." I got up and spoke in the passage outside but she was inclined to be querulous so I gave it up, but took her home at 4 a.m. in the motor with me – all the English going then. The Russians go here fairly constantly and frequently stay from midnight until 8 in the morning. So in this sort of way they are still some years behind us I think.

A much more sympathetic view of the gypsies and of this ceremony was given by Robert Bruce Lockhart, the flamboyant Russophile British diplomat and self-confessed spy, who was based in Moscow at the same time that Sybil was in Petrograd. Bruce Lockhart saw the gypsies as artists, especially the old gypsy singer Maria Nikolayevna, whom he went to see:

That night I heard her sing for the first time, and the memory of those great deep notes, which are the secret of the best women gypsy singers, will remain with me until I die. That night, too, I drank my first 'charochka' to her singing. For a novice it is rather a trying ordeal. A large champagne glass is filled to the brim. The gypsy singer places it on a plate and, facing the guest who is to drink the 'charochka', sings the following verse:

> *Like a scented flower*
> *Breathing out perfume,*
> *Bring the brimming glass;*
> *Let us drink a toast,*
> *Drink a toast to Roman,*
> *Roman our beloved,*

Until he drinks it down
Pour him out no more.

The last four lines are a chorus which is taken up with increasing frenzy by the whole troupe. The singer advances towards the guest whom she is honouring, and holds out the plate to him. He takes the glass, bows low, stands erect and then drinks the bumper in one draught.

It is an intimate ritual. Only the guest's Christian name is used, and, as there is no Robert in Russian, there and then Maria Nikolayevna christened me 'Roman', which I have remained to my Russian friends ever since.[5]

Moods and manners

Throughout the varied problems and setbacks in getting the hospital up and running, Sybil's mood was one of continuing optimism, despite short periods when she confessed to her mother that she occasionally felt lonely: 'You ask whether one gets lonely and depressed at times – Yes – sometimes, but it doesn't last long. I sometimes long for somebody who isn't a doctor or a nurse to discuss things with. But Ethel Lindley is useful in this way. It is delightful having her. I only tell you all this because you ask, but it doesn't amount to anything.'

Ethel Lindley was the wife of Francis Lindley, a senior diplomat at the Embassy, who later became British Consul General in Russia in 1919, after Sir George Buchanan left. Sybil used to stay with the Lindleys from time to time to relax from the pressures of running the hospital.

Another of her friends was the young Countess Olga Poutiatine who travelled out with her. Earlier she wrote to her mother: 'We should have been utterly and hopelessly lost without Countess Olga. She does everything for us. She is a dear and so good humoured and we all like her very much.' Countess Olga was seven years younger than Sybil and was clearly devoted to her with a touch of hero worship.[6]

Dr Fleming departed for the front and the hospital began to settle in. Sybil wrote: 'We are getting on slowly but we shan't be running smoothly for another three weeks. The sanitars [Russian orderlies] have all to be taught their duty and of course only talk Russian, and as the patients also talk only Russian it takes longer to get the hospital in running order than an English one would.'

They started to fill up with wounded: 'We have 124 patients, as many as we can manage for the moment. The authorities have been very good in sending us good cases and as many as we wanted. They filled us up in about three days and that was a real rush, so we have asked to have a week to settle down in. One man has died. All the others are doing fairly well, I think. We have some very badly wounded.'

She gave her view of Russian manners and eccentricities. In contrast to the

---

5 *Memoirs of a British Agent,* R. H. Bruce Lockhart.

6 An oddity about Olga Poutiatine was that on the death of her father, her mother insisted that she take on the position of head of the family, calling her 'Jack' and treating her henceforth as her son. Olga left Russia after the Revolution and settled for a time in South Africa. She suffered from mental breakdown and ultimately committed suicide in London in 1940.

punctilious manners of their friend Col. Fenoult, Russian behaviour could be crude. There was an extreme case when a patient spat at a doctor:

> Just before I left the hospital this evening Mr. Waterhouse came along very much annoyed as one of the new men had spat straight into his face in the Bandage Room. I admit an unpleasant experience. He says during his 25 years practice such a thing has never happened to him before!! Five new patients today bringing up our total to 142.

And she was censorious of the table manners of even cultured Russians: 'Another habit they have which I dislike is washing their mouths out in their finger bowls – I really don't know why they don't bring in their toothbrushes!'
But she loved Russian delicacies such as 'blenis':

> This is the week before Lent begins here and everybody therefore eats Blenies. They are round pancakes, a little thicker than our pancakes. They are brought in on a hot dish before anything else as an hors d'oeuvre. You start by taking a couple on your plate and then pour plenty of hot butter over them, then whipped cream and as much caviar as you want. It really is extremely good and I thoroughly enjoyed them. To my surprise I saw the servants returning with new dishes of hot pancakes, not once but many times. The Shakovsky children eat fifteen of these! and they all assured me that that was nothing unusual.

She also commented on a belated attempt to modernise Russia by bringing in income tax:

> At the Conseil d'État yesterday (it corresponds with our House of Lords) they passed the second reading of the income tax bill – much to the surprise of most Russians who were certain that it would be thrown out. It was passed by 84 to 53. The bill is not finally passed yet, but it is sure to now. It starts taxing incomes of 1,000 roubles. Up to 50,000 it is to be a 3% tax, after 50,000 a 6% tax. To have passed the principle of direct taxation is a tremendous thing. The first year (it only starts in 1917) it is only supposed to be going to bring in 70 million roubles.

Of course the new tax never came into being as it was overtaken by the Revolution. And she was charmed by the Russian capacity for the fantastical and unexpected – such as the introduction of a reindeer sleigh service from the far north. On 5 March she described this delightful means of wartime transport:

> Captain Kemp has just come from Alexanderoff by reindeer sleigh. The Russian Government really showed a lot of energy over organising the reindeer service. It put it in the hands of the Admiralty and have 1000s of reindeer working now. They collected them from all over the north. Captain Kemp said it was a most comfortable way of travelling. You lie down on your sleigh, like a dog sleigh and have two, three or four reindeer to each sleigh. They are harnessed abreast, have no reins of any sort but are guided by the driver with a long pole like a punt pole. They have collars and traces that go between their legs, one to each reindeer. They are delightful kindly animals and travel at the rate of about ten miles an hour. The first part of the country is flat and uninteresting with many lakes. Then later pretty country well wooded. The journey of over 500 miles in sleighs took eight days.

She knew that the ships trapped in the ice at Archangel were having a terrible time:

Some of the ship crews suffered severely this winter in the White Sea. One ship was badly damaged and her crew abandoned her and all perished in the cold poor people. Hope our goods off *Abarys* have been transhipped into *Laertes* or the breaker and that therefore we shall get them fairly soon.

And she was told by her 'landlord' of the dreadful carnage on the Western Front:

Dmitri Pavlovitch came round and inspected us today. He ran through the hospital as if he was racing for the Derby, but noticed a good deal, for he came down to my sitting room afterwards and asked dozens of questions about everything. He is a nice attractive-looking boy but very dissipated. He told me that the French had lost quite frightfully at Verdun and that between the French and the German lines 150,000 dead men were lying. I simply can't believe that it can be as appalling as that. What a ghastly war!

News of military reversals

Far away from the focus of the British war effort, Sybil found it frustrating and alarming to receive news of military reverses and crises. Information was often late and very incomplete, so she was left to draw the worst conclusions. At the end of April 1916, Dublin erupted with the Easter Rising by Irish nationalists. On Easter Monday, Irish Republicans led by the writer Patrick Pearse of the Irish Republican Brotherhood, the trade unionist James Connolly of the Irish Citizen Army and others, occupied key buildings in Dublin in armed revolt, proclaiming themselves to be the Provisional Government of Ireland. It was put down by the British Army after five day's heavy fighting, centring on the General Post Office building, and many of its leaders were executed. Sybil, whose father had left the Liberal Party over their plans to grant Home Rule to Ireland, and whose cousins the Antrims were leading Anglo-Irish landowners, was furious:

This Irish news is awful, the news we get is terribly scanty and one longs and yet dreads to hear more details. Of course everybody is talking about it, it is the one subject of conversation. I am afraid it will have a most disastrous effect. Will the Government for once play the man and put it down with an iron hand. One can't help feeling it is the only chance.

Shoot and hang right and left I believe and then perhaps you might stop it. Hanging is too good for Sir Roger. I suppose they will at least have the decency to hang him. His hanging is taken for a matter of course out here by the Russians. It really is awfully bitter isn't it that this should happen in Ireland now.

The British military authorities in Ireland certainly shared her view on the treatment of the ringleaders of the Uprising – fifteen of them including Pearse and Connolly were court-martialled and shot in Kilmainham Gaol. Sir Roger Casement, who combined being a British diplomat and an Irish nationalist, and who had tried to smuggle large quantities of German arms in by submarine, was tried for treason and hanged.

There had been widespread public apathy in Dublin towards the Rising when it broke out, and much has been made of how the British supposedly turned the leaders into martyrs by their ferocious response, but perhaps no other options would have been thinkable at the time. The Army was after all shooting its own soldiers convicted of cowardice on the Western Front, and in Ireland the British were confronted by what they saw as a treacherous insurrection in wartime in one of Britain's leading cities, using German arms. The Uprising left key areas of central Dublin extensively ruined, a sharp lesson had been delivered to the British state, and within five and a half years Ireland had in fact been partitioned with the creation of the independent Irish Free State ruled from Dublin by Eamon de Valera, one of the surviving leaders of the Rising.

News of the uprising coincided with another disaster, the surrender on 29 April of British troops under Major General Charles Townsend to Ottoman forces at Kut al Amara (in modern Iraq) after a four and a half month siege. Described by historian James Morris as 'the most abject capitulation in British military history', Kut al Amara had been cut off for months and attempts to relieve it having failed, it was starved into surrender. Mabel Grey's brother, Robert ('Bobby') Palmer, had been killed in the fighting around Kut in January.

Sybil saw the news of events in Ireland and at Kut as a terrible blow to Britain's reputation:

> Yesterday one of our wounded was having a heated argument with another man and we went up to stop it and ask what it was about. The answer was that the other man had said that the English had surrendered at Kut and he knew that to be a lie because the English would never surrender! We had to explain to him that it was true but that the floods had arisen and that the English were starved out; it apparently satisfied him for he said that nobody could withstand hunger.

Morale in Russia was superficially still strong, especially at a military parade Sybil witnessed where the Emperor reviewed 36,000 new Guards recruits on the Champs de Mars, near the British Embassy:

> It was a very fine sight – all the 36,000 on this huge open space. There were three broad avenues down between the ranks of men. It took a full half hour for the Emperor from the moment he arrived to ride up and down the avenues. The Empress with the Czarevitch followed in a small carriage with a couple of gorgeously dressed Cossacks behind them and then the members of the staff and Foreign Attachés. I had a splendid view of it all from the balcony of a house overlooking the ground. They have, I hear, reviewed 100,000 men on it, so you can imagine its size.
>
> It is a very moving sight because the moment the Czar appears the men nearest him start the cheering, the continuous roar that never stops. It completely drowns the bands playing the national anthem, and as the Czar gets near your end of the line the roar increases in crescendo as the battalions nearest you take it up. The most magnificent looking lot of men you ever saw. All great big strapping fellows. I was immensely impressed by their wonderful appearance after all these months of war. But I was interested at noticing that nearly half of them were without their rifles still. They were extremely well drilled for their lines were extraordinarily good.

Although its foundations were beginning to totter, the Tsarist state and its Army could nonetheless still put on a magnificent patriotic show.

17

The Field Hospital

The story now becomes a dialogue between Lady Sybil in Russia and her mother, Countess Alice Grey in England, both commenting on the momentous events and everyday life in time of war.

Russia

It soon became clear that the needs of the armies at the front could not be met by the base hospital in Petrograd and that a Field Hospital would be the best answer. With Dr Fleming back from the front they addressed the question of what sort of field hospital to deploy. Sybil wrote:

> We are going to have a long confab tomorrow – Mr Lindley, Doctor Fleming, Mr Waterhouse and self. It is difficult to settle exactly what kind of unit to be, whether we will pay so much a month to the Red X and then they have to keep us supplied with everything we need, or whether we will buy everything ourselves. I shall advise the former. How much motor transport we require and how much horse transport, whether we take tents and a dozen other important questions.

Dr Fleming explained:

> After much discussion it was decided that the most useful unit we could furnish would be the 'Lazaret' or field hospital with its own tents, staff and equipment, plus a limited number of horse ambulances, and three to six motor ambulances. The unit was thus a cross between the Russian 'Peredovoi Otriad' (casualty clearing station) and the 'Lazaret' (field hospital), combining the mobility of the former with the operating and nursing facilities of the latter.

The Russian Red Cross agreed to undertake the entire administration and supply of the unit (though not the cost of salaries and equipment), in return for the sum of 6,000 roubles a month. In late April 1916, Sybil made a reconnaissance of where the Anglo-Russian Hospital might send its Field Hospital:

> Last Sunday night I went to Reichitsa, a place between Riga and Dvinsk about 70 miles from the front line. It is the headquarters of the Guards Army which is in Reserve. The Guards Army consist of three Army Corps – 120,000 men – and this is the Army that my Field Hospital will be with. One couldn't be with a better, because if there is no fighting where they are, the Guards will move to where there is fighting and their hospitals of course go with them. However I think there is no doubt whatsoever about there being desperate fighting in May and June on this Northern Front.

It is not entirely clear where Reichitsa was. 'Between Riga and Dvinsk (modern Daugavpils)' would place it in modern Latvia, but there is no town of that name there. It was almost certainly Rechitsa (Rechytsa) in modern Belarus, south of Minsk, or could even have been further south still at Roshische (Rozhyshche) in the Ukraine where the Anglo-Russian Hospital did indeed send a detachment of their hospital in late June 1916, but both are a great deal further south than Dvinsk. Travelling by train, Sybil was perhaps not entirely clear of the geography herself.

Lady Muriel Paget

Muriel Paget was due to come out to Petrograd on 7 May to assume responsibility for the hospital. Sybil had written to her mother on 2 April about her own potential role once Muriel was in charge:

> I am glad that you say she is quite prepared for me to say that I want to start with the Field Hospital, because I am beginning to think that it is necessary for me to start with it, for the first six weeks I think. Our Red Cross delegate who will be head of it is a rich young man of quite a good family and he has had a lot of experience in this work and has many things to recommend him, but at the same time he is not popular with the Guards. So it is important for me to be there for the beginning and be able to keep an eye on him, and to go myself with him to see generals and other authorities, for they will do much more for a foreign woman than they will for a young man whom they do not much like. Of course Muriel could equally go down with the Field Hospital and would I know have much more effect on the generals and others, but I have the small advantage of knowing a certain number of people and the hospital staff, so on the whole I think I might be able to be of most use for the beginning.

Muriel Paget arrived in Petrograd on 7 May. Sybil commented: 'We have hardly talked plans of any sort yet and must wait a few more days before we do so, for her to feel her legs and see what she wishes to do.' Shortly after Muriel Paget arrived, the Tsarina revisited the hospital:

> Yesterday we had the young Empress and her four daughters at the hospital. I think we had it looking very smart and nice and that she was pleased. She was extremely affable and pleased all the men and the staff so that it was altogether a success. I will send you a photograph that was taken, if it comes out. We just had all the Russians in the Red Cross connected with the hospital and Sir George and Lady Buchanan.

Over time, the attitude of Countess Alice and Sybil to Lady Muriel Paget changed. Initially Muriel, who was Sybil's boss, was seen as a paragon – dynamic and successful at persuading people in official positions to back her plans for the hospital. As things progressed, they began to realise that as well as her formidable talents of commitment and persuasion Muriel also had significant faults. These included a tendency to change her mind about arrangements and not to inform others of her decisions, and a reputation for being too impulsive and unrealistic, and a vagueness and inconsistency about financial matters, particularly how much money was actually being raised and was available for the hospital. In November 1915, Alice wrote about Muriel's fundraising for the hospital, 'Muriel told me that they have £40,000 with the Canadian £10,000. I mentioned this to Jeanne and she said, Muriel was always changing the figures a little and that she says £40,000, and then when you press her, well nearly £40,000, so that it is difficult to be sure what it is.'

In February 1916, Alice had reluctantly advised Sybil to put off taking early leave back in England:

> Wait until Muriel has joined you and see how things go, I should very much doubt the wisdom of leaving her alone in charge, she is altogether too impulsive – she would probably get at loggerheads with some of our country women!! and so make the hospital a bone of contention – also she would more than likely suggest to people out there that you would branch out into all sorts of things and this while you were away, so that it would make it very difficult on your return to negate all her proposals, if they were wild.

At the same time Sybil wrote to her mother about Princess S, the aristocratic and very persistent volunteer allocated to help the Anglo-Russian Hospital, with whom Sybil had already had countless battles:

> You will be amused to hear that Princess Shakhovskoy and Matron and I are the best of good friends now. She has entirely defeated us and is staying on in this hospital although many elaborate plans were made by the Red Cross to transfer her to another hospital. She defeated both them and us and triumphant she remains but the curious part of the tale is that we are quite pleased that she should. She is very clever and has seen exactly how to endear herself to the English heart, and never dreams of attempting to interfere now and is really extremely useful in writing letters etc, for the men. In fact we should miss her if she left us now. She is extremely intelligent.

Sybil was able to concede defeat and recognise a good thing when she saw it, even when it came in the shape of as rough a diamond as Princess Shakovsky!

Jutland

Back in England, Countess Alice wrote to her daughter on 3 June with the first news of the great naval battle at Jutland, fought on 31 May and 1 June, 1916, the first and only face-to-face trial of strength of the war between the battleships of the Royal Navy and the German High Seas Fleet. Both sides claimed victory. The battle was costly, particularly for the British who lost more battle cruisers and destroyers than the Germans, and twice as many sailors. For some time it was not clear to the British public what the losses had been, leading Alice Grey to assume the worst. But in the end, the German fleet never again ventured out in force again, and remained cooped up in its ports for the rest of the war, and so the action came increasingly to be seen as victory for the British.

Alice Grey initially voiced fears that it may have been disastrous:

> Last night darling the news of this battle was received by the public late in the evening, and your father told me just before going to bed. No one knew any details but only that we had lost the *Queen Mary*, *Invincible*, *Indomitable*[1] and other ships, without knowing what loss we had inflicted on the Germans.

---

1 *Invincible* was blown in half by a direct hit on its magazine at Jutland, with only six survivors from a complement of 1,032. *Queen Mary* and *Indefatigable* were also sunk, but *Indomitable* survived.

She was preoccupied with the greater preparedness of the Germans:

> Evidently their Zepps, as <u>eyes</u> to their fleet, are going to give them great advantages over us, we shall seldom be able to surprise them.

She speculated on how the British cruisers had been taken at a disadvantage:

> Our battle cruisers – which are not sufficiently heavily armoured to be protected against their heavy dreadnoughts, came in too close contact with them and so we have to bear the loss of these six ships, which seem to have been engaged and destroyed before our heavier battle ships came up, to protect them and drive off the German fleet.

Above all she was dismayed by the boost to morale that it would give the Germans:

> I hate to think of the immense encouragement that this will be to the whole of the German people, it must buck them up tremendously – and rightly so – and it will discourage our Allies. Here to us Britons it will make little difference except to brace us to greater efforts, but to our enemies it will remain a great success against the world famed English Fleet. Ugh! How I wish it hadn't happened, a few more similar actions and our fighting power would suffer severely. They are so superiorly placed, able to hide in their holes and come out when they please choosing time and place, and with their Zepps to tell them exactly when we are coming up and how far off – they really do deserve success, they plan all these things so well.

The Government had not released any casualty figures and Alice feared that, 'our losses in officers and crews must be terrible, for we have been given <u>no information</u> in this morning's communiqués as to that, not one word to say any of the crews have been saved.'

Hard on the heels of Jutland, on 6 June, came the news of the loss of Lord Kitchener,[2] drowned at sea. Alice relayed the news:

> K. and all his staff have gone down in HMS *Hampshire* off the Orkneys on his way to Russia – either blown up by a mine or torpedoed! None apparently are saved. What a tragic and dramatic end. Lord K. will have certainly gone to his death believed by most people to be a great loss to the nation. Mercifully for England, he had accomplished the gathering together of our armies, and for long now having ceased to have any power in the commanding of our armies he will not be [the] loss that the unlearned will believe him to be.

She wrote: 'The German Nation will howl with delight I expect, but the higher command will probably judge aright that it will not affect the conduct of the War in any way.'

In Petrograd, Sybil was aghast at the lack of security which allowed news of Kitchener's voyage and its destination to be known in advance. Earlier that year, there had also been intriguing rumours of an engagement between Kitchener and Sybil's aunt, Countess Mary Minto, widow of the Earl of Minto. Sybil had written

---

2 Field Marshal Horatio Herbert Kitchener, 1st Earl Kitchener, (1850-1916). He won the Battle of Omdurman (1898) in the Sudan and as chief of staff helped Lord Roberts win the Second Boer War in South Africa (1901-2). In 1914 he became Secretary of State for War and was responsible for recruiting the largest volunteer army that Britain had ever seen, using posters declaring 'Your Country Needs You!'

to her mother at the time: 'Whether I really care to have Horace as an uncle or not I don't know.'

Field Hospital

In Russia, by late May, the Field Hospital was ready and the formal opening and blessing of the hospital was performed in the courtyard of the Corps des Pages on 28 May. The opening was attended by the Grand Duchess Vladimir, the religious ceremony being performed by the Metropolitan (Archbishop) of Petrograd. The field hospital was despatched to the Imperial Guards, on the Dvinsk-Minsk front.

Blessing of the Field Hospital (British Red Cross Museum and Archives).

On 10 June at 11.30 p.m., Sybil and her colleagues left Petrograd with the Field Hospital, bound for the front line. Two days later she wrote to her mother about their very slow progress:

We have at last started for the Field Hospital. We left Petrograd in our own train the night before last and have taken 44 hours so far to do 450 versts.[3] We go at the comfortable pace of about fifteen miles an hour and continually stop for periods of half an hour to three hours. We hope to reach our first destination, Polotsk,[4] tonight at about 10 o'clock. There we shall get our orders of where we are to go. I do hope it is at the front and not with an army in reserve for the moment. I do so want them to have work right away. I wish we had been down in Galicia a fortnight ago and had taken part in the so far victorious advance.

---

3 A verst was a Russian unit of distance equivalent to 1.06 km, so the train had taken nearly two days to travel 298 miles.

4 A city on the Dvina River, now in Belarus.

They travelled in a large train, with a huge complement of staff, horses and equipment. Later versions of the field hospital would be pared down considerably:

> We are a very long and imposing looking train, composed of I think 37 coaches, containing 105 horses, 125 sanitars, 44 transport carts and ambulances, two kitchens on wheels, a water boiler and a water barrel, and nineteen staff – the matron, three surgeons, four English sisters, two Russian sisters and one Russian cook, housekeeper, sister, five Russian men (the head man, who is head of the detachment, and two men to help him, a very nice young fellow who is in charge of the horses, and a man who corresponds to quartermaster and looks after the stores).

She didn't take to their Russian commandant (or *nachalnik*) a young aristocrat, H. E. Boris Ignatieff, whom she nicknamed Napoleon:

> He is not quite a gentleman and is a most obstinate and pig headed young man, but he doesn't mind what one says and I don't think bears any malice. I expect he and I will have some few words, as they say, before we all settle down comfortably.

She got on well with the other Russians in the party:

> The second man, Baron Meyendorff, is a dear, very clever and he is cynically amusing but most distinctly a man of letters and not of the sword. Mr. Martens, the third man, is a diplomat, nice person with a nervous twitch of the eyes. Then we have a young man, a nice youth who talks nothing but Russian and who is to look after the horses. Personally I think he knows very little about horses.

The British staff included Dr. Harmer (the surgeon in charge), Captain Gardner, Dr. Gould May, Mr. Harrison (dentist), Mr. McNally (dresser), Sister Robertson

Field Hospital Parade, 7 June 1916 (Leeds University Special Collections, Leeds Russian Archive, MS 781/6).

(matron), Sisters Cotton, Boykett, Carlill, Jessie Sutherland, and a Russian house-keeper and two interpreters, Anitchkova, Blicks and Istorina. They spent their time on the long train journey playing bridge and gambling. The train was garlanded:

> All the carriages are decorated with green branches, which makes us look gay. Trinity Sunday is the reason for these festive decorations: every train and every station that we have passed have been covered with green branches.
>
> The country we passed through yesterday was very flat and rather uninteresting. Today it is much more attractive, rather hilly with lots of lakes and pine trees, also nice looking pastures, little tumble down thatched roof houses very like the French part of Quebec. All the women walking about with bare legs and feet – in some places through mud nearly knee deep.

They arrived at Polotsk at midnight on 12 June. In some ways Sybil's expedition with the Anglo-Russian Hospital field hospital to what is now Belarus represented the high point of her time in Russia. All her life Sybil had enjoyed the outdoor life and was used to camping – in Canada on fishing expeditions to the northern wilder-nesses, in Africa, shooting big game, and in New Zealand under canvas at a remote fishing camp. She was a rider, so she found travelling on horseback for part of the way quite natural. And in taking the field hospital to the front, she felt that she was achieving the prime objective of the Anglo-Russian Hospital, to treat and care for wounded Russian soldiers at the heart of the fighting.

Negotiating with army commanders close to the front line on where to site the Anglo-Russian Hospital field hospital must have been exciting and satisfying in a way that talking about it in Petrograd simply couldn't be. Here she and her col-leagues were to be genuinely part of the war effort. They lived in sometimes prim-itive conditions and it could be startlingly cold for summer. They travelled by a range of transport, in the engine cabs of trains, by horse-drawn carts and on horse-back. But they clearly were bound together by a sense of mission – even their surly Russian *nachalnik* (literally 'commander'), Boris Ignatieff, seeking to make a suc-cess of the expedition as they were moved on from one place to another, in response to orders from the Russian Army, trying to get agreement on where they were to locate the hospital.

They were ordered to proceed to Veropaeva, a small town,[5] to be attached to the Guards regiment of the 2nd Army. On 15 June, they set off:

> Horses and carts left at 6 a.m. Grey but fine. Went over one of hospitals here – they are all in wooden low barracks and tents. They have room here for several thousand and the place is laid out like a freshly planned town in Canada with corduroy roads etc. The mud appalling. Dr. Harmer, Baron Meyendorf and the matron left by the 8 o'clock train for Veropaeva to choose the place for the hospital and to get something ready for the night. Started to rain about 5 o'clock. We reached Veropaeva at 11 – pouring wet. We were met by the trio who preceded us.

They were accommodated in a shed for the wounded:

> They took us to a neighbouring hospital where we were given a first-class meal, then

---

5 Varapaeva in modern Belarus.

we paddled home through the mud. They most cleverly got ready one of the wooden sheds for us. It was divided off into three. All the men went into the big end which we also divided by hanging up blankets to make a dining room. Then in the room that was built for the bandage room, three Russian and three English sisters slept, and matron, Sister Cotton and I took a little room at the end. Our room was open to the free air as most of the boards had cracks of an inch or two.

After a wet night they looked for a place to set up the field hospital:

We woke next morning to pouring rain and a wind. We walked about in mud and filth to try and find where we would pitch our tents and found quite a nice sandy spot at the top of the hill which would be very nice when dry.

She described Veropaeva and found it disconcertingly like the Home Counties:

It is a very pretty place, nice rolling country with lakes and pine woods. We are situated on the top of a hill where there are two hospitals in tents. We look across some very nice pasture land and a river to a hill covered with pines, and a pine forest behind us. The soil is all sandy. It is very like Woking and those places and one expects to come across a golf course at every turn, I could make a beautiful one here, but instead there are trenches and barbed wire entanglements.

Getting about was however very different to back home, as was the climate:

This place is 27 versts from the front. In the afternoon I drove off with Mr Ignatief to see the General of the Corps. It was a drive of about eight versts, but you never saw such roads. Up to the horses' knees in mud, quite awful it took us nearly two hours to do the six miles, but we got there – had a talk to the General, paid our respects etc. and were told to make our final arrangements with the head doctor of the Corps. The wind and the rain reminded one of late autumn not the middle of summer. I had on my brown riding coat and divided skirt, a jersey, a leather coat, an acquascutum and a scarf and was chilled to the bone. I have never worn so much before – that night we all nearly died of cold and hardly any of us slept; although I had my pyjamas, dressing grown, jaeger sleeping bag (Doctor Fleming's lent to me) and two rugs plus a hot bottle, I never got warm all night even in the morning. This is hot Russia in the middle of June!

On the 17 June the doctor in charge of the Corps visited them. He suggested that they should go to Volki which was closer to the front. There the Anglo-Russian Hospital would be able to use their horse ambulances to bring the wounded direct back to the Field Hospital and as they would be nearer the front and they would get many more wounded to treat.

The next day, while the main body of the Field Hospital stayed put in Veropaeva, Sybil and an advance party set out for Volki in the bitter cold:

We first of all drove through pine woods filled with horses and carts and ammunition boxes and all sorts of things. The road is quite awful. After about eight versts we got out of the rolling country into plains and woods. We reached Volki at 12 and went into one of the peasant's houses where the officers were. We met the lead doctor of the Corps and doctors of the two Divisions and talked over everything.

The Russian doctors wanted them to send the Anglo-Russian Hospital horse ambulances from Volki to Postavi in the firing line, so that they could bring the wounded straight back. They hoped that motors could also work there later when the roads dried.

> They also want us when there is a battle to have a tent three miles from the lines where a doctor and some sanitars should be to do the first dressings and then our carts would bring them straight on to us. We agreed to this. We shall have a hospital in tents and some of the staff will live in tents, they are also giving us two or three of the peasants' houses – they remind one the villages here of poor Irish houses, log cabins and thatched roofs.

Riding home, Sybil remarked that Ignatiev was no rider:

> He looks back view on a horse very like Napoleon and I am certain thinks he is a Napoleon. He rides with his feet sticking out at right angles, not pretty. The carriage stuck in the mud on the way back and had to be pulled out with ropes and men. It cleared up and was lovely and I shed my two coats and jersey.
>   There was a good deal of heavy artillery fire this afternoon. Got home at 6.30 having thoroughly enjoyed my day. Have settled to send the tents on Tuesday and for us all to go to Volki on Thursday.

On Monday 19 June, Sybil checked the condition of the horses and found them poorly cared for:

> Went to see the horses, Safronsky [the man in charge of the horses] is away for three days. I don't think either Ignatief or Safronsky knows anything about horses, the former admits that he doesn't. They had been put much, much too close together, the result was that two or three were fairly badly hurt this morning. I saw a man throw three bricks as hard as he could at the horse that he was grooming – reported him for extra duties for two days. It would have served him right if the horse had kicked him.

On 20 June, the advance party started off for Seslavino (which Sybil misspelled as Caclavena,[6] using the Cyrillic 'C', which she saw written at the railway station), expecting to meet Prof Wilheminof, head of the regional Russian Red Cross. They embarked on a train pulled by an engine as old as Sybil herself:

> We went in a Red Cross train as far as Caclavena and then had the good fortune to just have time to run and jump on the engine of a train of goods trucks filled with soldiers. On the engine there were three other officers beside Ignatief and a sister. There were even men on the roof of the carriages. It was a train of 64 coaches and the engine was built in 1882 so perhaps it wasn't surprising that we took one hour and a half to do 20 versts.

Arriving at their destination they were offered an empty railway carriage to sleep in by the doctor of the local *zemstvo* (district council) which they gratefully accepted. 'It had turned out into a lovely evening but cold. A glorious golden sunset with a beautiful church standing out black against a great number of pine trees.'

   On 21 June she wrote that she had seen Prof. Wilheminov, 'head doctor for the Guards', and she explained that the Russian Army's plan of campaign was to take Vilna [Vilnius] to the west:

---

6 'Seslavino' – a railway station at Dokshitsky (Dokšycy) just south of Varapaeva. Sybil was using the Russian alphabet 'C' meaning 'S'.

Field Hospital at camp with Lady Muriel Paget
(British Red Cross Museum and Archives).

So the Guards are being sent down to Molodechna[7] where the heaviest fighting is expected to take place. It if hadn't been for all these days of rain the attack would already have begun here, Molodechna, but the roads are appalling and I should imagine that it would be absolutely impossible to move heavy artillery. Of course an attack here is quite a different proposition to what the Russians have done in Galicia, as the enemy forces up here are entirely composed of Germans. I hear the Russians have lost terribly heavily in their victorious advance – in the 100,000s – but I suppose the result was well worth it.

She described their journey with a mix of humour and relish for the challenge of hard travel. She also enjoyed the glamour of being involved with an army on the march:

I drove over 40 versts of the worst roads I ever saw today in a little cart with no springs, one was really like a pea on a drum. It was pretty country and rather amusing as one passed a constant stream of wagons and transport moving to the new positions, either going to the station to take the train or going by road, and occasionally a most ornamental Cossack would gallop past. There is very little doubt that I shall elope with a Cossack one of these days. An army on the move is a picturesque thing.

At Veropaeva where the hospital is now there are a number of Austrian prisoners working. They look very well fed and extremely contented and happy. I have seen them working at trenches and barbed wire entanglements. There is a great deal of wire and trenches all round Veropaeva.

We shall move within the next few days near to Molodechna.

---

7 Maladzyechna in the Minsk region of Belarus, located on the Usha River. In World War One the headquarters of the Russian 10th Army of the Western Front.

They stayed the night in the Duc de Teutenberg's private railway car.

Thursday, June 22
Breakfasted at 7 and caught an 8 o'clock train. Teutenberg with beautiful manners up to see us off. He is going tonight to have a farewell dinner of his regiment – 50 officers and he has to drink each man's health. What a head next morning he will have. Got to Caclavena at 9 and had to wait till 12 when we got into the wagon of a goods train. Arrived at Veropaeva at 4 o'clock very hungry. Poured all morning. The Unit seemed quite content with the plans.

That afternoon they went to look at the horses and the Matron and some of the sisters tried riding. The Matron fell off her horse and hit her head and was knocked out. 'She walked home but kept asking what had happened and whether she had fallen. Her head was rather sore but she wouldn't go to bed before dinner as was the wise thing to do.'

Friday, June 23
Lovely morning. Matron had bad night with her head, stayed in bed with darkened room all day. I rode for half an hour to choose a horse, which I did, but wasn't feeling very fit so had a lazy day. Played skittles. The sanitars sang the evening prayer at 9 and then the Russian hymn. Played bridge and lost six roubles.

Saturday, June 24
Lovely day with very heavy showers. Matron better as to head, but has been badly poisoned by bites from flies, her arm swollen up and hard. It shows that she is not in a good state of health. Mr Harmer made her put it in a sling and said that she was to keep quiet. Did a lot of washing this morning.

Had the Colonel of the battery of air guns to luncheon.[8] After lunch and we went down and saw the guns at work – they wasted four shells for us to see. Then we went into the pine wood opposite and inspected the trenches which are made by the Austrian prisoners. They are extremely well made trenches, narrow and entirely lined with young saplings; most of the trenches are roofed over with loopholes to fire out and also places for the machine guns to fire from. There is also a great deal of barbed wire. We have heard very little firing these days.

Sisters Cotton, Sutherland, Carlill, Boykett and Brieks, Mr Gardner and Harrison and self all went for a picnic into the pine woods. A great success – buttered eggs, potatoes. We watched a lovely sunset and played some foolish games – 'Russian scandal' etc. Matron's arm quite bad and painful. She, Mr. Ignatief and Mr. Harmer started repacking the boxes, found them so badly packed that from fourteen boxes they managed to put in it all in eight boxes, saving six boxes.

Sunday, June 25
Read a novel most of the day and was thoroughly lazy. Went with Napoleon[9] and inspected all the horses. Then walked on and joined a party of Russians and shot with a revolver. The Commandant of the Camp came to dinner. The men after prayers started to play football, it was very amusing, they were very keen and roared with laughter most of the time. Played two rubbers of bridge and won thirteen roubles.

---

8 Anti-aircraft guns.
9 Ignatiev.

Monday, June 26
Lovely day got up at 7.30 for a change and wrote. Had two teeth stopped by Mr. Harrison[10] – very good and nice and painless. Went for a delightful picnic in the woods. We played word games and Sister Cotton and self had a great success with the 'lemon trick'.[11] Such a glorious evening.

On Tuesday 27 June, Matron and Sybil went and had a Turkish bath – the first time Sybil had ever indulged in it:

It was very hot and I expect it did one good. Just as we were coming out of the hot room to dry, in came three Russian sisters. I draped my towel as gracefully as possible round my figure but as it was only about one foot square it didn't cover much! The three Russians undressed and the oldest and fattest advanced attired in her birthday suit with a sponge in one hand and a piece of soap in the other and engaged us in lively and polite conversation. It was most amusing especially when the other two joined her.

Sybil's post from home caught up with her: 'A huge mail was brought in. Three letters from Mother, one from Evy etc and many newspaper cuttings.' Sybil also got a cable telling her that her sister Evy had had a second daughter, Dinah, born on 11 June. However Sister Cotton, the nurse from Canada, received tragic news:

Poor Sister Cotton got at the same time a cable saying that in the recent fighting in France her youngest brother was killed and the oldest one is still missing, but they hope he is a prisoner. Her eldest brother of all was killed in the South African War. Poor girl it is an awful blow for her but she is marvellously plucky, I don't think I have ever seen anybody pluckier.

Sybil admired the resilience of her Canadian friend and colleague – whom she was close to because of their shared experience of Canada: 'Had a long walk with Sister Cotton after dinner, she really is quite wonderful.'

Wednesday, June 28
Another glorious hot today – did washing and ironing in the morning and wrote letters. Also made a very creditable trout fly trying in the river on a sanitar-made rod. At 7 o'clock we got a wire from Wilhelminoff giving us permission to start for Molodechna tomorrow. Great rejoicings. I tried for a fish but didn't get a rise. Sister Cotton decided to go home as it makes such a difference to her mother. So we settled that Dr. Gardner should take her to Petrograd tomorrow after we had started for Molodechna and then Dr. G could bring back either of the Sisters Macdonald who we wired for, to come and replace Sister Cotton. Wrote letters and packed and then at midnight had a long walk with Sister Cotton, went to bed at 2.30.

Thursday, June 29
Cloudless morning – great hustle and bustle, we got off at 9. Very sorry to say goodbye to Sister Cotton.

Into this 'cloudless' existence catastrophe was about to burst. Two days later, on

---

10 The Anglo-Russian Hospital dental surgeon.
11 A conjuring trick, in which a playing card or bank note from the audience is apparently magically found inside a lemon fruit when it is sliced open.

1st July, at a small place called Dorlzumolv[12] near Molodechna, while watching a display of Russian Army hand grenade practice, from a supposedly protective bombproof shelter, Sybil was hit in the face by a grenade fragment, which entered her left cheek above the mouth and lodged in her skull. By a miracle it didn't do more damage – as Sybil wrote two days later in the train to Petrograd:

Beloveds, I do hope you won't worry very much when you get a cable to say I was wounded in the face the day before yesterday. Of course it was a piece of the most extraordinarily bad luck, but you mustn't look at it in that light, it was such wonderful luck that it didn't do real damage. An inch to the right it would have shattered my jaw and all the teeth that side, an inch and a half higher it would have got my eye and might probably have gone on into my brain and killed me. As it is it has made a round circular hole in my face which will eventually show only a very small scar. It is a very deep hole and they cannot feel the piece of shell or bullet with the probe, it is probably lodged somewhere in the upper jaw or antrum. I am writing this in the train on the way to Petrograd. We expect to get there tomorrow when they will X-ray me and Mr Harmer will operate before returning to the front. He is such a dear and so kind and very clever, curiously enough one of his specialities is operating on the face and making little or no scar – so it is very lucky that it is him.

She described the place where it happened:

It was a big wooden structure of heavy logs covered over with turf and then all along it about the height of one's eyes were slits to peep out of, 3 inches and $\frac{1}{16}$ deep and about a foot in length. It had been used for months and nobody hurt and here comes this little piece of shell and comes through this narrow opening and catches me, it certainly was a piece of bad luck.

Sister Robertson, the Matron had already written to Countess Alice:

The shock of the impact was tremendous, of course, and her poor eye and cheek were enormously swollen within the hour. Today after 24 hours, this is subsiding fast and will be almost gone tomorrow. She is, as one expected, as full of courage and spirit as possible, insisting that she has suffered more discomfort than actual pain. She really had a miserable night till 4 a.m. with increasing swelling and continuous slight haemorrhage. She had some morphia and after a sleepy day is almost herself again tonight, and we will motor her to Minsk where she will have a special carriage, one of our own sisters, Mr. Harmer our chief surgeon (fortunately a nose and throat specialist) and Baron Meyendorf to look after them.

She added:

It was only this time yesterday that Lady Sybil was talking in the highest spirits about our plans. We have had such an amusing pilgrimage and she has always been in the best of form and looking so well and gay. She has been riding astride ahead of our caravan with a group of Russian potentates and told me that she felt just as if we were all in a comic opera.

---

12 Dorzumolv – possibly Dolhinov or Dauhinava in modern Belarus. Dorlzumov is given as the site of the accident in Michael Harmer's *The Forgotten Hospital*.

Olga Poutiatine, in Petrograd, wrote to her own mother and sister in England on July 3, to report the news, using her pet name for Sybil (*Seraia*, Russian for 'grey'):

> This evening there came two telegrams from the front, from our First [Field] Unit, which I had to translate orally right there. My dear Seraia has been wounded in the cheek and upper jaw by a fragment of a hand grenade. The wound is regarded as serious but not dangerous. She is being brought here for X-raying.

On 11 July Olga further reported to her mother with a tone of hero worship:

> My dear Seraia is doing really well and except for neuralgia of the left eye and toothache occasionally has not much pain. All admire her plucky right way of taking this, and I can't say how much this has strengthened my love for her.[13]

Doctors Douglas Harmer and Herbert Waterhouse also wrote from Petrograd, re-assuring Countess Alice that the operation to extract the grenade splinter would be successful. Dr Harmer wrote:

> Our x-ray photograph shows that there is a fairly large piece of metal, perhaps half an inch across the widest part, lying deeply in the wound, immediately below the back part of the orbit. We have localised it as carefully as possible and tomorrow morning, if she is sufficiently rested, an operation will be performed for its removal. I do not ex-pect that it will be necessary to make any fresh scar during the removal.

Letters were also received from Muriel Paget in Petrograd, from the Russian Red Cross (written in both French and English); and from Queen Alexandra (widow of Edward VII) who sent a letter to Sybil's father from Marlborough House:

> My Dear Lord Grey, Very many thanks for your letters about your poor daughter Sybil. Thank God she is doing well so far and got through the operation successfully – I trust you will soon be able to get her home which certainly will be the best thing for her. What a terrible shock it must have been to you and your poor wife when you first heard the news of her having been wounded, like a soldier!! But excuse me I am sure the dear girl ought never to have gone where she did!

The Dowager Empress of Russia, Maria Feodorovna, had telegraphed from Kiev to say how horrified she was.

Her mother, Alice, described her shock at hearing that Sybil had been wounded:

> My Most beloved, What a fright you have given us all. As someone wrote to me this morning, it is bad enough having one's son at the front, but to have a daughter too, in the firing zone is really too much!! We are filled with thankfulness that it is no worse, for I imagine a very little fraction higher and it would have gone into your eye or temple – too horrible to contemplate.

She was reassured by friends and by doctors that the wound would heal with very little if any scarring. She and Earl Grey had read and re-read the Reuters news re-port in order to understand its message:

> You can imagine how we dwelt on every word that might throw a little light on your

---

13 *War and Revolution, Excerpts from the Letters and Diaries of the Countess Olga Poutiatine,* edited by George Alexander Lensen (The Dipolomatic Press, 1971).

state, and I was greatly comforted by the apparent preciseness of Reuters' information, they spoke of the splinter from the hand grenade having pierced your left cheek and upper jaw – 'splinter' and 'pierced' gave me the comforting feeling that it was pointed and went straight in without being likely to make a big ragged wound. And now that we have got a cable through the Foreign Office from the British Embassy saying you had the fragment taken out in a few minutes with very little trouble, 'condition quite satisfactory, wound healthy, sends back love', we are for the first time really at peace about you.

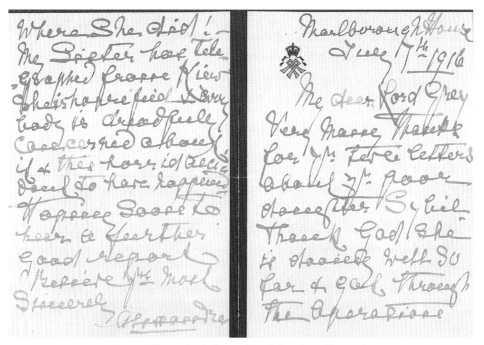

Queen Alexandra's letter (Boyd family collection).

Alice and Albert had learnt the news while out at lunch at Devonshire House with Victor Cavendish, Duke of Devonshire and his wife lady Evelyn – Lord Cavendish was about to become Governor General of Canada.

> After lunch Albert went off with Victor (and I thought he had left the house), the other guests departed and I remained on talking to Evy. The butler came in and asked if I could speak to my secretary on the telephone, then Gilly's voice was heard saying that she had rung me up, in case I should be frightened by seeing in the evening papers an announcement that you had been wounded.
>
> You can imagine my feelings. I told Evy and her daughter who were full of sympathy, and I ran downstairs to see if I could find out where your father had gone, then found to my intense relief that he was still in the house. We took a cab and went straight off to the Red Cross in Pall Mall to know if they had communicated the news.

The Red Cross had no news. The Greys ran into the Russian Ambassador, Count Benkendorf, who promised to send a cable to Petrograd immediately. On their way home they also met Alice's cousin David Lindsay, Earl of Crawford and Balcarres, who had just returned from serving in the ranks in France with the Royal Army Medical Corps to take up the post of Minister of Agriculture and Fisheries in the coalition government. He advised them to check the exact information that Reuters had received. Reuters confirmed that it came from a very reliable correspondent of theirs in Petrograd.

Alice must of course have thought immediately of how her eldest daughter, Vera, had died unexpectedly nine years earlier. The Greys requested their passports from the Foreign Office and began to plan to travel out to Petrograd to be with Sybil, notwithstanding Albert's poor health. But they found it impossible to get berths on a ship leaving for Norway. And they learnt from Petrograd that Sybil had been successfully operated on and was out of danger.

They finally decided, after the arrival of a telegraph from Petrograd with a message from Sybil herself, to postpone their journey. Alice told Sybil, 'You know darling don't you, how we have both longed to be with you, as also has little Evy, to cheer you and amuse you and look after you and pet you. Of course I know you are splendidly looked after and nursed by all around you. I suppose you are in your own hospital?'

She sent out letters of sympathy from Sybil's friends and her dressmaker, Marta, and particularly from Sybil's friend, Aileen Roberts, who came round to dine with the family. 'We had as you can imagine a very nice little evening and talked almost entirely of you or the War.'

It was ironic that in all the time that Sybil was in charge of the field hospital they never treated any Russians, and the only casualty was to be herself. In its various later incarnations, the field hospital went on to do sterling work in treating the wounded after the battle of Stokhod, at Lutsk and among the green mountains of the Carpathians in Bukovina

18

Recovery at Home

We can imagine the scenes in mid July when Sybil returned home to England to recuperate, to be greeted by her parents, by Evy, Jonah, Charlie and Mabel, by her nieces and by her friends such as Aileen, Zella and 'Chip' and her many cousins – the Bensons, the Parkers, the 'Mintos' and the 'Antrims'. She must have spent the three months of her recuperation partly in London, probably seeing a number of her father's doctors, and of course chiefly back home in Northumberland at Howick.

She arrived back in England only a few weeks after the terrible results of the Battle of the Somme had become known. The battle began on 1st July and raged until 13th July; with associated actions lasting right up until November, but it is the first day that is remembered chiefly for its astronomic losses – 60,000 British casualties, of which 20,000 were fatalities.

The German lines had come under massive bombardment for five days before the advance intended to break down their resistance and cut the wire, whereupon the British troops would go over the top and advance across a wide front to take the German positions. Several huge underground mines were also exploded under key parts of the German line.

Unfortunately the German defences were well dug in, enabling their forward troops to survive the bombardment and their machine gunners to scramble up when they heard the British whistles signalling the advance. Huge numbers were simply mown down as they walked forward in line at a 'steady speed' and never reached the German lines. The British troops did break through in parts of the line but in most areas the Germans held out, and the Somme has become synonymous with huge loss of life, with families grieving across the country, and little or no worthwhile advance to show for all the suffering and dying. It has come to symbolise the apocalyptic scale of loss in the war.

Alice had already sent an account from their friend John Buchan of the terrible power of machine guns:

> The Bosch has been fighting like the devil and shows little or no loss of morale. What we suffer so terribly from is their machine guns. They have shown the most marvellous organisation in using them. They have dugouts 30 feet deep with flights of steps standardised that lead down into them. When our bombardment begins the men and machine guns go down into them. The moment our guns raise their fire for the advance of our men, in a second or two they are up with their guns, or else they let us make our rush and take their first line trenches, and then emerge like rabbits from their holes with their machine guns, behind us and mow us down while we have to turn round and retake

the trench in reverse, losing of course heavily. The only way to obviate this is to bomb every dugout before moving a step on, no shells or big gun fire has any effect in destroying their deep dugouts.

There are no letters from Sybil giving her views on the Somme, but she must have been shocked at the scale of losses, despite her knowledge of the heavy loss of life already experienced in Russia and of the slaughter around Verdun earlier in the year. She must have had friends among the wounded and dead, although thankfully no close family members were involved.

As someone interested in cinema, she was almost certainly among the estimated 20 million people in Britain who saw the first official film of the Battle of the Somme, shot in France by Geoffrey Malins for the War Office. Seen by record numbers in August and September 1916,[1] it was a new kind of 'documentary' film which brought home some of the horrors of the front to an audience back in Britain.

Sybil learned about personal tragedies among their friends. The death had just been announced of a close family friend, Lord Hugo 'Ego' Elcho, 11th Earl of Wemyss, killed in Egypt at the age of 32. His wife Lady Violet ('Letty') Elcho had been on a cruel emotional roller coaster as it was first of all reported that he was 'missing', then that he was 'known' to be a prisoner in Damascus, before confirmation came of his death – 'after about three weeks of wonderful hope and relief comes this final blow'.

Another close family friend, Lady Ethel ('Ettie') Desborough, wife of William Grenfell, Baron Desborough, had by a huge effort of will pulled herself up from 'her terrible state of prostration' after her own two sons, Julian Grenfell and Billy Grenfell, were killed. Ettie Desborough was drafted in to console Letty Elcho, 'But Ettie said there was no way by which you can help her. She says herself she has no faith or belief whatsoever in anything, so can give no support or comfort from her inner self, and she sits in a huddled heap in the corner of the room (that is how Ettie found her) in a sort of state of despairing tension and terror. One's heart aches for these poor things who take their sufferings in this terrible way.'

Five years later, in July 1921, Letty Elcho married again, this time to Sybil's cousin Guy Benson.

During the months Sybil spent recovering in England, events took place in Europe, including the entry of Romania into the war on the Allied side in late August, and continuing battles on the Western Front, including the first tank battle at Flers-Courcelette. On 23 September, a major German air raid on London and Essex resulted in 170 deaths and the downing of a German airship by a British airplane.[2]

By October Sybil was well enough to return to Russia. Before that she and Mabel Grey made a short visit to Paris to meet Charlie Grey. They arrived in Paris in the evening of 21 September: 'Charlie was at the station to meet us. Looking awfully well and delighted to see us. He is very cheerful as to the way things are

---

1 Described in Jeremy Paxman's book *Great Britain's Great War*. An estimated one million people saw it in its first week, and perhaps 20 million within six weeks.

2 Greatwar.co.uk/timeline

going.' Sybil had to be reminded to hand over to her brother a protective body shield which their mother Alice had sent out with them to keep him safe. Charlie wrote to thank his mother: 'It was lucky that you told me about the body shield for I really believe that Sybil would have taken it away again at the bottom of her bag if I had not demanded it.[3] It really does not feel heavy when on and of course I should wear it in a battle. Thank you so much for it. Also for the kippers which were excellent.' Seeing his sister for the first time since she was wounded he added, 'Sybil's scar is very small and barely noticeable. It is wonderful to think that such a wound will leave no scar at all.'

Sybil and Mabel stayed at the Ritz Hotel for a couple of nights where they were wined and dined. They were taken off to visit two hospitals, the first an American hospital run by Mildred Barnes Bliss, heiress and wife of an American diplomat in Paris, who organized the American Distributing Service to transfer medical supplies to French hospitals and funded vehicles for the Ambulance Corps. Sybil described the hospital: 'It is a beautiful place on 600 beds and most awfully good.' The next day, Lord Esher sent a car to take Mabel and Sybil to St Cloud to see the French Canadian hospital of 1,800 beds.

They went to the theatre to see a comedy about sexual liaisons and infidelity: 'Last night we went to play at the Palais Royal called *Madame et son Filleul*. A real farce and we never stopped laughing the whole time.' The following day they returned to England and Charlie returned to the front.

Russia

While Sybil was recuperating in England, in Russia the Anglo-Russian Hospital continued to deploy its field hospital to best advantage. Lady Muriel Paget and Dr Fleming had visited Rovno, the headquarters of the Russian 8th Army in Galicia, in the middle of June to see what assistance was required. Russian armies under General Brusilov had captured the nearby town of Lutsk, with 'enormous numbers of wounded pouring into the base and field hospitals', and General Lerche, head of the Russian Red Cross with the 8th Army, had eagerly accepted the offer of assistance from the Anglo-Russian Hospital.[4]

Lady Muriel Paget arranged that the field hospital should be immediately transferred to Galicia to work with the 8th Army. At the same time a separate surgical detachment was set up under the charge of Dr Flavelle, with Mr Jefferson as operating surgeon, and four nurses and three motor ambulances and drivers. This small operating unit was designed to be attached to an existing base hospital at the front. Working at Rozjhische and at Lutsk, 'it was one of the most useful of our field organisations, treating in three and a half months altogether 2,111 new cases, and performing 285 operations and 4,300 dressings.'

The field hospital arrived at Lutsk in July and was sent on to Rozjhische in the salient in front of the River Stokhod, about six versts from the firing line. During

---

3 A range of different sorts of body armour were produced during the First World War, ranging from kapok and silk strengthened with resin, to ones incorporating steel plates, or chain mail visors.
4 Described in Michael Harmer's *The Forgotten Hospital,* pp. 91-93.

the late summer and autumn of 1916 the fighting on the Stokhod was particularly fierce, and the Anglo-Russian Hospital went through an arduous time. At Stokhod its members were cited for their bravery under fire during a fierce battle – even Sybil was cited for valour at Stokhod, although she had actually been wounded and returned to Petrograd several weeks beforehand. At Lutsk they worked under great pressure for days on end treating the wounded. The young neuro-surgeon Geoffrey Jefferson wrote in June 1916: 'The wounded came in by rail on a narrow gauge and in trucks drawn by horses; and here they all lay dead and dying mixed together. It was terrible; but it was an experience I wouldn't have missed for anything. In the past seven days I've dressed 340 major wounds and done thirty-three operations.'[5]

Dr Fleming reported: 'There was no question now of insufficient work or any complaints that British hospitals were not wanted in Russia. Though only equipped for 100 beds our hospital accommodated 165 cases one night, and passed through 250 severe cases in one day, all requiring operation or extensive dressing.'[6] They were also bombed almost daily by German and Austrian aeroplanes.

At the same time a fleet of fifteen Vulcan motor ambulances and an X-Ray car arrived with their drivers from England, and eventually proceeded to Bukovina with the field hospital.

Over the course of nearly a year, from June 1916 until the early summer of 1917, the Anglo-Russian Hospital continued to deploy its various field units on different parts of the Russian front – the field hospital moved south to Kirlibaba and as far east as Stary Ply in Bukovina, while the separate surgical unit aided existing hospitals at Lutsk and Rozhyshche. In some places they also had use of a depot or base, e.g. Seliatyn was a base for Stary Ply, and some ambulances were based for a time in Czernowitz in the Ukraine. These field hospitals at Lutsk, Rozhyshche and Kirlibaba probably saw much more action than the base hospital back in Petrograd, treating many hundreds of wounded men – it was the greatest contribution that the Anglo-Russian Hospital made to the Russian war effort.

Dr Fleming's summed up the Anglo-Russian Hospital's first year up to September 1916:

It was a year of many vicissitudes, many failures and yet of much achieved. I have made no attempt to gloss over the troubles and difficulties that arose. That faults were committed and mistakes made there is no doubt, and probably with more knowledge of the language, the people, and local conditions, many pitfalls might have been avoided. That every member of the staff did his best there is no doubt, and the results were good. We had established a base hospital in the capital second to none, we had organised in the field two most useful units, and had running a large fleet of motor ambulances, which was of immense value at the Russian front with its great distances and absence of railway facilities. We had, moreover, established good relations with our Russian allies, and had been to them a sign manual of British appreciation and sympathy.

---

5 Geoffrey Jefferson quoted in Michael Harmer, *Forgotten Hospital,* p. 92.
6 Quoted from the report on the Anglo-Russian Hospital by Dr Fleming and Dr Jefferson, 1917, (British Red Cross Archives).

The autumn of 1916 when the weather had broken saw the return of the field detachments of the Anglo-Russian Hospital, the field hospital returning first and then the Lutsk detachment in October.[7]

Fighting on the South Western front had been extraordinarily severe, and almost incessant for many months. 'On one occasion we had 127 severely wounded men in wards with beds for only 92, and room had to be made by pushing beds together and laying three men on two beds and so on.'

On their return to Petrograd, the new commandant, Dr Flavelle, left for Bukovina to arrange details of the field hospital which was to be re-opened as soon as possible in one of the passes of the Carpathian Mountains. The motor column ambulances at Lutsk were also moved to Bukovina, working at Czernowitz for the winter. 'The field hospital was to be located at Stary Ply on an upland mountain pass some 100 versts south west of Czernowitz at the side of a newly made military 'corduroy' road cut through the forest.'

---

7 Anglo-Russian Hospital Report, 1917, *ibid.*

19
Return to Russia

In mid October, Sybil Grey, returned to Russia, and took over again from Lady Muriel who was due to return to England by the start of November. Almost immediately on her return, Sybil was back at the front, in November visiting Kiev, in the present day Ukraine,to help plan for the field detachment in Bukovina. She was bowled over by the city:

> Kiev is an extraordinarily beautiful place. You approach it through Prairie Country (which I always love) but with a good few forests near Kiev. The place it reminds me of more than any other is Quebec. It is most beautiful. The river is huge and in two arms and you stand on the bluff where the town is built and look down, just like you do at the Citadel at Quebec. To the left, like at Quebec, on a level with the river is a large commercial part of the town and all the rest of the town is built on the hill. Across the river there are many small houses and trees and then comes the other arm of the river… then beyond, miles and miles of prairie – such a view. The town is full of the most beautiful churches with their glittering gold domes and cupolas and coloured roofs. It is amazingly picturesque and beautiful.

Above all she marvelled at the Pecherska Lavra, the great 'monastery of the caves', to the east of the city, overlooking the Dneiper River. It was so called because its cavernous catacombs preserved the bodies of generations of monks, naturally embalmed by the saltpetre in the soil. It was the third holiest site in the Russian Orthodox Church. It simply took her breath away:

> On the high bluff of land above the river on the outskirts of the town the most famous monastery of Russia stands. I saw it one afternoon when the sun was setting. It is a huge place composed of many buildings and many churches and gardens and is built on terraces of different heights above the river. Standing on the top by the main church and cloisters one looks down the hill on the buildings and the gardens across a little valley to the farthest away part of the monastery on the other side of the valley on the same level where one is standing. The buildings are all white with bright green roofs and gold domes, etc. Then straight down below over the river, the plains and the blue distance. Behind the monastery the setting sun turning the gold into a sort of crimson. It was quite, quite beautiful.

She described its human population:

> The peasant women adding picturesque colours to the whole picture – in their leather coats tied with bright worked belts, their scarlet leather high boots, their bright coloured handkerchiefs over their heads, carrying their heavy burdens by means of a long pole

balanced across the shoulder, with green and brown bottles made of some cheap pottery in which they bring the milk from the country, etc. Seeing them walking down the flights of steps leading from one part of the monastery grounds to the other, and meeting the monks all dressed in black with tall black hats, the shape of a top hat only broader at the top and with a long black veil hanging behind, adding much to the charm of the whole. You really would have revelled in it.

I, too, was lucky enough to see the monastery one afternoon in July 2014. In many ways things were remarkably unchanged from Sybil's description written 98 years before, although the Ukraine is now independent. The buildings were still gleaming white, the roofs still green, the domes dazzled with gold and blue. The priests still wore black robes and hats with black veils hanging down the back, and the country was still at war, although now its foes were pro-Russian secessionists in the east. Only the peasant women were absent – they had been replaced by groups of Ukrainian tourists taking snaps of each other at the view overlooking the river. Gazing across the river one no longer saw the distant blue plains of Sybil's day, but rank after rank of massive brutalist high-rise housing developments stretching across the horizon.

   I went into one of the churches on the site and found a shop selling postcards and souvenirs. The girl behind the desk was studying to teach English. I showed her Sybil's description of the monastery written the year before the Revolution. 'Ah, what a wonderful story,' she said, 'you must write a book and send me a copy.' The purpose of Sybil's visit to Kiev was to sort out problems of the Anglo-Russian Hospital, both with the Russians and the internal disputes between its staff:

> On the whole my visit to Kieff was satisfactory and I was able to settle a good many points with Flavelle, but of course exactly where the hospital is to be and exactly what type of hospital it is, whether a base or an advanced one with our transport, can only finally be settled on the spot with the authorities of the Eighth Army.

The Anglo-Russian Hospital had become unpopular with the Russians in the south and there was a need for tact and sensitivity, something which both the fiery Dr Flavelle and impulsive Lady Muriel seem to have lacked.

> Our one great object is to be as little in the limelight as possible this winter and so gain the approval of the Russian Red Cross and the Army we are working with. At the present minute down here the name 'Anglo-Russian Hospital' stinks in the nostrils of the Russians. It is a 1000 pities as the work that was done was jolly good and I think the Russians who know about it thoroughly recognise it, but the bother we have been to them and our constant wants and changes of plans have got on their nerves.
>   The only thing to do now is to try to get placed in as good a position as possible with the 8th Army and then quietly remain working and making no effort of any kind to put ourselves forward in the limelight. Let the Russian Generals and Red Cross authorities forget if they like that we exist.

Sybil felt that a more sensitive approach earlier on by Muriel Paget would have been better. 'I think M[1] had a dreadfully difficult task this summer, far more difficult

---

1 Lady Muriel Paget,

Kiev, Pecherska Lavra postcard collected by Lady Sybil (Boyd family collection).

than we realised, but even then I think she might, had she gone more tactfully to work, and have made a greater success of it.'

As well as the Anglo-Russian Hospital's unpopularity with the Russians, the hospital was beset by internal divisions, jealousies and conflicting personalities. Once again, she felt these could have been better handled:

> The more I see of it the more the difficulties overwhelm one. First one has to contend with all the wishes and jealousies of one's staff. They are by no means easy to settle. Muriel said she had left me with the most contented family as far as the doctors were concerned. I am afraid the wish was father to the thought – there is a great deal of discontent in certain quarters to a certain extent the result of her talking vaguely and promising them things that are difficult to carry out.

In particular, Dr Flavelle, the new head of their medical team, had a habit of riding roughshod over others:

> Flavelle has started very badly by getting all their backs up by his unfortunate manner. Being a red hot socialist and having been one of the chief critics of Fleming for having as he said taken too much on himself and consulted the staff too little – he starts himself by making the mistake of outdoing Fleming in this respect. With me he couldn't be nicer so far. The doctors, two of them, already in the week that Flavelle was at Petrograd, complained to me of his high handedness and the way he shut them up whenever they asked a question. I preach to him conciliating the doctors as much as possible and asking their advice even if he doesn't mean to take it. The difficulty is to keep a steady course and not to side with the doctors against Flavelle or with Flavelle against the doctors.

She was critical too of the Russian Red Cross members of the team, particularly Alexei Homiakov, their *nachalnik* in charge of the field hospital. We have been introduced to him earlier in the book – a lazy dreamer:

> You want to get a paper written for the Red Cross? You take the pen, put it into his hands and stand over him and say, 'Now that paper is to be written straight away'. I find it hard work being patient and keeping my temper and long to stick a pin into him, and then he looks at you with those eyes of his, a 100 years old with the weariness and boredom of life, eyes whose lids come half over them as if it was too much trouble to keep them open but all the same that look at you half humorously and seem to say, 'Don't worry, when you understand life like me you will realize that today, tomorrow, or 100 years hence is all the same'. It is very typical of the rich young Russian who cannot imagine why one should ever work.

She set out her plan for the future of the field hospital in the south: 'Flavelle and matron will get the hospital going and then will return to Petrograd at the beginning of December, this if all goes well. I shall wait till after Xmas to go down and then probably shall stay a month or six weeks.' This plan was of course overtaken by the revolution in Petrograd in February 1917.

On her return journey to Petrograd, she narrowly missed being involved in a terrible train accident, which must have brought Alice's heart into her mouth when she read of it:

> It was a terrible accident. One train caught fire and so stopped, and was run into by a train from behind and almost directly afterwards was run into from a train in front from the opposite direction – 86 were killed and 400 wounded.

Sitting in the train behind, they were delayed for a day. She said:

> Being by myself and being in the depth of the Russian country I haven't dared leave the train as nobody I could talk to knew, or knows when we shall go on. Otherwise I would have walked down the line six versts to where the accident took place.

England

At the start of November 1916, Alice reflected on the brevity of Sybil's return to England:

> You will have been gone a week tomorrow and I shall soon think it has all been a dream and that you have never been back at all! But it was delightful while it lasted to have you back with us.

She described how she and Albert were invited to see the inspection of the Dismounted Battalion of the Household Brigade in London – the infantry counterpart to the Life Guards.

> You never saw a more magnificent body of men. It made one's heart ache to think of the number that would never return to see their homeland and their dear ones.
>
> It took place opposite the Knightsbridge Barracks, and I think to be accurate 830 men paraded. Young Wyndham Portal who is just 30 I think, goes as their Colonel, and he must be immensely proud of his Battalion. The King and Queen, Queen Alexandra,

Princess Victoria and Princess Mary arrived on the scene and were greeted by Lord French, Uncle Francis, who is Colonel of the Life Guards isn't he, and lots of other well-known officers.

Uncle Francis was Field Marshal Francis Wallace Grenfell, former Governor of Malta, with whom Sybil and Vera had stayed fourteen years earlier. Alice continued:

The King and his staff marched all down and between the lines and inspected them. Then the massed bands played and all the regiments marched past. After the march past, the King went out and made them a farewell speech. Then Wyndham Portal an-swered for the regiment, and made a short but excellent little reply thanking the King for the honour he had done them, etc. It was just right and delivered in a ringing voice so that we all could hear every word he said; after that they gave three cheers for the King, shaking their caps high in the air at the end of their bayonets (I suppose) and the ceremonial was over.

Two months later (in January 1917) she wrote to tell Sybil of the tragic outcome of the regiment's involvement in action in France, where they were pitched unprepared into battle and return shattered by the experience, with their young commander, Wyndham Portal,[2] ill and dispirited:

They were not given any time to learn the ropes or get seasoned, and in these awful conditions that prevail as to wet and mud, they were sent at once to the trenches without being given a single pair of trench boots – at the moment when thousands of men are being invalided with trench feet.

Sir George Holford, Alice's brother, heard this direct from Wyndham Portal (now at home suffering from laryngitis and complete exhaustion), and repeated it to one of the Generals in high office:

'I don't believe it,' said the General, 'No man is now sent into the trenches without trench boots.' But it was so, and they were not even sent to trenches, but they took over from the Warwicks, shell holes full of water and mud, up to their knees and some-times much higher. Wyndham Portal said there was ground 150 yards further back where they could have been comparatively dry, but they were not allowed to move there, and in a few days several hundred out of the 1,000 were down with sickness and had to be sent back.

If this could happen to an elite regiment of the British Army, conditions for ordinary units must have been even worse.

Russia

By the end of 1916, the war had taken a huge toll on the Russian economy, attempts to resume the offensive had failed, and the massive casualties created disaffection and mutinous attitudes in the Army. At the same time food shortages in the major

---

2 Wyndham Portal, later 1st Viscount Portal (1885-1949). He was a soldier and a politician. After commanding the Household Battalion he returned to France. He served in the Government 1940-44, was the last Chairman of the Great Western Railway and President of the Olympic Games in London in 1948.

urban centres, the result of chronic transport and storage and distribution problems, but popularly believed to be deliberately encouraged by the authorities, caused civil unrest in the cities, especially Petrograd. Meanwhile the Duma, which held no actual executive power, was becoming ever more vocal in its criticism of the Tsar and his ministers, particularly voiced by deputies belonging to the Socialist Revolutionary Party, but also by some liberal deputies. Former reasonably effective ministers, such as Sazonov, had been replaced by ever more reactionary ministers such as Alexander Protopopov, the Minister of the Interior, often at the urging of the Tsarina, herself very unpopular.

Sybil returned in mid-November to a Petrograd alive with excitement and rumour. The newspapers were not allowed to report on the proceedings of the Duma and they vented their frustration by featuring headings 'The Sitting of the Duma', followed by columns of blank white space. Sybil commented:

> Still one hears a great deal. Never have people talked so openly before in public in Russia. It is almost unbelievable the things that have been said. Sturmer[3] [the unpopular Foreign Minister who had replaced Sazonov] was accused of all sorts of things, principally of taking money from the Germans. Now there are rumours that his fall is imminent; that he cannot stand any longer against this outcry for his blood. I heard yesterday that Sazonov was at the Staffka [the Tsar's Army Headquarters] and that he is to come back as Minister of Foreign Affairs. Whether this is likely to be or not, I don't know.

She described the rapturous reception given by the Duma to the British Ambassador:

> Sir George had the most wonderful reception at the Opening of the Duma the other day. When he entered the box which is set aside for the Ambassadors the Duma got on its feet and shouted for nearly ten minutes. I am told it really was thrilling and no foreigner has ever had such a reception.

Sir George had also been made a Fellow of the University of Moscow, an honour never before bestowed on a foreigner. Sybil wrote, 'There is no doubt that they love him and I suggested that in case there should be really mighty upheavals here he might form the next dynasty! But joking apart it all is extraordinarily interesting here now and a great deal may happen.'

Clearly people were beginning to think the unthinkable, but Sybil and her colleagues could scarcely have guessed at the 'mighty upheavals' that would come in just four months' time.

---

3 Boris Sturmer (1848-1917), a civil servant and an opponent of democratic government, he was appointed Minister of the Interior by the Tsar in 1916 and then replaced Sazonov at the Foreign Office. He was hated by the Duma and after the February 1917 Revolution he was arrested by the Provisional Government and died in prison.

England

The perennial subject of Earl Grey's health came up again. Alice wrote:

> We really hear the same from all doctors, that what is wrong with him is an excess of acidity, produced by an over fatigued brain which induces this excess of acidity, which in its turn prevents his food from nourishing him, hence his falling away in flesh, for he is getting very thin again, and his neck is all cord. This being the universal dictum, the only real remedy is rest and proper nourishment, and your father thoroughly likes and trusts Byles Mori and will do more what he tells him is really necessary than anyone else.

Dr Mori didn't mince his words, warning Earl Grey that he must 'pull up' and rest or the consequences for his health would be grave:

> Dr. B.M. spoke very seriously to him and said that he was seeing similar cases, many more every day, men of your father's age and much younger keep coming to him over-wrought and over fatigued by these anxious times and worries, and unless they will pull up, he said over and over again, the consequences have proved really serious, either the man goes on until there comes a stroke and he goes out, or serious illnesses are generated in the inside from this continued acidity and irritability. Your father has got over one very serious breakdown, and cannot afford another… he must get rest.

Alice thought that Dr Mori would like to send them to Switzerland after Christmas to recover in the mountain air. (Travel to other parts of Europe was of course possible in the First World War if you had the money). But the trouble was that Albert still wanted to be involved in political debate:

> It is terribly unfortunate, as the things he has stood for all his life, such as Proportional Representation for one thing, are just coming to the front as practical politics, if they are carefully pushed and striven for. He is as you know a member of this Electoral Conference, and has been having unlooked for success at the meetings with his P.R. [proportional representation] which he has been advocating there with great energy. It is hard to feel he should drop it and not attend to further his views which he considers so important.

She hoped that others would now take forward the campaign for Proportional Representation.

The Electoral Conference Alice referred to was a Speaker's Conference on Electoral Reform, set up in 1916 which reported in 1917. It recommended a limited form of Women's Suffrage, which was later included in the Representation of the People Act of 1918, but its recommendations for the use of proportional representation were voted down in the Lords.

Alice also reported that Arthur Grenfell was recovering from a bad wound to his leg, and that she herself had been diagnosed with a bad attack of her old bugbear, nettle rash – 'hives'.

The British Government had taken over food regulation and was appointing a Minister for Food, but Alice was critical of the lack of urgency in addressing the problem of feeding the nation and of defending merchant shipping against German U-boats:

We have not yet been told who our Food Dictator is to be, they do seem so slow over things. They talk a great deal and we are left without any further directions. These horrible submarines go sinking our tonnage right and left and we may be face to face next year with a very serious position regarding our food supplies, and yet the Government does nothing to oblige the country to grow more foodstuffs to make provision for a shortage, nor does it arm our mercantile ships with guns to protect themselves against the submarines. Our seamen would certainly know how to fight and they would risk nothing for as it is their ship is invariably sunk to the bottom and the crew left to get to land in their boats as best they can.

Things were so bad that local people in the fishing village of Craster could no longer get fresh fish which was all sent off to London.

Alice herself continued to be busy with war work. Although the convalescent hospital for officers at Howick Hall had by now closed, she remained involved with the Red Cross, sitting on its committee in Newcastle and raising funds through events like 'Our Day'. On 18 November 1916, she described the mix of work she did in London – packing supplies for prisoners of war and serving in one of the street canteens set up for soldiers:

I have been pretty busy this week. Tuesday and Wednesday mornings I packed at the new central office for the Prisoners of War. One has to give in one's name as a packer to the War Office and answer whole strings of questions about one's parentage until the 3rd or 4th generation back, before one is permitted to be used as a packer, dealing directly with Germany. Thursday I spent the whole morning at a work party for medical things – pneumonia jackets,[4] bandages, abdominal etc, etc – that Connie Balcarres[5] holds at her house, where she has about sixteen ladies working for one of the big societies, Queen Mary's Needlework Guild I think. I like going there – it is so peaceful, in alternation with a morning's packing which is most strenuous, all the time on one's legs and working at express speed. Then yesterday afternoon or rather evening, I was again at the London Bridge Canteen, and that again is strenuous if you like, hundreds of Tommies clamouring for a cup of hot tea or coffee, cake, bread and butter and sandwiches, one has not one moment's peace, either serving that or cutting fresh sandwiches and cake for dear life, I got home at 11 o'clock.

After a particularly busy week, she was pleased that more work on prisoner of war parcels wouldn't be needed until after December.

Russia
Meanwhile, in Petrograd, Sybil received a series of reports from the roving Field Hospital in Bukovina. On 19 November, the young Dr Humphrey Thompson, wrote from a place called Krugla Keecherka, close to the site of the battle of Kirlibaba:

We are 5,000 feet up, sixteen versts north west of Kirlibaba[6] in the wildest part of the

4 These jackets were made of flannelette by volunteers, and were sleeveless and fastened down the front to make them easy to put on pneumonia patients.
5 Constance Lilian Pelly, who married Lord Crawford, Earl Balcarres. Earl Balcarres was a Lindsay of Balcarres, of the same family that Alice's mother Mary Anne Lindsay came from.
6 Cârlibaba is a commune located in Suceava County in modern Romania. It is composed of six villages.

country – just in Hungary and three versts from the Front. There is only a corduroy road from here to the base, up to the front one can only go on horseback. On Wednesday, the day on which the Russian attack began, we had only just got up the big white tent, on the top of the hill, when patients began to arrive. Our own little living tent was hurriedly put up and the Sanitars were at once made to transport the wounded. We admitted 156 wounded and Dr Flavelle and I did 62 dressings. The tent you can imagine was crowded and we had patients lying outside in the wet round a large fire.

Today (Thursday) we were lucky in getting from Seletin[7] a little round tent – we intended to use it as a dressing tent, but wounded had to be put into it and a large open summer tent without ends – we only had one stove for all three tents and about 30 blankets – this night was a nightmare, we had 165 lying cases and between 150 to 200 walking cases – a beastly cold night with a raw mist and only one hurricane lamp to see by – dressings were done under great difficulties. Unfortunately, also, our tent was so placed that it could be seen from the German lines, so we had two or three shells sent over to cheer us up – no damage done.

The Russian attack he witnessed had failed: 'They succeeded wonderfully the first day and we heard had captured Kirlibaba but since then they have been driven back to their old positions with awful casualties.' The plan was now that the hospital should be moved back to a new site twelve versts away, either in Selatin or on the road between Selatin and Kimpolong[8] – this is the location of the field hospital known as Stary Ply near the current border of Romania and Ukraine. Professor Pares, matron and a number of sisters were there, together with the staff of the motor column under Keeble (head of the Anglo-Russian Hospital chauffeurs). But Flavelle decided to send the X-ray car, the only one in the area, back to Kiev, as it was underused – it had only done a dozen screenings in a month: 'The Russian operator does not understand the car and is careless, and the driver like all Russians would drive furiously and knock the car to pieces.'

Of all the sites of the Anglo-Russian Hospital field hospitals, I find Stary Ply ('old meadow') the most alluring – perched on a mountain pass of the pine forested Carpathians, it was probably an old farmstead – it had been declared unfit to stable horses in by the Imperial Russian Army so it must have been very dilapidated indeed. It is not on any map, but was in the hills above the modern Romanian-Ukraine border – perhaps above Seliatyn on the Romanian side or at Storonetz Putillay in the Ukraine. It remains an idyllic spot, a Shangri-la, lost in the mountains. The doctor in charge, Dr Thomson, wrote:

We are all very comfortable here in a log hut which looks rather like a garret. We have a good Russian mud stove and can make the heat so hot that even Rosher [the Anglo-Russian Hospital's bacteriologist] would enjoy himself. The climate here and scenery is wonderful, we have had quite a lot of snow and fine sunny weather. There is a lot of game here too – wolves, bear, boar, deer and smaller animals like foxes, hares etc. I have seen numerous tracks and a few days ago saw two large brown deer.

7 Now Selyatyn, just inside the Ukrainian border with Romania.
8 Champolung, in modern northern Romania (literally 'Long Field')

England

In December a crisis erupted in the British Coalition Government, with both the Liberal left under Lloyd George and the Conservatives under Bonar Law challenging the authority of Herbert Asquith, the Prime Minister. On 7 December, Alice wrote:

> We are in the middle of the most violent Government crisis, and it is impossible to tell what will happen. Will Lloyd George form a Cabinet with Bonar Law, Sir E. Carson and others, or will he fail to get sufficient support?[9]
>
> One really hardly knows what one wishes, but now that the crash has come, I think it must be better to go on and try and secure a vigorous government – with a small cabinet, and a War Council of four who will determine to push the war for all we are worth.

She called for strong and determined leadership which would harness the energies of everyone, including women:

> We cannot revert to the drift policy, which seems to get worse week by week, when the whole nation is champing the bit and almost crying out for stronger measures and for being organised as a nation of women as well as men for war purposes. Why don't we arm all our merchant ships and fight every submarine that shows its nose? We are all ready and begging to be put to the proof in every way, and nothing is done to use all this good will and readiness to subordinate everything to win the War.

She was under no illusions about the enemy's determination:

> Germany meantime is working feverishly with her whole nation's powers, and has now made herself mistress of Bucharest. I do not see how we are to save the oil and wheat fields she will have won, it is heart breaking. She really almost deserves to win, she is so united and determined and one idea'd – unless we prove ourselves as determined we shall for all intents and purposes lose the War and its fruits.

And she overcame her instinctive aversion to the radical Lloyd George – whom she referred to as 'Taffy' – in her desire to see decisive leadership:

> I cannot help but think that a government under him would wake up the nation; no that is not it, the nation are woken up, but would drive ahead, and put an enormous added pressure on Germany. One has only to look at the press comments of Germany, to see how terrified they are lest Lloyd George should become Prime Minister for they know what that would stand for. The Allies and America would also understand that it means the 'wait and see' policy being chucked overboard and we should go full steam ahead.

The next day, 8 December, Alice enclosed press reports that Lloyd George would form a new cabinet, backed by the Labour Party.

> I hope it will be a strong one, for events lately have been moving far too well and quickly for the Germans. It is terrible to see their continued success in Roumania and the awful mess we are in in Greece. I confess I feel relieved that Mr. Asquith's cabinet

---

9 After the troubles of 1916, the members of the coalition lost faith in Asquith's conduct of the war. Asquith was persuaded to resign and his place was taken by Lloyd George as Prime Minister, with Bonar Law as Chancellor of the Exchequer and Balfour as Foreign Secretary.

has gone, and that sterner measures will be the order of the day.

Alice like all her family was steeped in politics, which were her husband Albert's consuming interest. Her comments on Sir Edward Grey's handling of foreign policy were particularly cutting, given that he was her cousin and a close friend and neighbour:

> I felt no confidence in Edward's grip of foreign things and he always had far too much admiration of his friend Lord Haldane.[10] They really seem to have lost all power of clear outlook and quick decision, and I imagine it is not that we shall have to complain of now, we may be praying soon for not quite so much precipitancy. Still such a lot of valuable time has been lost in every direction that it has cost us very dear already, and who knows if we shall be able to make up for it, however much we try.

Sir Edward left government after twelve years, exhausted and delighted to be rid of the burdens of office.

Sybil also received a series of letters from Muriel Paget, now back in Britain. They covered all kinds of issues – financial, administrative, and regarding the criticism the Anglo-Russian Hospital had encountered from its own former members returning to Britain at the end of their contracts, who had questioned whether the Anglo-Russian Hospital was succeeding or failing. And behind these, there were the differences in approach and temperament between Muriel and Sybil – which caused the propagandist-novelist Hugh Walpole to describe them as like 'Seidlitz Powder' – two salts which when mixed effervesce violently and bubble over.

Muriel wrote about a plethora of financial issues, great and small: about the minutiae of the sponsorship of the Anglo-Russian Hospital by British towns at £100 a bed – 'there must be a plate stating the nature of the gift over a bed for a year, so that the men should realise that the English are helping'; and about Sybil's request for £15,000 more funding, which Muriel thought should be forthcoming from fresh funds: 'The Flag Day telephoned me they have a cheque for £19,000 which will be paid in after they receive my report and if they approve of forecast of work.' A week later however Mabel wrote that she had not been able to get the full sum: 'Am sorry the Committee would not pass more than £10,000 but hope that with the other £1,000 sent you will have enough for the time.'

Muriel outlined administrative arrangements she wanted made in Russia, enabling Anglo-Russian Hospital staff from Petrograd to serve in Kiev and vice versa, and she discussed which members of Anglo-Russian Hospital staff and their Russian advisers should receive British medals for their assistance to the Anglo-Russian Hospital, nominating 'Polotsoff, Tchamansky, Col. Fénoult, and the smallest possible pin for Ignatieff!' She was seeking awards of the OBE to doctors Fleming,

---

10 Richard Burton Haldane, 1st Viscount Haldane (1856-1928), was an influential Liberal Imperialist and later Labour politician, lawyer and philosopher. He was Secretary of State for War between 1905 and 1912, and was Lord Chancellor between 1912 and 1915, when he was forced to resign because of his supposed and unproven German sympathies. He later joined the Labour Party and once again served as Lord Chancellor in 1924 the first ever Labour administration. Haldane was also an influential writer on philosophy.

Waterhouse and Harmer, and also a Red Cross order for matron.

Muriel then turned to the criticisms that had surfaced among returning Anglo-Russian Hospital staff, regarding the lack of work. She was particularly furious with Dr Gould May: 'Dr. May has proved a real rotter – he wrote to the War Office that our hospital was not wanted and that it was the opinion of the medical staff that young men like Jefferson and Marshall should be recalled as their work could equally well be done by older and less efficient men.' This had been sent to Lord Cheylesmore[11] who responded that if a man was so disloyal he should not be employed by the War Office.

The Australian doctor Captain Gardner who had been with Sybil at Verapaeva was also critical of the lack of work, writing to his sister about an Australian proposal to equip a hospital in Russia: 'The Russians don't want foreign hospitals and the difficulties in the way are so great and it costs so much money that it isn't worth it. Give Russia the money and let them do what they like with it – then of course they will be delighted.'[12] This view may well have been shared at times by many of the staff of the Anglo-Russian Hospital on the ground in Russia.

Muriel then addressed the more sensitive matter of differences between herself and Sybil, voiced to her by Hugh Walpole, a friend in whom Sybil had confided, recently returned from Petrograd: 'He seemed to think we were like a Seidlitz powder and that our views never coincide. I pointed out that if this were so, we should not be working together now, because it is impossible to run two policies – or two anythings – in an organisation like this.'

Muriel claimed that discipline was very poor when she had come out in May 1916:

> There was too much of everyone wanting to run the show in the beginning. When I came out last year I had a very difficult time from the moment I arrived – as you know there was almost mutiny among the medical staff and a certain amount of dissatisfaction among the nursing staff – and very general outside criticism.'

She voiced her suspicions that the Russian staff seconded to the field hospital had tried to undermine the Anglo-Russian Hospital; and referred to other problems, such as conflicts between senior staff such as the matron and Dr Fleming, and rumours that pro-German agents were spreading criticisms of the hospital. 'With all these difficulties to face and no strong man as commanding officer, in fact practically no commanding officer at all, the only thing was to make the best of things all round till better conditions prevailed.'

She implored Sybil: 'I see no real points of difference between us but if you feel they exist as strongly as Mr Walpole leads me to believe do tell me what they are.' She added: 'You are bound to hear as many criticisms of my work as I heard of yours, people enjoy nothing more than repeating things generally in a different way to which they are said, with intent of mischief making.' She concluded:

> So tell me what you have at the back of your head Sybil dear and what your points of

11 Chairman of the committee in London responsible for the Anglo-Russian Hospital.
12 From the file of Gardner manuscripts belonging to Richard Gardner.

difference are so that there shall be no misunderstandings in a work about which there can be no two opinions can there. You know I thoroughly appreciate everything you have done for the hospital and the splendid way in which you got the thing going in Petrograd.

The correspondence between Sybil and her her mother shows a growing wariness and exasperation of Muriel Paget's leadership, but they still pay tribute to her energy and determination in getting things started, and Sybil remained loyal and was loath to publicly criticise Muriel. By the time that January 1917 came round Alice was writing to Sybil:

> She has so many talents in initiative, wonderful energy and drive and persuasiveness, here at home at any rate, that people cannot help but recognise it, and it is difficult therefore for people who only know her as a charming personality to realise that she can have been a failure in Russia, all the more as she of course leads them to believe the contrary... Think of the way you looked upon her yourself a year and a half ago and you will understand all this.

Clearly Alice was being partisan, speaking as she saw it in defence of her daughter. But it did represent a temporary rift between the Greys and Muriel Paget.

Muriel too was critical to some extent of Sybil's more laissez faire leadership before Muriel arrived in Petrograd, and she later wrote suggesting that Sybil was good at carrying out instructions but lacked initiative. Clearly the pressures of having to deliver success in a high profile venture in a foreign land, were beginning to drive a wedge between Muriel and Sybil, as well as Sybil's criticism to her mother of Muriel's impulsiveness and vagueness on matters of finance.

A few days later, Muriel wrote again, of her desire to return to Russia, hoping to secure large new funds. She wanted to visit towns in southern Russia, perhaps with Sybil, 'but all this will be more easily settled and schemes made on the spot and I shall then know what money we shall have to rely on – anyhow another £50,000 next year is more or less assured and as soon as the gifts are made from the towns here.' However she was also heavily committed to setting up the Russia Exhibition at the Grafton Gallery in London, an exhibition in May 1917 devoted to displays of Russian culture. Muriel Paget and the Anglo-Russian Hospital were involved in helping gather exhibits. She asked Sybil to 'send any photographs which are typically Russian and anything that would attract attention and be interesting in way of exhibits. A case of leather things made by patients would also be excellent.' Two books of photographs of the work of the Anglo-Russian Hospital with the Russian Army were later published as a result of this exhibition.

Lady Muriel was a complex character. She was a visionary who could inspire (and sometimes even bully) other people and officialdom into achieving her goals. She was a great humanitarian who was moved by compassion to help people of completely different backgrounds and nationality to her own; who after the end of the Anglo-Russian Hospital went on to set up humanitarian ventures in many places in eastern and central Europe, from Czechoslovakia, to Romania and the Baltic states, including for Distressed British Subjects (usually widows) in Stalin's Russia.

She was extraordinarily brave and completely undeferential to 'authority' – be it to bureaucrats in Britain or to the aristocratic elite in Imperial Russia. She was the driving force who created and inspired the Anglo-Russian Hospital, but when it came to running it on the ground in the increasingly chaotic state of imperial Russia, her over optimism and perhaps lack of a sure touch in managing others seem to have hampered her.

20

The Murder of the 'Mad Monk'

Back in Petrograd an event occurred which rocked the country and further desta-
bilised the monarchy – the assassination of Rasputin.

Grigori 'Grishka' Rasputin[1] was the son of peasants from the village of
Pokrovskoe, in western Siberia. A sexual philanderer, he nevertheless made a pilgrimage to Mt Athos in Greece and to Jerusalem, and proclaimed himself a *staretz*
or Holy Man, claiming he could effect cures. He became known among circles at
court and was introduced to the Tsarina, whose son, the Tsarevitch suffered from
haemophilia, which prevented his blood from clotting. Rasputin seems to have had
an influence over the boy's condition and successfully predicted his recovery from
some attacks. Sybil said that he manipulated the Tsarina – by arranging for fake accidents to happen in the Palace which he, Rasputin, would 'predict' and engineer
in advance. By 1916, he had huge influence on the Tsarina and through her on the
appointment of ministers and the running of Russia. He was hated by many of the
aristocratic families, but had a devoted circle of noble women – Sybil tells a story
of how he would eat with his fingers and then hold his hands out to be licked by
this group of women!

In December 1916, a group of aristocrats, led by Prince Felix Yusupov and by
Grand Duke Dmitri Pavlovitch, owner of the palace in which the Anglo-Russian
Hospital resided, decided to kill Rasputin. They involved Vladimir Purishkevich,
a right wing member of the Duma who had denounced Rasputin, and a Dr Lazovert,
whose job was to supply poison. On 29 December, they lured Rasputin at 1 a.m. at
night to Yusupov's palace on the Moika Canal, with the promise of meeting
Yusupov's wife, Irina. There they fed Rasputin with cakes and wine laced with
potassium cyanide. When, after several hours, this failed to kill him, Yusupov shot
him with a revolver in a basement room, but Rasputin revived, attacked Yusupov
and tried to escape. He was finally beaten and shot in the snow outside the palace
and his body dumped through a hole in the ice in the frozen Neva. When the body
was recovered by the police, he was found to have finally died by drowning! He
was buried in the grounds of the Imperial Palace at Tsarskoe Selo, on the orders of
a grieving Tsar and Tsarina.

On 15 February, Sybil, in bed with mumps, wrote to her father to tell him of the
stories circulating about the end of Rasputin:

---

1 Grigori Rasputin (1869-1916), self-proclaimed holy man and libertine who came to wield influence
over the Russian Imperial family.

Isn't it extraordinary that the state of affairs that this place is in now can continue as it does? For even if they had one strong man to organise a determined resistance they could do what they wanted instead of having to resort to murder – which after all is but a poor way of arranging matters.

She thought that the murder of Rasputin 'no doubt did good but he has still power, although removed from the Earth. I will try to tell you all the gossip, it is difficult to tell truth from fiction at such a time as this.'

Rasputin was supposed to be better guarded than the Emperor – with guards who never left him night and day. He was a tall thin man with something of a stoop, not good-looking but with these strange compelling eyes. Most Russians say he was a pro-German, but people like Sazonov (who hated him with a deadly hatred) said no, that was wrong, if anything he was rather more of a Russian patriot; that he was indirectly used by the Germans there is no doubt of, but that that was never one of the considerations that controlled his actions; that his character and mode of living was of the lowest is admitted by all. There are many stories about his end, but the one most believed is the following and is, as far as one can make out, the correct one.

He was in the habit of meeting some of these Grand Dukes at different times in more or less drunken orgies. They used to see what they could get out of him in the way of information when his tongue got rather loosened. Things were getting so bad that a great many people were implicated in the plot to do away with him. That Dmitri Pavlovitch was at the bottom of the whole thing I believe, but I do not definitely know. That all the different families of Grand Dukes were in it I think is accepted as a fact.[2]

She wrote about the night of the murder at Yusupov's palace:

I suppose nobody will ever know the exact truth of what took place. At 2 a.m. a shot was heard and the police approached the house and asked what was the matter. They were told that some of the Grand Dukes were supping inside and that they were practising with a revolver and that one of the shots by mistake had gone through the window, and they were shown broken glass in the street and sent away.

In Russia no police can ever enter the house in which a Grand Duke is, so whatever happened they would have no right to enter the house as long as a Grand Duke was there! Shortly after the shot a motor car drove up and very soon afterwards two struggling women were put into it. At 6 a.m. two or three more shots were heard and when the police again went to the door young Yusupov answered it and said 'Rasputin is dead'. When they asked him where his body was the only answer he gave was: 'The body is where it should be, that is enough'. What happened between 2 and 6 nobody rightly knows. One story is that they offered him to commit suicide and that they gave him a revolver and that he had a shot at Dmitri Pavlovitch and that the shot missed him and went out of the window. If this is true I should have thought they would have finished him off at once instead of waiting another four hours. In the end I expect two or three of them shot at him so that nobody knows exactly who dealt the fatal shot. That they did not necessarily do it as gentlemen should but tried to make him confess certain things before he died I think is more than probable – horrible isn't it?

There are all sorts of stories: that they had never intended to do it that night but that R. said such things of the Empress and of the Grand Duchesses that it quite finished

---

2 Lady Sybil to her father (quoted by permission of William Harmer).

him. He is supposed amongst other things to have said that not one of them would dare to kill the Empress's lover. They tried to sink him in the river but, I think unfortunately, the ice cut away the weight and then caught his body and it was found. Some people think it was a good thing because had this not happened it would always have been said afterwards that he had never been killed at all. The order was given from Tsarskoe that the river and bay were to be searched and Kronstadt if necessary, but the body was to be found. Unfortunately it was and was buried in one of the chapels at Tsarskoe at 3 a.m. in the presence of the Emperor, Empress, some of the family, Protopopov,[3] Minister of the Interior, and the service was taken by the Metropolitan of Petrograd.[4]

Can you understand what the average Russian would feel about such a thing – the bitter humiliation of it and the fury? It would be difficult to keep much feeling of loyalty or respect after that wouldn't it? Now the story goes that every day a wreath is put on his grave by order of the Empress and that at night tongues of fire are seen playing around the grave. The Empress is supposed to thoroughly believe that Rasputin was a manifestation of Christ, and that just as Christ was despised and rejected of men 1900 years ago so it was today and that she and a very few others were the only people who recognised him; that Rasputin explained some of the things that he did by saying that God liked you to sin much so that much could be forgiven. If this is really true, and I think it is quite possible, for I do not think she is sane where religion and mysticism are concerned, it is one of the most tragic and pathetic things that have ever happened. Protopopov told somebody the other day that Christ has appeared to both him and the Empress together since Rasputin died.

Now are you surprised that the right kind of men will not work with a man like Protopopov? When the Emperor asked Trepov to form a Cabinet it was on the distinct understanding that he had a free hand. He formed his Cabinet and went to H.M. who told him that on no account was Protopopov to go. Deadlock at once, and it doesn't help the people to believe that the Emperor means fairly and squarely by them. Can you imagine anything more utterly stupid of the Emperor?

Sybil told her father that after the murder Dmitri Pavlovitch hid Prince Yusupov in the Dmitri Palace, which the police could not search:

The day that Rasputin was killed, Dmitri Pavlovitch brought young Yusupov up into the hospital to take a bone out of the boy's throat. Think what interest there would have been had we realised the truth. We did not know it till late that day. Then for the next week Dmitri Pavlovitch was in the palace under arrest (Emperor's orders). The guard with fixed bayonets used to go in and out of his rooms just in front of my door. The police wanted Yusupov. He is not a Grand Duke, but only married to a Grand Duchess, so that the police could arrest him but he was hidden here by Dmitri Pavlovitch and of course the police could not get into the palace. Strange people used to come to the hospital door and ask all sorts of questions, but of course we know nothing.

Dmitri Pavlovitch asked a special favour of Sybil to keep the conspirators safe:

From my rooms to the hospital I have to go up a flight of stairs and along a passage at

3 Alexander Protopopov (1866-1918). A conservative politician and an ally of Sturmer. He apparently favoured signing a separate peace with Germany.
4 Saint (Hieromartyr) Benjamin (1873-1922), elected archbishop of Petrograd in early 1917. After the October Revolution he came into conflict with the communists and was executed in 1922.

the end of which is a corkscrew staircase leading down into Dmitri Pavlovitch's rooms. At the head of the stairs are two solid double-folding doors which lead into the linen room of the hospital where all the staff have tea, etc. To these doors there is a huge ornamental brass key the size of a very large cellar key. This, the day after the event was put into my hands and I solemnly swore that never should it leave me – that nobody should even go through the doors for one second without me and that I would religiously keep them shut. So for the next week I walked about like a goaler with a gigantic key hanging from my waist. It weighed a ton! I wore it under my dress as there was supposed to be deep secrecy about it. We heard a rumour that Protopopov had told someone that he was going to get somebody into the palace by hook or by crook. However he didn't succeed through us.

Years later, when giving a talk to her local Women's Institute in the 1950s, Sybil commented that it was the only time she had ever knowingly sheltered a murderer!

The Tsar was furious that members of his family were involved, and Dmitri Pavlovitch was bundled off at night on a train to exile in Persia:

The train is not allowed to stop more than 2 minutes at Moscow or Odessa so that he shouldn't see anyone, and sends him to an appalling climate which is the very worst place possible for consumption, which the boy has. The first three weeks he was there he lived in a mud hut of two tiny rooms. Yusupov was treated better: sent off to one of his estates where his wife and Father and Mother were allowed to join him. He was sent in a second class carriage hooked on to a goods train with not a morsel of food on it and it took 30 hours to arrive at Moscow.

One of the older and richest of the Grand Dukes who remonstrated with the Tsar was also banished to one of his estates:

He is immensely rich and has many fine estates but was sent to the only one on which there was no house. It is awfully dangerous behaving like this when you have the people against you – to go deliberately to work to set the entire Imperial family against you as well. They – the Emperor and Empress – are supposed to have said that now is the time to show the people who is master and not to give way one inch. Isn't it desperately pathetic?

Sybil had a clear vision of the sort of courageous leadership required, but which the Tsar was quite incapable of providing:

It cannot go on like this. It must end badly and if only the little man would play the game he could make them adore him. If only when the Duma opens in a fortnight he would boldly go to the Duma himself and say, 'I don't mean to hear things through my Ministers. I have come myself to hear all you have got to say. Tell me your grievances. Tell me the truth. Tell me what you wish me to do and then we will see if we cannot agree together.' Were he to do that they would adore him, but instead what does he do? Three Cavalry divisions of Guards have been ordered back from the Front to guard him. Two refused to come, but one I believe is coming and many of the officers are trying to get quickly exchanged into the Infantry so as not to come. Can you imagine what the people feel like, that their Emperor is bringing back soldiers from the Front to guard him and his family, instead of going himself and facing the music and playing the man.

Sybil herself was of course not sure how it would all turn out:

> It will be extremely thrilling to see what happens when the Duma meets. Anything might happen and nothing might happen. You see I don't wish to be a false prophet! But honestly, in this country you never know. You think everything is at boiling pitch and then curiously things seem to fizzle out in a strange way although underneath everything is in the same white heat. I think the real thing is that people are very loth to do anything during the war.

Stary Ply

In mid-January 1917, Sybil heard from Dr Aspland, now at Stary Ply in Bukovina. He reported on their work or lack of it: 'I need not stop to record the fact that this Selatin Valley and our hill is the most beautiful I have seen in Russia – you will have heard this from Matron.' He however was very conscious of a very light workload: 'Don't worry about the surgeon coming down; I can manage here perfectly for the present and am very happy.' He suggested that the sisters return to Petrograd. 'There is no nursing to do here as it is only dressing station – the few dressings there are daily I can manage easily done myself.'

Conditions were basic at the Stary Ply Field Hospital: 'Tell anyone coming here to bring their old clothes – for we cannot help but be piggy – in our huts and dugouts and being entirely alone – it is a good opportunity to spare good ones.'

Nevertheless, life in the Carpathians was good and had its moments of humour. He described how he, a lifelong teetotaller, was made to take pride of place as the guest at the Russian Army's local festival, 'The Blessing of the Waters':

> The ceremony was very interesting. I approached with officers and kissed the cross and had my head sprinkled with the 'Blessed Water'. Then came the 'Hurrahs' for the Emperor, the band playing the traditional anthem, then speeches and hurrahs for the General in Chief, Brigadiers and Colonels; a long performance in the cold, and finally the General proposed the Anglo-Russian Hospital and Great Britain. The Band played *God Save the King* and I had to march before all the soldiers, and salute the Generals and Colonels who advanced, saluted and shook hands with me. This finished we tried to get away – but it was the Festival Day of the Division – so no excuse availed. We had to stay to dinner. A most sumptuous board was spread – with unlimited vodka, Cognac, port and champagne. I had seat of honour next to the General in Chief, and by the time every toast had been drunk and *God Save the King* had been played a few more times by the Band, I was getting distinctly worse for their hospitality. Being a lifelong abstainer except at functions I cannot stand it – there could be no refusal – they hurrahed and shouted – until I was compelled – with the result that I barely remember coming home – and had a frightful headache after. However they are all devoted to us, and certainly we are amongst the nicest people I have met in Russia – alas I was kissed 50 times by the Colonel.

A more melancholy view of Stary Ply was given by the young Countess Olga Poutiatine, working there as a nurse. Looking down from her hilltop, Olga reflected on Stary Ply and saw beyond its stunning scenery and forested mountains to the fundamental tragedy of war:

Stary Ply must hardly recognise itself these days and the great sentinel firs must have much to watch and think of and grow sad over when their peaceful mountains are invaded by thousands of little khaki and grey coloured men. They fell the giant firs down to make log roads for the artillery, log shelters for men, log fires to heat themselves by, fir posts for wire entanglements and to strengthen and line their trenches and dugouts, and plane the fir tree boards for the little white crosses with their black name boards in the wee cemeteries one finds everywhere in these mountains as in the plain country of Lutsk.[5]

'I see no real hope for the country'

In February Sybil went down with mumps, as mentioned briefly previously, landing her in her own hospital for the second time and preventing her from meeting the members of a high level British government delegation, sent out to conduct an Inter-Allied conference with the Russians on the conduct of the war in the east which was going badly. She knew all the members of the British delegation – Lord Milner (her father's mentor), Lord Revelstoke (a member of the Baring family) and General Sir Henry Wilson, as well as Sir George Buchanan. Her friend, Sir John Hanbury-Williams, wrote to her parents to reassure them, no doubt echoing Sybil's own exasperated words: 'Sybil is "all right" – "all right" – "all right" – notwithstanding having had mumps! It is such bad luck her being laid up at this moment – as her talks are always useful, and she would have enjoyed seeing more of [the Conference visitors].'

He may have been flattering her, but I prefer to believe that he took Sybil's views seriously on matters such as politics, Russia and the war. On 28 February, fully recovered, Sybil attended the opening of the Duma:

Of course nothing happened. It was hardly politic to make a row today for the authorities were too well prepared for it. Secondly, it would be foolish to take action before giving the Duma the chance of improving things. If they fail then anything may happen. Today you weren't allowed to even stop as you were crossing a street, or look into a shop window before a policeman made you move along. There were patrols of Cossacks riding down the streets and the police had machine guns in hiding. We had a Cossack patrol of about 30 men in our yard all day and a sentry with fixed bayonet inside the hospital doors and one by the Grand Duke's and my private entrances. Is it likely that on a day like this the people would try to make a row?

It was stuck up on posters at the corner of streets yesterday that if there was any row anywhere the police would shoot. The peasants stood and read these notices in the streets and went away smiling. There was a speech in the Duma this afternoon made by a member of the extreme left, who said that the Government that Russia now had was such a Government that no civilised country in the world would stand for a week, and even an uncivilised barbarian country would be ashamed of it and turn it out: that it did not represent the people, the Zemstvos, the aristocracy, in fact it represented nobody but its own rotten self and didn't even know what it wanted itself for the ministers changed every week. The speaker turned to the Government side and said, "Isn't it absolutely true what I am saying. You are leading the country straight into Revolution and you will even make a mess of that?" He continued to say that the present time in

---

5 *War and Revolution: excerpts from the letters and diaries of Countess Olga Poutiatine*, George A, Lensen (The Diplomatic Press, 1971).

Russia resembled the end of the eighteenth century in France and that it would end in the same way. His speech was listened to pretty well in silence and Rodzianko[6] never once stopped him.

I was told that never has anybody been allowed to say such things without being stopped at least a dozen times by the President. But today they seem to be allowed free speech. They did not allude to the Imperial family or Rasputin, but I only heard the first three speeches and there may have been all sorts of things said later. But I think they wanted to keep things quiet and orderly to start with.

The speeches in the Duma were presumably conducted in Russian, and Sybil's knowledge of the language would not have been sufficient to follow the flow. So she must have had someone with her, translating.

She wrote of the terrible food shortages:

It is the food question that is so appalling. It is terribly difficult to get bread now – butter is almost prohibited in price – sugar very difficult, etc. Can you imagine what it must be like when the temperature is below zero like it has been for the last fortnight – standing out all night in the street waiting in a queue to get bread! It is damnable.

Miss Seymour[7] who has just been to Moscow on holiday tells me that people have died frozen to death in the streets and at the same time the nouveau riche who have made money out of the war can go to a restaurant and pay 100 roubles for a bottle of champagne and 50 roubles a lb. of caviar.

The Government's approach was riddled with inefficiency and inconsistency:

They stopped all passenger traffic for a fortnight and now they have extended it for another fortnight in order to bring food into the cities. Then one hears that it half fails because they haven't got the trucks to move the stuff with. Then for some utterly unknown reason it is prohibited to bring foodstuffs from Finland to Russia. Finland used to export eggs, butter, timber, etc. She cannot export now but could send her big surplus into Russia (Petrograd being a few hours by train from one of the rich centres) were it not prohibited. The result is that butter is about four roubles a lb here and two or three hours away from here it is being made into soap because they cannot use it at all. In Siberia it is being used to grease the engines and railway wheels. Also it is forbidden in many instances for one Government to sell its produce to another. Result, in the province where Princess Shakhovsky lives they have a super-abundance of potatoes: in the next province they are short of potatoes, but as it is forbidden for potatoes to be sold out of that province they are rotting where they lie. This is all done, or anyhow not undone, by Protopopov.

Finally Sybil lost all patience:

If I were a Russian I should be a red hot revolutionary. There is nothing else for it. I am beginning to think this is the most hopeless country that one could possibly imagine,

---

6 Mikhail Rodzianko (1859-1924), Chairman of the Duma. He failed to persuade the Tsar to introduce reforms. After the February Revolution, he became a leader of the new Provisional Government, and conducted talks on abdication with the Tsar.
7 Dorothy Nina Seymour (1882-1953), daughter of Gen. Lord William Seymour. She was a Woman of the Bedchamber to HRH Princess Christian. She was with the British Red Cross during the First World War.

one sees no light anywhere. They will have a terrible revolution some time. I hope not before the end of the war, but it wouldn't surprise me if it came at any moment. I can't see that they will be much better if they sweep away the whole Romanov family and the Government. The country and people are corrupt from top to toe. It is heart-breaking. How they are ever to get straight I cannot think.

Protopopov, the Prime Minister was claiming that 'Christ comes to him and the Empress when they are together and tells them how to save Russia. So now poor Russia is being governed by a weak man (the Emperor) and two people of unbalanced mind.'

> The Emperor won't see what he is doing and I think he will end by losing his head over it. If only, as I have said before, he will dismiss Protopopov (who doesn't dare enter the Duma) and if only he had gone and faced the Duma today they might have made a hero of him. But instead of that he sits at Tsarskoe with a division of cavalry brought back from the front to guard him. There is so much I could tell you if only I could talk to you.

Her friend Dorothy Seymour had visited the Grand Duchess Sergei (sister of the Tsarina, and original owner of the Dmitri Palace) and found the Grand Duchess distraught about the country:

> The Grand Duchess was utterly miserable and could talk of nothing else: said that owing to the mismanagement of the food question thousands were starving in Moscow; that she quite understood and sympathised with the revolutionaries, but that her sister would not understand – and a great deal more. As a matter of fact I believe the Grand Duchess who was at Tsarskoe a week before Rasputin was murdered, prayed her sister on her knees to send R. away and told her the truth. She was returned to Moscow with thanks and told not to come back. Moscow talks red-hot revolution – everywhere – in the streets, in the restaurants and among all classes of society. Many factories will soon have to be shut down for want of fuel. The street cars will probably soon stop for the same reason. A good number of factories have already stopped.

Sybil summed up the situation:

> England need never be afraid of Russia. Nothing will ever convince me to the contrary. Colossal confusion and inefficiency reigns everywhere. They are corrupt financially and morally. When I think of how I used to talk glibly during the first year of the war of Russia and of what the Russian steam roller was going to do to the Germans – one would laugh if one didn't feel more like crying. However Russia is a bright spot compared to Roumania! The people and the Roumanian army are starving; the wounded dying in thousands unattended.

Sir George Buchanan, a sympathetic but despairing friend of the Tsar, in vain urged him to change course just weeks before the February 1917 revolution: 'Your Majesty… has but one safe course open to you – namely, to break down the barriers that separate you from your people and to regain their confidence.' And he warned:

> If I were to see a friend walking through a wood on a dark night along a path which I knew ended in a precipice, would it not be my duty, sir, to warn him of his danger? And is it not equally my duty to warn Your Majesty of the abyss that lies ahead of you?

You have, sir, come to the parting of the ways, and you have now to choose between two paths. The one will lead you to victory and a glorious peace – and the other to revolution and disaster.[8]

Sybil however doubted that a revolution would yet succeed in Russia:

I don't think these people will have a real revolution before the end of the war or make a separate peace. The Police are all absolutely loyal and have machine guns! Then you cannot make a successful revolution before you are certain that 75 per cent of the Army is revolutionary. I doubt if 75 per cent is so, although I should say it was growing fast. I believe that the Petrograd regiments were tested the other day and more than 60 per cent were ready but the others remained loyal.

And she assured her parents: 'If there is a revolution (and it is always possible) don't fuss about us. We have got a stock of food in the shape of enough flour for some time, etc, and we are living in the palace of a man who killed Rasputin and is in banishment in consequence, so that will safeguard us.'

She related the result of a petition for clemency on behalf of the exiled Dmitry Pavlovich, from members of the Royal family:

I saw a copy of the letter written to the Emperor by the entire Royal family the other day and the Emperor's answer. The Grand Duke Paul, Dmitri Pavlovitch's father, had given it to the person who showed it to me. It was the most charming and respectful and loyal letter from the entire Imperial family (signed by practically every G. Duke and Duchess) begging the Emperor to reconsider his decision of sending Dmitri to Persia.

The answer was short, saying that the Emperor doesn't understand how they dare write to him like that: that never in the course of his reign had he condoned murder and that he did not wish them ever to speak of the subject again. Hardly the sort of letter to write to the Imperial family when you have practically got the nation at large against you. Isn't it pathetic?

She added: 'Don't think I am depressed because of this letter. I am not in the least. If I were a Russian I should be in the depths. I see no real hope for the country for many, many years.'

---

8 Sir George Buchanan, *My Mission to Russia,* (Cassell, 1923).

21

Revolution

The events of 8-16 March 1917 (Russian dates, 23 February- 3 March) were some of the most profoundly shattering of the twentieth century, toppling the Romanov dynasty and opening the way to the coming of the first communist government nine months later. They were chronicled by Sybil Grey who witnessed them at first hand from the windows of the Anglo-Russian Hospital, and in the streets of Petrograd. Her diary, kept hour by hour during the first days of the Revolution, gives a vivid picture of what an historic insurrection looks like to someone caught up in the middle of it.

Thursday, 8 March (23 February, Russian date)
On Thursday, 8 March a poor woman entered a bread shop on the Morskaia (the Bond Street of Petrograd) and asked for bread. She was told there was none. On leaving the shop, seeing bread in the window, she broke the window and took it.

A General, passing in his motor, stopped and remonstrated with her. A crowd collected round them, smashed his motor car, and, increasing in size, paraded the streets, asking for bread.

On the other side of the river, where the factories are, a factory hand beat his wife because she had failed to find him bread. Other women ran in saying that they had waited hours only to be told there was no bread. The men agreed the women were not at fault and that they must all strike and demonstrate in the street demanding bread.

Friday, 9 March
I went to the bank early with Dr. Rosher. Some trams overturned, driving handles of others removed.

Great crowds in the streets of both well-to-do and working men, all in the best humour, gathering on the Nevski and opposite the Kazan Cathedral.

Cossacks were riding up and down through the crowds and on the pavements, when the Prefect of Police got out of his car, and ordered them to charge with their swords. The officer in charge said, 'I cannot give this order; the people only asking for bread.' The only thing that people called out was: 'Give us bread.'

All was quiet until 12 o'clock, when great crowds came again; the factory hands having all come out on strike. The police used the backs of their swords to beat the people off the Fontanka bridge.

Miss Danzas saw the crowd on their knees saying to the Cossacks, 'You must not shoot; we are only asking for bread,' and the Cossacks said, 'We won't.' They treated the crowds with great gentleness and received an ovation, such sympathy being unknown in Russian history. One Cossack fell off his horse and the crowd gently picked him up and put him back on his horse again. Immense crowds cheered them all that day.

At 5.30 p.m. Baron Meyerdorf, Member of the Duma appointed to help the Anglo-Russian Hospital, arrived and said that the Minister of Agriculture had just made a speech saying there was plenty of bread but that it had been badly distributed.

On Saturday, 10 March

No food was coming into the city, as whatever organisation had existed disappeared overnight.

Baron Meyerdorf said that there had been a short Duma sitting; the organisation of the food supply was handed over by the government to the municipal authorities

A man was killed on our bridge by a sudden shot in the afternoon; and shooting had taken place near the Kazan; this was said to be not by Cossacks, but by police dressed as soldiers.

We have about 70 soldiers in the palace and four Siniousky guards stand at the doors.

At night the lights were extinguished on the Nevski, and a searchlight played down the street from the Admiralty.

Sunday, 11 March, 'Revolution Day'

A glorious – sunny – cloudless – day. Martial law was proclaimed, people warned not to be outside their houses next day. I had all hospital staff brought over in ambulances. Quite peaceful all morning, but we were warned that things would happen in the afternoon.

At about 3 p.m. I went to the window to look out. It was a glorious day, people on the bridge were laughing and talking, about ten deep across the road; when looking down the Nevski Prospect, I suddenly saw soldiers lie down in the snow, about 100 yards down by Sedovia, and fire a volley into the people on the bridge. As soon as the people saw the soldiers lie down, they scattered; but about seven men were caught by the volley while others crawled away on their hands and knees. We had ten casualties brought in, three died, (two women), almost immediately. After that the fat was in the fire. Soldiers had fired on the people; nothing now to stop the Revolution.

The following day, taxis and motor cars were going up and down the Nevski all the time, machine guns firing just for fun while two men with rifles and fixed bayonets were lying on the running boards, in front as they drove along the street. After the firing, the Nevski filled rapidly; people did not seem to mind and continued crowding onto the bridge.

A police officer was torn to pieces. Bridges all stopped and guarded, but the crowd crossed by the ice all day. I saw fourteen ambulances go by at a great pace in under a minute.

Red flags appeared 'Down with the War'. By night motor cars drove round distributing arms to the people.

All through Monday and the following 48 hours there was a great deal of fighting. It was interesting to see big motor lorries going around town distributing arms and ammunition to soldiers and civilians alike. Red flags were now to be seen everywhere. The soldiers tied strips of red to their bayonets; the civilians wore red armlets or streamers from their buttonholes. The police were armed with machine guns which had been placed several weeks before on roofs and in attics of houses commanding the principal thoroughfares. Machine guns had also been placed on the Duma building, and even on the churches and on St. Isaac's Cathedral.[1]

Monday, 12 March

There were no newspapers; but newsheets and proclamations were issued daily from the Duma, also from Petrograd Council of Labour Deputies, distributed by motors to the various centres of the town. As soon as the motors were seen approaching, they were surrounded by eager and impatient crowds, who fought to obtain a copy.

Regiments marching on the Duma. The Siniousky Guards join the revolutionaries. All our palace guards left us about noon. Great crowds, everyone armed, promiscuous shooting. Burning of police courts and the Courts of Justice; with all records. They also broke into the prisons, releasing criminal prisoners as well as political. The fire engines were turned back and not allowed to extinguish fires.

Heavy guns fired, the Duma was 'closed' but kept open by members, and surrounded by revolutionary troops.

Sir George's[2] motor was stopped on the way back from the Foreign Office by a very big crowd of revolutionaries. He quickly put his head on one side of the car and said, 'English Ambassador'; Paleologue[3] popped his head out of the other side and said 'French Ambassador'; upon which they were conducted by a cheering crowd, all waving red flags, to their separate Embassies.

Col. Knox went to the barracks of the Guards where he had left his 'British warm' by mistake. The soldiers had just revolted, locked up the officers and were very excited. [But] they gave him his coat back and formed a guard of honour to escort him back to the Embassy. He had a pretty nasty time and saw some very grim sights.

At Helsingfors[4] the port of the Navy, three Admirals of the Baltic Fleet and a number of officers were killed. Much fighting. Trouble at Reval[5] also.

Much firing all day and wounded coming in.

During the evening a big number of Cossacks rode down the Nevski at a walk, with their lances. The light was just fading and they looked splendid in the grey

---

1 Sybil Grey's *National Review* article.
2 Sir George Buchanan, British Ambassador.
3 Maurice Paleologue, French Ambassador.
4 Former name of Helsinki in Finland.
5 Now Tallinn in Estonia.

failing light; but just as they got onto the bridge, shots were fired. They leant down over the necks of their horses and galloped away. Two saddles were empty.

7.30 p.m. Quieter. Some staff went to Vladimirsky (Staff House) but had to run for it. Heavy firing. I refused to allow night sisters over and kept all day staff in.

8.30 p.m. Crowds broke into the palace, by the front door, and said we had machine guns firing from the roof; Gen Leyman[6] spoke to them. He delivered up his sword and revolver and asked them to go and search for themselves. This they refused to do. All doors were then opened to give free access all through the hospital. We hung a very big Union Jack from the balcony.

We made as many Red Cross flags as we could out of old sheets and an old Father Christmas coat; we also put a lantern with a Red Cross on it outside the door. Three flags were stolen as soon as put up; feverish haste to make more.

Continuous and heavy firing. New crowds met by staff from the wards, came in from the street; insisting that machine guns were on our roof, but none would go and look.

11:30 p.m. As I was going round the wards, four soldiers with fixed bayonets came in, officered by a young student. He carried a revolver, and came up to me pointing the revolver at my chest and started a speech in Russian, which I understood enough to realise that he was talking about wine; and felt it prudent to offer him all we had. I then found to my amusement, that he was offering us wine at the point of the revolver, as Kerensky[7] had ordered all wine cellars to be emptied and given to the hospitals in order to prevent drunkenness.

Tuesday, 13 March
3 a.m. Things quietening here; but at 3 a.m., Mr Garstin rang up from the Astoria asking whether we wanted help, as big, angry crowds were then threatening the Astoria.

4 a.m. I went down to my room, taking Dorothy Cotton and one or two others. We laid down in our clothes until 6 a.m. when renewed outbursts of firing took me upstairs. The Morskaia Hotel at the corner of the Vladimirski, stronghold of the police, was attacked. Staff quartered at the club had a terrible night.

At 8 a.m. on Tuesday the crowd attacked the Astoria Hotel which had been taken over by the government several months before, and turned into a military hotel. [Despite receiving guarantees that no-one would fire on them from the hotel, the police or German agents hidden on the roof of the building fired on passing revolutionary troops and workmen with machine guns.]

Revolutionaries, infuriated, stormed the building, and after an hour and a half of hot fighting took the hotel. They rushed in – a howling, raging mob, armed to the teeth; sacked the ground floor, killed some Russian officers, and surged up the staircase, shooting up the lift and in every direction.

Some British officers there thought that their last moment had come, but the moment the crowd saw English uniforms they stopped. Some even took off their

---

6 Chief of Dimitri Pavlovitch's staff.
7 Alexander Kerensky, lawyer and political leader of the moderate socialist party.

hats and said, 'English officers, forgive us, we do not wish to bother you,' and passed on in the most courteous manner possible to do more destruction to the hotel and its inmates. They got into the cellars, where there were thousands of bottles of wine, and many barrels of spirit. A few were just beginning to drink when soldiers coming in said, 'No my friends, do not let us spoil our fight for freedom by drinking and looting' and straightaway they broke all bottles with the butt ends of their rifles.

This and similar examples of self-restraint saved the town. Had all the wine shops been looted and people been drunk by their contents nothing would have averted a second French Revolution.

Every man and boy from the age of twelve was armed from this day.

During all Tuesday, Allied officers have been going around the barracks, speaking to soldiers, telling them of the necessity to go on with the War. Soldiers interested and ask questions: did soldiers salute their officers in France and England? At first refused to believe they did. Regiments then selected small committees to advise on their future conduct. Results satisfactory, in nearly every case soldiers selected by their fellows were unanimous in wanting to go on with the War.

A good number of criminals are going about armed and dressed as soldiers, entering houses and stealing.

11.30 p.m. I had just got all sisters settled for the night, when drunken soldiers came into the hospital; three brandished naked swords, and one with a loaded rifle wanting his fingers bandaged. They were quite nice about it and we were very nice and civil to them.

Wednesday, 14 March
Snowing slightly, crowds collecting early, regiment passes, band playing – cars and lorries filled with soldiers and civilians, rushing up and down the Nevski. Men holding rifles, at every angle, others brandishing naked swords and bayonets.

9 a.m. Some are drunk – this is the danger. Olga Poutiatine was stopped in her ambulance by an armed soldier, who begged her to telephone 'the committee' asking for a bigger guard to save the wine shop from being looted.

I saw several drunken men being arrested by soldiers with officers and by sailors with an admiral at their head.

Notices were out everywhere calling people to order, 'not to drink', 'not to loot', and a 'Council of Labour Proclamation' said: 'Bands of hooligans are beginning to rob the shops and property of the inhabitants. The revolutionary people and the army must on no account allow this; looting by hooligans might cast a shadow on the holy work of freeing the revolutionary people; and the army should arrest hooligans who are found looting and hand them over to the Governor of Petrograd, appointed by the State Duma.'

2 p.m. The revolutionaries brought two machine guns onto the bridge and bombarded the Anitchkova Palace opposite. Arrests were being made, and people being taken away – all motors carry a Red Cross flag.

I saw one car with a big Red Cross flag as well as red flags, with rifles in front, and two maxims pointing out of the back.

The wounded were being brought in all the afternoon.

A student member of the Duma came into the hospital, stood on a chair and read a proclamation saying 'there was ample bread in Petrograd and that all hospitals will be well supplied.' After telephoning to one committee after another, at last bread was promised us for the next day.

6.30 p.m. Very heavy firing. Bullet through the window of Ward C, high up. Patients panicky. Moved some of the worst cases into Ward B. The crowds still believe we have machine guns on the roof of the palace – our soldiers think this also – got General Leyman down to speak to the soldiers and tell them they might go and look for themselves. He also telephoned to the Duma, to send soldiers to search the palace. They promised to do this.

The Duma Executive is in a difficulty, as there are three parties: 1) For a republic; 2) For compromise with the Emperor, who has not yet answered the telegrams; 3) For a Regency with his son Alexei.

Fortunately Rodzianko came to an understanding with the extreme left on Tuesday night, and thereby kept control of the people, which saved the situation.

Heard that the Imperial Guard has left Tsarskoe Selo to join the revolutionaries and many of the palace servants have also deserted; the Empress and the Grand Duchesses are ill with measles. The Duma sent off post-haste a revolutionary regiment to guard her and her family.

British officers are treated with wonderful courtesy and an English uniform is as good as a passport.

The lack of any answers to telegrams sent to the Emperor by the Duma and an appeal by members of the Council of the Empire, which called on the Emperor to sack his cabinet and replace it with a new one.[8]

Thursday, 15 March (Russian date 29 February)
Not much shooting, but crowds enormous and nervous – there is a bad and uncomfortable feeling. Soldiers saluting officers much less than yesterday. Still no answer from the Emperor to the Duma – no decisions.

An armed guard of sixteen men came in here, with an officer, demanding 25 suits of underlinen for soldiers. When challenged to produce his authority, he looked most insolent and said: 'It is not a request – it is a command.' Sixteen bayonets won the day. I asked the Duma for a guard.

The Embassy motor was sent for me and I lunched there. Col. Knox said 'feeling was very bad and things at the Duma chaotic.'

Three regiments have arrived from Riga and joined the rebels; 2,000 police are expected from the Baltic provinces; also light artillery from the front.

The family at Tsarskoe Selo still know nothing. Rumours that troops stopped the Emperor's train and that he has been arrested.

General Poole trying to get us a guard all afternoon. At 8 p.m. he came with

---

8 Only later was it discovered that the Emperor's entourage never showed him the telegrams until too late.

two officers to say he hoped a guard would arrive soon, but thought it right to warn me that they expected all hotels to be sacked; and anything might happen that night – very gloomy. He advised us to hang out a bigger Union Jack, as the best protection, and I hung it on the inside of the stairs.

Things seem quieter.

10.30 p.m. Capt. Lessing telephoned saying 'A guard is impossible. Were we alright?'

JOINT WAR COMMITTEE

of the

BRITISH RED CROSS SOCIETY AND THE ORDER OF ST. JOHN.

To *Lady Sybil Grey*

I have the honour to inform you that your name was brought to the notice of the Secretary of State for War for valuable services rendered to the sick and wounded men of H.M. Forces during the War.

I am desired by the Members of the Joint War Committee to convey to you their sincere congratulations on this public recognition of your war work.

Chairman.

Sybil's award for bravery from the Red Cross (Boyd family collection).

Sybil's OBE and medals, the Russian St. George medal is on the right
(Boyd family collection).

Friday, 16 March

Dr. Flavelle, Head of the Field Hospital, arrived at 3 a.m. having heard nothing of any trouble within 50 versts (about 30 miles) of Petrograd!

The Abdication is announced of the Emperor and his son, and of Grand Duke Michael.

The Revolutionary flag had been hoisted on the Winter Palace. All crowns – double eagles – and Imperial ciphers were hastily torn down in the streets and thrown into the canals. Only the eagles on the Emperor's huge Winter Palace were left and draped in red.

The feeling of the crowd is much better. Processions singing the *Marseillaise*, free dining rooms opening everywhere for soldiers and students; soldiers selling butter at a low prices and long lines of carts going up and down with bread and flour.

Rumours: the Grand Duke has died of measles. There has been a three-day revolution in Berlin. The Kaiser is a prisoner. The Crown Prince is killed. The Germans have taken Riga.

Facts: Heavy snow storms and many carts of provisions. People happier.[9]

[end of diary]

There was much uncertainty about what the future would bring. 'Two privates were overheard discussing the future. One of them said that the Emperor should remain

---

9 Lady Sybil Grey's manuscript diary of the Russian Revolution.

Emperor with a Constitutional Government, for God had anointed him, and that once God anointed him man could not undo his work. "Yes," replied the other, "but since God anointed him, Rasputin has covered him with his dirt, and God would never re-anoint a man".'[10]

Sybil commented: 'The amazing success of the Revolution in so short a time, with comparatively small loss of life, was due to the fact that there was hardly a dissentient voice. All classes in all parts of Russia were in sympathy with the revolutionaries in the overthrow of an incompetent and hated Government.'[11]

---

10 Sybil Grey's published *National Review* article, 'Sidelights on the Russian Revolution'.
11 Sybil Grey's contemporaneous account is of course limited to what she saw and heard about day to day. Her diary understates the degree of violence involved in the February Revolution (estimates of at least 4,000 deaths, particularly of policemen butchered by the populace) which ironically was more violent than the Bolshevik Revolution in October.

22

Home again; Dorchester House Hospital

'The Revolution must seem like a long way away from you now, part of a life that was lived last year,' Sybil's friend, E. Barnard Lintott, one of the more florid and blustery members of the British Embassy staff in Petrograd, wrote in March 1917 just after Sybil had returned to Britain from Russia. A talented watercolour artist – signing himself as 'the Hoododjnik' (*khudozhnik* is Russian for artist) – Lintott was instinctively reactionary and unburdened himself of his deep dislike of the Revolution, referring to it as 'just a fluke', and to the Russians as, 'Eastern barbarians with a veneer of Western civilisation'. Quoting the French revolutionary Madame Roland, executed during the Terror, he perceptively anticipated that it would end in dictatorship and bloodshed: '"Liberty, what crimes are committed in thy name", that is what I anticipate here. I do not believe that the mental or moral state of Russia is fitted for a democratic form of government as yet.'

Sybil had been summoned home by her parents. After being unwell for many years Earl Grey had finally been diagnosed with terminal cancer. With her father's illness and the Revolution in Russia, the Greys were understandably determined that Sybil shouldn't stay any longer in a dangerously unpredictable Petrograd. She left Russia on 21 March 1917, never to return.

Sybil returned home to help look after her father but continued to received news from her many friends at the British Embassy, Petrograd. They referred to her as 'the Old Grey Fox', missing her imperturbable calmness and good sense. One wrote, 'There is no one now to clear our minds for us as you did.'

It was indeed a time of huge uncertainty in Russia. The Revolution had turned everything upside down – soldiers were no longer required to salute their officers, workers demanded huge pay increases – doubled wages backdated two or three years. The opera and theatre had been opened up to the masses and the imperial decor such as the curtain bearing the royal coat of arms had been ripped down. Playbills proclaimed that the performances were staged on behalf of the Workers' Soviet – and this was even before the second revolution later that year which brought the Bolsheviks to power.

As under the Tsar, there were shortages of key goods and foodstuffs. Threats of general strikes and even worse of violence came and went. Banks did brisk business as the better off took their jewels and valuables there for safekeeping or sent them out of the country to safety in Finland or Sweden. Nothing was certain any more.

Countess Olga Poutiatine, Sybil's young half English, half Russian friend, wrote, 'It was a great relief to hear that you were safe and sound in your horrid old, staid and level headed country. I should love to hear what people think of our great, grand, poor, absurd country and its doings,' She added 'Easter was too anxious to be joyful.' She signed herself, 'Your loving Petrograd Child'.

The British ambassador's daughter, Meriel Buchanan, author of a rather sentimentalised memoir of life in Russia (*Petrograd – City of Troubles*) wrote: 'I was so fond of the Russians, and it's horrid to see everything crumbling away.'

Not all her Embassy friends shared Lintott's gloomy dystopian view of the Revolution. Herbert Brooks who had often accompanied Sybil to the theatre and with whom she had lunched at Donon's[1] and dined at his flat, wrote in a remarkably unruffled mood. The general strike hadn't occurred, Brooks continued to go to the opera – he sent a playbill of *Esmeralda* starring Tamara Karsavina, wife of the British diplomat Henry Bruce, and featuring the opera singer Feodor Chaliapin. He grumbled a bit about the Imperial Box being turned over to an audience of Baltic sailors, but life for him continued on phlegmatically.

Some like Denis Garstin, an army captain and an enthusiastic socialist sympathiser, were brimming over with excitement and enthusiasm: 'I'm jolly fond of these people. They're not like children, they are children, and they do want so tremendously to grow up, which is their idea of being good.' He went on: 'We are still shaking our poor foolish heads and grumbling at the Russians. They've neither gone on with the war, like good allies, nor have they murdered us in our beds, like good revolutionaries, nor yet have they declared a separate peace, like good social democrats. In fact they shock us. They're so confoundedly unconventional.' Garstin viewed Russians as just beginning to learn how to live free lives, too given to talking and unused to taking action or responsibility. 'I saw a little crowd outside your hospital the other day; they were awfully excited about carrying on the war, and just when it seemed as if the only thing left for them to do was to march off to the Stokhod and recapture that as a prelude to the rest of the world, the orator suddenly paused, spreading out his arms to the sun and the Nevski and his Tovarishtchi [comrades], gave a little yelp of joy and said, "See, we talk and no-one stops us," and they forgot the war and fell to congratulating each other.'[2]

Within the year Garstin himself would be dead, machine-gunned by the Bolsheviks on a mysterious British War Office mission to Archangel.

These letters help us to glimpse more of Sybil's life while in Russia. With each of these friends one can envisage her having very different conversations – with Herbert Brooks she would doubtless have discussed music, theatre and the arts; with Lintott, she took an interest in his painting and discussed the quirkiness of the Russian character; with Denis Garstin she may have debated politics and perhaps helped rein in his naïve enthusiasm with a dose of her hard headed realism. Each of them valued Sybil's friendship and her clear headed advice. They wished that she was back with them in Petrogad.

The new Provisional Government of Russia never succeeded in uniting the

---

1 A fashionable Petrograd restaurant.
2 Denis Norman Garstin (1890-1918), author of *Friendly Russia,* published posthumously. He worked in the British Propaganda Unit in Petrograd, and was also an intelligence officer.

country. Formed by the Duma and essentially representing the bourgoisie (although it saw itself as ruling for the benefit of all Russia), it hoped to forge a democratic constitutional republic. Alongside it grew up a rival centre of power, the Soviet (Council) of Soldiers' and Workers' Deputies, also based in Petrograd. It was the Soviet which came to represent the interests of working people and was dominated by deputies from the socialist party and the revolutionary parties, the Mensheviks and the Bolsheviks.

The Provisional Government began well by introducing extensive democratic reforms, civil rights and religious freedom, replaced the monarchy with a republic and prepared for elections to a new constituent assembly; but it was increasingly undermined by the rival power of the Soviet and by continued failure in the war. A socialist deputy, Alexander Kerensky, joined the government and duly became Prime Minister. In July, Kerensky launched a last and unsuccessful offensive against the Germans. Also in July, an attempted Bolshevik Revolution failed – 'the July Days' – leading to the temporary flight into exile of Lenin and the imprison-ment of Trotsky. In August, Kerensky and his field marshal General Kornilov fell out, with Kornilov marching on Petrograd, only to surrender himself. Two months later, with the return of Lenin, the Bolsheviks, grabbed their chance in the October Revolution 1917, ushering in the Soviet Government.

The achievement of the Anglo-Russian-Hospital
How successful was the Anglo-Russian Hospital? No venture can be a complete success and the Anglo-Russian Hospital had more than its share of problems. To start with it took three months to convert the Dimitry Palace and its stores were held up for half a year in the ice of the White Sea. It initially had too little work to do in St Petersburg – and some of its doctors went home complaining that their time was being wasted. There was dissension among its senior staff, particularly over the role of first head doctor, Andrew Fleming, who was forced to stand down.

The Anglo-Russian Hospital took on huge challenges – working in a foreign land, in the depths of winter, in the middle of a titanic war and in a country where power was slipping away from the government – challenges still faced by organi-sations like the Red Cross today. Its field hospitals in particular gave sterling service – at Lutsk particularly where its doctors worked flat out for days on end treating thousands and doing hundreds of major operations. The staff showed great bravery in the face of the danger and chaos of the Russian Revolution – treating the injured from both sides. And the hospital kept the Union Jack flying bravely on the Nevsky Prospekt through the darkest days of the war and represented Britain's commitment to its Russian ally.

In March 1918, Lady Muriel Paget finally evacuated the last remnants of the Anglo-Russian Hospital in a heroic journey right across Russia by the Trans-Siber-ian Railway to Vladivostok on the Pacific coast, and home via Japan and the United States.

Propaganda and intelligence[3]

It has been suggested that the Anglo-Russian Hospital might knowingly or not have been used as a cover by British intelligence, particularly in the plot to assassinate Rasputin. Britain did indeed have spies amongst its diplomats at the time, such as Robert Bruce Lockhart in Moscow, and alongside the formal diplomacy of the British Embassy and the Military Attachés, Britain did run a propaganda bureau and a secret service liaison with Russian intelligence.

Sybil didn't know Bruce Lockhart (if she had, she probably would have found him very entertaining). But she did know the Military Attachés, Sir John Hanbury-Williams and Col. Knox – she was particularly fond of Sir John. She may very well have known Sir Samuel Hoare, MP for Chelsea and the Secret Service Liaison officer in Petrograd.[4]

She was also good friend of Hugh Walpole, head of the British Propaganda Bureau. Walpole was a successful young novelist who had served at the front with the Russian Army as an officer of Sanitar (orderlies). He knew both Sybil and Lady Muriel and commented on their sometimes turbulent relationship.

Propaganda was a vital activity – it was felt important to counteract German influence in Russia. In a sense the Anglo-Russian Hospital had been part of British propaganda from the start – it was intended to win hearts and minds in the battle to counteract Russian cynicism about Britain's commitment to the war effort. The British propaganda effort had begun with Prof. Bernard Pares, a noted Russian scholar, touring the Russian front on a bicycle. The reports he had sent back had first suggested the idea of the Anglo-Russian Hospital to Lady Muriel.

By 1916, the British Propaganda Bureau under Hugh Walpole was established with a staff of twelve, in conjunction with a separate intelligence mission, at a small office on the Fontanka, near the Nevsky Prospekt – within spitting distance of the Anglo-Russian Hospital. It was described as 'like a comfortable English club'. Propaganda and the intelligence community certainly used bright young British writers – as well as Walpole, Somerset Maugham and probably Arthur Ransome were involved. Some like the young soldier Denis Garstin probably had a foot in both camps, propaganda and intelligence.

Back in Britain, the author John Buchan had just been put in charge of the new government Information Department which coordinated all British propaganda, producing quantities of material for distribution in Russia as well. Another aspect of propaganda was the innovative use of film, on which Sybil herself had offered advice. In 1916-17, Capt. Bromhead, future head of Gaumont Cinemas, toured the Russian front with lorries fitted with projectors and showed British military films to 100,000 Russian troops and 3,000 officers.

It seems very unlikely that the hospital and its staff of doctors and nurses were

3 This section draws on a journal article: *Joy Rides? British Intelligence and Propaganda in Russia in 1914-17,* Keith Neilson, Royal Military College of Canada, Kingston, Ontario. The Historical Journal, 24, 4 (1981), pp 885-906.
4 Sir Samuel Hoare (1880-1959), 1st Viscount Templewood. He went on to become Secretary of State for Air in the 1920s, Foreign Secretary (1935), First Lord of the Admiralty (1936) and Home Secretary (1937-9).

involved in espionage of any kind. Sybil's letters do not give any hint of any such activity – they are personal and are concerned with setting up and running the hospital and her impressions of life in Russia. She was frank and critical in her assessment of the failings of Imperial Russia, occasionally asking that some sections should be treated as private. Her letters were circulated – she was a bit alarmed to hear that they might be read by the King – and her cousin the Foreign Secretary, Sir Edward Grey, expressed his admiration of them; but they were personal accounts of Russia not espionage assessments. It would surely have been reckless and dangerous for the Anglo-Russian Hospital and for Sybil had British officials misused her letters in this way.

It is, however, alleged that two young British Secret Intelligence Service agents in Petrograd, Oswald Rayner and Capt. Stephen Alley, associates of Yusupov, may have been involved in the plot to kill Rasputin, perhaps with the knowledge of Ambassador Buchanan, (Rayner himself perhaps even firing the fatal shot with his Webley service revolver). Rayner made several trips to the Yusupov Palace at the time, driven by his chauffeur, William Compton, who it just happened was also included in the Anglo-Russian Hospital staff list of chauffeurs.[5]

Twenty years later, in 1938, Lady Muriel Paget was actually accused of being a link between British intelligence and a senior Russian diplomat, K G Rakovskii, who was on trial for his life in one of Stalin's notorious show trials. The accusation was dismissed by both Muriel Paget herself and by the Prime Minister, Neville Chamberlain, in the House of Commons. Whatever the truth, it is much more likely that British humanitarians might have been used as a cover for espionage against a hostile Soviet Russia in the late 1930s than against our Imperial Russian ally in 1916-17.

Earl Grey's death

Earl Grey died on 29 August 1917. He had continued to waste away as a result of the cancer that afflicted him, until as his wife Alice put it, his skin resembled the ivory colour of a beautiful Venetian Doge, but he remained amused, caring and committed to the last.

His sister, Lady Victoria Dawnay (Auntie Tora) came to help look after him and entertained him by reading old letters from Howick from a trunk they discovered– the two of them swopping reminiscences about the house and its occupants fifty years before.

A couple of weeks before his death, he asked to see some improvements which had been made at the graveyard at the small church in Howick's grounds, and his family took him there in a wheel chair. The nurse who was looking after him in his final illness was shocked at such apparent callous insensitivity, saying in disgust, 'You might just as well leave him there!' When told of what she had said, Albert Grey gave a hearty laugh.

His funeral service was held at Howick, with messages received from the King,

---

5 Source, 'The prince, the spy and the Mad Monk', article by Christopher Danziger in *Oxford Today*, Vol. 29 No 1, 2016.

from Queen Alexandra and from former Prime Minister Laurier of Canada.

His political ambitions had to some extent been thwarted – he had never played a national role in government at home and some of the causes he fought for such as proportional representation had not been rewarded with success. His contribution was rather to building an ideal of Empire and to the generous, broad minded and caring attitude of mind he brought towards all people and all aspects of life.

His mentor, Lord Milner, caught his qualities well: 'He had a record of public service of which any man might be proud. But it is entirely dwarfed by his personality. He was the most lovable and inspiring human being. His sympathies were always with the right things and with big things. He was always on the side of harmony and of good understanding, always against discord and disintegration. And thus, in an almost impalpable way, by what he was rather than anything he did, he probably contributed as much to promoting unity of spirit amongst the peoples of the Empire, and to counteracting estrangement between different classes at home, as any man of his time.'[6]

He remained a shining example and an inspiration to Sybil for the rest of her life.

Dorchester House

From February until December 1918, Sybil was commandant of the Astley Hospital for officers based at her uncle Sir George Holford's magnificent mansion, Dorchester House, on Park Lane. With its massive marble staircase and grand Italianate halls and reception rooms, it is difficult to imagine anywhere less suited to function as a hospital. Its magnificent collection of Renaissance art was presumably stored carefully away. Her young cousin Rosalind Benson worked as a parlour maid at the hospital.

Sybil was once more at the centre of London society and spent a good deal of time dining with friends and family, and going to the theatre. Looking after the administration of the hospital, preparing it for inspection, doing the accounts, getting in provisions and seeking to raise funds for the hospital took up part of her time, but she enjoyed her return to London – writing to her mother: 'five nights running I have been to the theatre, isn't it disgraceful.'

There was chaos over the supply of foodstuffs to hospitals – lacking food coupons they were not able to secure supplies of chicken from butchers or poulterers: 'I went down to the R.C. [Red Cross] offices in Eaton Square, and found agitated and infuriated matrons waiting to see the authorities, all of us wanting to know the same sort of questions.' She described trips to get provisions for the hospital, when she and Mrs Woodward, the housekeeper, 'staggered home from Piccadilly Tube Station carrying between us a huge sack of vegetables', both unable to stop laughing as they struggled with their burden.

The war made its presence felt even in London – one day 'airplanes kept flying above us and an airship flew over us very low and we could see about twelve men waving at us.' As in the Second World War, people used to take refuge from air

---

6 Lord Milner quoted by Harold Begbie in *Albert Fourth Earl Grey: A Last Word* (1918.)

Charlie, 5th Earl Grey, his wife Mabel and children Molly and Nisset (standing)
(Howick Hall Trustees).

raids in the Tube stations. More worryingly, her brother-in-law Jonah Jones was reported missing. Her sister Evy was very distressed with her emotions veering from high to low, at times seeing visions of Jonah 'at his last gasp' and at others sensing that he was sublimely happy. An unattributed report that he had been shot in the stomach happily proved untrue. To Evy's huge relief, Jonah was finally posted by the Red Cross as a prisoner of war.

It was a time of austerity and the King angrily refused to attend a ball held in his honour on Easter Sunday, rounding furiously on its organisers, thundering: 'Not only did they choose to hold it whilst their country was in extreme peril, and their relatives and friends were being killed, but they chose Holy Week.'

The fortunes of Sybil's friends and relatives were mixed. Her friend Jeanne Malcolm had a baby; Rhoda, another friend of Sybil's, died in childbirth. Her relative Claire was badly burned on a hospital operating table in the course of an operation! News reached Sybil that her father's former secretary, Gilly, had had a nervous breakdown and she went to visit Gilly's family in 'the Garden City' – perhaps Hampstead or Welwyn.

Jonah Jones on his return from Prisoner of War captivity in Germany
(Jones family collection).

Her cousin Constantine (Con) Benson was at No. 1 Red Cross Hospital at Le Touquet with what were said to be 'severe gunshot wounds to his side'. Sybil commented: 'We all think it is rather a satisfactory telegram, for "severe" doesn't mean anything very bad in the War Office language. I think Aunt Evy is very thankful to know where he is and that although wounded he is out of it.'

She kept her own spirits up – visiting Ciro's, a classy restaurant and cabaret venue during the First World War, set up by an Italian born Egyptian. And she went to the theatre with her cousins Daisy, Rex and Con Benson, Daisy's husband Hereward Wake, and her brother Charlie and his wife Mabel, dining beforehand at the Berkley. Her friend Zella Leather-Culley visited from Northumberland , 'telling me all the northern country gossip… Howick has been let to some people who are going to open up the entire house and many rooms that had never been opened up for years and years.'

She also saw her favourite cousin Angus McDonnell, now married, Sybil making a gibe at his wife Susan: 'I lunched with Angus in the Carlton Grill Room and we had a real old gossip. He may come with us to 'Dear Brutus' on Friday night, if Susan allows him to.'

Dorchester House was also the home of Stewart Menzies when he was in London and not with Haig's GHQ staff in France. He occasionally kept her informed of the progress of the war: 'Stewart has just come in with better news. He says that the French have started to attack near Bailleul and have taken two villages.'

There were Sybil's old bugbear, accounts, to attend to. Fortunately when they were audited the accounts proved to be trouble free: 'They were finished yesterday afternoon and found correct to a halfpenny.' The auditor complimented her: 'he said he wished that he always had as easy a job as this had been and that they were very well kept. I was awfully pleased because I had taken a great deal of trouble about them.'

In June she wrote to Jonah, now a prisoner of war, using Dorchester House Hospital headed paper with her name 'Lady Sybil Grey' printed on it. After posting the letter she was assailed with worry that the Germans would notice it and think that Jonah was a relative of Sir Edward Grey, and that they would single him out for reprisals. Sybil immediately talked to the secretary of the Postmaster General and two hours later the letter was returned to her, unopened, at Dorchester House!

She was invited to be part of a new British committee on relief to Russia, headed by the Buchanans (the former British Ambassador and his wife) and the polar explorer Sir Ernest Shackleton. At a meeting in September 1918 at the Mansion House they learned the news of the murder of the Tsar and his family – 'Did I tell you that the King had heard that all four little Grand Duchesses had been murdered. It must be pretty horrible there now.'

The Germans launched a major new offensive in spring 1918, which initially made great gains. In June Sybil spoke of 'the fear that Germany may be about to defeat us. Utterly unbelievable… one cannot admit such a possibility.' But it proved to be Germany's last offensive, which was ultimately defeated by the British, French and Americans.

Russia remained in her thoughts. Early in the year, Lord Hardinge, a leading British diplomat told her that there had been over 2,000 executions in Kieff alone and commented that if he was an educated Russian and a Patriot, that he would welcome the Germans as the only hope and means of saving his country from utter ruin.

At the end of July, she met Muriel Paget and was impressed by her continuing commitment to aiding the Russians: 'She is absolutely undefeated. Means to take three units back at once – but I hear the authorities do not mean to allow her to. Somehow I expect she will win.' Lady Muriel told Sybil 'that she is bombarding everyone, that she works twelve hours a day in America bringing round public opinion to helping Russia, addressed meetings in the open of 2,000 people, had long interviews with Wilson, and ended by changing the whole American attitude towards Russia.' Sybil commented: 'She is a marvel.' However she was painfully aware that Lady Muriel spent most of her time away from her young children, adding 'of course her family and husband do not count much if she thinks of straightway returning to Russia.'

The Voluntary Aid Detachment (VAD) organization was run by the Joint War Committee of the British Red Cross and the Order of St John, based at Devonshire House in Piccadilly which had been loaned by the Duke and Duchess of Devonshire. On 25 July, Sybil went to Devonshire House: 'I arrived to find everybody lined up in the hall awaiting the arrival of the Queen – so I was roped in. She didn't look very fat and was quite well dressed all in black. Princess Mary looking very pretty with her – but I think how stupid it was, she was not dressed in her VAD uniform. If ever there was an appropriate moment this was it. There were 36 VADs just over from Canada all thrilled at seeing the Queen and they would have been so pleased if Princess Mary had been in uniform. They haven't much imagination I am afraid.'

She also became involved with Americans in London who were responsible for the care of American wounded troops in Britain and France. She already knew Mrs Whitelaw Reid, a rich American philanthropist and social activist whom the Greys had met in San Francisco in 1914. The wife of Whitelaw Reid the newspaper man and American Ambassador to Paris, Elizabeth Whitelaw Reid had helped to run the Red Cross Society in the United States and in the Philippines. In 1918 she served as Chairman of the England chapter of the American Red Cross, in London.

Sybil found herself in the position to influence the kind of hospitals the Americans established in England. The Americans had a preference for hospitals exclusively treating their own troops, whereas Sybil was keen to see integrated wards with both American and British patients: 'I am trying to work that the Americans and British should be mixed up in hospitals and convalescent homes here. It is our one chance of making friends and getting to know one another. I am going to see Mrs Whitelaw Reid about it tomorrow morning and General Goodwin.' She secured General Goodwin's agreement that Americans would not be segregated in their own hospitals, and she challenged the arrogant assumption of one American, Major Griscomb, that only their own doctors were any good.

As the Great War drew towards its close in 1918, a new threat raised its head – the so-called Spanish Flu became an epidemic which swept the world killing more people quicker than the war itself. In June Sybil noted that many people were catching flu: 'Everybody is getting this flu – most of the parlour maids are down with it. I have been feeling like a wet rag for two days but after taking cachets every four hours for the last three days I have warded off the Spanish disease.'

Politics was also never completely absent from her thoughts. 1918 saw a number of strikes, as workers, aware of the revolutionary situation in Rusia, challenged the British Government on pay and conditions. The most critical of these was the railway strike. Sybil commented: 'I think and hope it looks as if the Government are really going to stand firm over the Strike. I trust so, if we don't we shall be lost.'

Despite the situation it was still possible to enjoy oneself. In late summer, Sybil made plans to join her young Benson cousins at their holiday retreat at Grogary on South Uist. The Bensons had gone on in advance, and Sybil received a telegram asking her to bring a few additional items: '"Bring Rex's two guns, 200 cartridges also marmalade, bacon, bicycle and books." I wired back "I am bringing two elephants and a ton of potatoes." Do they think that I'd travel on Bank Holiday with a furniture van?'

23

Peace, France and the Women's Legion

In many ways the year she spent in France immediately after World War I was Sybil's most professionally satisfying.

She felt the need to continue to contribute more rather than just remaining as head of the Dorchester House Hospital at her uncle's London home. Her instincts took her to serve as commandant in France of the Women's Legion – one of the first uniformed detachments of women attached to the British Army, providing drivers of staff cars and ambulances, taking over the role of men who were either required for other military duties or who were being demobbed.

In many ways Sybil was well suited to joining the army – we've seen how she viewed herself as having masculine qualities – the 'Palmist' had colourfully told that she had lived several previous lives as a man and had fought as a soldier.

Commanding the Women's Legion in France brought out Sybil's strengths – she took the role of organising and administering the Legion very seriously, addressing issues as wide-ranging as housing the girls, inspecting their units, drawing up rules and enforcing discipline when wearing the King's uniform, winning over grumpy and distrustful commanding officers who resented having to work with women, and resolving disputes with the local French population. Most of all she had to address the problem of keeping 500 young and not so young women from getting too amorously involved with their opposite numbers – the young officers whom they drove round and with whom they went off on expeditions for days at a time.

Sybil wrote to her mother: 'You see, they have such opportunities... they are the constant companion for a week's time with one officer... and the officers are not all what they used to be! So don't be surprised if I return with a white head!' She had to take aside the worst offenders, and give them the choice of reining in their instincts or being sent home. She became quite unpopular with some of the Women's Legion staff, who took her to be an unbending disciplinarian.

She soon got used to being in uniform and touring the many units which the Legion had scattered all across northern France, Flanders and Belgium. She wrote to her mother: 'I now walk quite unconcernedly into a strange officers' mess to dine with their officers'. Afterwards she would go off to their office to discuss their needs in terms of drivers, cars, accommodation, discipline and the like. It was the job which most involved her in administration and planning, from the initial expansion of numbers of staff car and ambulance drivers required, and then just as rapidly the requirements to downsize and finally demobilise the Legion in response to War Office directives.

Sybil in the uniform of the Women's Legion (Boyd family collection).

It also gave her scope for social activity – visiting far-flung units of the Women's Legion to have tea in their camps – sometimes in Nissen huts lovingly decorated by the girls, sometimes under canvas. Divisional commanders gave dances which the Women's Legion were happy to attend. Sybil also had the opportunity to play golf – at Wimereux where the Women's Legion were headquartered, there were wonderful links on the green sward all along the coastal cliffs – one day Sybil recorded playing 32 holes! She took out a six-month subscription to the local golf club for Fr. 75 (a little over £2!)

And she found the time and opportunity to visit defeated and occupied Germany, visiting her friend Violet Carruthers and her husband Col Jim Carruthers, and experiencing the enormous disparity in purchasing power between the English whose money could afford almost anything in the shops, and the Germans who experienced a horrendous fall in the value of their currency and savings, together with the numerous other slights and humiliations suffered by a conquered people. Presciently, she warned of the terrible consequences of heaping indignities on the Germans.

It had all begun earlier that year in 1919, when Sybil travelled to France for a quick trip with her sister-in-law Mabel and her brother Charlie. They visited a detachment of women driving ambulances for the army at Étaples – which may have given Sybil the idea of working with the Women's Legion later that year.

They went on to Paris, where they mingled in distinguished political circles. The great Versailles Peace Conference was in full swing which established the terms of the reparations and territorial losses imposed on the vanquished nations, and the shape of the New World order. Four great empires had foundered in the war – Russia, Austria-Hungary, Germany and Ottoman Turkey. The world would literally never be the same again. Sybil's cousin Rex Benson was attached to the British delegation at Versailles, and they were invited to dinner at the flat of the Foreign Secretary and former Prime Minister, A. J. Balfour, in the company of Robert ('Bob') Cecil (later Viscount Cecil), Under Secretary of State for Foreign Affairs who had helped facilitate Sybil's passage to and from Russia and who became one of the architects of the League of Nations.

Sybil found herself seated beside T. E. Lawrence 'Lawrence of Arabia': 'I had expected rather a fine imposing-looking person, and instead found a very small rather insignificant looking little man. He was very amusing and entertained me considerably by giving me candid opinions on all the great men in Paris – but I couldn't make up my mind on what I really thought about him.' Also at the dinner were the Aubrey Herberts, Sir Henry Wilson (Britain's Chief Military Adviser at the Versailles talks), Rex Benson and a 'bosom friend' of Rex's from Ireland, and a clever Frenchman called Dillon. There were several interconnected circles operating at this party. First, T. E. Lawrence was at Versailles to advise on the Middle East. So too was Aubrey Herbert, a maverick MP and a legendary traveller in Mesopotamia, Albania and Turkey (said to be the original of John Buchan's hero Sandy Arbuthnot in *Greenmantle*, he was twice offered the crown of Albania). And Balfour himself was forever associated with the Balfour Declaration of 1917, establishing the right to a Jewish homeland in Palestine.

Intelligence was also a focus – Rex Benson was involved in intelligence, as was Aubrey Herbert and, at some stages, Lawrence. And finally Ireland – Sir Henry Wilson was one of the senior British officers most antipathetic to Irish nationalism (he was murdered by the IRA in 1922), and Rex Benson had served in Ireland after the Easter Rising was put down in 1916, as perhaps had his 'bosom' friend. Rex's brief involvement in the pacification of Ireland after the Rising (which disgusted him and led him to request a transfer to Haig's intelligence staff in France) may explain my mother's odd story that Sybil had once been on an IRA death list.

As well as visiting Paris, Mabel and Sybil stayed at Rex Benson's residence in Chantilly, where he was quartered in a house belonging to the Rothschilds. While they were there they were the subject of an elaborate prank – they were arrested (at Rex's request) by the local French commander for not having the right papers, only to be told that it was an 'April Fool'. They also had their first flight in an open light aeroplane – also at Rex's invitation. Sybil wrote to Evy: 'I had no idea what a marvellous view of all the country one had… Looking over the side doesn't make one in the least giddy.' But she asked Evy to keep the news of such a dangerous adventure secret from their mother.

When the job in charge of the Women's Legion in France came up in the summer of 1919, Sybil applied for it eagerly. She wrote to her mother – 'You are absolutely angelic about my going… I can't help thinking that this is a very good job and that I'm very lucky to have got it.' She arrived in Wimereux, headquarters of the

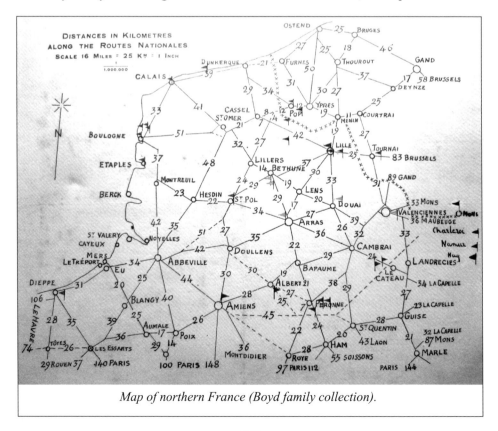

Map of northern France (Boyd family collection).

Women's Legion, to find that her predecessor Lady Margaret Lock was pregnant and ill, and had done virtually no administrative work – it was all in chaos. Wimereux was then (and is now) a small resort town near Calais, with a large British presence that had been established in World War I. Sybil stayed at the Hotel Splendide on the seafront overlooking the huge expanse of beach, frequently covered with bathers. She wrote: 'My room looks out over the sea… At high tide I could almost throw an orange into the water.'

The Women's Legion had established administrative areas across northern France and Belgium – each with their own sub-areas – ranging from Brussels down to Rouen, with headquarters at Valenciennes, Flixecourt, Namur and Lille. Many of the sub-areas were names well-known to the British Army in the First World War – Bethune, Arras, Mons, St Quentin, Cambrai and Ypres – all associated with battles.

Sybil outlined the administrative structure and the Army's requirements: 'In each area we have to fill up all the ambulance cars before we put girls on to the HQ cars (staff cars) and in this area (Flixecourt) there are seven CCS (casualty clearing stations) where we have to send six to eight drivers and a head driver to look after them. The superintendent lives with the lot at HQ and is given a motor of her own in which she visits all the scattered units in her area.'

Accommodation for the Women's Legion varied enormously, ranging from uncomfortable Nissen huts to purpose built camps. Elsewhere they caused a sensation. At Lille they were housed in the great Monastery St André, where they had sent three units of the Women's Legion: 'We found them settling down quite comfortably, but with no stove to work with – …So for the moment they're sharing the monks' kitchen with them – *scandal terrible!* …I saw the Prior and he said he didn't mind at all.'

She drove to visit her units through the devastated countryside of Flanders, visiting towns that had been reduced to rubble in the war. She wrote to her mother:

> There is not the slightest doubt that from Menin to Ypres shows you the best what the battlefields are like… In so many places they have filled up all the shell holes and have crops growing – but here there is nothing of that and all the shattered trees look so desolate – shattered as far as you can look in any direction and here you see numerous derelict tanks and altogether it is awful.

She saw little hamlets on the 160 mile drive to Ypres where nothing remained standing: 'From Ypres to Albert we didn't see a single whole house, even the little houses along the roadside, or in the small villages one passed, which by the way you often didn't even realise there had been a village there – all traces obliterated except for a few heaps of stones.'

She described the extraordinary detritus of the ruins:

> We found one woman at Bailleul whose house was down a little cul-de-sac… that home seemed to be the only standing thing amongst acres and acres of chaos composed of bricks and mortar and every conceivable thing peeking out of the heaps of stones, old velvet chairs, innumerable dud shells of every size, unexploded hand grenades, broken crockery, old bits of bedding and beds, clothes, whole parts of house blown out and the upper storeys hanging down as if by a hair.

Women's Legion and ambulances (de Wesselow collection).

She nevertheless was enjoying her stay at the hotel and observing its inmates and owner: 'Monsieur Le Patron is a very smart young man of about 40 who I think was trained as an opera singer. He has a beautiful trained voice and all the family play and dance and sing.' She described how after dinner was cleared away every evening, the tables were pushed to one side and M. Le Patron's wife, children, brother and sister-in-law and cousins all sat in a long straight line beside the piano, 'and then our friend with a captivating smile enters the arena, and sings like a bird'. Sybil enjoyed the spectacle but watched from a distance through the glass doors of the dining room: 'I hadn't the courage to enter the room to face the long line of relatives.'

Her 'boss', Miss Christabel Ellis, came out on a two-day visit from England and Sybil arranged a whirlwind tour of as many units as possible: 'Miss Ellis and I start out at 7 a.m. tomorrow for Hesdigneul, Bethune, Douai, Valenciennes and Mons. Monday we go to Arras, Poulanville, Flexicourt, and back to Boulogne and try to catch the 5 o'clock boat. It will be a rush but I think we can do it.' Miss Ellis was pleased with what she saw 'she found all the girls very happy and doing good work'. In the General's HQ Mess they heard great praise of some of the girls, principally because they'd turned out to be very good riders – 'One of them they assured us was a marvellous rider and was going to train their polo ponies for them.' Sybil shot back a reply: 'I suggested that if her car was in the workshop oftener than it ought to be that we should institute an enquiry into it.'

She liked and admired Miss Ellis: 'She is a very cheery companion and I thought

very tactful – and a very strong will, which one could see by the shape of her chin.'
She reminded Sybil of another strong woman – her brother Charlie's mother-in-
law Lady Selborne – who had journeyed to the Middle East and India in the middle
of the war in fruitless search for her missing son Robert Palmer. 'I should think
that like Lady Selborne she would start for the uttermost ends of the Earth at a moment's notice just because someone told her that she wouldn't. …A great sense of
humour. I can quite believe that she would never work under anybody.' But she
conceded that Miss Ellis would be difficult to work for.

Miss Ellis wanted propaganda pictures to be taken of the Women's Legion at
work and play – and commissioned Sybil to tour with a 'tame photographer'. Sybil
commented: 'I am now on a photographic tour – tomorrow I go to Charleroi and
Namur taking fascinating photographs of fascinating motors, driven by fascinating
Women's Legion drivers.'

Miss Ellis's visit was a success and Sybil commented: 'It was very useful her
coming out because she could see for herself the reason for certain things we wanted
done, and also things we did not want done. She also saw the crying need for drivers, drivers and yet more drivers being sent out immediately.'

On her return home, Miss Ellis made injudicious light hearted remarks to the
press about having seen generals dancing at a party in Wimereux. It led to criticism
of the role of the Women's Legion in France, giving the impression that it was
purely frivolous.

Just as Sybil painted a sympathetic and entertaining picture of Miss Ellis, she
also perceptively described her army opposite number, Colonel McLeod, at the office in Wimereux: 'He's been in the office for four years now, he is a tremendously
hard worker, rarely takes holidays and you find him always between 9 a.m. and
7.30 p.m. He is terribly tired, his eyes twitch and he bites his nails, and in this hot
weather mops his brow and says his life is a washout and that he hopes he will
never hear the word transport again. Then every few minutes one of the areas rings
up on the telephone.' With dry amusement she commented: 'Poor Col. McLeod
can't swear whilst I'm in the office so all he can do to relieve his feelings is to bite
his nails a little more persistently.'

Out in France, Sybil faced the problems of enforcing discipline. She wrote: 'I've
just had to make a second-class Supt revert to being a head driver, not because she
had misbehaved but because she couldn't keep sufficient discipline and didn't realise quite what the girls can't do. I felt an awful brute.' She also faced girls whose
hearts had led them astray. She talked to one driver at Poperinghe: 'Her trouble is
that she is very pretty and she loses her head completely over men;' and to another
at Flexicourt: 'She's been engaged to one officer, thrown him over and was talked
about with another officer, and all the time was engaged to somebody back in London.' The girl told her that she couldn't help it if men were so silly. There followed
'a long but very kind lecture from Sybil Grey and removal from Flexicourt to the
Base.'

She shared her problem with Gen Williams who sympathised: 'I have two gentlemen in the area, that is all! Some of my officers are out and outers and there are

many very bad hats who are not be trusted with a woman.' She also commented that the Belgians and French 'can't begin to understand the British girls consorting with officers', a position made worse by the fact that the authorities had housed one lot of girls in a building used by the Germans as a 'house of ill fame'.

Sybil finally had to lay down the law. She wrote to her sister Evy:

> My Darling Popsqueak, I'm having a stormy time, my Supt told 70 girls here that I would in future rigidly enforce certain rules re wine and late passes. They all asked to see me, so last night I made them a speech (very carefully thought out) on general deportment when you are wearing the King's uniform.

The girls weren't happy and petitioned Sybil to change her mind. Sybil wrote:

> they really wanted to dance every night – I allowed them one late pass a week till 1.30 so that they could dance at the Casino in Boulogne, one late pass for dinner and bridge and one dance every week in their own mess. I call it liberal, most liberal, and then they dare to grouse. I asked them whether they'd come out to dance or drive motors. After she left she heard that they complained what was the use of a discussion when all they came up against was a stone wall!

Her great friend Aileen Roberts visited, and Sybil took her to see the Menin Ridge and Sanctuary Wood which was 'crawling with trippers and their motors'. Aileen was the daughter of Field Marshall Lord Roberts and had known the Greys at least since their time in Canada. References to Aileen crop up often in both Sybil's and

Women's Legion staff cars (de Wesselow collection).

Countess Alice's letters, and I wasn't able to place who she was until I read that she and Sybil had visited the scene of Aileen's father's death in France – Field Marshall Roberts had died of pneumonia at St Omer in November 1914 while visiting the troops. Aileen succeeded to her father's title as Countess Roberts of Kandahar, Waterford and Pretoria. She was twelve years older than Sybil, who seems to have been drawn to older women, perhaps remembering her elder sister Vera. Aileen remained a close friend of Sybil's until her own death in 1944.

Sybil was having to wrestle with the often contradictory demands for increasing or decreasing the size of the Women's Legion. They absorbed 50 WAACs drivers into the Legion, and in the late summer she noted 'our last draft comes out on Tuesday – 90 strong – we will then have 540 in the country. By the middle of October we'll be sending people home because the areas are closing and the cars are naturally being reduced.'

The women in the Legion put up surprisingly cheerfully with rough conditions. Some girls had rats in their bedrooms – one girl told Sybil 'two were playing on the table by my bed last night but when one slipped out of my pillow by mistake it was rather tiresome!' Sybil commented: 'tiresome isn't the word I would use!'

She joined them in a woodland camp at Hesdigneul near Bethune where a unit of about 30 was under canvas. 'Nobody had ever thought of having a campfire at night! So after supper I organised a fatigue party to collect wood – we had a glorious campfire. I don't think any of them had ever camped before.' She commented: 'It is rather sad the way most of them have no idea what they're going to do when they are demobilised. The greater majority of them must earn their livelihood and I think they are dreading the day they have to be demobilised.'

By November things became increasingly difficult. Sybil wrote:

> I'm not having a very easy time just now. It is impossible to get things done because there aren't enough people in the country to do them. They all say they feel more uncomfortable now than they were during the war. Transport is becoming increasingly difficult – no fitters or mechanics left to mend ambulances and motors. One unit has perhaps 30 in a rotten wooden camp and in deep mud, with two roofs leaking. Snow stops work. The ambulances are literally tumbling to pieces. They have run since 1914. It is pretty disheartening trying to keep that sort of broken down thing on the road and then come back to a cold damp hut with the rations not having arrived because they had been snowed up.
>
> Five girls came in this morning from Lille, they'd started in their ambulance at 12 a.m. on Saturday and they arrived here at midnight on Monday – spent 60 hours on the road.

Some of the women were indeed very tough – she was told: 'One of the WAACs we took over from Calais had come down in a parachute 360 times! The officer who she is driving told me that she had once saved a girl's life by bringing her down in the parachute with her. She is a very good looking girl but very tall and powerfully built. The officer says that if anything goes wrong with the car he leaves it to her. I immediately obey because I feel she could take me up between her finger and thumb and drop me in the ditch.' It is difficult to believe that any woman could have made 360 parachute drops at that time – Sybil was said by some relatives to be very credulous.

An idea of the demands of the job can be gleaned from this account of convoy work:

> I had to go and see about 20 girls down at Rouen who are doing convoy work – bringing a hundred cars up to Abbeville from Rouen. Very hard work it is because they are very old cars. They generally leave Rouen about 10 a.m. and arriving at Abbeville, the lucky ones with decent cars, about 5 p.m., but the majority with dud ones arrive about 3 a.m. The next day they have to come down in a huge charabanc which shakes them to pieces on these roads.

The girls were nevertheless all very cheerful and full of their different adventures, despite sometimes facing danger.

> One girl had broken down just as it was getting dark in the Forêt de Eu, a huge place. She was there 4½ hours before she was rescued by the fitters who are supposed to be with the convoy instead of 4½ hours behind it. The girl had been terrified having heard terrible stories of British soldiers who been sandbagged by ruffians living near the forest.

They later heard reports of the murder of two uniformed women, ironically blamed by the French newspapers on two Scottish soldiers.

In the midst of all this Sybil took the opportunity of travelling to Germany to visit her friends Violet Carruthers and her husband in Cologne, where Col Carruthers was stationed as part of the occupying British Army.

It seems that Sybil had in fact already visited Germany the previous year and she was interested in the relationship between the Germans and their occupiers:

> It is deeply interesting here. The shops are wonderful and I ache to buy everything. The rate of exchange is terrible for the Germans but as far as buying goes it is wonderful for us. 180 Marks to the pound. When I came to Cologne after the Armistice the exchange rate was 40 – so the man who had a capital of £100,000 a year ago is now worth about £12,000. You can see very good hats for 160 Marks, not £1 to us English.

She and Violet Carruthers went window shopping and were able to think about buying almost anything – from life like toy dolls to excellent Zeiss binoculars. Sybil was increasingly sympathetic to the Germans.

> Of course this is out and out the cheapest place for English people to live today – but what is actually going to happen to the Germans I can't think. They're much more bitter with the French than with us. The French are much harder on them than we are – I believe this is a great mistake for it simply makes them more determined to get their own back just as soon as they're strong enough to do it – as Violet says 30,000 cannot sit on 60 million for ever.

The French had decided to deliberately quarter black colonial troops on German households instead of putting them in barracks. Sybil heard that a 'French officer of high standing told one of our generals here that they were doing this… in order to deteriorate the German blood.' Sybil was scandalised and the French practice of billeting colonial troops in this way led to questions being asked in the House of Commons.

Sybil concluded: 'It can only mean another huge war if you deliberately drive strong people to desperation whatever the crimes they may have committed. One can only put oneself in their shoes and realise what one would feel oneself.' Nevertheless she enjoyed visits to the opera: 'We went to Tannhauser last night which was really superbly given. The orchestra was splendid, the acting and singing very good and the *mis en scéne* wonderful.'

Another British military couple, Gen Hutchinson and his wife, lived in a beautiful house in Cologne filled with lovely tapestries and beautiful old Italian furniture, formerly used by the Kaiser on his visits to Cologne. Sybil described the humiliation felt by the owners of the house – a German Baron and his wife.

> The Baron and Baronne also live in the house but in the backrooms and she loathes these foreign conquerors. At first she gave them nothing but inferior china and table linen, etc. So the general said he was not accustomed to eat off such common stuff and will they at once put out a proper service for him. Apparently he stands no nonsense and is now at once given what he asks for... How galling it must be for them passing these English on the stairs every day as you try and sneak out of your own house by the back door, seeing these foreigners sitting in your rooms using your furniture and sending you curt notes if they don't get all they wanted. How should we stand for it – Tottie at Dorchester House for instance?

But the Germans remained inscrutable – 'I thought they take it remarkably well, outwardly at any rate. What they feel in their inmost heart nobody can tell. But I don't think their thoughts can be pleasant.' Of the French she says, 'I'm sure that if you make your period of occupation a time of unnecessary hardship – then you're only shortening the time before the next war. The idea of billeting black troops on people in order to degrade them is hardly one that can help the future peace of the world.'

Her mother Countess Alice visited Sybil in France in mid-November. There is no record of the visit (as most of Sybil's letters were written to her mother) but it seems that she was driven around to see the sights including the battlefields. Later Sybil had other guests including her cousins Guy Benson and his sister Rosalind Benson.

On Christmas Day 1919 the various Women's Legion areas gave Sybil presents – Area 1 presented her with an umbrella chosen by her mother Countess Alice, Headquarters gave her a silver centrepiece for a table and Area 3 a lovely silver box. Rather ungratefully she says: 'It means I have to make speeches of thanks wherever I go at every lunch and dinner for the next four days, it's awful.' Sybil did not like speaking in public.

She also claimed not to enjoy dances but was persuaded to drive to St Pol for the general's dinner dance, hoping to get home by 12.30 a.m. Instead she and her driver, Crosbie, broke down in a flooded part of the coast road near Boulogne and had to sleep in the nearly flooded car. 'The sea kept landing in heavy thuds on the hood and the motor, and the water kept on getting deeper until there was nearly eighteen inches and I wondered how soon it would get into the engine and the mag-

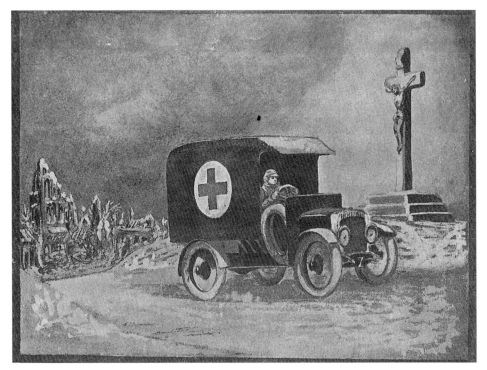

Women's Legion Christmas card (de Wesselow collection).

neto. You feel so silly at 3 a.m. sitting in a motor that is literally being rocked by the sea.' They were rescued early next morning.

She was a close observer of social situations, with a writerly talent for description. She left an amusing account of her visit to her friend, Mrs Turner, at whose house a young Mademoiselle de Tître had arranged to meet the love of her life – a young English officer. The English officer's train was delayed and the young lady's frustration and feverish anticipation mounted. She told Sybil that marriage to a Frenchman would be out of the question:

> She was absolutely open telling me how hateful French marriages were – how no Frenchman believed in real love, and how the whole thing was buying and selling. How her Mother was dead, so luckily she had some money of her own that her Father couldn't touch and how he had said that if she married this Englishman that he would turn her out of his house and that she wouldn't get a penny of his money. How she had two brothers, one who like her believed in love and wished to marry an English girl and backed her up – and the other brother was nothing but a traitor and was dead against her.

She remained absolutely determined to marry her 'chic anglais'. The young Englishman arrived (Sybil thought him very disappointing – 'a washed out canary') but as they embraced each other in the next door room, the maid announced the arrival of Mademoiselle's brother. Sybil was enthralled at witnessing the scene: 'I was thrilled to the marrow, was this 'le traiteur' or the good brother? In my heart of hearts I rather hoped it was 'le traiteur'. I felt a really dramatic scene would follow but it turned out to be Gui who sympathised with his sister.' Sybil added: 'I now find that the brother Gui is pursuing two very nice Legion girls at Boulogne and that he asked someone the other day which had the biggest dot (dowry)! Aren't they funny. I must say I haven't enjoyed a tea so much for ages.'

In her travels round Flanders and northern France, Sybil could not help seeing the new British military cemeteries. She was full of praise for their uniform design and for the headstones designed by Lutyens. She described one such cemetery at Forceville:

> All the 2,800 British cemeteries are to be done the same. It will take years and be very expensive, but I was much impressed by it. The whole cemetery is walled round by a wall of smooth white stone. And at the east end, in the centre, there is a tall cross made with the same stone. In the centre of the cross is a long metal sword with a gilt handle.

She provided a sketch of the sword and of the uniform headstones. 'At the opposite end of the cemetery, the west side, is a sort of Cenotaph of the same white stone. Every grave has a white tombstone all in long rows with the inscriptions towards the cross at the east.' She approved of all the ranks being buried together: 'I think it is quite right that all the graves should be done the same – the same tombstones for general and private and as a *tout ensemble.*'

While in France, Sybil also heard about Arthur Grenfell's latest business venture in Roumania: 'I hear from Evy that Arthur has gone back to Roumania and that he hopes to be back in three weeks. Does that mean that he will have got his concession through? It is most exciting. If it is, will it mean in a few years a great deal of money to A?' It is not clear what Arthur's new venture was but Sybil's other brother-in-law, Jonah Jones, travelled out about this time on the Orient Express to Bucharest on behalf of the British Overseas Bank to negotiate a large loan for the Roumanian Government.

In due course the time came for the demobilisation of the Women's Legion and their return from France. By the end of March she wrote to her mother 'I have settled that I'm coming home on 24th of April – by then I shall have demobilised everyone with the exception of here and at Calais.' The Legion had done important work, showing that women could efficiently drive ambulances and staff cars, relieving the pressure on the Army to provide manpower. After she left France, Brigadier General E. Gibb wrote to the War Office to express his appreciation of her service:

> She has held the appointment of overseas commandant since July 1919 and throughout this period her administration has been marked by success. She has combined sympathy and tact with firmness and good disciplinary powers. She has displayed great energy and vitality, and her frequent visits of inspection to all detachments of the Women's Legion distributed over this large area has resulted not only in the maintenance of a high standard of discipline in the contingent but has also secured for them the maximum welfare and comfort which circumstances have permitted. No case of serious indiscipline has occurred amongst the personnel of the Women's Legion and I attribute this largely to the efficiency of their commandant.

He added:

Lady Sybil Grey has helped in no small degree in the administrative work at these Headquarters by cooperating with and establishing the most happy relations with other heads of Women's Corps serving in France and Flanders, and her advice based on sound common sense and good judgement has always proved of the greatest assistance to my staff and to me.

PART III

Estevan Lodge, Grand Metis (Reford family collection).

24

Grand Metis, 1920

Sybil had given her all in her work for the Women's Legion in France (with time off for the occasional game of golf). She needed to recharge her batteries and have a complete change, and she inevitably thought of Canada, Grand Metis and Elsie Reford.[1]

The Greys had known the Refords since at least 1906 when Earl Grey described Sybil's first fishing expedition in New Brunswick in the company of the Refords: 'Sybil has enjoyed her trip down the Restigouche immensely. I wish you could have seen her, the Tiger and Mrs Reford in moccasins and short petticoats, looking like three Howick bondagers. They all enjoyed the camping out life, notwithstanding that the mosquitoes made heavy incursions, with disfiguring results upon them all.'

Elsie Reford had helped Earl Grey with the setting up of the Quebec Tercentenary and had kept up a close personal correspondence with him. She was ten years older than Sybil Grey, a friend of her father and mother as well as of Sybil. Talking to Elsie Reford's great-grandson, Alexander Reford and his partner Trish they described Elsie as gifted and driven, a headstrong woman, even at times almost tyrannical, who would perhaps have preferred to have been a man. (Her act of 'tyranny' was to bar her son Bruce from Montreal because of his heavy drinking, although she nevertheless in the end gave him Grand Metis). She had hoped that her husband would become a politician, as she herself perhaps would have wished to be.

Elsie Reford had been given Grand Metis by her uncle Lord Mount Stephen – a self-made millionaire, railroad and banking magnate who originally came over penniless to Canada from Scotland. The heart of Grand Metis was a fishing lodge on the south shore of the St Lawrence. Estevan Lodge was a large rambling two-storey white wooden building with a wide veranda and lawn looking out over the great seaway. The Metis River, full of wild salmon in June and July, ran out into the St Lawrence below it. In the woods and on the slopes around the house, Elsie would later establish the most northerly garden in Canada, famous for its blue Himalyan poppies (*Meconopsis Betonicifolia*) and other exotic species.

Grand Metis was Sybil's idyll of a wild existence. Life was relatively simple there, certainly compared to the formal and lavish lifestyle of Ottawa and Montreal. Estevan Lodge was in essence a fishing lodge – although its servants wore livery, life was stripped down to the basic purpose of catching wild salmon. Sybil craved

---

1 Elsie Reford (née Meighen, 1872-1967). She married Robert Reford and had two sons, Bruce and Eric. She was a close acquaintance of Albert, 4th Earl Grey, working with him on the Quebec Tercentenary in 1908. She was a close friend of Sybil.

that kind of simplicity, a life without adornment, which was nevertheless comfortable and spent relaxing with friends, in a beautiful wild environment. During a later crisis in her life she described the place as 'soul satisfying' – and she returned there throughout her life at times of crisis or when she faced a great decision.

Sybil set off for Canada in mid June 1920. On the train she overheard a fellow passenger declare that she had 'fidgety legs… when one can't keep still'. Sybil commented 'I felt inclined to say "Oh, so have I"… Evidently it is not purely a Grey disease.'

On board the steamship *Mimedosa*, she complained that the weather was bitterly cold and blowing a gale. She declared 'the Atlantic is a beastly place. I've come to the conclusion that I must like Elsie and the salmon very much indeed.' They could not get daily news on board because they had sailed without Marconi men – the steamer line had refused to employ unionised radio operators. The captain however secretly had a backup Marconi operator travelling in third class in case of emergencies.

She was dismissive about most of her fellow passengers, but was very intrigued by one cabin class passenger – a 56-year-old barber from Bristol – who was travelling to Canada to fulfil his ambition to go over the Niagara Falls in a barrel. Sybil said, 'I'm told that he's quite happy and not thinking of suicide… It's a curious ambition to have at the age of 56 isn't it?' She described the barrel:

> It is 6 foot 2 long, well-padded. It has a weight of 160 lbs at the bottom so it should ride on the water. He meanwhile is strapped in in the right position. He takes breathing apparatus which would last him eight hours if necessary, also a battery to give himself electric light. He is put in 1,000 yards above the falls and he expects to be in the water 10 minutes before he is picked up.

The Englishman's name was Charles Stephens and he duly went over the Falls two weeks later on 11 July 1920. Sadly, he did not survive, but sank to the bottom and only one of his arms was recovered.

Arriving in the St Lawrence Seaway she asked to be dropped off with the locals at Rimouski, a small port halfway up the St Lawrence. She was taken ashore by the Pilot Boat and driven the final 30 miles to Grand Metis:

> A 60 horse power motor – very bad sandy roads and all turns and twists, but we flew round them, I hanging on with both hands. My driver hoped that I was not scared and said that he had driven over 150,000 miles. I said oh, oh n no, and resigned myself to my fate. We accomplished the 30 miles in 55 minutes. It was a wonderful night – moon out over the river and the heavy scent of pine trees and the place alive with fireflies. I found Elsie and Mr Reford, the Bruces and Evie. Their motor was broken otherwise they would have met me.

She relaxed in the environment she loved: 'Sunday, a lovely day. I unpacked and lay out on the veranda in one of those comfortable Canadian bed hammocks like yours at Howick. It was most peaceful and delicious looking over the river.'

They told her that there were hardly any fish in the river: 'either it's going to be a very bad year or the fish owing to a great deal of late ice are only just beginning to come in. Seven fish, their catch to date.' The problem was blamed on many different things – on late ice preventing the fish from coming into the rivers; on hot bright sunshine which made it difficult to fish during the morning and afternoon; and finally on torrential rain which turned the river into a muddy flood.

> Having quarrelled with the lovely fine dry weather and longed for rain we are now having it to our undoing. It has rained steadily since Friday night and now it is still raining at 11 a.m. Monday. The river has risen over a foot and is a dark chocolate. The glass gets tapped every hour but still shows signs of falling. The farmers who were praying for rain now fear that the roots will be washed away – are farmers or fishermen ever satisfied with the weather? I don't expect they are.

They waited in enforced idleness for the rain to stop and the river level to fall:

> whilst it rains we can't take exercise, we overeat ourselves so disgustingly on Elsie's supreme food that it is very bad for us. We had a huge birchwood fire in the open hearth yesterday and all sat round reading, popping corn and eating it and talking between meals. By evening I came to the conclusion that corn must swell at least five times after it gets inside you, and a walk in the pouring rain in the evening was the only thing that saved my life.

Finally, a week after she arrived she began to get good catches: 'Friday evening I had an excellent evening's fishing, getting three fish 26 lbs, 24 lbs, and 19lbs. Last week all total I got six fish averaging 22 lbs – quite good.'

She appreciated the beauty of her surroundings and of the huge river, 'The grass all round the house is one mass of daisies, a lovely blue and purple vetch and pink clover – it is a real carpet of colour. This morning the north shore of the St Lawrence, 40 miles away, is a lovely misty blue ridge of mountains over the still bluer river.'

They spent a day picnicking on a promontory jutting out into the river, 'We shall take books and cushions and I shall also take field glasses to scan the passing ships and there we shall idle away the morning – the men in canoes fetching us in time for luncheon and fresh grilled salmon. Sounds all right doesn't it?'

She told her mother who was a keen watercolour artist, 'we had a most lovely sunset here two nights ago. I longed for you and your paint box. I think you would have refused to sketch it, but you would have thoroughly enjoyed seeing it. I wish I could sketch – there are so many things I would like to sketch here.'

She also commented on Canadian politics. 'So Sir Robert Borden (the Canadian Prime Minister) has finally resigned and there is great excitement in the papers as to who will be his successor. I think Elsie hopes Arthur Meighen will get it – and from what the papers say he seems to be the first favourite.' A week later, Meighen was the Conservative politician chosen in succession to Borden and Sybil commented on his virtues:

> From all one can hear Mr Meighen the new Prime Minister must be very fine fellow – 44, very able and cultivated, courageous, absolutely straight, with very few intimate friends, not caring for society, a tremendous worker and looked upon as cold and reserved by the man in the street, very modest and unassuming – all the newspapers seem

to have more or less agreed on this.

But she saw problems ahead for him: 'He is not at all liked by Quebec and without their support will have a very difficult time.'

She picked up on news from Britain where Mary Pickford, the Canadian movie actress, was touring with her husband Douglas Fairbanks on their six-week honey-moon tour of Europe. Upon their arrival in London, Pickford and Fairbanks were mobbed by a crowd that was desperate to see them and which got out of control. A Canadian correspondent Alexander Woollcott, reported that fans 'hung from factory windows and mounted running boards and fell under the wheels.' The authorities had had to step in to protect the visitors from 'having their clothes lovingly torn from them.' Sybil commented, 'I've been reading *The Times* of June 23rd and 24th. Poor Mary Pickford, she seems almost to have been killed.'

She then heard the extraordinary news that Fernande Boutet,[2] her mother's for-mer French lady's maid and friend of the family, was accompanying Pickford:

> I'm really thrilled to hear it. I would love to be maid to Mary Pickford on a tour through France, Belgium, Germany and Italy, etc. I think it would be the greatest fun. Fernande has certainly fallen on her feet and as you say she will probably spend the remainder of her life associated with the movies in some form or other. I wonder how she got in touch with Mary Pickford. How interested and delighted Father would have been.

In fact, Fernande Boutet was to go on to an even more dramatic career. In 1938, she became the first Frenchwoman to cross Arabia, accompanying the Count of Athlone and Princess Alice of Albany. Princess Alice, was the last surviving grand-child of Queen Victoria, and was married to her German cousin Prince Alexander of Teck (who adopted the surname Cambridge and became the Earl of Athlone).

Sybil's holiday had in general been a disappointment. She wrote in mid-July, 'We have been very unfortunate over the fishing. The whole of last week the river was practically unfishable. It rose over two feet and was chocolate coloured.' And the weather then became too hot and blowy:

> We are all feeling like limp rags unable to move – temperature 90° in the shade and a howling gale blowing hot sirocco wind. We all sit about limply in chairs unable to do anything. I hope before the evening is out that a thunder storm will relieve us. Fishing today out of the question, the river still remains very high.

Fishing was also disrupted by the annual lumber industry:

> We should have had excellent fishing for the last four or five days if it hadn't been that they are having a lumber drive up the river and that every morning they open the dam of the lake 40 miles up. The river in consequence starts to rise about 9 a.m. and rises between 8 inches and a foot bringing down much driftwood. This with the natural height of the river with all the rain we have had, so unsettles the fish that it is a pure toss up

---

2 Fernande Boutet was born in 1884 in Sainte-Hermaine in the Vendée region of France. She was Countess Alice's lady's maid certainly from the time of the Grey's round the world trip in 1914 when Fernande accompanied them (and probably before), until late in the First World War. After accompanying Mary Pickford as translator on her European tour in 1929, Fernande later travelled with the Countess of Athlone and her husband across Arabia.

whether we get any or not. It is just bad luck that I should have hit upon it this year.

Returning home, her doctor, Becket Overy insisted that she should immediately take a month's rest in a nursing home. Sybil told her mother:

B.O. said he would probably allow me to get up for an hour or two every day during the fourth week but that he wanted me to have one of his own nurses who would massage me (I who hate massage) and give me exercises. I then suggested at the end of the month in bed that perhaps I might go to Englemere for ten days whilst you finished with Evy.

Elsie Reford with catch (Reford family collection).

The visit to Englemere, Aileen Roberts's home at Ascot, didn't come off. Her sister Evy wrote to their mother about Sybil's health:

Instead of arriving with Aileen, she has to go to bed in London for a month and have a hospital nurse. I think she is too tired throughout to feel much disappointment for herself, but she is acutely wretched for you, and also poor old Aileen.

The one thing to be thankful for however is that she has nothing really wrong – thank God. [B.O.] is certain of that, but her heart is a very tired one, has only part 1 instead of part 7 blood pressure. She told him that she felt generally tired out, and slack all the time, and that the one time she had played tennis her heart raced madly, and became intermittent and she had to go and lie down.

Sybil had also told her that on board ship coming home, her heart began to race badly again, just from nervousness at having to speak a few words at the concert. Evy continued:

Seeing her here, resting all day in pouring rain, she had a nice pinky colour and although seemed very tired, didn't show it so much; but last night, after a day in London, she looked very white and dragged and a wreck, and was tired out. There is no doubt, bed is the only thing. She is to be allowed to read and see a few people but not knit, and must have massage.

Evy wrote, 'She is not worrying about herself – very glad I think, to know definitely from B.O. that he was certain there was nothing organically wrong, but he wouldn't hear of her going anywhere except to bed – saying if she didn't she would very likely crack up her heart for life.' Evy thought it was due to the strain Sybil had been under: 'As we said, last night, after all Sybil has had 1½ years more war work than most of us, and never a real long holiday or rest, and a good deal of strain. Mentally her Canadian trip has done her immense good she says, and she would not have missed it for the world.'

Whatever was wrong with Sybil's health, whether due to nerves or to a physical problem, she continued to suffer periodically from these symptoms. A racing or intermittent heart is mentioned and low blood pressure is hinted at. Her concerns about her health may have been at the root of her interest in Monsieur Coué's apparently miraculous cures which we hear of in the next chapter.

25

The Healer

In February 1922, Sybil and her friend Jeanne Malcolm visited the fashionable healer, Emile Coué, in Nancy, in north east France. Coué claimed to cure patients by autosuggestion, using the mantra: 'every day in every way I get better and better'. He said that the technique allowed the unconscious mind to act positively to cure a large range of illnesses, ranging from nerves, depression, sleeplessness and asthma to those suffering from paralysis and war wounds. Patients were treated in group 'séances', and came from all levels of society – from poor French people to rich English socialites.

Jeanne was the illegitimate daughter of actress Lily Langtry and probably Prince Louis of Battenberg (although Jeanne herself apparently claimed her father was Edward VII, the former Prince of Wales). She suffered from a nervous condition, depression and asthma. Under Coué's treatment she made a recovery and she and Sybil became committed converts. They invited others to come out from England, including Lady Beatty, wife of Admiral Beatty, who also became a believer. Lambert Middleton also joined them. It may well be that Sybil's sympathy and desire to help Lambert led to their increasing attraction to each other and to their decision to marry to have a family before it was too late for them both.

Emile Coué de la Châtaigneraie was a French psychologist and pharmacist who introduced a method of psychotherapy based on autosuggestion. He trained as a pharmacist and quickly discovered the placebo effect – when he reassured clients about the efficacy of a remedy they got better quicker than those to whom he gave no reassurance.

Coué developed a comprehensive theory about how his cure worked; his guiding principle being to harness the subconscious or unconscious mind, which he believed was stronger than rational thought or the will. He taught that if a person firmly believed that his asthma is going to disappear, then this could actually happen through the power of autosuggestion. If on the other hand a patient thought negatively about the illness (e.g. 'I'm not feeling well… I'll never get better') it would encourage both his mind and body to accept this state of affairs.[1]

His treatment also seems to have relied heavily on the dynamics of group therapy – typically there would be a mix of new patients and patients who had already been cured or partly cured by Coué, who would report their progress and reinforce the

---

1 Coué's cure probably tapped into the French psychological tradition that was interested in subconscious and automatic phenomena. Hypnosis was also widely practised. (Acknowledgement is due to Ann Jefferies).

positive belief of other patients at what Sybil referred to as 'séances'.

Why did Sybil Grey, who had some professional familiarity with hospitals and nursing come to rely on a therapy that amounted to little more than the patient intoning 'I will get better'? It was a more superstitious age when it was easier to believe in 'miracle cures' which were dressed up in apparently scientific explanations. Even today many people believe, as Sybil and her friends certainly did, in complementary medicines such as homeopathy which defy scientific explanation. Also, she herself was suffering from symptoms – an 'intermittent' heart, fatigue etc – which her doctors struggled to diagnose or cure.

Her letters home showed that although she did not initially swallow all of Coué's claims, she became increasingly a 'believer' in the cure, mainly due to the apparently great improvements in the health of Jeanne Malcolm and people like Lady Beatty. It points perhaps to an unexpectedly credulous and unquestioning side of Sybil's character – one of her great nieces, Anne Dawnay described her as 'very gullible'.

Emile Coué may well have helped some people temporarily, but his methods were akin to those of faith healers, religious charismatics and cult leaders who have exploited peoples' desire to get better. His method may have had kernel of truth – that a positive attitude pays dividends in confronting disease – but sounds to have contained much that was bogus wish fulfilment.

Sybil had been to hear Coué speak in London and it was this that encouraged her to take Jeanne out to Nancy to meet him. She described Jeanne's poor state of health: 'Jeanne's nerves, although a casual outsider would notice nothing, are all to pot. She can't bear being spoken to by any stranger here about these sorts of things. She is unreasonable and she knows it. I do feel for her future happiness this trip is terribly important – if only Coué can help give her a new perspective.' She adds however that 'Jeanne is very keen, deeply interested and very much inclined to become a real believer'.

On their first visit to Coué's house they were astonished to find that instead of a plush set of consulting rooms, his sessions were held in an unassuming chalet in the garden of his house in Nancy. 'We came to a tiny house, the size of a two storied cottage… we went up a little wooden stair and were ushered into a small room. There were about 23 people sitting there packed like sardines.'

Coué's assistant, Monsieur Brasbois, asked what they were suffering from: 'Jeanne said that she was suffering from nerves and that everything worried and aggassèd (irritated) her, and I said that mon coeur était fatigué.' M. Brasbois, who referred to Coué as 'The Master', assured them that their various complaints would be completely healed or else very much improved.

She wrote: 'I was very much impressed by the humbleness of the shabby little room. People who come out with the idea that they will find a regular clinic with a big lecture room will be very much taken aback.' It was claimed also that Coué never asked for money for his treatments. The next day Coué addressed an eclectic audience of patients of different nationalities and classes, crammed into his tiny room.

Besides myself there were eight English people and about twelve French people. There was an Englishman who had been paralyzed through a wound – he can painfully walk dragging his leg and has his arm in a sling. He has been going for some time to the lectures. M. Coué was delighted because he can move slightly three fingers of his paralysed hand and thinks he will get back practically complete use of his arm and leg.

The patients had a bewildering variety of complaints. A little French boy of about twelve years old, 'such a jolly looking boy' – proudly announced that he had had no '*crises nerveuses*' since his last visit a fortnight before. A French woman had brought her thirteen year old daughter because she could not understand mathematics at school – Coué claimed that another young man attained mastery of mathematics after undergoing his treatment. Another woman brought a lame child because her friend had been cured of a long term alcohol problem by Coué.

Jokingly, Sybil wrote: 'I wish Coué could make me like writing letters. I suppose if I go the right way about it, I could bring about the desired effect.'

The following day, the patients gathered again in two interconnected tiny rooms: 'It is big enough for 22 people to sit on camp stools and chairs all touching each other as close as possible round the four walls.' They were joined by an English artist who had been cured by reading a book about Coué's method; by an Eton master, H. V. Macnaughten and his sister; and by a well to do young French merchant suffering from insomnia and '*des mauvaises idées dans la tête.*'

Some of the patients argued with Coué.

A rather smart up to date young woman from another part of France who was suffering terribly from stomach trouble… exasperated Coué by saying it was not true when he said he could guarantee that she would be cured. She wouldn't have it at any price and said that no doctor had been able to cure her and it was therefore ridiculous for Coué to say he was certain to cure her.

Coué told her bluntly, '*Quand des personnes parlent des choses qu'on ne connaisent pas, on dit Madame de grande bêtises*',[2] and she stormed out. The Eton master, Macnaughten, suffered from insomnia and '*habituelle tristesse*'.

Anything sadder or more mournful than his face I have seldom seen – he argued with Coué for at least a quarter of an hour, he told him that he didn't believe and wouldn't believe that he could make his sister walk without pain in her foot.

Watching him, Sybil felt how hard it was for highly educated people to accept Coué's method: 'One realised that it is far more difficult for people who will bring their intellect to bear on it than for the peasant who comes in with faith and questions nothing that he is told.'

Miss Macnaughten, had her foot rubbed by Coué while rapidly reciting *çe passe* at breakneck speed for 20 seconds, following which she walked round the room and admitted that the pain had lessened. Her insomniac brother was told that he would get a good night's sleep if he made no effort about it but simply thought that he would go to sleep. When he protested that he had often tried this and failed, he

---

2 'When people talk about what they don't know about, they say very stupid things.'

was told that in the past he had always had doubts at the back of his mind which prevented him being cured: '*Vous avez toujours dans votre idée une petite reservation que vous ne dormirez pas.*'

Coué explained his theory about the power of the unconscious mind. 'If one repeats at night '*Tous les jours, à tous points de vue, je vais de mieux en mieux*' – it doesn't matter if your conscious mind is thinking about something else – as long as you go on repeating this your subconscious mind will hear it.' He drew the analogy of hearing a barrel organ playing a tune in the distance – even if one was absorbed in one's tasks, one's subconscious mind would have heard it and you might find yourself whistling the tune later. He told them: 'that if they had a pain, on the first day they should close their eyes and say '*çe passe*' up to 50, 80 or 150 times as quickly as possible; each day they would find that they had to repeat it fewer and fewer times until the pain had completely gone.'

That night Jeanne put it into practice. Very sensitive to asthma, she feared she would get an attack simply walking home to the hotel. They decided that she would use the technique to 'Coué away' any manifestation of the disease.

> This morning, with great excitement, she told me that she woke up in the middle of the night with a choking sensation almost unable to breathe or to speak above a whisper. Her first thought was – heavens, I have bronchitis – no she said I will Coué, so she sat up in bed and Coué'd hard for a couple of minutes – she realised quickly that it was a bad attack of asthma. It completely went in five minutes and in another five she was asleep again. Two hours later she woke up again with the same tight choking feeling unable to breathe, with exactly the same result – to her absolutely miraculous. This morning she is bright eyed and alert a different creature. Thrilled over the possibilities of the future, whereas a week ago she honestly saw no future and felt that she would never feel well again.

However, there were ups and downs. Next day they visited a small local town and had dinner with Coué and the Macnaughtens afterwards. It exhausted both Jeanne and Mr Macnaughten, who spent sleepless nights despite repeating '*je vais dormir*'. The next morning, informed about the failure of his method, Coué rounded on the unfortunate pair: '*Mais, ce n'est pas ma faute, c'est vous qui l'avez mal appliqué.*'

They were told they should settle themselves in the most comfortable position for sleep and repeat '*Je vais dormir*' in a low voice that sounded like the droning of a bumble bee – 'go on bumble bee-ing for 10-20 minutes if necessary, and you can't help but fall asleep.'

This appeared to work. 'Both our sleepless patients went to bed droning like bumble bees with the result that they both slept nearly nine hours.' Next morning Mr Macnaughten was quite different; he was now wreathed in smiles instead of being lugubrious.

Coué's sessions continued and a succession of patients thanked him, crediting his method with curing them – including a 35 year old French workman, an epileptic, who had not had a fit since his visit to Coué a month before. A 30 year old man arrived, suffering from neurasthenia and suicidal tendencies. Coué stroked the man's head as he gabbled '*ça passe*' and the man announced that his habitual headache has disappeared.

A much more taxing problem arrived in the form of an ill looking boy of 27 with locomotor ataxia (a degenerative disease of the nervous system resulting in lack of control over bodily movements). He walked with great effort with a stick, throwing his feet out very much to the side.

> Coué made him walk without a stick and managed to get him to put his feet out straight in front of him instead of throwing them out with a sort of involuntary kick to the side. His relatives said it was the first time he had walked without a stick for six years. I think it was a great effort – he was trembling all over when he sat down – he was very afraid of falling but he did better when he got into the garden after the séance.

Coué said he ought to get infinitely better but admitted he doubted the boy would ever get really well.

Sybil herself was also taking the cure, for a variety of conditions, including varicose veins and supposed problems with her heart rate. Jeanne wrote to Countess Alice about Sybil:

> It is a real delight to see her looking better and better every day; I do assure you that her face is visibly filling out, the few wrinkles that she had are fast disappearing and quite frankly, she looks ten years younger. She told me yesterday that she felt sure her heart was better and as for her knee, she can now bend it in a way she assures me was impossible to her before and I am convinced that the swelling is less. One cannot help feeling better when at every sitting one sees and hears of the improvement in the other , 'patients' – it is little short of marvellous and almost impossible to take in at times.

Coue's assistant, M. Brasbois, offered a pseudo-scientific explanation of how the cure 'invariably works' for varicose veins:

> Inside the veins and arteries are a particularly sensitive sheaf of nerves… like an inside tube to the veins, and therefore when the subconscious mind orders them to contract they do so at once. You simply touch your leg (to draw the subconscious mind's attention to it) and think it is getting better and your subconscious mind does the rest.

Sybil herself joined in the language of conviction. She said of Jeanne:

> She is a totally different woman to what she was ten days ago. I couldn't have believed such a change possible. She looks years younger she is bright and alive etc – but naturally there is no reserve strength whatsoever yet. Her cold and her asthma were a godsend to her because she was able to Coué away both absolutely successfully. It has given her wonderful faith in Coué's teaching and confidence in her own powers of applying it. To her both things have been miraculous. She now says she will never dread asthma, she knows she is its master.

Sybil was delighted with Jeanne's progress and clearly understood the psychology of the cure:

> She had a wonderful night's sleep. I hope and trust it will be repeated again tonight – that will be one step further on – but you will understand when we have all that right, there is still much to work at, and if she is to be a happy contented woman she has to learn to think differently about nearly everything in life – that is going to take us time

and hard work, and we can only accomplish it by doing Coué all day long.

Success with the cure was dependent on a complete transformation of one's outlook:

> One has to learn to think differently about nearly everything in life –one had so often said, 'Oh, I shall never be able to do that', or 'Oh! I have such a difficult letter to write', putting such suggestions into one's subconscious mind. We have to at once undo that thought and think as Coué does that everything is easy so long as it is in the realms of possibility.

Coué said that Jeanne was particularly susceptible to suggestion, and had done herself harm in the past though being open to 'wrong suggestion'. Sybil recognised that there were likely to be setbacks. She stopped short of expressing complete confidence and belief herself: 'Of course if I were a good pupil of Coué I should have no doubts at all!'

She had very few illusions about her friend Jeanne and her health fads:

> She has foolish little fussy ideas about nearly everything in life. She now begins to realise that they only become true because she is expecting them to. If she goes outside for a second in the winter after dark without her head covered she will catch a cold. She can't possibly have her [hair] washed by a new person because her head is so tender it would hurt her and so on and so on. Jeanne realises that all this is pure imagination. But we still have a very long way to go if she is going to go home with really a new mental outlook. I rather despair of it at times – but I daresay it will come alright.

Two other very significant patients arrived on the scene, both invited by Sybil and Jeanne – Lady Beatty, wife of the First Sea Lord, Admiral David Beatty,[3] and Lambert Middleton who would become Sybil's husband later that year.

Sybil had been to see Lambert Middleton in a nursing home in England where he was being treated for his chronic illnesses – including stomach problems and skin conditions affecting his legs. She had urged him to come out to see Coué and try his cure and had lent him Coué's book, *Self Mastery*. She commented: 'my letter seems to have arrived just *à propos* when he was in the depths of despair.' It is impossible to know how often Sybil had met Lambert – this seems to be the first mention of him in her correspondence since 1910 when he worked for Earl Grey in Canada. She very obviously sympathised greatly with him and perhaps their relationship was already much closer than she revealed. Visiting him in a nursing home would certainly have furnished a preview of an aspect of their married life, when Lambert was often in nursing homes in the 1930s.

Meanwhile, Evy was involved in planning an evening conference for Coué at Jeanne's house in London, to encourage prospective patients to visit him at Nancy. And Sybil heard the good news of the marriage of her father's former ADC in Canada – Lord Harry Lascelles who had travelled with them to the Yukon in 1909. Now the 6th Earl of Harewood – he married Princess Mary, the only daughter of King George V and Queen Mary, at Westminster Abbey, on 28 February 1922. Sybil wrote: 'Fancy if ten years ago we had predicted that Harry, millionaire, wear-

---

3 Lady Beatty (née Ethel Field) American divorcee and wife of Admiral Lord David Beatty (1871-1936), British commander at the battle of Jutland, 1916.

ing the Garter would drive through the packed London streets in a golden and glass coach with the King's daughter as his bride. We should have rocked with merriment at the mere thought of it. How strange life is.'

Sybil continued to give an honest assessment of the failures of Coué's method, but usually with a qualification. She commented: 'You ask about Miss Macnaughten – no I don't think she felt much improvement – for she admitted in the end that she had a misplaced bone, so that it probably would not do her much good.' Miss Seymour another of Coué's English patients was not much better: 'she finds it very hard to walk and her hands tremble all the time. She has the courage of a lion.' Miss Seymour had been out there for three months living in a convent with a lengthy journey each day.

However, for Jeanne, the treatment seemed an undoubted success. Sybil wrote:

> I honestly believe that Jeanne has completely got it. From the very first day she under-
> stood and took in the method. I think she really is absolutely cured. She told me yes-
> terday that she never makes the slightest effort but from the first day has believed it
> blindly. She thinks this is the reason. She was so down and out on arrival and so ex-
> hausted in mind that she was incapable of reasoning at all, or trying to. She simply took
> everything that was told her without questioning in her mind the why or the wherefore.

Jeanne had believed from the first day that either Coué would be the answer or it meant drugs and misery for the rest of her life. She felt beaten and utterly exhausted 'so that her conscious mind as it were stood aside and allowed her subconscious mind to drink it all in.'

Jeanne herself felt something had fundamentally altered in her. 'She is not the same. Things that all her life have worried her will never worry her again. At first I thought that she would feel this whilst she was out here, surrounded by Coué's atmosphere and no worries, and that it might be very different when she gets home– but now I am convinced I was wrong – she has got it and has got it for good – it is wonderful.'

Lady Beatty was to become perhaps Coué's most eminent and surprising con-vert. She arrived with her husband, Admiral Lord Beatty, her young American niece, two ladies maids and one valet. She was in a much worse state of nerves than Jeanne had been on arrival and declared that she only wished to attend the 'séances' with Coué alone and not in group with other patients, or she would immediately return to Britain with her husband.

Jeanne took her under her wing and Sybil noticed how this responsibility changed Jeanne as well:

> I think it is doing Jeanne a lot of good. First she has to think of others. Secondly it is a
> terrible object lesson, she fully realises the seriousness of Lady B's condition and how
> utterly impossible she makes it for anyone round her. Oh we are all so sorry for him
> [Admiral Beatty], and for her too. How strange life is, here is a woman married to a
> man she worships and adores and who she cannot bear out of her sight, two sons she
> adores, money galore so that her slightest wish is gratified and yet who is supremely
> miserable.

Two weeks later, Sybil reported to her mother a complete turn around in Lady Beatty, who had begun by sobbing throughout her first two séances.

> Last night at dinner she laughed and talked quite happily and her little niece looked on open eyed. She hasn't seen her laugh for months. Last night she slept well and woke happy. Jeanne and I can't get over the change in her – instead of miserable eyes they are smiling today. And she says of her own accord without prompting suddenly – 'I am getting better and better'.

Lady Beatty had started to send telegrams to her ill friends urging them to come out and see Coué. Jeanne seemed also to benefit from having to look after her – 'instead of it tiring her out she throve on it and gloried in her new found strength'.

Mrs Barnett, Lambert Middleton's sister, was also fast becoming an enthusiast, having apparently had her rheumatism eased by Coué: 'She more or less creeps out of bed to unstiffen the rheumatic joints, but today she jumped out of bed and felt absolutely nothing besides Couéing a cold with absolute success, so she is an absolute believer.' By this stage, Jeanne and Sybil had been pressed into service as secretaries, enthusiastically writing English language letters of reply to Coué's prospective patients in England.

Shortly afterwards, Sybil and Jeanne left for Strasbourg, to continue their holiday on Lake Como. Before that they had the satisfaction of seeing Lady Beatty off to Paris, 'an absolutely transformed person… I have never seen anybody change in five days like Lady Beatty did. I honestly believe that, like Jeanne, she is really cured.' Lady Beatty now slept soundly, happy and no longer suffering from constipation. Back home in Paris she began to evangelise Coué's treatment to all and sundry. Her American niece wrote: 'the list of converts rapidly increases – today's bag consists of the lift man, suffering from shellshock, the manager of the hotel, Aunt Ethel's vendeuse at Callot Soeurs [a fashion house] and Sir William Orpen.'

Sybil also heard from Lambert Middleton. He said that he 'feels like a different man' and had recovered from a cold that prevented him taking Coué's treatment. It may be that Lambert was being diplomatic in saying that the cure had helped him, but he also reported that the wounded British soldier, Captain Rogerson, had convulsively moved his paralysed right leg in his sleep, as well as moving his fingers. Sybil concluded 'it shows that life is returning very gradually to the paralysed parts'.

Finally she recounted the story of the Prince of Siam and his family who were also staying at the hotel in Nancy. Sybil and Jeanne made their acquaintance only at the very end of their stay and recommended Coué to one of the women in the Prince's party who was suffering from sleeplessness, want of appetite, giddiness and '*battements de coeur*'. They took her to Coué who treated her apparently successfully. As a result the Prince, his wife and ADC attended Coué and the Prince vowed to have his method taught in Siam!

On reaching Lake Como, at the end of March, they stayed in the idyllic surroundings of the Hotel Tremezzo on the lakeside opposite the town of Bellagio. Sybil described it:

> I am writing this while sitting on the side of a hill in the most glorious sunshine. Oh, it

is such a wonderful day, it almost makes one stand up on top of the hill and shout for joy at the mere happiness of being alive. Such a wonderful view of the lake and the lovely snow-capped mountains beyond. The birds are singing, the wild flowers beginning, some of the fruit trees in blossom and quite a number of mimosa trees just getting to their best. It is a divine day as warm as June – the longer we stay here the more we like the place and the more beautiful we think it.

She reviewed the success of their visit to Coué – Lady Beatty a completely different person, Lambert Middleton and his sister improved, Jeanne transformed by the experience and by her role in helping Lady Beatty.

There is a little hesitancy when Sybil writes to her mother:

You ask about myself, what I shall say; you see I wasn't ill when I came out. Undoubtedly as far as my own feelings go my heart is infinitely better. I am practically never conscious of its intermitting now. I should say it was absolutely right and I should think my blood pressure much better.

My leg is more difficult to say. Jeanne who sees it every ten days or so says it is infinitely better. I who see it every day can't judge half so well. I think the veins are flatter and not so blue looking.

She found she could now press hard on the varicose veins and not feel it in the slightest – before they were very tender. She could bend her knee easier. Her leg still got tired, 'but I think that is to do with my thinking a good deal about it. Jeanne says I look much better, that again I am not much judge of. I am certainly very well, so I think you can be happy about me.' Sybil was clearly pleased for her friends, even if she doesn't appear to conclusively believe that the treatment had improved her own health.

What does this month with Coué tell us? Certainly that a group of fellow sufferers can be affected by a collective desire to experience a cure, which can override their individual doubts and fears. It also suggests that the treatment of neurosis benefitted to some extent from such techniques. For Sybil was it a brief interlude of shared belief with a group of sufferers who hoped desperately for a cure and were literally 'suggestible'? Or did it point to a more deep seated gullibility in Sybil about complementary and unproven medicine – which she seems to have shared with her mother Alice and with her sister Evy, and which she certainly passed on to her own family?

An interesting epilogue took place in April that year in London when Coué visited to demonstrate his technique at the big neurasthenic Pensions Hospital at Tooting. The hospital was used after the First World War as a neurological hospital for shell-shocked ex-servicemen, all badly affected by the war. Sybil's sister Evy went down to the hospital and was introduced to the doctor in charge as someone who was interested in suggestion. She told him: 'I'm very interested in Emile Coué.' The doctor responded, 'Oh, I don't think there's anything in Coué,' but a visit by the Frenchman was arranged for the following Wednesday evening.

Coué's visit to the hospital however went terribly wrong. A contemporary *New York Times* journalist told how, faced with a patient suffering from bodily tremors, Coué passed his hands with lightning rapidity up and down the man's legs and hands, intoning his mantra. The patient shrieked, contorted his face and fell to the ground. The effect of his frenzy on the rest of the shell shocked patients was swift and terrible. Man after man moaned, shrieked and flung themselves to the ground. Doctors and nurses had to run round calming the distraught patients and removing those who couldn't be controlled. The British medical establishment used the incident as a stick with which to beat Coué and to dismiss him as a charlatan.[4]

4 Source: quoted on a BBC Radio 4 programme, *Every Day in Every Way,* presented by Gillian Darley, 30.12.2012.

26

Marriage and the General Strike

Six months after their visit to Coué, on 21 September 1922, Sybil and Lambert got married at Howick. She was 40 and he was 45, and they both knew it was their last chance to start a family. Although he was habitually in poor health, he had a quirky sense of humour, an independent outlook on life and was completely trustworthy.

The following day *The Scotsman* printed a report of the wedding. Inevitably, it was most interested in the bride's dress. At 40, Sybil clearly was not going to wear virginal white, which she would probably have thought of as 'mutton dressed as lamb'. Instead she was stylishly dressed in silver grey crêpe romaine, with a flamboyant grey hat touched with black and adorned with a large drooping ostrich feather. Her sister Evy's eldest daughters, Nancy aged nine and Dinah aged six, were bridesmaids, dressed in frocks of yellow shot silk, holding wreaths of real marigolds, and wearing seed pearl necklaces given them by Lambert.

The bride was given away by her brother Charlie, 5th Earl Grey and the ceremony was performed by Archdeacon Blackett-Ord, assisted by the Rev J. Mitchell, vicar of Howick. Afterwards a small reception was held at Howick Hall for near relations only. It was clearly a deliberately low key affair.

They spent their honeymoon at Bywell House, home of Mrs Alice Barnet, a Middleton relative, where Lambert and his parents had stayed during the 1911 census.

Sybil and Lambert were old friends – they had known each other for well over ten years, ever since he had been her father's banker in Newcastle. When Lambert had been brought out to replace Arthur Sladden as Comptroller of Earl Grey's finances in Canada in 1910, Sybil had written to congratulate her mother on their new members of staff: 'They sound quite splendid, especially Mr Middleton, I somehow felt all the time that he would be a great success.' She admired him and trusted him as a safe pair of hands – her father had had several disastrous financial advisers including Sybil's brother-in-law Arthur Grenfell, who lost the Earl a great deal of money.

Who broached the subject of marriage first, and when? It was not a leap year and anyway it was not customary in those days for women to propose. Perhaps Lambert had proposed several times over the years, but there is no evidence that he did. He simply doesn't feature in Sybil's extant correspondence between 1910 and February 1922 when she went out with her friend Jeanne Malcolm to take Emile Coué's unconventional cure in Nancy.

When she does mention him to her mother in March 1922 she speaks of him as

'Mr Middleton' or 'Lambert Middleton' – never as 'dear Lambert'. He had been ill and she had visited him at his nursing home in England, had obviously felt sorry for him and had urged him to come out to try the cure. She told her mother, 'He arrives in just the same state as Jeanne did, only she says with much more real reason. He is absolutely down and out, looking on Coué as his last card.' It seems, incidentally, that Lambert Middleton did indeed have much to feel 'down' about, as he had recently had an only partially successful operation on his stomach, that left him with problems for the rest of his life.

It is not clear whether they were in love or whether it was what might be called 'a marriage of convenience'. It was probably a bit of both. They must have been drawn to shared qualities they recognised in each other – a similar sense of humour, a sense of the ridiculous. Lambert at the age of nineteen had written a pastiche of Edward Lear's nonsense poetry – called the *Book of Bosh* – for his younger siblings. One senses in him a ready and irreverent wit. Later he wrote a poem for his children, *The Lay of the Pessimist*, beginning: 'Nothing to eat but food, Nothing to breathe but air, Nothing but clothes to wear, To keep one from going nude.' It is very difficult however to be sure of his feelings as very few of his letters have survived – the ones which do have precise careful handwriting whereas Sybil's is much more flowing and free. There must have been letters between them, particularly about marriage, but Sybil doesn't seem to have saved them with her other correspondence, or perhaps she destroyed them after Lambert's death?

Lambert William Middleton, son of Henry Nicholas Middleton, was born in 1877 in Quebec. He had family links to Canada – his grandmother (née Sophia Holmes) seems to have been Canadian and his mother (née Sophia Meredith) appears also to have been born in Canada. His father's original surname was Monck, which he changed to Middleton in February 1876, just before Lambert was born. Henry Nicholas Middleton was a banker as well as being vice chairman of Northumberland County Council and a justice of the peace. From the age of three, Lambert grew up in Northumberland, first at Fenham Hall, now a suburb of Newcastle, and the family later moved to Dissington Hall, a much larger house in North Dissington near Ponteland. Lambert is recorded as living at Dissington in the censuses of 1891 and 1901. The house belonged to the Collingwood family and was rented by the Middletons. In 1901 it had a large retinue of almost twenty servants.

Lambert's grandfather, Sir Charles Atticus Monck, was a Hellenophile who as a young man was greatly struck by classical architecture on his grand tour of Greece. Although he already owned Belsay Castle (a semi-ruined mediaeval fortified house) he built Belsay Hall on the lines of a huge Doric temple incongruously positioned in the rolling Northumbrian countryside close to Newcastle. It is built of heavy masonry including thick internal stone walls and must have been very uncomfortable to live in.

In the 1901 census Lambert listed his occupation as 'banker', but in 1911 census he is recorded as 'barrister'. Perhaps in between he tired of banking which was his father's profession and studied and began to practise law. But by the 1920s he was certainly once more employed by a bank – Lloyds – which involved travel to foreign branches. He travelled on business quite regularly to Milan, the centre of finance in Italy, and in 1927 made a trip to visit the branches of the Bank of London and South America (BOLSA) in a number of South American countries, accompanied by Sybil.

Although he was witty and humorous he suffered from ill health, perhaps from his youth and increasingly as he grew older. In 1927 he found their journey to South America very trying, during which he suffered amongst other things from a poorly fitting dental plate that made it difficult for him to eat. In the late 1920s and in the 1930s he had repeated crisises because of a very painful condition of his legs and feet involving blisters, shedding skin and with open wounds, which involved treatment in various private sanatoria. He was given an alarming cocktail of drugs and medicines including morphine, strychnine, heroin, and certain 'inoculations' to help him to bear and overcome the painful condition in his legs. His health problems and his alarming medication had repercussions for the rest of his life. In photographs he invariably looks thin and ill – with a sallow complexion and with the skin stretched taut over his cheekbones and deep hollow shadows under his eyes.

Over the years Lambert's health problems never went away – reaching various peaks and climaxes. There were many days when he didn't get up until lunch time and or later, or days when he was plainly depressed, refusing to see visitors. It must have been very wearing for Sybil and one gets an impression of how the constant anxiety, and her husband's understandable fatigue and depression must have had an effect on Sybil's own spirits. However it is a burden she seems to have accepted, and at the back of her mind she must often have thought about how her own father had become an invalid in his old age and had required constant support by her mother.

Their marriage was certainly not just a picture of gloom. There are glimpses of tenderness: Lambert writing from London to his young children, ending: 'Tell your Mama that I will come and kiss her on the nose on my return,' and even in Sybil's letters in mid-1936 when she escaped to Grand Metis in Canada, suffering it seems almost from a nervous breakdown and questioning their relationship. She wrote: 'I miss you terribly, man, and just long for you, I miss your companionship and love, I miss not being able to share everything with you,' but she also talked of them getting too dependent on each other, of the need for them to recover a sense of perspective. Above all, Sybil and Lambert each entered upon marriage late in life, after 40 years of independent existence. It must have involved great adjustments to both their individual habits and life styles, and the change was perhaps greatest for Sybil. She had embraced the new freedoms available to women of her class that came with the war, and it must have in some senses felt restricting to become a wife and mother; however their choice and the desire for a family was obviously of overwhelming importance.

At this distance in time Lambert Middleton is a difficult figure to know and understand. My mother treasured the memory of her father as an amusing man and a loving father. He wrote humorous letters to his children – one in 1931, when Molly was six, told them how he had watched a 'mother water hen' on the pond racing off to save its young from straying, whilst the 'daddy water hen just swam about bobbing his head up and down and did not come to help at all, and I think he is a lazy old pig!' An adherent of the maxim 'never apologise, never explain', he seems to have adopted an amused scepticism, approaching pessimism, expecting things to go wrong. He also offered the advice (unusual today) never to mount a horse unless armed with a revolver to shoot it dead if it bolted!

Both he and Sybil shared an interest in writers and literature. They were friends of the author and politician John Buchan, who went on in 1935 as Lord Tweedsmuir to become Governor General of Canada. Lambert and Sybil suggested to Buchan the plot of one of his novels – *The Gap in the Curtain* – in which guests at a house party are involved in a madcap occult experiment in which they are each granted a momentary vision of an issue of *The Times* a year in the future, three of them reading their own obituaries. The book explores how they use that time and that knowledge.

Lambert probably encouraged Sybil's interest in photography and film and he was keenly interested in the scouting movement for boys. But overall, I get the impression that he was predisposed to be a rather solitary character, whose world was bound up in his work at the bank, where illness forced him into frequent absences. Sybil, with a much more outgoing and lively disposition, enjoyed travel whereas Lambert probably preferred to stay at home.

I can of course never know what my grandfather was like (he died eight years before I was born). He gave Sybil the children she wanted, the security of their life together and 'made an honest woman out of her'. They obviously grew together in their love and affection for each other. As Lady Sybil Middleston she adapted to family life, but perhaps he knew all too well what it sometimes cost her and the limitations it put on the world that she had been so actively a part of.

He was probably a mixture – at times an engaging companion and at others a fretful invalid. She was also a mixture – an intrepid traveller seeking new experiences, but someone who increasingly put home and family at the centre of all she lived for.

Their son Harry was born on 23 August 1923 and their daughter Molly on 4 July 1925. Sybil must have been relieved that she was able to conceive children. She settled down to a life as a proud mother. The Middletons lived in London where Lambert worked in the city at Lloyds Bank, and they periodically visited his parents who lived at Lowood, a house near Melrose in the Scottish Borders.

In the autumn of 1925, shortly after the birth of Molly, Sybil was advised by her doctors to recuperate over the winter at Folkestone with its mild climate. It was the scene of a confrontation that very nearly proved fatal. With the approval of the local council, the Middletons built a temporary wooden shelter on a cliff, where Sybil could sit out overlooking the bay. However, it was built on a beauty spot where local people were accustomed to sit and admire the view. 'A violation of public rights; push it over men' was written on the shack and one day an attempt was made to do just that and push it over, with Sybil actually inside. The story made the local press and the London papers, and Sybil kept a press clipping.

On one level, the world after the First World War appeared deceptively un-changed. Britain still retained its empire while other European Powers had lost theirs. The British Empire was indeed at its greatest geographical extent, ruling al-most a quarter of the globe, but Britain was no longer the pre-eminent industrial and military power. It would take 30 more years and another world war for pressure to build up for colonial independence. But change was underway, and Ireland was a precursor to the breaking apart of Empire. The years 1919-21 saw the Irish War of Independence, and the establishment of the Irish Free State in December 1922. Political, economic and social change also swept mainland Britain. The Represen-tation of the People Act in 1918 gave the vote to all men over 21 and to women over 30. In 1919, Nancy Astor, whom Sybil knew well, became the first woman to take her seat in Parliament.[1] Nowhere was the change in economic and political fortunes more dramatic than in the pressure for better conditions that showed itself in the General Strike of 1926.

General strike

Industrial unrest erupted in the coal mines because of cheap imported German coal and wage cuts. The Trades Union Congress (TUC) declared a general strike which lasted ten days, from 4 to 13 May 1926. Over one and a half million workers, in-cluding miners, railwaymen, dockers, and iron and steel workers, went on strike, 'from John o'Groats to Land's End'. The government enlisted large numbers of often middle-class and upper-class volunteers to help run essential services and ef-fectively break the strike.

Sybil wrote to her friend Dorothy Onslow, wife of Edward Wood, 1st Earl of Halifax, who was away in India: 'The chief feeling one has is of immense pride for one's country and the English race. To think of the general strike lasting nine days and not a single shot fired is really a magnificent achievement and I am sure it could only have happened in this country and nowhere else in the world.'[2]

Lambert enrolled as a special constable based at Scotland Yard. Sybil travelled down from Scotland on the night train to be with him 'to bind up his broken head if need be' – her one year old daughter Molly sleeping comfortably in Sybil's open suitcase. Sybil described Lambert's duties as a special constable, where many of his confrères were young medical students and members of the Harlequin Football Club:

> He spent one very lengthy day from 9.30 a.m. to 7.30 p.m. standing outside a Commu-nist office watching it, trying to capture a badly wanted Communist. His hat well pulled

---

1 Nancy (née Witcher) Viscountess Astor (1879-1964). Wealthy American socialite who married Lord Waldorf Astor. She was sharply critical of the British class system and of her husband's ac-ceptance of a peerage. She nevertheless stood for and won his old seat in Parliament. The first woman elected an an MP was the Anglo Irish Countess Constance Markievicz, elected as a Sinn Fein can-didate in 1918 but who declined to take her seat.
2 Lady Sybil Middleton to Countess Halifax. Copyright in this letter: Borthwick Institute, University of York.

over his eyes – I made him leave his eyeglass at home so he should not be tempted to use it – and eating peas and splitting the skins into the gutter – a thing he said he'd never done in London before.

They arrested the young communist, George Mills, who Lambert described as 'such a nice young boy, very well educated and talking perfect English without any accent'. Mills predicted that the failure of the General Strike would act as a recruiting sergeant for the Communist Party – Sybil wondered if he was right, the detective who accompanied Lambert thought not.

Sybil told stories of how their aristocratic friends volunteered as dockers, porters and dustmen: 'Lord Portalington was head porter at Paddington; Sir Rennel Rodd in order to set a good example went as a dustman, but he dropped a big dustbin on his foot and was put out of action for the remainder of the strike.' Her cousin Viscount Grey (the former Foreign Secretary) went and hauled on a rope in the docks, 'so you see the old and the distinguished had a variety of jobs'.

Undergraduates drove the London buses, with either a regular policeman or a 'special' sitting beside them. And Sybil delighted in telling the story of the Great Western Railway train that made the journey from Bristol to Paddington in record time because its volunteer drivers didn't know how to stop at red lights! Her cousin Rex Benson was involved in organising the distribution of the Government Gazette, a propaganda news sheet, by means of fast cars driven at night at dangerously high speeds.

The General Strike was brought to a halt by the TUC, after a court ruling that the strike was not covered by legal immunity, leaving unions liable for breach of contract and sequestration of their assets. The aftermath of the strike saw many strikers remaining unemployed or re-employed at lower wages, and a legacy of bitterness persisted.

On a personal level, Sybil saw changes which altered some of her family's homes and consigned others to history. In February 1926, a fire all but destroyed Howick Hall. It broke out at 3 a.m. in the morning while the Grey family (her brother Charles, his wife Mabel and daughters Molly and Nisset) were all asleep. The fire engine took several hours to reach the hall and on arrival it found that there was no ready source of water, which had instead to be pumped from the burn. The entire central block was gutted, but the Greys, their staff and local people managed to save many of their most prized possessions. Sadly all the rooms and interiors which Sybil had known as a child and as a young woman had been destroyed.

It took several years before Howick was rebuilt, reconfiguring the front aspect and lowering it by one storey and adding a new ornamental pool in front of the house to provide a ready supply of water in emergencies.

The period from 1928 to the mid-1930s was of course the Great Depression, and the North West and Wales were particularly badly affected. The North, home to most of Britain's heavy industry, such as coal mining, steel, textiles and shipbuilding, was particularly hard hit. The downturn obviously hit all of society, even affecting better off families such as the Middletons and Greys. Shares, which the well to do held, had lost a great deal of their value in the crash – although Lambert

Middleton was probably a very cautious investor. It was a time of great change. The Grey family in the person of Charles 5th Earl Grey, sold a lot of land in the 1930s and 1940s to pay off the huge family mortgage.

Death duties and the lack of an heir to big estates also meant an end to some great houses. The late 1920s saw the sale of two of the Holford family's iconic homes – Dorchester House, sold in 1927 and subsequently demolished to make way for the new Dorchester Hotel – and Westonbirt – sold in 1928 to become a girls' school. Both houses were victims of the death duties which fell due after the death of Sir George Holford in 1926 and of their impracticability as family homes. Westonbirt had cost Sir George's father £235,000 to build in 1864 and was sold for a mere £30,000.

The death duties also triggered the sale of the fabulous Holford collection of Italian Renaissance art and Dutch masterpieces which was auctioned in two sales at Sotheby's in 1927 and 1928, raising over £2 million (probably over £100 million at today's value) distributed between Sir George Holford's Morley and Benson relatives and his Grey nieces.

27

South America

In January 1927, Lambert and Sybil embarked on a four-month trip to South America. It was a business visit – Lambert was a director of Lloyds Bank and the trip took in all the head branches of the Bank of London and South America (BOLSA) a subsidiary of Lloyds. They travelled out by sea – there were no intercontinental passenger flights then – the first ever air crossing of the Atlantic by Allcock and Brown having only been accomplished in 1919. It was also planned by Sybil as a restful trip for Lambert – unfortunately that was not to be.

Their itinerary took them aboard the *Orduna*, a liner of 15,500 tonnes, nearly 10,000 km from Liverpool to Rio de Janeiro in Brazil, the outward journey lasting eighteen days. From Rio they went on to nearby Montevideo in Uruguay, before sailing for the Falkland Islands and then via the Straits of Magellan into the Pacific and up the coast to Santiago in Chile. From there they took the train back across the continent – some 2,900 km – crossing the Andes by the extraordinary TransAndine line. They traversed Argentina before returning to the east coast and Buenos Aires, São Paulo and Rio de Janeiro, from where they shipped back to Britain.

It was an overall journey of over 23,000 km. They were well into their mid-age – Sybil was 45 and Lambert was 50. The trip was made more difficult by the death of Lambert's mother Sophia Middleton aged 79 back at home in Scotland,which they learnt of three days after their arrival in in Rio. Their first instinct was to return home as they learnt that Lambert's father Henry Middleton had been badly affected by his wife's death, but they were persuaded by his sisters that old Mr Middleton was recovering.

Lambert himself suffered from a number of ailments – his stomach continued to be susceptible to problems, and he had just had many of his teeth taken out to be replaced by ill-fitting upper and lower dental plates which made it difficult for him to eat. Both Lambert and Sybil lost a good deal of weight during the trip. They both found the trip wearing from the start and Sybil wrote to her mother on arrival in Rio – 'no words can say how happy and pleased we shall both be to get back – for this trip is pretty heavy work – not physically but mentally.'

They had left behind their very young children – Harry was three and a half and Molly was just one and a half years old. It was of course an age of nannies and the children were left in the care of Sybil's mother Countess Alice at her home Piperscroft near Slough, but one must wonder a bit at Sybil going on such a long trip when Molly was such a tender age. But she enjoyed travel and the challenge of a new continent which she had never visited before, and she was perhaps unsure whether Lambert was robust enough to tackle the trip alone. Anyway, she went.

The trip out on the *Orduna* was uneventful, with Lambert and Sybil seeking out solitude and relaxation on the upper deck while other passengers enjoyed tennis and a variety of water sports in the pool. Sybil did take part in clock golf and played bridge in the evening and they enjoyed the 'race meetings' where 'horse races' were conducted at the throw of a dice – Lambert and Sybil winning £4 on the first 'race meet'. They also enjoyed the ceremony of Lord Neptune coming on board as they crossed the equator, the hardiest passengers receiving a ducking and the rest getting a certificate granting them the freedom of the deep.

Lambert and Sybil were travelling with Mr Simmons, one of the BOLSA managers, and his wife, a rather stout woman whom Lambert and Sybil probably unfairly took a dislike to, calling her 'the Google'. Sybil called her 'a vulgar, second-rate woman who talks continually about good manners and other people's rudeness – she is awful.' As the trip round South America proceeded, Sybil came to admire Mrs Simmons's excellence as a photographer, something which Sybil herself was very keen on. Pictures show Lambert and Sybil both holding cameras during this trip.

Father Neptune charter for Lady Sybil Middleton (Boyd family collection).

Their first taste of South America was when they reached Rio de Janeiro, then capital of Brazil, on 24 January. As they approached from the sea, Sybil was captivated to see an extraordinary mirage of the shore, islands and ships reflected again and again, making a weird and compelling image. As they entered the harbour, she was struck by the city's magnificent surroundings with its islands and high hills and peaks, on one side the Sugarloaf and on the other landside a range of low mountains. At first she did not think it was as stunning as Sydney, 'but later on when we were getting into the huge harbour I changed my mind and thought it more beautiful.'

The weather was exceptionally hot – too hot for sightseeing which they left for later in the trip when they were due to return to Rio at the end of their journey; but she admired the well laid out town set in a grid pattern with 'several great broad avenues with four rows of trees, and all the side streets very, very narrow, just room for two vehicles abreast – this being done for shade and coolness.'

They stayed at a hotel on the great Copocabana Bay, about twenty minutes from the town centre facing the open Atlantic – 'a long curving beach a mile and a half long of very silver white sand, the sea very deep blue and white breakers rolling in one after another and making a continuous roar.' She envied the people who crowded the beach in wonderful garments and cloaks for a delicious cool bathe.

At night Lambert and Sybil found it hard to sleep for the sound of the breakers. But the hotel had a very fine casino attached and Sybil indulged in gambling which she had enjoyed ever since her time in Petrograd. 'I had varying fortune and ended up about ten shillings to the bad, so not much harm was done… dinner at the hotel was excellent, but the band played such loud jazz that it was difficult to hear what was said. People danced and smoked during and between each course, which I think is a tiresome habit.'

During dinner, Sybil began to learn about the country. The bank manager from Bahia, about two days north by boat, told her how yellow fever had been practically stamped out by the Rockefeller Institute. 'The town has about 300,000 inhabitants and the Rockefeller doctors and staff inspect every house and hovel once a week. Every tank, every gutter, every tap is inspected by these men.' The strategy was to eliminate the insects which spread the fever and which laid their eggs in water. 'Whenever there is a shower of rain these men go out and squirt every single puddle.' The Japanese man who first isolated the yellow fever germ, and who Sybil noted was paid £20,000 a year, was a frequent visitor to Bahia.

When they reached Montevideo, capital of Uruguay, they learnt of the death of Lambert's mother Sophia Middleton back home in Scotland. Lambert wrote to Countess Alice: 'I have never seen Sybil so well as she looks now. She is of course anxious for news and longing to know that Harry and Molly are well… She means to get all the health and interest out of this tour that is possible.' He added 'I can never tell you how dear and good she has been to me at this sad time.'

Sybil had also taken a leaf out of her mother's book when it came to long-distance travel – this time she was accompanied by a maid to look after her. Sybil wrote to her mother: 'McFarlane is excellent and saves me a great deal of trouble – washes my things and keeps me tidy' – and she also sent her love to Harry and Molly – her 'two little bandicoots'.

By 31 January they were at sea again, at the start of the trip round the tip of South America. The weather was colder and they saw their first iceberg. Two days later they woke to find themselves in the Falkland Islands. Sybil was unimpressed – 'large bare islands of grass and rock, rather like Lambert's pictures of the Hebrides. Not a tree on the whole island or islands which are about the size of Wales.'

The governor's wife Mrs Beatty visited them on board. She told them that she had no one speak to on the islands and she expressed how awkward it could be entertaining in such a small community, where you might find that your parlour maid was the sister or aunt of your luncheon guests. According to Mrs Beatty the islands' 2,000 inhabitants 'are deteriorating owing to constant and continual inter-marriage.'

On the trip round South America, Sybil frequently found that many of the wives of expatriate managers were isolated and lonely. Couples could be out there for fifteen years or more and would only rarely have the chance to see their growing children who were being educated back home in England. Sybil acknowledged 'I should hate it.'

They reached Punta Arenas, where the Magellan Straits divide mainland South America from Tierra del Fuego. Here they visited the golf club and played two holes in order to say that they had played on the southernmost course in the world. Sybil described how they 'sat on the links by the water's edge looking at the cobalt blue hills across the Straits of Magellan – a glorious sky with wonderful cloud ef-

Lambert on deck (Boyd family collection).

fects resulting in marvellous lights and shades.' She commented how peaceful it was – 'far the most perfect time we've had since leaving England.'

As they sailed through them, Sybil at first found the Straits disappointing 'very much like parts of the Labrador coast.' Later the landscape became wilder with 'snow-capped mountains and several glaciers but no sign of animal life anywhere; a good deal of mist, cloud and frequent scuds of rain with a tremendous wind blowing.' She decided, 'once I've seen the Straits I never wish to see them again.'

They progressed up the coast to Valparaiso, one of the chief ports of Chile. Sybil was impressed with the wild coastline north of the city, where they visited Can Can, the home of Mr Maycock, the bank's manager responsible for Chile. She described the coastline, 'very big volcanic rocks that look very much as if some giant had been tossing them into the air and then playing Spillicans with them.'

The next day they drove into the country to visit Mr Rogers who owned an attractive farm looking out at the foothills of the Andes. Sybil described the scene: 'there were about eighteen children and young people having a great time – bathing in the river and riding bare backed on about six horses and ponies that Mr Rogers has. Big orchards of excellent peaches, quinces, grapes et cetera all irrigated from the river. He grows six to seven crops of alfalfa a year in his orchards to feed livestock.'

They also visited the coastal town of Vina del Mar outside Valparaiso, the home of Mr and Mrs Chilcote (the sub manager of the bank) and Mr and Mrs Hoare (the accountant). Everyone seemed depressed and took a very gloomy view of the future of business in Chile. Sybil commented:

> Rather a sticky luncheon – Mr Chilcote a very tired and nervy man whose home leave is overdue by eighteen months. Mr and Mrs Chilcote have not seen their boy aged seventeen for six years. I understand that Valparaiso is a very nervy place, quite apart from earthquakes, so with business being difficult and bad in Chile I should say it is high time the Chilcotes went home for a bit.

She felt sorry for Mrs Hoare, a young Irish woman from County Kerry, who was due to have a baby but who was very bored and lonely, rarely seeing other British people. Sybil said: 'I don't think bank wives are seeing anything of each other. Mrs Hoare tells me that her husband leaves at 8.30 in the morning and rarely returns before 8 o'clock at night.' However, many expatriate entrepreneurs were very comfortably well-off and had beautiful houses outside Valparaiso.

Lambert's job was to meet all the local managers of the Bank of London and South America and to recommend any necessary changes to banking practice or even to how they projected the bank in society. He gave an entertainment allowance to one of the bank's managers (their competitors entertained liberally) and he insisted on BOLSA men being invited to the networks of English firms represented in Chile. He also met a deputy of clerks asking for higher salaries.

The Middletons stayed with the British Consul in Santiago, Sir Thomas Hohler and his wife. Hohler had acquired 160 acres to set up a country club for British expatriates outside Santiago. Sybil was invited and loved it.

It is a glorious spot with the Andes on three sides of it. They have already got quite a good cricket ground (four of our bank men are in the Santiago cricket XI), four tile tennis courts have already been built and four red tennis courts are in the course of construction. A large open-air pool which was opened a short time ago. So far there is no club house and the golf course has not been yet been commenced. Eventually there is to be a croquet ground, children's playground, etc. If it can be kept from being too expensive it ought to be a charming club in absolutely ideal surroundings.

Sybil took a small cine camera with her and filmed guests disporting themselves in the swimming pool. While in Santiago they also visited the racecourse, and again Sybil was impressed:

It is the most beautiful course with a gorgeous view of the snow capped Andes. A wonderful luxurious stand with a roof garden where you can have refreshments and watch the whole race. The big Jockey Club stand has armchair seats and one of these huge new concrete roofs that have no pillar supports but are kept up by some form of balance.

They had been told that the racecourse was only used for horse races for nine months of the year – during the other three months races were held in nearby Valparaiso. However when they visited Lambert and Sybil were surprised to find that the stands, especially the second class stand, were very nearly full. They learned that when the racing was held in Valparaiso 'people at Santiago still go to their own racecourse to bet on the races just as they do at an ordinary meeting, only there are no horses and a man on the course tells them through a megaphone how the race in Valparaiso is going. We were very much amused. They had a band playing and everything with the exception of horses, just as if the races were taking place there.'

Sybil always responded to the mystery and attraction of wild places. So it is no surprise to find that her diary is alive with descriptions of the next part of their journey – by train across the Andes via the extraordinary TransAndine railway. They left Santiago and travelled on a broad gauge railway to Los Andes through very attractive country – great broad fertile valleys, looking very green as they were all under cultivation and irrigated. She described big fields of maize, gold in colour and standing twelve feet high; many herds of cattle and horses in brilliant fields of green alfalfa; the two great trees of this part of Chile, the poplar and the weeping willow, adding charm and picturesqueness to the scenery. Some of the fields which they passed were blue with chicory and the railway embankments were smothered with brilliant gentian blue morning glory.

At Los Andes they changed to a narrow gauged cogwheel railway: 'We were in a very comfortable Pullman car with big stuffed wicker armchairs and large plate glass windows that opened and shut very easily.' They were supplied with huge baskets of fruit and set off across the Andes. 'It took us from 10 a.m. to 2.30 p.m. to climb the 43 miles to the top of the pass. At the top at 10,500 feet, in a tunnel of one mile of length, you cross from Chile into the Argentine.' She wrote:

It is amazing how steeply and rapidly the train rises in certain places, and the engineering feat of the line, I'm told, is far more remarkable than that of the CPR (Canadian Pacific Railway). Two brothers called Clark, more or less unknown engineers who had nothing of any account to their credit, are responsible for the line. They made a mess of the financial side of the enterprise, but succeeded magnificently in the far more difficult task of overcoming the appalling engineering difficulties of making a railway across the Andes.

As they ascended, Sybil initially felt that these mountains were less beautiful than the Canadian Rockies. They rose steeply on either side and there were no great splendid vistas of mountains to see. However after waiting for an hour at the top for the Argentine train to arrive they started down. Immediately she noted that the scenery changed completely. Aconcagua, 23,000 feet high, towered above covered in snow. The rest of the mountains appeared to be of sandstone which had been sculptured by the wind and weather into every imaginable shape. She found the Argentine side of the mountains infinitely more beautiful.

> No sign of life or vegetation – for we were not lucky enough to see condors – but the colouring of the mountains is superb. Every shade of pink, terracotta, brown, yellow, saffron and pale greens – and as the sun set behind us and lit up brilliantly the peaks, the shadows were of the darkest purple. I've never seen anything more beautiful – Barbaric splendour!

She was particularly impressed by a mountain mass called 'Los Penitentes':

> It is a curious rock formation giving the illusion of a number of cowelled penitents climbing upwards towards a huge cathedral which crowns the top of the mountain. As we suddenly came on this mountain standing back between two nearer ones, the sun was setting full on the rocks which looked like a magnificent sculptured cathedral, painting them a brilliant red – the mountain below being in deep shadow was dark purple. It looked like some wonderful fairy like building and reminded one of the drawings of Du Lac[1] – I cannot describe the beauty or mystery of it.

Before taking their journey they had been advised not to eat too much as that would make it more likely that they would suffer from altitude sickness. Sybil however felt well enough to have a big afternoon tea 'which was my undoing, for it gave me a violent headache and mountain sickness.' They were pleased to fall into their beds in a comfortable hotel in Mendoza on the Argentinian side of the mountains.

They continued their journey a couple of days later by train to Buenos Aires, in great comfort 'in a special coach with cabins, dining room, observation car that the authorities gave us free.' They travelled all day across the Argentine Pampas, which Sybil described as dead flat like the Prairies, enabling one to see for miles and miles. 'It was mostly grazing land carrying 100,000s of cattle and 10,000s of horses; we saw no wheat but a good deal of maize. All along the way we came were enormous estancias, but no small farms.' They were less impressed with the railway line itself – a single track, 'with a very badly kept look about it – you can just see the rails among the grass and weeds.'

They were similarly unimpressed when that evening they pulled into Buenos Aires through the favelas and were horrified at 'the utter squalor of the suburbs of

---

1 Edmund Dulac (1882-1953), a French born but British naturalised book illustrator.

B.A. right up to the station… which seem to consist principally of a number of tin huts made of old kerosene tins put up just hugger mugger anyhow and anywhere. Coming into a tremendously rich city of over two million people in a new country it gives one a very bad impression.'

The Middletons were perhaps unprepared for the huge discrepancy in wealth between the rich and poor in a country such as Argentina, but they certainly admired the energy and success of self-made entrepreneurs whom they met there. Many were European men who had forged their success over many years spent out there. Some were real rough diamonds, such as the landowner, 'an Argentine-Basque of the roughest type', who took Lambert and Sybil over his vast estate. Sybil described him:

> a man of about 55, very fat, dressed in a dirty old pyjama coat and black trousers and bedroom slippers, with four days growth on his chin, met us with a couple of Ford cars and a very high old dogcart. I thought he was a farmhand but found that he rented all this land and other huge tracts at the enormous rent of over £80,000 a year and that he is worth one million sterling. I drove with him in his old dogcart through a forest of thistles, in places so high that they came up to the top of the motors.

There were also businessmen visiting the country, some of whom had built their own fortunes back home in Britain. One such whom Lambert introduced to Sybil was Mr Morris, creator of Britain's great modern motor manufacturing success story.

> He is 48, looks younger, a small dark man with a keen face, blue eyes and a shock of black hair. He started as an assistant in a small bicycle shop in Oxford, and is now worth £20 million. Mr Holt says his income last year was £1,250,000. The other day he gave £104,000 to St Thomas' Hospital. He turns out one car a minute now and is here to see what he can do with the South American market.

Mr Morris explained that selling cars to South America was exceedingly difficult, because although Morris cars were robust enough for Argentine roads, the American Ford company paid just third of the price he had to for steel and so could undercut him.

There are quirky and sometimes comic sidelights on the activities of upper class English visitors. Sybil wrote:

> A whole crowd of English people, the Beauchamps, two of the Lygon girls and dozens of other English people one knows arrive tomorrow on a boat that is making a maiden trip – they are all guests of the company belonging to the Vesteys, the big meat people, who are just starting this new passenger line.

The Beauchamps were the family of William Lygon, the 7th Earl Beauchamp, the leader of the Liberal Party in the House of Lords and supposedly the model for Lord Marchmain in *Brideshead Revisited*, his wife Lady Beauchamp and her teenage children. The Vestey brothers, originally family butchers in Liverpool, had established a huge empire importing beef products from their ranches and factories in South America, New Zealand and Australia, William Vestey being ennobled as Baron Vestey in 1922.

Sybil met Lady Beauchamp who seemed particularly disorganised and ill dressed in the lift of their hotel. 'She hadn't one penny'… so Sybil took her to the Bank of London and South America. 'Anybody more helpless or at sea I have seldom seen. She looked like an old overblown sort of housekeeper, very badly dressed in a crushed old pink dirty linen.' Her children, two teenage girls and her ten year old son, were also poorly dressed, 'the boy in quite the grubbiest white flannel trousers I have ever seen. He looked a darling, but he might have been clean.' Rather censoriously, Sybil remarked of the family: 'such a pity to come to the smartest hotel in B.A. looking like that – especially when they had two maids and a nurse with them.'

Sybil, with her eye for unusual stories, was intrigued by another young British aristocrat living in town – seemingly the Hon. George Spencer, aged 23, younger son of Earl Spencer, who had briefly served in the Navy and after a slightly wild time had been shipped out to South America to earn his fortune in the railways. Sybil wrote:

> I understand (it is difficult to get the exact true story) that when he was working as a clerk here in the railway, he was behaving like a young fool with some woman, when her Papa came along and shot him through the mouth with a revolver from a yard off. The bullet went between the jugular vein and the carotid artery, touched his vocal cords, so that he will never be able to speak above a whisper again, and went out at the back of his neck just missing his spine. After that he was two months in hospital and is still going daily to the dentist as the back of his jaw was damaged. The poor boy looks awfully ill, and one can't help being very sorry for him.

She added: 'I think he is a weak youth, but this last episode should sober him up a bit.' The weak youth went on to marry and became the great uncle of Lady Diana Spencer, Princess of Wales.

As Lambert completed the final weeks of his tour of South America, Sybil visited a range of places. Nearby La Plata had received a great deal of investment because it was the capital of Buenos Aires Province. But although it was elaborately laid out on the Washington plan, and had cost £20 million to build, its future was in doubt. Sybil saw its huge cathedral which remained unfinished for lack of money and its excellent museum of prehistory featuring the largest dinosaur ever discovered. But despite its fine parks and avenues, Sybil felt that 'La Plata looks like a city that it is half dead.'

In São Paulo, she visited the British hospital, a big airy building with both private rooms and public wards, and a British matron. We are reminded that Sybil was very much a woman of her time when, going through the public wards, she noted 'What surprised me most was seeing a white woman between two black ones.' Sybil spoke to the matron about it who said, 'Yes, I can never get used to it myself, but here there is no feeling about it whatsoever.' Clearly, Sybil and the matron's imperial background made equality between the races difficult and uncomfortable to contemplate whereas in South America's multiracial heritage it was more accepted.

They made final expeditions up the spectacular mountains overlooking Rio – going to the top of the Sugarloaf Mountain in a swaying cable car, and on the cog-

Rio de Janeiro Bay, photographed by Sybil from the summit of Corcovado,
(Boyd family collection).

wheel railway up Corcovado, in places rising on a gradient of one in three. She
marvelled at the view from the top, 2,200 feet up right over the city, bay and surrounding mountains – she described it as 'simply stupendous… it is far beyond
anything one can imagine.'

They spent an hour at the top, watching the glorious sunset behind Gavea and
Tijuca, 'these mountains standing out inky black, with red and gold clouds behind,
and an opalescent sea on the Atlantic side.'

On 1 April, three days before they sailed for home, Sybil and Lambert played
an April Fool on Lambert's colleague Mr Simmons. They wrote him an anonymous
letter saying that it had caused great anxiety and uneasiness to well-wishers of the
Bank to see Lambert and Sybil gambling at the casino at Copacabana. In particular,
'I had been heard to say, when reproached by Lambert for putting in a specially
high hazard, "What does it matter Humbert for I am playing with the Bank's
money".' Poor Mr Simmons was thoroughly taken in, as was his colleague Mr
Stark. It was perhaps rather an unfair position to put Mr Simmons in as he was
Lambert's junior at the bank, but April Fools were a favourite in Sybil's family.

They sailed back on the *Alcantara*, calling at Madeira. It had been a long trip
but, despite all the problems of Lambert's ill-health, the visit had proved a success
– enabling Lambert to meet all the regional managers in Brazil, Argentina, Uruguay
and Chile. The countries they visited had been of great and varied interest. In Brazil
Lambert had written to Countess Alice, 'Sybil has announced her intention of coming back here and seeing more of the country some day, with or without me!' As
they sailed home, Lambert and Sybil even concluded that they should return to
South America in the next four to five years for a follow-up trip.

28

Family Life

In December 1928, Lambert's father, Henry Middleton, died and the family moved to Lowood near Melrose in the Scottish Borders. They returned to London from time to time, usually dictated by Lambert's health.

Lowood is on the Tweed, which literally flows past the front door. A long drive leads to the house itself which is surprisingly low – a ground floor and a single first storey – built of Borders stone and rendered. An entrance hall leads in to the dining room and the drawing room, two large, light, well-proportioned rooms overlooking the front garden. The only evidence that now remains of the Middleton's tenure is a set of electric bells in the servants' passage with the names 'Mr Middleton's room', 'Lady Sybil's room', 'Miss Molly's room'.

It must have been a wonderful place for Sybil's young family – Harry and Molly – to grow up in, with riding and fishing very much a part of everyday life, tennis in the summer and skating in the winter and children's parties throughout the year.

Sybil's diaries from the early 1920s on give a day by day record of her life. Written in chunky desk diaries, with a page a day, they are disciplined and systematic – each page recording the events of that day, headed by where she was living (London, Lowood, Piperscroft, etc) and the weather, and listing at the bottom expenditure (cost of travel, her purchases, tips, etc). The diaries of course devoted a lot of space to her young family, how they were growing up and what they were doing.

In London, she received a large number of visitors – sometimes four or five a day. The people whom she entertained included members of the family including the Bensons, Grenfells, and the Joneses, her mother, sister Evy and brother Charlie; and friends of hers such as Dorothy Streatfield, Dorothy Wood (wife of the Earl of Halifax), the Elphinstones, Aileen Roberts, Zella Leather Culley and nursing friends like Miss Chipman (Chip).

Lambert worked for Lloyd's Bank in the City and made occasional business trips to Milan and Turin, centres of Italian banking services, in the 1920s. In London, Sybil also undertook charitable work with organisations such as the Paddington Dispensary (a free dispensary for sick children based in Paddington Green), and the Docklands Settlement (which promoted social and religious work by public school boys and university students among the poor of east London).

At Lowood, Sybil busied herself with improving her new home – building new rooms and making it more comfortable, adding central heating and electricity, and above all planting new copses and woodlands, and a great variety of flower beds in the garden.

She of course made the most of the wonderful fishing on the Tweed – there was scarcely a day in the fishing season when she was not out on the river. And she enjoyed the spectacular Border scenery and wildlife – admiring the glorious autumn colours or standing transfixed by the sight of a huge flight of geese passing over the Northumbrian coast.

Young family – Sybil, Harry and Molly (Boyd family collection).

1929

In April, her nephew Reggie Grenfell announced his engagement to Joyce Phipps, the American actress and entertainer who became famous as Joyce Grenfell. Sybil was delighted: 'She is very good-looking and quite charming and so natural and delightful and perfectly at ease with Mother. I am enchanted with her and I think

Reggie is very lucky.'

Photography was a major interest, and she took many cine films and photographs. The cine films built into a collection that she would show to different audiences: films of her young children in 1927-28, nature films of swans swimming at Courteenhall in Northampton, and of ducks at Fallodon being fed by her cousin Sir Edward Grey. She filmed village life in Darnwick and Melrose – the Darnwick film was found decades later in a junkshop and screened on a BBC programme as 'a masterpiece of anonymous amateur cinema'. She filmed salmon leaping up the river caulds at Selkirk and Philliphaugh. Sybil bought her cameras from Bell and Howell and would occasionally get the owner, Mr Bell, to come and demonstrate a new camera or projector. She was meticulous in recording the settings, aperture and timing and speed at which she shot the pictures.

In May 1929 she went to see a new anti-war play in London – *Journey's End* by R. C. Sherriff – about doomed British soldiers in the front line in the First World War: 'House absolutely crowded with people standing. Very well acted. Painful but an admirable play for the young who don't remember the war.'

Also in May, she, Evy and Jonah spent the evening in Selfridges listening to the result of the General Election relayed presumably on the radio: 'it was all very well done except that the cabaret show and bands rather drowned the announcing.' Labour, under Ramsay MacDonald, took power.

In August, back in the Borders, Lambert and she opened the gardens to the local population. 'Lambert had put up a notice at the Lodge saying that anybody who liked could walk up the drive through the garden and back by the pond field. Sixty-four people came to our great delight.' She was also involved in many local charitable bodies – especially the Women's Institute at Darnwick, putting on teas for school children, and becoming involved with the Brownies, whilst Lambert was involved in the Scouts, giving prizes at Scout meetings and holding the annual Scout camp at Lowood.

In September, while at Lowood, there is also an intriguing note in her diary: 'After tea I dressed up as a man to Molly's horror and Harry's surprise. Completely took in Bill [Lambert's brother in law] for about ten minutes.' It was clearly not something that she did often. It may have been a practical joke or might have been linked to her feelings that there was a masculine side to her character. On another occasion, the whole family dressed in each other's clothes for dinner.

Early 1930s
Until August 1931, Lambert and Sybil still maintained a house in London (presumably rented) at Hyde Park Street, although they were progressively improving their house at Lowood, in the Scottish borders. At Lowood they had regular visitors, particularly Grey relatives from Howick (e.g. her nieces Molly and Nisset) and Middleton relatives (e.g. her sisters-in-law, Laura, married to William Barnett, and Harriet, married to Rear Admiral William Baker Baker, and their respective children, William and Alice (Alsie) and Roger Barnett, and Oswald and Conyers Baker Baker). In 1931 Molly and Nisset arranged a week-long camp for girl guides at Lowood.

Sybil was passionately interested in gardening. In 1931 she visited Mark Fenwick, a celebrated gardener who lived at Abbotswood in Gloucestershire. Fenwick also came to stay with her at Lowood in September 1931 where he helped with her plans. She and Lambert set about comprehensively replanning and replanting the whole of the Lowood estate – setting out a new garden and planting new woods, e.g. the Pond Wood and the Lodge Wood. It involved large numbers of new trees – at one point her diary says that 20,000 trees were being delivered, which seems an incredibly high number for a relatively small estate.

In good weather theirs was very much an outdoor country life. Sybil's greatest passion was fishing – for the adults the great prize were the salmon in the Tweed, which could weigh up to 20 lbs or more. Young Harry learnt how to fish with a trout rod and fly and Molly, two years younger, learned the craft of fishing with a worm. Other country pursuits also featured. When well enough, Lambert and guests went out shooting around Lowood and there was regular shooting at Howick, with large 'bags' of pheasant and other game. Sybil also took part – at Lowood she owned a rook rifle and a shotgun.

The children began to learn the skill of riding ponies and they also 'followed' the hunt on foot. In 1932, Harry hunted regularly on his pony, and on February 3 he arrived first at the kill (through taking a short cut) and was 'blooded' and awarded the fox's mask (its head). Molly, aged seven, also hunted.

At the same time both Lambert and Sybil remained very concerned about their health. Lambert's main complaint was his legs and feet which suffered from skin complaints and ulceration. Not surprisingly he seems to have been easily depressed judging by the amount of time that he slept poorly, was said to be 'feeling rotten' or spent time off work. He suffered repeated crises in the condition of his legs, and spent many months in private nursing homes, no doubt suffering also from the alarming mixture of drugs with which he was treated.

Lambert Middleton was a complex and contradictory character. He was remembered as being great fun and with a strong sense of humour who wrote comic nonsense verse for his children. But he was also undeniably a demanding invalid whose illness made life hard for Sybil and the rest of the family. It must have been a considerable strain for someone of Sybil's active and positive outlook, and it clearly led to strains in her marriage which surfaced in her trip to Grand Metis in 1936.

He was taken ill at the end of January 1929 and finally returned to work in October that year, eight months later. He spent several months in the Preston Deanery sanatorium in Northampton, followed by recuperation on the south coast and at home at Lowood.

In April 1932, he was again confined to a nursing home, this time in Putney, under different doctors, being treated with an experimental Octozone treatment (giving oxygen to the legs). In July he was back in London staying at the Putney nursing home to see Dr Castellani, who diagnosed hepatitis of the liver. It was not until mid-September that he returned to Scotland. Sister Leader, a nurse, stayed at Lowood for many months to look after him.

In early May 1933 there was another crisis and Lambert was again confined to the nursing home in Putney. His legs were in a terrible condition – in places he had to have dead, 'gangrenous' flesh cut away, and the ulcers were again treated with oxygen.

However Lambert's legs did recover sufficiently to allow him to go back to work. It seemed that they were however always prone to relapses and the long term effects of the medication he had to take (particularly heroin) must have affected his health and outlook.

Sybil was also concerned also about her own health, especially long-term heart problems she believed she was suffering an 'intermitting' heart, etc. Her doctors seem not to have been convinced that it was a problem, repeatedly reassuring her despite a slight murmur that her heart 'would not let her down'. She was being treated with *digitalis* ('pink pills'). And she was also concerned about Harry's health. In 1933 she got Harry's heart X-rayed and an electrical test done (presumably an ECG). Fortunately it showed that his heart was 'quite normal and in the right place' and the doctor saw no bar to an active games playing life.

Lambert Middleton, (Boyd family collection).

When in London they regularly made an excursion to Ranelagh Gardens (beside the Royal Chelsea Hospital – near the site of the Chelsea Flower Show) where the Ranelagh Pleasure gardens had been set out as a 'quiet green retreat with shady walks', essential relaxation to a family that was most at home in the countryside.

Sybil of course took Harry and Molly to children's parties, and on Monday, 6 July 1931, Sybil's diary records that she 'took the children to a party at Nina Balfour's[1] for Princess Elizabeth.' Princess Elizabeth would have been five years old at the time and Molly was six – it appears that Molly was privileged to meet the princesses very early in life.

---

1 Helena McDonnell, sister of Sybil's uncle, William Randal McDonnell, who was married to Capt. Charles Balfour. She was usually known as Nina.

In the Borders, Sybil was much involved in the Women's Rural Institute at Darnick, which invited speakers regularly on a wide range of topics. She gave its members a talk on the Russian Revolution. She also arranged for her cousin, Sir Edward Grey, to act as a speaker in 1932 on the centenary of Walter Scott's death.

She became a founding supporter of the Melrose Amateur Operatic Society which had its first performance, of Gilbert and Sullivan's *The Sorcerer's Apprentice*, on 1 April 1933 in Melrose. Sybil and Molly attended: 'The cast were all well made up and they acted and sang awfully well – a crowded house. At the end I made a short speech – so did Mr Jones.' She then gave all 72 performers and helpers a tea at Patterson's.

Details of national politics found their way into the diary – for example on 8 September 1931 she noted that the King and Prince of Wales were each giving up part of their 'vote' (£50,000 and £10,000 respectively) in response to the Great Depression. It was an early indication of Royal sensitivity about being seen to be receiving excessive funds at a time of national austerity. They listened to historic broadcasts on the radio. That year the Schneider Trophy was broadcast, an annual race for sea planes and flying boats, which fostered innovative aircraft design. It was the crucial testing ground in 1931 for the new Supermarine aircraft which was to become known as the Spitfire.

Sybil's interest in photography and in amateur cinema kept growing. In the early 1930s she experimented with colour photography and became proficient at taking cine films on a series of cameras of increasing sophistication. She edited films at home, on 25 February 1933 noting: 'did four hours work on the fishing film.' She was delighted with the local women's response to seeing themselves on screen in the Darnwick film. On 6 March 1933, she showed the Darnwick WI four films presumably filmed by her: 'Helping salmon over the cauld', 'Fishing for salmon', 'Oxford canoeists' and 'the London film' – adding 'I gave a little lecture at the same time; I think they all enjoyed it.'

She also occasionally showed library films on health or public information matters. She enjoyed going to the cinema and theatre to see the latest films and plays, particularly when in London. She was a keen theatre goer, going to a wide range of different plays and giving her frank assessment of each – 'very poor' or 'very exciting'. She also joined the Red Cross course in first aid given locally near Lowood.

They lived in a changing society where great families and grand houses of the past felt the chill wind of new realities. In April 1932, Sybil visited Lambton Castle, home of the Earl of Durham, which was being sold with all its contents to pay for death duties (the Lambtons were related by marriage to the Greys). She bid for a print of Lady Grey and her children and a set of bedroom china.

The family also honoured the past. On 5 June 1932, Sybil and her children attended a party at Howick, celebrating the centenary of the Reform Bill which Sybil's great grandfather, Charles 2nd Earl Grey, had enacted in 1832. A happy gathering of descendants of Earl Grey was present – Sybil and her brother Charlie, her mother, Molly and Nisset, and members of the Halifax family. The next day they were guests of honour at the Mayor's dinner at the Town Hall, Newcastle, where members of the family made speeches.

Local customs, such as the Border Common Ridings, were also a part of life. The menfolk of towns like Selkirk and Hawick, calling themselves the 'Braw Lads', rode out to patrol their boundaries, as their ancestors had done for generations. In 1932 Harry joined them for the first time.

Lambert Middleton's chronic ill health continued, treated by doctors using a range of alarming and sometimes experimental medications over a prolonged period. On many days, Sybil's diary noted 'L feeling rotten... did not get up'. He sometimes refused to see visitors, and on 4 July 1932 he remained in bed and saw nobody despite it being Molly's seventh birthday. His constant illness must from time to time have cast a pall over Sybil's and the family's life, but he was always remembered as a kind, loving and very humorous man. Lambert appeared to recover considerably, and he played a role in helping the Scouts and Cubs locally, with Lord Baden Powell himself coming to stay at Lowood in autumn 1932 to meet the local scout masters.

Two stories give a lighter picture of Lambert, as a humorous, tolerant and amusing man with a ready wit. On one occasion, patrolling the river's privately owned fishing 'beats', he came upon a poacher. The man assured him that he was only experimenting by using a potato (a 'tattie') as bait, and Lambert was taken in. Returning some hours later he found the fisherman with four good sized trout beside him. 'You surely didn't catch them with the potato?' asked Lambert.

'No,' the man replied, 'I caught the fish on a fly; it was you I caught on the tattie.' Lambert was so delighted with the reply that he gave the man free fishing for life.

On another occasion he took Harry to Eton's great summer festivity on the Fourth of June, where they sat in a large crowd on the bank of the Thames to watch fireworks. A large man directly in front blocked Lambert's view and refused to move until Lambert said, 'If you don't move I'll light your trousers.'

On Christmas Day, 1932, the family listened to the first Christmas greetings radio broadcast by King George V to the Empire, which launched the Empire Service (now the World Service). This was followed by a children's party at Lowood on 3 January 1933. It was a Cotillion, an old fashioned type of dance from Sybil's own childhood, which involved children giving each other gifts. Sybil and her sister in law Harriet Baker Baker prepared for the festivities: 'General dance; girls' sprays of flowers; boys' buttonholes; boys racing on cushions; girls' fans; girls powdering boys' faces; driving race; noses all round; blow outs; boys wiping girls off looking glasses; whistles, torches and tassels; balloons, coloured balls.'

The dining room carpet was taken up; French chalk was put on the floor to make it easy to dance on. They borrowed the Women's Institute piano. The guests all came from the main families and the Middletons' friends in the Borders. Intriguingly one was a young member of the Boyd family (probably my father John) from nearby Whiterigg.

Winter sports included skating on the pond at Lowood, which they opened up to everyone. On 28 January 1933, Sybil wrote:

Lambert has had all men sweeping the ice every day and all day. The brazier he has had filled with coke, and it makes an excellent warm fire, which people can stand around without getting smoke in their eyes. Seats and chairs covered with the Canadian fur rugs. In the afternoon he takes down a kettle and a jug of soup – and a number of potatoes which are roasted in the house and then put under the fire of the brazier to keep hot and a couple of loaves and brown bread. I added a box of ginger nuts.

In April 1933, the whole family (Lambert, Sybil, Harry, Molly) accompanied by their driver Henderson, set out on a visit to the Highlands. They first journeyed to Stirling, which impressed Sybil, then to Pitlochrie, and on via the Pass of Killi-crankie along Loch Ness to Inverness. They saw the battlefield of Culloden with its memorials to the conquered Highland clans. They fished on Loch Ness, played golf and walked to see local sights. In all they drove 632 miles in six days before returning to Lowood.

Money remained somewhat of a concern, although they were sending Harry to Hawtreys and later to Eton, and they bought a new car. Sybil's diary in 1933 shows that she managed her own portfolio of investments, listing those she sold and for what value and gain. She was also inveigled into buying 'a small holding' in Arthur Grenfell's latest scheme – a gold mine (we don't learn where the mine was located or whether it proved a reliable investment or a disaster).

Mid 1930s

The year 1936 began with Lambert apparently vigorous and not suffering so much from his legs. Sybil was surprised to note several times that 'Lambert is on his feet the whole day'. By contrast it was often Sybil who was ill in January 1936 in bed for many days in a row.

The diary gives an intriguing account of a trip that the whole family made to Germany in April of that year. This was just after Hitler's re-militarisation of the Rhineland on 7 March. The Middletons and their children set out from London on 17 April for 'our first continental trip'. They visited Bruges for a night, then stayed at Brussels and went on to stay in Cologne, Koblenz and Bingen (a small town on the Rhine not far from Mainz). These towns were all in the Rhineland, and for three of the four days of their stay in Germany Sybil's diary was completely blank, which contrasted surprisingly with her enthusiastic descriptions of Bruges and Brussels, with its flower markets in the Grand Place. On their way to Cologne she did remark that 'red swastika flags flutter from the windows of every house' – they only dis-covered that it was Hitler's birthday when they arrived in the city. Sybil was ap-parently disappointed to miss the Nazi rally: 'alas we arrived too late to see the soldiers' parade.'

She was probably being prudent while travelling with her young family and kept any thoughts or observations out of her diary. It may be too fanciful to suggest that the Middleton's trip to the Rhineland, only about a month after the Nazi troops had marched back in, might have involved a subsequent report back on conditions there from Sybil to her cousin Stewart Menzies, then deputy head of MI6.

At the end of the year the papers reported a constitutional crisis between the

King and the Cabinet over the new King Edward VIII's desire to marry Mrs Simpson an American divorcee. On 5 December Sybil wrote: 'We are all anxiously awaiting news of what King will settle – he seems to think that the Empire might allow him to make a morganatic marriage.'[2] However the Cabinet, the Prime Minister and the Church of England were opposed and on 10 December the King abdicated in favour of his younger brother, the Duke of York, who was to become George VI. Sybil wrote, 'It is all too pathetic but I think it is by far the best thing for the country. We emerge from this crisis strengthened and absolutely united in the face of the world. Hitler and Mussolini, etc. will have to realise that they still have to reckon with the British Empire as a united whole.'

In May 1937, Harry became a Page to Edward Wood, 1st Earl of Halifax, at the Coronation of King George VI. Sybil had to find a way to kit out Harry in the splendid uniform of a Page (in blue velvet coat and trousers, with chocolate brown cuffs, lace facings, silver buckled shoes and a silver and ivory sword) at a reasonable price. They had a number of rehearsals in Westminster Abbey, which Sybil and her mother witnessed, and then the great day came, which Sybil described from a seat in the House of Lords. 'Very amusing watching the Peers come out and walk about in their Robes before the arrival of the King. The most beautiful part of the Procession was I think the band of the Scots Greys followed by the Yeoman of Guard and then followed by the King's Burgesses.'

In April 1937, Lambert, Sybil and the two children went for a six day motor trip with the chauffeur Henderson, which took in the Lake District, Liverpool and North Wales. They went first to Greystoke Castle, near Penrith, owned by the Howard family, which Sybil knew, and were saddened to find it empty and deserted. They went on to stay with the Cavendishs at Holker Hall, on the Cumbrian coast, well known for its beautiful gardens. They then drove on to Liverpool to see the new Protestant cathedral, then only half built. Sybil was very enthusiastic: 'It is going to be quite beautiful, of red sandstone. It will take another 20 years to build. I thought the glass was lovely.' They finally proceeded to Nannau House in Dolgellau, North Wales, described as one of the most beautiful estates in the country – perched above the coast and combining both mountain and sea air, it was ideal for both shooting and fishing. They returned via Lake Windermere where they stayed the night and so home to Lowood.

All through the early part of 1937, Sybil and her gardeners and friends were involved in a huge planting programme at Lowood – first of trees in her new woods and then of flowers to beautify the woodland. She got plants from far and wide – from her mother's garden, from Howick, from Dobbie's the big nursery garden and from the Royal Botanical Garden in Edinburgh, from the Chelsea Flower Show and even Himalayan blue poppies from her friend Elsie Reford in Metis, Canada.

At the end of May 1937 Sybil herself came in for a taste of the frustrations of being laid up for a month in a nursing home. She had been invited by her brother Charlie to visit Southampton to witness the Coronation Naval Review on 20 May. They sailed

2 A marriage between two people of unequal social standing where the senior partner's titles and privileges do not transmit to the offspring of the marriage.

Molly and Harry in Lowood Garden, (Boyd family collection).

down the double line of warships moored off Spithead. It was a magnificent affair with wonderful hospitality and a glittering guest list, but whilst scrambling to see a fly past of the latest aircraft, Sybil slipped over a high railing and fell breaking her hip. She was taken to the Empire Nursing Home in London, just beside Westminster Boys' School, where she could hear the boys playing cricket below her window.

There she remained in bed for a month while her hip mended. She was visited by all her London friends and had time to read. She also appreciated Lambert's devotion and help – she wrote, 'Lambert is an angel – the way he looks after me.' Returning to Lowood at the end of July, Sybil found that the garden had been neglected by her gardeners: 'Mr Brown has yet to learn that I hate brown earth.' But the weather improved and by the middle of August things were going well. Lambert went off to shoot grouse for the first time in 25 years, and Sybil held a party for the WRI: 'Almost sixty came. The boy at Brown's the chemist brought up his pipes and they danced on the lawn – had a high jump competition won by Joe Scott – a

Harry, Lambert and Molly, (Boyd family collection).

putting competition won by Nellie scoring 23 – a cricket match of tip and run, etc. The garden looking pretty and I think they all enjoyed it.'

The young Norfolk artist Edward (Ted) Seago, also visited Lowood to paint portraits of Harry and Molly, pictured on their ponies bedside the Tweed with the Eildons as a backdrop. He also drew them 'a delightful picture of a farmer with a pot of beer', and played them energetically at tennis.

In October 1937, Sybil visited Howick and heard from her brother Charlie about his participation in September in an official visit by British Parliamentarians and others to Germany to see the country's new autobahns which were Hitler's personal project. She wrote: '200 went, 57 MPs, a few House of Lords and the rest all road experts from all over England and Scotland.[3] They were taken all over Germany and Charlie said the organisation was wonderful.' It was obviously a large official visit to keep up with new developments in road making – but perhaps also to assess their military and strategic significance.

In November, Lambert and Sybil went to Westheath School, at Sevenoaks, to see about a school for Molly: 'We saw Miss Elliott and Lambert liked her. She was very sensible in the way she talked. 70 girls – nine tennis courts – charming house, high rooms with lots of windows, etc. She says one thing she can guarantee is the teaching.' They came away determined to send Molly there in 1939. But in the event Molly went instead to Longstowe Hall in Cambridge.

---

3 German autobahns were inspected by a group of British MPs and representatives, on a visit to Germany in 1937 to look at the famous state roads. The party later attended a rally at the Olympic Stadium where both Hitler and Mussolini gave speeches.

29

Recuperation at Grand Metis (1936)

In the summer of 1936, Sybil revisited one of her favourite places – Grand Metis in Canada. She went alone for a five-week fishing holiday – leaving her husband Lambert and two young children, even though it meant missing Harry's important Common Entrance exam and Molly's eleventh birthday (the fishing season in Canada was less than two month's duration). She was run down and needed a break, but still longed for Lambert and felt guilty at coming away alone. There were also hints of a crisis in her marriage with which she was struggling – in letters home she repeated Lambert's view that they had become too dependent on each other, and spoke of gaining a sense of proportion, as well as regaining her health (recovering from her recurrent heart problem as well as anxiety) and even restoring her religious faith. Perhaps living with a man who was a chronic invalid, and even the loss of independence after 40 years as a single woman, had been weighing down on her and affecting her own health and well-being. She was after all 52 years old, and may also have been going through the menopause with its emotional effects.

Sybil, date unknown, possibly in the late 1920s (de Wesselow collection).

Grand Metis was an ideal place to regain her equilibrium. She described it as a place that was 'soul satisfying'. She found that there were changes – her friend, Elsie Reford, was establishing an outstanding garden at Estevan Lodge overlooking the St Lawrence (the garden has since become a national attraction). Yet the place remained as Sybil had remembered, and she longed for Lambert to see Grand Metis and to love it as she did. These letters show Sybil's powers of description of the countryside and places that she loved in Canada, but they are also deeply affecting love letters to her husband for whom she longed but from whom she apparently needed a breathing space.

She wrote to Lambert on the voyage out, on the *Empress of Britain*, about their parting: 'It was pretty hateful this afternoon wasn't it? The more I think of it the more I dislike it – and wonder why am I doing it? Oh my darling, how I hate to think of you in a hot train now going back to London and feeling lonely.'

Arriving at Grand Metis on 25 June, she wrote: 'No, Lambert I am not the least disappointed it is all just as I remembered it, one of the most heavenly places in the world. In fact it is much better now because there is Elsie's garden.' Sybil marvelled

Sybil with Harry and Molly, Eton for 4th June, late 1930s (de Wesselow collection).

at the world her friend had created:

> Elsie is completely wrapped up in her garden and spends most of her day there. What impresses me is the wonderful way in which the plants are growing. Most of the garden or gardens are rock, she doesn't really care for herbaceous – a lovely tumbling gurgling laughing stream flows through a good deal of it, and wherever you sit you can hear the sound of tumbling water.

She wrote to Lambert:

> I miss you terribly, man, and just long for your companionship and love, I miss not being able to share everything with you, and I long for you to see this place and love it as I do.
>
> I have had three heavenly days here. The vividness of colouring, the clearness of the atmosphere, and the beauty of the skies is unsurpassed here, and the view from the verandah of the house is soul satisfying, I cannot say more. I am never tired of looking at it.

Sybil and Elsie Reford shared a view of Grand Metis as a haven:

> Elsie and I just glance at the headlines of the newspapers and then just throw them down in disgust. We agree that this place is far too beautiful and peaceful to allow the outside world to come in and interfere with our pleasure or enjoyment of it. So we just ignore the world and all its beastliness. We feel that if anything out the ordinary happens it will be forced upon our consciousness whether we like it or not!

They drove out into the country and saw a magnificent sunset:

> We went high up into the hills and coming home we looked down over a rolling wooded country about 20 miles to the St Lawrence and then 30 miles across to the blue hills on the other side, with a marvellous sky and clouds of every conceivable brilliant light and shadow. Gradually the blue hills over 50 miles away became rose pink and the St Lawrence a rim of pure gold. Never in my life have I seen anything more beautiful – of course I had left my cameras behind!

As Molly's eleventh birthday approached, Sybil wrote: 'Oh how much I shall be thinking of my three beloveds the day after tomorrow.' On the day, 4 July, she wrote to Lambert: 'eleven years ago great happiness came into our lives. I hope that you and I may be spared to see her on her 22nd birthday.' (Lambert in fact would die just over five years later).

That same day, she received Lambert's letter, written a fortnight before when she had left. She was overwhelmed again by self-reproach. 'Oh my darling, my heart ached and ached when I read your letter. Those that are left behind always have the worst time; they return, I always feel to a complete emptiness whilst there is all the bustle of departure and novelty on the part of the traveller.' Nevertheless, she said: 'I agree with you old man that it is good for both of us being apart like this – we were getting too utterly dependant on each other, but how good it will be when we are together again.'

She continued to bask in the beauty of Grand Metis:

> I kept shutting my eyes and opening them again wondering if it was all a dream, or whether it could be real, it was so lovely. At these times I so long for you with a positive

ache and not only you but Harry too.

Sybil threw herself into fishing:

The real run of the salmon started yesterday. From all their accounts they seem terrific fish, taking nearly all the backing out and careering madly all over the river. I got in a week eleven fish and lost two and pricked one… I am feeling marvellously better in the last week. I haven't felt so well for ages – my heart which was intermitting a lot when I arrived has settled down splendidly and seems to like fishing! Elsie says I look a different person – I certainly feel one.

She described how they watched Elsie's son, Eric, fishing in the swift running river:

We sat up above the Pool and watched and about the third cast Eric was into a 25 lb fish. Elsie and I sat breathless watching and criticising – "He will never keep him in the pool," and sure enough he didn't and they had to go down the first part of the rapids and were very lucky and got him before they reached the unpassable part.

Sybil took part in the friendly rivalry between the two fishing canoes and their 'ghillies':

I had a great compliment paid me by my head canoe man on Saturday – he asked me who had taught me to fish as I was certainly A1 in every department!! The old lady was quite bucked. There is tremendous rivalry between the two canoes – and on Saturday night when I had only one fish, he looked sadly at me and said "Sure you are not going to lose me my money?" I said, "Certainly not," and just managed to get the necessary second fish before coming in.

She returned to Lambert's comments on the two of them:

I agree with you darling that I think this five weeks will have done us both a lot of good. It will adjust one's sense of proportion. It has given me a lot of time to think – and I have been, and am trying to get a greater sense of peace and faith into my soul, a feeling of being nearer to God and a greater sense of the reality of prayer. This place is wonderfully suited to help such a frame of mind.

She added, 'I certainly was feeling pretty rotten when I arrived and found that Christ's words "let not your heart be troubled neither let it be afraid" was a great help to me.' And she looked forward to the moment that she would arrive back: 'What a joyous moment it will be. I shall be wearing one huge grin.'

Clearly the haven of Metis, fishing, the Canadian wilderness and her friendship with Elsie Reford were of immense importance to Sybil. On this occasion as so often they helped her to recuperate and to revive and restate her commitment to Lambert and her marriage, while taking advantage of the space and distance to rejuvenate her feelings and outlook on the world.

My wife Julia and I visited Grand Metis in October 2015, where we were welcomed very hospitably by Alexander Reford, Elsie Reford's great grandson. I looked forward to encountering a place which was so dear to Sybil's heart, and of perhaps being able to share some of her feelings for it. We stayed at a nearby beach hotel overlooking the St Lawrence and gazing out at the magnificent expanse of the river and the spectacular sunset on the first evening it was easy to feel in communion with the spirit of the place that had so moved Sybil 80 years before. We were lucky enough to be shown round Grand Metis and Estevan Lodge by Alexander Reford himself.

The gardens were spectacular, even so late in the season – featuring walks through the woods which Elsie and her gardeners had created with a huge variety of flora. Estevan Lodge was impressive and very well maintained – the Reford family had re-asummed ownership after its many years in the care of the state, and its rooms were an interesting mix of domestic interiors as well as acting as a small museum devoted to Elsie, her family, fishing and gardening. It is no longer lived in and I think that is where I felt a sense of some disappointment and distance. It was possible to visit the splendid veranda on which Sybil and her friends had relaxed after fishing, and to see the beautiful fireside hearth and wood panelled staircase leading up to the bedrooms and to Bruce Reford's darkroom which would have fascinated Sybil. But I couldn't of course feel the same way as Sybil had felt about the place – so much of our engagement with and love of a place is bound up with the friends one shares it with, and Sybil, Elsie and their friends were all long gone.

30
World War II (1939-45)

The 1930s had been dominated by developments in Germany and the rise of Nazism, attempts at appeasement and belated recognition of the need for rearmament. Germany under Hitler aimed to reverse the Treaty of Versailles by rebuilding Germany's armed forces, taking back control of lands it had lost, expanding its borders and uniting all German-speaking peoples under the Third Reich.

The response of the British and French governments was initially a policy of appeasement. This reflected real fears and dilemmas. The huge scale of loss of life in World War I dominated people's memories and politicians were understandably anxious to avoid a second catastrophe. Some believed that Germany had been unfairly treated at Versailles and that its grievances could be solved by negotiation. And in the Depression, the government prioritised greater spending on social welfare and infrastructure above rearmament.

Voices on the left, some in the Labour Party and even the British Communist party, as well as Winston Churchill on the right, warning of the dangers of Nazism, were pitted against the tide of public opinion which favoured peace at almost any price. Famously in February 1933, the Oxford Union debating society voted in favour of the motion 'This house will under no circumstances fight for King and Country'. It was only much later, after Germany's annexation of Austria and invasion of Czechoslovakia in March and September 1938 respectively, that the British government woke up, almost too late, to the need to rearm and confront the menace of Nazism.

Sybil and Lambert's views on German resurgence aren't spelled out anywhere. They were supporters of the Conservative governments of Baldwin and Chamberlain, and Sybil was a very close friend of Dorothy Onslow, the wife of Edward Wood, 1st Earl of Halifax, a leading British politician who like many was associated with the appeasement policy. But Sybil and Lambert almost certainly viewed Germany with distrust as the enemy during World War I which was now fomenting further trouble. Sybil was used to holding her own opinions, and she was also a long-time admirer of Winston Churchill, whom she had met early on. When war broke out in September 1939, everyone backed the government and the war effort.

1940

Opening Sybil Middleton's diary for 1940, one is immediately aware of something new. As well as her usual personal entries about her family life, she includes press cuttings from an authoritative newspaper source, giving daily news of the military campaigns and of political and social developments in Britain (such as conscription and rationing, etc).

The entries are very dramatic indeed. After a period of 'phoney war' lasting until March 1940, with few reports of combat except for distant attacks by Germany on Poland, Denmark and Norway, the tempo quickens with the blitzkrieg on Holland and France culminating in the fall of Paris and the collapse of the French government. The entries seem almost breathless and the drama mounts as British troops were outflanked and the British Expeditionary Force (BEF) was driven back to Dunkirk, hopefully to be evacuated. Sybil's skill in selecting the most significant news posting for each day gives an almost unique view of the progress of the war.

On 14 June 1940, the news described the fall of Paris:

> German motorised forces entered Paris at about 7 o'clock this morning. It was a silent city: all the shops were closed and shuttered and no one was in the streets except police and civil guards now without weapons. Armament factories in or near Paris were blown up last night. Allied troops covering the city retreated to new positions. Early this morning the British government renewed their pledge to the French government to continue the struggle at all costs.

Sybil recorded her shock and disbelief:

> Who could have imagined such a thing possible five weeks ago today when the Germans invaded Holland. The tragedy of it. I suppose the fifth column which is said to be very large in France and the millions of refugees have all helped towards this dreadful climax.

Incongruously, the same day, she recorded Molly's progress at learning to type – 'she is apparently extraordinarily quick.'

Churchill's response to the surrender of the French Government was swift: 'It makes no difference to British faith and purpose. We shall fight on unconquerable until the curse of Hitler is removed from the brows of men.' Sybil's diary recorded the evacuation of the greater part of the BEF from Dunkirk, the British bombing of the elements of the French fleet that had surrendered to the Germans, and the rapidly escalating air war against Britain. By late June air raids were nightly occurrences and the diary records the shifting fortunes of the bombing campaign, each day listing the very high German losses as they tried to bludgeon Britain into surrender, as well as those of the British defenders, the 'few' to whom Churchill paid tribute.

Although most of the action was in the South East and Midlands, and occasionally against cities in the North East, on 4 September 1940 Sybil recorded the dropping of four bombs on Red Stead Farm at Howick. 'Charlie and I went to see the craters made by the bombs: two in the field opposite Frank's Plantation, one in the hayfield and a fourth just near the railway.' The target had probably been a passing train.

We also have her notes about her own involvement – she attended First Aid lectures, was involved in the Women's Voluntary Service (WVS) and took part in air raid precautions (ARP) at the local ARP stations in Galashiels and Darnwick. She described an exercise at Lowood: 'At 7 p.m. we had 37 people on the lawn for the first lecture on what to do in air raids. We lit three incendiary bombs and put them out with both sand and stirrup pumps.'

She was involved also in war work with charities – with the Polish Relief Fund and with Weapons Week which raised huge sums in December 1940. And we are given a picture of the nation tightening its belt, with the announcement of rationing of tea, sugar and meat.

This is interspersed with comments on her personal life and the life of her family and community, and on visits by relations and friends. Her children were brought back home from schools in the south – Harry from Eton and Molly from Longstowe Hall near Cambridge – and their young cousin Vivien Jones, daughter of Evy and Jonah, also joined the family from London 'until the fear of invasion is passed'. For Vivien, the autumn and spring she spent at Lowood were a bright interlude from her own childhood in Norfolk. She found Aunt Sybil was warm and welcoming, encouraging her to make her own decisions, and much easier to relate to than her own parents. Vivien also warmed to Lambert whom she thought sweet and witty.

Sybil's diary nevertheless covered Lambert's deteriorating health, and provided a shock of its own the day after the fall of France when Lambert was judged by a doctor in Bristol to have had a gastroenterostomy (an operation linking his stomach to a lower part of his intestine) 22 years before, seemingly without his being fully informed of it. This was challenged later in Edinburgh, on the basis of X-rays, but it does show that poor Lambert Middleton had indeed been suffering from long-

Evacuee children at Lowood.

term and serious gastric intestinal problems.

While dining at a Bristol hotel, Lambert and Sybil admired a young woman in the dark blue uniform of the Fleet Air Arm, with two gold bars on her shoulder straps, a gold wing on her breast and the ribbon of the Distinguished Flying Medal awarded for exceptionally long distance flights. She was presumably a member of the Air Transport Auxiliary, women pilots who delivered warplanes such as the Spitfire to operational airfields.

In November, Sybil approvingly noted: 'Mr Bevin, Minister of Labour, told the House of Commons that a much larger number of women ought to be employed in engineering factories. Half a million women may be required for full time work.'

We learn that evacuee children were sent to Lowood – Sybil held a party for them at the end of August 1940: 'We gave them tea, some small presents, and took them all to the cinema, Mrs MacDonald, Ian, Sheila, Billy and Elna Henderson and James Hogg.' She and Molly were also involved in cooking a day a week at the Atholl Crescent Domestic Science College in Edinburgh – possibly following a wartime course on food preparation.

On 11 September the newspaper reported fears that invasion was imminent:

> "Next week may be a very important week in our history," Mr Churchill observed; and as he recounted our strength on the sea and land and in the air one felt his confidence that any attempt at invasion will utterly fail.

Sybil and a number of other parents however decided not to send their sons back south to Eton until the danger was passed.

On 21 September, Churchill gave an 'inspiring broadcast to the French nation' – speaking first in English then in French, he told Britain's former allies: 'We seek to beat the life and soul out of Hitler and Hitlerism. That alone, that all the time, that to the end.'

On 26 October, Ralph Ingersoll, a New York newspaper proprietor visiting London, wrote to his New York office:

> What you cannot realise unless you've been here is the constant unremitting and uninterrupted pressure of danger to every man, woman and child in a city under siege from the air, or the fantastic courage which people find somewhere in themselves with which to meet it. This is not baloney. It is something to make one proud to be a member of the human race – to know that there are people who can and are resisting what is evil and repulsive to them as a matter of course.

As always, Sybil had an eye for oddity. On 1 September 1940 she noted in her diary: 'An Edinburgh lady sent the enclosed lines to the newspaper which she said can be read on a 500-year-old tombstone at Church Campsie, Essex:

> When pictures look alive with movements free
> When ships like fishes swim below the sea,
> When men outstripping birds can span the sky
> Then half the world deep drenched in blood shall be.

Others also spotted the unlikely 'prophecy' and commented sceptically that there was no such place as Campsie in Essex, although one existed in Stirlingshire, and that a 500-year-old gravestone was unlikely to be legible. If proved true, the seer's prophetic powers would be truly the equal of Old Mother Shipton's!

Sybil had a wide circle of friends from the Borders and beyond. They included her aunt by marriage, Nina Balfour, who lived at Newton Don, and Dinah Colquhoun (née Tenant), presumably a relative of Muriel Paget. They visited or dined with Sybil frequently, as did Grizel Riddell Carr a close friend who lived nearby. Others included Violet Egerton, Mary Elphinstone (wife of 'Lord E' with whom Sybil's name had once briefly been amorously linked), Doushka Landale and other families such as the Maxwell Scotts and Milligans, together with Zella Leather Culley from Northumberland, Jeanne Malcolm from London, and her old friend Aileen Roberts from Ascot.

Clearly Lambert's health was sinking. At the end of July 1940 Sybil wrote: 'Lambert has had a slightly better night. But he forgets things easily and is still slow at understanding.' On many days he lay in bed feeling miserable.

1941

The pressures of running a large house in the war were beginning to tell and Sybil wrote to tell Molly that she was downsizing the establishment at Lowood. ' By the time that you return we shall be down to Henderson, Sanderson and three maids – instead of the seven maids we had before the war. Quite a difference.' She warned them: 'If Harry and you want your sitting room, you will have to do it and any fire entirely yourselves, and you will have to help in our bedroom too. Harry will have to carry wood and coal every day.'

In the autumn Harry went up to New College, Oxford. He commented to Molly, after being invited to dine as a guest at high table, 'the amount of drink these dons consume must be tremendous in a week.'

Some members of Sybil's family – Lady Mary (Molly) Baring and her children and her sister Lady Elizabeth (Nisset) Dawnay and her children – spent part of war in Canada. It was there that Nisset died prematurely of a brain tumour in 1941, leaving her children to be brought up by her sister Molly Baring. At the end of November

Sybil portrait in 1941 by Molly Bishop,
(de Wesselow collection).

there was a final crisis in Lambert's health. Harry wrote to Molly: 'Isn't it awful about Daddy, I am so sorry for him having such a dreadful time and for Mummy having to look after him.'

Not long afterwards, on 10 December 1941, Lambert Middleton died aged 64. He had suffered for a long time from many ailments, but his death was unexpected and it came as a shock to Sybil and the family. They all gathered at Lowood, and Lambert's funeral was held at the family church of Bolam near Belsay, in Northumberland. Molly's young cousin, Penelope Palmer, wrote to her: 'I can't tell you how sorry I am. I have only met your father once but even in that little time his charm made a great impression on me. I can only imagine what you must feel and what it would be like if my father was taken from me.'

Lambert's photograph remained on Sybil's dressing table for the rest of her life.

1942

Sybil's diary opened: 'A sad new year but I hope it will see peace of a kind,' although she didn't expect real peace until ten years after the war had ended. She looked back to New Year 1922, the year she had been married, and all the happy memories since then – 'a priceless possession'.

The family were all in mourning but almost immediately they suffered another setback as Harry was hospitalised in Edinburgh with back problems, which left him immobilised for some three months. He was treated in Edinburgh and in February 1942 returned home in a plaster cast to convalesce at Lowood under the care of a nursing sister who tried to engage him in exercise. 'She said brightly, "Now we are going to be very gay this morning, and we will do our exercises which will be great fun".' Sybil sympathised with her depressed son and told her, 'Sister, if you said that to me I think I should murder you and slowly at that.'

By now the United States were in the war and were committing huge resources to the defence of Britain – 'an essential fortress' – and to fighting the Japanese in the Far East. This did not prevent the fall of Singapore and the threat to Burma, Papua New Guinea and even to Australia. All through the war, Sybil continued to do her bit through involvement in the WVS, the ARP, the First Aid Post and in taking responsibility for collection of salvage in the Melrose area. She was involved in packing the Red Cross parcels for prisoners of war, and in what she termed 'blood transfusion' – in fact helping set up blood donor clinics.

A bomb fell on the nearby village of Bowden and failed to explode, all 170 of the inhabitants having to be evacuated until it could be defused.

In March, Sybil visited Cambridge for Molly's confirmation. The Bishop gave a moving and simple address. Sybil felt the loss of her husband: 'It was everything one could wish for Molly and I longed for Lambert.'

In the summer, with Molly by now at a finishing school in Oxford, and Harry back at university, Sybil was free to consider the future. Should she continue to live at Lambert's old family home in the Borders or move south to be closer to where her children were studying and would ultimately live and work? The Army sought to acquire Lowood for its officers, and offered to pay the cost of fuel for central heating, prompting her to consider whether to leave. She ultimately decided to keep Lowood on for the present but to search for a new house in Hampshire.

By the early autumn the course of the war had begun to turn, with the Americans inflicting defeat on the Japanese at the Battle of Midway, with Britain's 8th Army rolling back Rommel's Afrika Korps at El Alamein, and the Russians' epic resistance at Stalingrad.

In December, Sybil wrote to Molly about the new house in the New Forest: 'You will be glad to hear that the survey of Burley Grange was successful so we are going through with the deal.' She had then to tell her long time servants – the Hendersons, Darries and Sandersons and their neighbours. She wrote: 'I rather dread it all. I wonder what your father would have said and whether considering the circumstances he would have approved or not? He died a year ago today; how badly we miss his love and advice, and oh, how much I wish we could discuss Harry's future with him.'

On 10 December she noted in her diary: 'a year ago Lambert died. It seems very long ago and yet so short a time. A sad day full of memories and longings.' She added: 'I told Grizel about Burley Grange. She was very very sad.'

1942 ended with a further tragedy for the family with the death on Christmas Day of Sybil's niece Dinah Jones, at the age of only 26, from tuberculosis. Dinah had been the most vivacious and glamorous of the Jones sisters and her mother Evy never really recovered from her death and the earlier death of another of her daughters, Delia, aged only six, also from tuberculosis.[1] Evy resorted increasingly to spiritualism in a sad attempt to remain in contact with her dead children.

1943

Despite the sad circumstances, Sybil held a New Year's tea party at Lowood and 67 local friends and neighbours came. Her diary lists the wartime provender set before them: 'five dozen small cakes, five dozen finger scones, three Madeira cakes and four small flat round ones.' She hired a taxi to ferry guests through the snow from the lodge at the bottom of the drive.

At the end of January, Roosevelt and Churchill and their military, naval and air chiefs met in Casablanca, for what Roosevelt called the 'Unconditional Surrender meeting', stating 'the aim of the United Nations being the unconditional surrender of Germany, Italy and Japan, but not the destruction of the peoples of the hostile countries.'

On leaving Oxford, in February 1943, Harry decided his future and joined the BBC. He wrote: 'It is impossible to try and describe to you the sort of work I am learning. In short it is to do with how records are made, acoustics and the general organisation that is needed to put a programme on the air, which I assure you is most involved.'

In March 1943, Sybil oversaw the packing of two furniture vans which left for

---

1 Tuberculosis was one of Britain's biggest killers for much of the first half of the twentieth century and only declined after the Second World War with the introduction of vaccination and antibacterial drugs. There is now sadly a resurgence in some quarters.

One of the rooms presumably inside Lowood, (Boyd family collection).

Burley Grange in Hampshire, with Sybil and Helen (Nellie) Barlow, who became her housekeeper and constant companion, travelling down to unpack and begin to move in to the new house. However, Lowood remained in use as the family home in the north and it was not until the end of 1945 that Sybil finally left for good. Indeed, in May Sybil arranged with the Board of Agriculture that the whole of the back of Lowood would provide premises for 26 land girls who would be 'digging for victory'.

On 8 September, Sybil noted with satisfaction that Italy had unconditionally surrendered to the Allies. The previous day, Sybil's Aunt Evy, her mother's sister, had died. Also by September 1943, Molly was in secretarial college in Egham. After a struggle to become fast enough at typing and shorthand, in November 1943 she enrolled in the Foreign Office. There she joined her friends, Margaret Elphinstone (later to become Hon. Margaret Rhodes), Liz Lambart (later Lady Elizabeth Longman), and Diana Legh (later Lady Diana Colville) all girls from well-to-do families working as secretaries for the intelligence services MI5 and MI6. Molly told the story of hearing the approach of a 'doodlebug' flying bomb while taking dictation – she herself took cover under the desk but her boss continued dictating unperturbed and uninterrupted.

MI6 was run by Stewart Menzies – a cousin by marriage (son of Molly's great aunt Tottie Holford). Menzies was the model for 'M' and was responsible for Bletchley Park and its decoding operation, and relaying its intelligence personally to Churchill. Molly remembered that he always signed in green ink.

1944

In June 1944, the Guards' Chapel in London was demolished by a bomb during a service. Molly was working nearby in the MI6 office off Petty France and was luckily unhurt.

Later, as the Blitz in London intensified, Molly was moved for her protection to Windsor where she lived with an elderly Canon of the Church of England in a tower of Windsor Castle. The Royal family heard that this young girl was there all alone and very kindly invited her to tea. Afterwards they played the card game 'Racing Demon' in which each player has a separate pack of cards which they race to discard to finish first. Princess Margaret, prevented from finishing the game by holding high-value court cards, exclaimed 'Damn these kings and queens' – only to be gently rebuked by her mother.

Sybil's mother, Countess Alice, was by now living with her at Lowood. She was 85 and had been soldiering on despite failing health through the previous winter in a seriously under heated house. In September, her ill-health finally caught up with her. On 4 September, after making tomato chutney all afternoon with the cook Mrs Sanderson, Alice felt tired. She woke in the night and found that she had lost the use of her left arm and feared it had been a stroke.

The next day, while Harry and Sybil were chatting to her, Alice suffered another stroke 'I suddenly saw Mother's mouth go crooked for a couple of moments and she could not speak.' She was nursed but continued to decline, Sybil noting 'Mother feels that she is going to die and is anxious to do so.' Evy and Charlie were both summoned and Alice took her leave of Harry who was returning south: 'Goodbye darling you have been a very good grandson to me.'

On 12 September, Sybil was woken in the middle of the night. Alice had taken a very powerful sleeping draught but had woken unable to speak. Sybil stayed with her all night, 'Mother trying and praying to die – very painful. In the morning Dr Graham gave her 16th of heroin.' Ten days later, Alice died: 'She just slowly and very peacefully ceased to breathe.'

She was cremated on 25 September, at Edinburgh Crematorium – 'a very simple nice service like Lambert.' The next day a service was held at Howick: 'all old Howick people who still knew Mother came. Six choirboys from Alnwick sang beautifully two hymns. A lovely peaceful service Mother would have called it.'

The following day, a new member of the family was born – Sybil's niece Nancy Morse had a daughter whom she called Annabel.

In October that year, Aileen Roberts also died. She was older than Sybil and had long been her close friend and confidante.

1945

The year saw Sybil moving about from Lowood, to Alice's former home Pipers Croft to prepare for probate, to Burley which was being converted and extended, and back to Lowood where the final auction of their furniture and contents took place. On 30 April, the Germans announced the death of Hitler. The next day, the Lowood sale began: '3 to 400 people came. A great many cars. The auctioneer (Mr

Muir) stood on the steps of the garden entrance and people sat on the grass.' The sale netted £2,375 on the first day, £394 on the second.

On 8 May, Churchill made an announcement of the German surrender and declared the following day to be Victory in Europe Day (VE Day). They listened to a wonderful radio broadcast 'a tribute to the King from all the Dominions and Colonies which gave them an excuse to relate all they had done in the last six years. Brilliantly done and most moving.'

On 10 May, a momentous domestic event took place – Sybil left Lowood for the last time: 'at last the sad day arrived but we were so busy that we did not have leisure to think about it. I got off in the car with two dogs at 4.15; had tea with Grizel and just stopped off to see Nina.' The next day she and Harry set off southwards from Howick on a journey dogged by mechanical breakdowns.

> We took the car into a garage in Darlington where a young boy put the ignition wrong with the result that it could only start when being towed. Went to the garage at Beverley and again at Doncaster – continued trouble with starting, five times in garages, a white fog by 11 p.m. so at 3 a.m., when we reached Market Harborough and the car stopped, we decided to sleep by the roadside which we did till 7 a.m. The dogs thought it a strange day.

They completed their journey the next day, calling in at the Wake's family home at Courteenhall near Northampton and at Oxford to pick up Molly, before finally driving to Burley. They had now truly left the Borders for good.

The following month Sybil spent time moving into Burley, hanging pictures and unpacking case after case, beginning to plant her new garden, helped on weekends by Harry and Molly. She began to get to know and enjoy her new surroundings – walking her dogs, shopping in nearby Ringwood and bathing at Mudeford down on the coast near Christchurch.

At the start of August came further astonishing and unnerving news – the explosion of the first atomic bomb over Hiroshima. Sybil wrote:

> A new era has set in. It all sounds very frightening. It has cost £500,000,000 to produce and American and British scientists have worked together. It is 22,000 times more powerful than one ten ton bomb. It sounds devastatingly frightful. Will man destroy himself by his own ingenuity?

On 13 August after the second bomb was dropped on Nagasaki, America announced the unconditional surrender of Japan. 15 August was declared the first VJ Day and coincided with the opening of Parliament. Sybil wrote: 'Immense and frantically happy crowds throng the London streets and cheer the procession. Great rejoicing and huge crowds all over the country.'

Sybil's Aunt Louisa, aged 90, came to tea, 'a little deaf but wonderfully alert in mind and interest.' On the following days Sybil worked in her kitchen garden and Aunt Louisa sat out on the lawn reading and sketching. It was time for new plans and Molly was invited out to Cape Town by her cousin Molly Baring, the wife of the British High Commissioner to South Africa, Evelyn Baring. The last entry in Sybil's 1945 diary reads: '10 December: Molly sails for South Africa from Liverpool with Harry Grenfell.'

31

Over to the children

Harry and Molly were both now living and working in London and of course Sybil's interests and concerns were increasingly wrapped up in what they were doing. Harry was a new executive in the BBC where he became a newsreader at the time when they were required to don a dinner jacket and black tie in order to read the news even on the radio! He loved horse racing and began to acquire of a succession of horses.

Television was an exciting new communications medium which almost defined the new post-war era. The BBC's television service had closed during the war years, and was reopened in 1946. Television news began with the programme *Newsreel* in 1948, and the first great outside broadcast was the coronation of Queen Elizabeth II in June 1953. Harry made his name in outside broadcasting. He was very much a man about town and remained a bachelor until 1964, when he married Jennifer Berry.

Molly visits South Africa

In 1946, Molly travelled to South Africa for six months with her cousin Harry Grenfell, who had lost his legs in the war and who was going to work in Rhodesia. The trip was a present for her 21st birthday and she was going out to stay with and help her cousin Lady Mary Baring (confusingly also called Molly) in Cape Town where her husband Sir Evelyn Baring[1] was now British High Commissioner to South Africa. Evelyn Baring distinguished the two Mollys by calling his wife 'Auntie' and Molly Middleton 'Agatha'.

Colonial administration, and particularly Rhodesia, could almost be said to be in the family's DNA. Molly's grandfather, Albert 4th Earl Grey had been Administrator of Rhodesia 50 years earlier. Familiarity with the strangely different, almost nineteenth century, world of colonial Africa, was part of the family's experience, but South Africa was a breath of fresh air to Molly. There was none of the rationing or food shortages of post-war Britain. It was an insight quite literally into another world – with beautiful houses, exotic flowers, and black servants at one's beck and call, of parties, receptions, tennis and bathing. Molly wrote to her mother: 'I'm thrilled with this country and I am enjoying it to the full – I've got my love of travel

---

1 Sir Evelyn Baring, 1st Baron Howick of Glendale (1903-73). Younger son of the 1st Earl of Cromer. He married Lady Mary (Molly) Grey in 1935. He was Governor of Southern Rhodesia (1942-4), High Commissioner for Southern Africa (1944-51) and Governor of Kenya (1952-9). He was created 1st Baron Howick of Glendale in 1960 and a Knight of the Garter in 1972.

Molly, photographed circa 1948,
(Boyd family collection).

from you.'

She described the High Commissioner's house in Wynberg, a low, rambling, white thatched house at the foot of Table Mountain, overlooking Cape Town: 'At night it is especially beautiful, as the town lights twinkle like hundreds of stars below and the mountain rears up like a protective wall on the left.'

It was of course very much a European dominated Africa which she encountered – living in the High Commission was a bit like living in a 'bubble' – protected and with one's every whim met by an army of black servants. And the High Commissioner's house at Wynberg would have seemed reassuringly British – its airy rooms furnished with a mix of comfortable furniture from home and adorned with some exotic African artefacts. The parties they went to were predominantly of the white European elite. Molly Middleton probably only rarely had the opportunity to meet many Africans except for the household staff.

Even then Cape Town could be threatening. A murder had made the roads outside the High Commission compound too dangerous to walk down at night. 'Here no one dares go out after dark. A gory murder took place last week and the murderer was seen escaping onto the side of the mountain, where he is still at large. Every time one goes outside the gate one is met by a native policeman and a bloodhound.'

She went surfing on Muisenberg Beach and experienced South African style horseracing: 'It is the crookedest thing on Earth. They decide in advance which horse is to win each race, and it may be the favourite or a rank outsider.' She and Evelyn Baring, an accomplished mountaineer, climbed 2,000 feet on a steep path up Table Mountain in broiling sun to join a Remembrance Day service on its summit addressed by Jan Smuts, Prime Minister of South Africa and a hero to both the Afrikaners and to the British. She wrote: 'He's a great man and I'm terribly glad I was there. It's something I shall always remember.'

She was also taken to see the proceedings of the National Parliament in Cape Town, a body based on the Westminster Parliament, whose byzantine ways bemused her: 'Although out here is an absolute duplicate of what goes on at home, I was amazed by the whole procedure. Neither the Speaker nor the other members seem to pay attention to what he said, either going to sleep or gossiping among themselves! How do they get anything done?'

She went with Molly Baring to see a Cape Town slum:

> It is a large area called Pondochi, on some mud flats near to the sea. Very often the sea floods the natives out but they always return and continue to live in the same squalor. An organisation called Cafa is starting to help them, but there are so many similar slums out here that what one person does is just a drop in the ocean. Still I suppose it is better than nothing.

She was taken to hear Evelyn Baring speak on native development. 'He speaks awfully well making every point very clear and concise. We were introduced to the overall Chief of Bechuanaland, a brilliant man who is a qualified lawyer.[2] It is E's private belief that he would make a very suitable Governor General of S.A.!' The brilliant young lawyer might have been Seretse Khama, who did indeed later go on to be President of Basutoland.

After a month or so of Cape Town society, Molly went 'up country' to Salisbury, in Southern Rhodesia. She was warned in advance of the health risks:

> It seems that there are thousands of things that one has to take precautions against. Boiling all water and milk; not wearing any clothes rough dried or else you get some terrible bug; seeing that the mosquito nets are cleaned each day; not touching running water or you collect a parasite, and oh endless other things.

She nevertheless revelled in the outdoor life of the Marandella Hills, staying with her hosts the McIlwaines in a cottage they had built themselves:

> We're 7,000 feet up here and the cottage is beside the river with a waterfall just a few yards away. It is too high for either malaria or bilharzia so bathing and fishing has no drawbacks. It is very snug but one has to live a hardy life. No hot water, about a mile to the PK and one guttering candle. I'm loving it all.

But she was less impressed by the atrocious state of the roads in the bush, where they took an hour to travel six miles.

She went on to Lusaka in Northern Rhodesia (now Zambia), where by this time Harry Grenfell had found a house. Hitherto her interaction with black Africans had been very limited, just a quick visit to a black slum in Cape Town and meeting black house servants at the High Commissioner's house. In Lusaka she became responsible for running Harry Grenfell's house and managing his black servants. She fell out with one called 'Motorcar' whom she thought rude and lazy, but became firm friends with the others, Joseph, Cook and Johnny the gardener. She particularly enjoyed gardening – the speed at which plants grew was a revelation: 'The garden is coming up fast. The sweet peas grow inches every day, the carnation seedlings have begun to show. It is thrilling going out each morning to see how much bigger they have all got. Johnny is thrilled too.'

---

2 Perhaps Seretse Khama, (1921-80), who joined the Inner Temple in London in 1946. He became first President of independent Basutoland in 1965. Although very young to have been pre-eminent chief in 1946, his uncle had been regent while he was a minor.

John Boyd, photographed circa 1948,
(Boyd family collection).

Molly obviously had a problem with Motorcar, the servant with whom she didn't get on: 'Motorcar is still here, as lazy and as unpleasant as ever. I've got a new method of dealing with him. Instead of following him around all day to see that he does some work, I leave him alone (until he should have finished the job) and then if it hasn't been done he has to do it in his spare time.'

She had amusing family stories to relate. Her aunt Hilda Grenfell, who was visiting Washington, had telexed her family back home: 'Invited to lunch at the White House, must have my feather boa, please send it by special plane so as to arrive tomorrow morning without fail!' Molly commented that only Aunt Hilda could make such a demand. She also had admirers, particularly Edgar, a young officer who hoped to marry her: 'Edgar is a very unexciting lover, but a very persistent one.'

Despite regular 'sundowner 'parties, they were in fact very cut off in Lusaka. They didn't get the Cape Town newspapers until three days late and the radio signal was intermittent. It was possible to feel quite lonely and isolated, particularly if like Harry Grenfell you were disabled.

Molly met some feisty characters, including Anne Botha Reid, a girl her own age, granddaughter of the legendary Boer commander General Louis Botha. Working as a secretary for the British Army, Anne Botha Reid was unconventional and far from compliant, taking weeks over and above her holiday allowance. When denied a day off to celebrate Dingaans Day, which she claimed as a great Zulu holiday, she responded by heaping old files in the middle of her office, lighting them and doing a Zulu war dance around the fire. Molly wrote: 'They must now know what they are dealing with.'

Out riding in the bush one day, Molly and a friend saw what appeared to be a big cat close by: 'About 150 yards in front of us was quite definitely an animal of sorts, standing up in the long grass. We could just see its head and the outline of a catlike tail. It may have been a leopard or a cheetah. We were riding around Leopard's Hill, so I firmly believe it was one!' The two girls retreated a safe distance to a kopje (hill) from where they surveyed the country once more. 'There was the

Sybil at Molly's wedding, flanked by the author's other grandparents Commander J G Boyd and Violet Boyd, and Harry, (Boyd family collection).

animal only it was in a different position, still practically hidden in the grass. Needless to say no-one believes our story.'

She participated in the ceremonial occasions – a military parade bidding farewell to the outgoing governor – where she was mildly critical of the pomposity: 'Lusaka society turned out for the show in all its finest feathers: high heels, silk stockings, some absurdly beveiled hats, and tightfitting dresses.'

Molly turned 21 in Africa, and was presented with innumerable parcels and bouquets of flowers 'which made me feel like a filmstar!' She went out to South Africa an inexperienced girl and returned six months later, a self-confident young woman. Her cousin Harry Grenfell wrote to Sybil: 'Your Molly is now an accomplished housewife. She has learnt to take it all in her stride; to meet all sorts of ages, and that is a liberal education in itself.'

On her return home that summer, Molly Middleton fell in love with Captain John Boyd, of the King's Own Scottish Borders, who had been wounded in France, losing his leg. In fact they had grown up less than five miles apart in the Scottish Borders – the Boyds living at Whiterigg, a farm the other side of the Eildon Hills from Lowood – and the two had met at tennis parties and other children's parties. Now Molly and John fell in love and Sybil, realising that it might be the real thing, took Molly off on a visit to Grand Metis in Canada, where she felt that the peace and quiet of the place would help Molly to reach her great decision. John continued to send letters to her in Canada which left Molly in no doubt of the strength of his feelings.

They became engaged and married on 20 February 1948.

32

Sybil revisits Africa

In the 1950s, Sybil paid two visits to stay with her niece, Lady Molly Baring, in Africa. The first was to Cape Town in 1950 where Molly's husband Sir Evelyn Baring was High Commissioner; the second, when Sybil was 74, was to Kenya in 1956 during Britain's final decade of Empire, when Evelyn Baring was Governor and facing the Mau Mau rebellion.

It is of course easy to overstate the importance of Africa in Sybil's life. It was certainly the place which had been the proving ground for her father's service in colonial administration, as Administrator of Rhodesia. And other members of the Grey family were also associated with the continent, such as George Grey (Sir Edward Grey's brother). Sybil had visited South Africa and Rhodesia in 1912 with her father, but although she was aware of its importance in the family's history, it wasn't as significant to her as Canada and Russia. However, through Sybil's visits to Africa in the 1950s we can glimpse a picture of the final stages of the Empire which had been so central to her father's life and beliefs.

Sybil visits South Africa, 1950
At the start of 1950, following her daughter's example, Sybil visited South Africa where she was a guest of the Barings at the High Commission's beautiful house in Wynberg, Cape Town. She would have relaxed and enjoyed the balmy weather while Britain faced a cold and austere winter.

She described a government house garden party, the first of a number of exotic scenes: 'It was one of the best shows I have seen for quite a long time. It is a very big garden and there are extensive lawns and big oak trees. All the ministers and the diplomats stay on a top lawn to themselves, with the other 2,300 guests being on the lower lawns at hundreds of tables. Rather like being below the salt.' They rubbed shoulders with General Smuts and Dr Malan the South African Prime Minister as a detachment of Scottish soldiers in white uniforms marched up and down the lawns playing the bagpipes.

Sybil was delighted to be taken on a three day trip round a game reserve by Mrs Stevenson Hamilton, 'the lion woman!' who promised to show her 'lions and every conceivable wild animal!' She had to fly 3½ hours to Johannesburg and she was uneasy: 'I rather wonder how I shall like flying – I am not that keen on it, but everyone says that if you have a chance to go into Kruger National Game Reserve with Mrs S. H. you would be mad to refuse the offer.'

She gave an amusing, rather acerbic account of one of their dinner guests, Miss

Attlee, sister of the British Prime Minister Clement Attlee. 'She is rather a fearsome old lady, with a will of iron. She has spent 40 years out here, her life's work being to convert Mohammedans to Christianity. She has converted nine and there are another two half converted. We feel it is rather a poor return for 40 years of intense effort.'

In Britain there was a General Election in February in which Labour held on by a slim majority of five. Britain was still trapped in post war austerity and rationing, which contrasted markedly with the more opulent lifestyle in colonial Africa, so she sent packets of food and stores home: 'I have sent you a parcel of 4 lbs. of ham and chicken and one tin of lard, also one of soap, consisting of six lavender toilet soap and 3½ lbs. bag of soap flakes.'

Burley, 1955

At home in Hampshire, she had her grandchildren to stay and prepared to hold a children's party: 'I am writing this on the terrace just after breakfast, the scent of the wisteria is almost overpowering — and there is a delicious soft summer wind blowing. We have a party of 20 children this afternoon and what we shall do if they are all in the house I have no idea! I understand they all mean to be bandits and very wild. They all have paper swords, daggers made of cardboard with gilt handles, water pistols and small gold dirks to put in the tops of their socks.' Many of Sybil's grandchildren and great nieces and nephews remembered her enthusiasm making paper swords and hats for them.

In mid-1955 she listened to the Prime Minister, Anthony Eden, speaking on the radio about the developing Suez crisis. She thought him dull and a poor communicator compared to Churchill: 'The trouble is that for sixteen years, whenever there has been a crisis, we have been accustomed to listen to a genius speaking, and now everyone falls painfully short.'

Kenya 1956

1956 was a year of two major international crises – the failed Hungarian Uprising against Soviet occupation and the Suez crisis – the last fling of British imperial adventuring to try to gain control of the Suez Canal that was snuffed out by the USA.

It was also a time of ongoing crisis in Kenya, where Britain confronted the Mau Mau rebellion which began in 1952 and lasted eight years. The Mau Mau was drawn from the largest tribe, the Kikuyu, who had suffered particularly from the colonial practice of reserving the best agricultural land in the highlands for white settlers. It was a ferocious insurgency which saw murderous attacks and atrocities against isolated white settler families and farms as well as fraticidal attacks on the villages of loyalist elements of the Kikuyu. The British brought in 20,000 troops to help quell the uprising as well as using deportation of Kikuyu to giant reservations. Many thousands of Africans, both rebels and loyalists, were killed during the eight year insurgency, whereas only 32 settlers died. By 1956 when Sybil visited the troubled colony, the military phase was largely over and it had become chiefly a policing operation against the terrorists. It remained a bloody affair, with atrocities on both sides, and with Mau Mau prisoners held in detention camps sometimes under appalling conditions.

Sybil flew out to Kenya to stay with her niece Molly Baring, wife of Sir Evelyn Baring, the Governor. She was unprepared for the contrast between the appearance of Nairobi and the opulence of Government House. She was driven through the city, 'through what I thought were very squalid surroundings and drab looking buildings – so I was completely unprepared for what I was to see on entering Government House – it is fantastic it is out of this world of 1956 – I feel I am living in a dream. The house is beautiful, very large and supremely comfortable. It is built round two big open courtyards with green grass, fountains in the centre and lovely creepers. All the main sitting rooms open out onto the biggest of the courtyards with a wide corridor running all round and then big arches all round, so from one set of rooms you can look through the arches across the courtyard, gay with flowers, through the opposite white arches to the rooms on the other side.' She included a small pen and ink sketch of the arches in her letter.

Coming down to dinner she was entranced by the brilliantly lit rooms and courtyard: 'As I crossed the green grass of the courtyard the smell of the *stephanotis* blooms on one of the creepers was almost overpowering – the stars above brilliant, I felt it couldn't be real, it must be some beautifully staged show.'

She was given the most comfortable bedroom and was amazed at the attentiveness of the staff: 'Black boys in long white coats and red fezzes fall over each other. My own boy is quite embarrassingly attentive. He unpacked for me and arranged all my clothes quite as well as an absolutely first-class lady's maid. He is always popping in and out of my room to see that nothing is wanted.' She joked: 'I never know what he will do next and quite expect him to help me dress!'

The garden was just as superlative: 'Just outside is a most comfortable large loggia with the most expensive and luxurious garden furniture. I spent all yesterday afternoon lying on one of its long chairs looking out onto a brilliant border of flowers – lovely roses, lilies, etc – with an enticing blue swimming pool on one side and all looking onto an extensive garden, lawns, flowering shrubs, etc.'

Sybil did not just lie in the garden – she made a number of trips out into the country to visit owners of some of the great estates. The first was 50 miles away, the home of an Irishman, Major Joyce, whose American wife Sybil had known in Canada 45 years before. 'Their house is most comfortable and built half way up a 600 foot hill, with a most superb view, you look down onto a plain which extends for miles and miles, and hills in the distance. I should never be tired of looking at it. As Mary Joyce says, it is a very African view.'

Major Joyce farmed 20,000 acres with nearly all dairy cattle. Sybil was told that he was one of the best farmers in Kenya and was one of the first white settlers back in 1910. He was also known for having given 5,000 acres over to the local people who worked for him:

They are called squatters for they all live on these 5,000 acres – they grow their maize and their crops – they each have three cows, or one cow and seven sheep. There are 1,250 men, women and children living on this area, and Major Joyce has built a school and provides a teacher, and has just built a shop where they can buy the necessaries of life instead of having to go into the nearest town miles away. There they all work for him and get wages of about 70 shillings a month, some of the more expert ones get more.

The workers were from a different tribe to the Kikuyu and had never joined the Mau Mau, and Major Joyce left his windows and doors open, but kept a revolver handy at night, just in case.

A week later she, Molly Baring and Charlie her brother went to stay the night with a Major Sharpe who lived on the slopes of the Aberdare Mountains, 160 miles from Nairobi. She described him as 'a great character has a lovely garden with peacocks, ducks and geese and all sorts of birds and lots of elephant all round in the forest and bang in the heart of the Mau Mau country. The strange thing is he has never been attacked.' Major Sharpe had armed night watchmen and he also kept his revolver at his side.

The next day they drove further to visit Michael Blundell and his wife, also in Mau Mau country. Blundell was Minister of Agriculture and a member of Evelyn Bar-

Sybil in Kenya in 1956 on safari,
(Anne Dawnay collection).

ing's War Council. Sybil viewed him as the most important white politician in Kenya: 'a real charmer, he started life with the idea of being an opera singer, is now aged 45 and a farmer and a man of immense character and very amusing.' Blundell was indeed highly regarded by all sides, black and white, and helped Evelyn Baring to end the Mau Mau rebellion by bringing in land reforms. Following Kenyan independence he led a short lived multiracial New Kenya Party.

In the evening Blundell took them up the hill behind his house at just over 8,000 feet to 'the most superb view I have ever seen... as we stood on the top we could see 300 miles from north to south and 150 miles from east to west. I have never seen anything like it – plains, forests, mountains, lakes laid out in front of our eyes and the sun setting over the furthest range opposite us 150 miles away. This is certainly a most beautiful and fascinating country.'

She reflected soberly on what she had seen:

> Now that I have seen the forest on the slopes of the Aberdare Mountains with dense undergrowth, I cannot see how the Mau Mau can be mopped up. Regiments of soldiers could force their way through the forest and could easily miss the natives. Black men are much much easier hidden than white men – for they fade into the earth. However it is all so much better than a few months ago – although nobody knows how many terrorists still remain active, probably about 2,000.

There was a large party of people staying at Government House, many family members, including Charlie and Mabel Grey, and Sybil's great niece Anne Dawnay, and her cousins Peregrine Pollen, and Patricia Dawnay (née Wake). Others included William (Willie) and Polly Percy, Davina Bowes Lyon, and Claire Baring.

Sybil writing, (Anne Dawnay collection).

Sybil and nine others went on a safari to Marsabit, 400 miles north of Nairobi. It was a demanding journey, travelling in two Land Rovers and a Humber Super Snipe, along barely made up roads and tracks in the far north of Kenya. Sybil sketched their itinerary:

> We skirt round the base of Mount Kenya (17,500 feet) and I think we go on to a place called Isiola where I think we camp for three days where we shall see an incredible number of birds. Then we spend five days at Marsabit where we shall be surrounded on all sides by elephants, crocodiles, etc, scorpions and snakes abound. That sounds fun doesn't it – you shake your shoes and everything you wear before putting it on in case it holds a scorpion. It is all volcanic country with huge craters, one particular one where you lie on the mouth of the crater and watch all the animals 2 to 300 feet below coming to drink.

She gave her daughter Molly a picture of her in safari clothing: 'I am, don't laugh, wearing trousers and short coat of a light khaki colour. You will be sent photographs and will see that your mother does not look too bad in them.'

She described their camp halfway to Marsabit:

> We have been for the last five days camping in supreme luxury – there are four wooden huts with straw roofs, Molly and Anne share one, the Percys another, and Davina and

Claire, and I have the fourth to myself – for Peregrine and James Simmons the aide-de-camp are in a tent. Each hut has a small bathroom with a long bath which is filled with hot water by boys whenever one wants it! We have ten boys with us to attend to our cooking and the camp generally.

Each day they went out on expeditions to see wildlife, in Land Rovers across very rough ground:

There is not the slightest doubt that it is the most incredibly beautiful country. Yesterday we started at 7 a.m. and went 35 miles from the camp and back, 70 in all, but it took over seven hours allowing for stopping and looking at animals. We passed a mountain of 9,000 feet, to the top of which elephant will go. A wild country of mountains, plains with scrubby bush on them, very very red earth, and then suddenly into more trees with those lovely flat thorns which remind one of cedar trees. We have seen elephant, rhino, buffalo, crocodile, oryx, impala, baboons, giraffe, two kinds of zebra, warthogs, waterbuck, genets, camels and two or three kinds of antelope. We haven't seen any lion although there are quite a lot here. The elephants and giraffes are my favourite.

They pressed on to Marsabit, on roads through arid desert country and so little travelled that often no other car would pass that way for three or four days and anyone stranded could easily die of thirst. They reached Marsabit, 'about 70 miles from the Abyssinian border' where they were once more very comfortably accommodated in a little stone house for the women and the men in tents:

The superintendent of police of the Northern Province lives here and we have been dining with him and his wife. She gave us a wonderful meal – a table laden with every kind of cold meats, egg dishes, salads, etc, and we took our plate, knife and fork and walked round the table taking what we fancied, like at the small restaurant at Claridges.

Marsabit is a national reserve of about 1,500 square kilometres which consists of a forested mountain that rises like an oasis in the middle of a desert wilderness. It has three spectacular crater lakes that provide a habitat for wildlife. Sybil wrote from the most famous of these, Paradise Crater:

It is 3.30 p.m. and we are all sitting in canvas chairs at the top of a big hill or small mountain, overlooking a crater which is 400 feet below us. It is an incredible flat green amphitheatre quite circular, about 1,000 yards across, and it is completely encircled by the forest – in the middle is about six acres of slush and water. There is very little water in this country a lot of which is desert, so that the animals come to drink at any place where there is water. The day before yesterday when we were here twelve elephants and a giraffe came. We are too high above them for them to be conscious of us at all. They neither can see nor smell us so behave absolutely naturally.

We suddenly saw a long line of elephants come out of the forest and very slowly and sedately march in single file across the arena to the water and the slush. They were all sizes, two very small babies and one or two very big ones – the biggest old bull in the rear. We watched them for a couple of hours amusing themselves, first having a good drink, and then squirting water over themselves and their friends and finally several of them getting right down and rolling in the mud. It was very amusing and we all had field glasses.

She described the way up through the forest with 'trees covered with silver grey green lichen hanging down from the branches like long bits of seaweed, like a Rackham picture, mysterious and rather sinister.'

Revealingly she commented: 'It is a grim but fascinating country, very beautiful to see but I have no wish to live in it, especially up here for it is mostly desert and very very little water. It is not a white man's country.'

On their way back to Nairobi they stopped off at the home of George Adamson, and his Austrian wife Joy. Sybil wrote:

> They had three lion cubs of not quite four weeks old. They had been after a man eating lion – and a lioness suddenly charged them forcing them to shoot her – and they then found three small helpless cubs three days old. They were now delicious little balls of fluff with pale blue eyes taking their meals out of a baby's bottle and holding the neck of the bottle with their two front paws just like a baby.

Anne Dawnay with three lion cubs at the Adamson's house.
One of the lions was Elsa star of the book 'Born Free' (Anne Dawnay collection).

Sybil and party at Government House in Mombasa, left to right: Peter Carthew, aide-de-camp; Molly Howick; Walter Douglas Scott (Duke of Buccleugh); Mabel Grey; Charlie Grey; Lady De La Warr; Sybil Middleton; Polly Percy; Buck (Lord De La Warr). (Anne Dawnay collection).

One of the three cubs, a little lioness, was hand raised by the Adamsons at their home and became famous as Elsa the lioness in *Born Free*. Her two brothers were later returned to the wild. A delightful photograph shows Sybil's great niece Anne Dawnay holding all the three cubs on her lap.

Their final visit was to the Barings' second home, Government House in Mombasa, on the south eastern coast. Sybil described its setting: 'This is a dream house and place. I am sitting in the most comfortable armchair on the veranda of my immense bedroom – the sea just below us; it's like living on a ship. The continual noise of the long rollers, the bluest of blue green seas with occasional white sails on it, two gigantic palms just to the right of my windows – and the flamboyant trees smothered in brilliant orange and red on the other side of the house, making an unforgettable picture.'

She said of her niece: 'The more I see of Molly the more I admire her. She is always serene and happy and gay and quite charming to everyone. She seems to me much younger than she was at the Cape.'

Sybil would of course never have compared the life of the British colonial elite and white settlers with that of the average African – the huge gulf in lifestyles was an accepted fact of life. And she would naturally have shared the view that the British colonial regime was justified in putting down the murderous rebellion. For much of her life Britain had been at war somewhere in the world – against African peoples in the 1880-90s, against the Boers at the turn of the twentieth century, twice in global wars against Germany and her allies, and subsequently in 'emergencies' in Malaysia and Cyprus. The counter-insurgency in Kenya was seen as just another such war. Sybil did ponder the huge discrepancy in lifestyle between her niece

Molly Baring and the everyday experience of ordinary people back home in Britain in the 1950s, suffering from austerity and rationing. She wrote:

> What Molly will do when she comes home for good I just can't imagine, after sixteen years of this sort of life. Everything is left to a first-class lady housekeeper or an aide-de-camp. She just says what she wants and then never worries again. It certainly is a wonderful life. I knew it well 45 years ago and have immensely enjoyed meeting it again for a couple of months with the knowledge that I shall never see it again.

Fifteen years later, by contrast, I found myself in independent Kenya in very different circumstances – as a young volunteer teacher, travelling the country on local trains and buses and taxis, staying at youth hostels, admiring the wildlife and looking curiously at the home made guns and knives of the 'freedom fighters' displayed in glass cabinets at the National Museum in Nairobi.

Sybil flew home via Khartoum in the Sudan, leaving at 1 a.m. in the morning on a four engine piston aircraft.

> The Captain of our DC6 said on the loudspeaker: 'Goodnight. I hope you will all sleep well. I shall not be speaking to you again until just before we reach Athens,' but at 5.30 he spoke again and said that one engine had failed completely and that another one was giving trouble so that he was going to fly back to Wadi Halfa . As a matter of fact, two engines had stopped and he had to jettison 5,600 gallons of petrol. He made a beautiful landing to all our relief, at a very small aerodrome in the desert.

Later the journey home continued without further incident.

Evelyn Baring's seven years in Kenya were first and foremost that of a colonial governor putting down a major insurgency. He did however have long African experience and a forward looking outlook which favoured long term transition to multiracial participation in the colonial government of Kenya. He mapped out a series of new constitutions that ended the monopoly of white settlers on ministerial input to the Kenyan administration. And he also introduced agrarian reforms which similarly broke the white monopoly on commercial farming and opened it up to successful African farmers to get loans to grow cash crops. Although these reforms were limited, they did help provide a transitional foundation for a more modern Kenya to emerge.

The British did go on to defeat the Mau Mau, with bloodshed and atrocities on both sides. The most damaging incident for the British side occurred in 1959, three years after Sybil's visit. At Hola Camp, a government authorised policy of 'compelling force' was introduced to force recalcitrant black prisoners to work.[1] Eleven prisoners were beaten to death and several dozen wounded. The deaths were at first covered up but then exposed and finally debated in the House of Commons, with Conservative MP Enoch Powell denouncing the government for not punishing the killings.

---

1 A court case in 2013 ultimately led to British Foreign Secretary, William Hague, giving an apology for the ill-treatment of the Mau Mau prisoners nearly 60 years before, and to payment of compensation.

33

Last decade

The last decade of Sybil's life was spent at Burley Grange, her home in the New Forest. Burley was an attractive house, approached by a short drive from the road, and which looked out on to a garden and grassy fields at the rear. Sybil lived there with Nellie Barlow her faithful retainer and companion and her black spaniel Sally.

I remember Burley as a wonderful oasis – its peaceful garden, the green sward of grass outside the drive gates through which ran a stream where small fish and tadpoles could be found, the forest all around for miles, where wild ponies roamed free. We grandchildren went there in our summer holidays and were always welcome. And there were wonderful excursions to the beach at Mudeford on the coast.

Sybil inherited her mother's love of gardens and gardening. She set about extending the garden at the suggestion of her son Harry – taking in a part of the field at the rear of the house which became 'H.G.' (Harry's garden) planted with a mix of roses, shrubs and herbaceous borders. The heavy work of digging and planting was of course done by others, and among a host of other flowers were included her

Burley Grange, Ringwood, in the New Forest, Sybil's final home.
(Boyd family collection).

pride and joy, blue Himalayan poppies from her friend Elsie Reford's garden at Grand Metis.

In 1954, Molly and John Boyd had moved to Frankfurt-am-Main, where John founded ICI Germany. Sybil visited them at Christmas, when the Weihnachsmärkte was held in the Römer Platz, with brighty lit stalls selling pretzels, gingerbread men, gifts, decorations and Christmas trees down by the river, and they all packed into the family car to listen to the Queen's speech on the radio. She visited them in summer when the family holidayed in Bavaria or closer to home in the Taunus Mountains. And she enjoyed being driven at over 100 mph on Germany's speed limit-free autobahn. She later visited them when they moved to Yorkshire.

Molly, Pat Natirbov, and Sybil in Gstaad, on one of Sybil's visits to the Boyd family on the continent in the 1950s. (Boyd family collection).

In April 1956, Sybil went up to London for 'four days of intensive personal reparation. My oculist, my dentist, Blackie, and Miss Grace for treatment of my hair to help I hope some bald patches.' Dr Marjorie Blackie was Sybil's friend and doctor, a specialist in homoeopathy, who was incidentally also the Queen's homeopath. On the way back Sybil stayed with her friends the Astors[1] at their home Hever Castle, a restored Elizabethan castle surrounded by a moat (once the home of Anne Boleyn).

Sybil continued to take a proprietary interest in Harry's racehorses. In August 1957 she was at Goodwood, watching the race from the BBC television outside broadcasting van, fascinated by the making of the programme: 'I haven't the faintest idea who won, it was so exciting so enthralling watching the production of it. I adored every minute of it.'

---

1 Sybil's cousin, Lady Violet Astor (née Kynynmound, 1889-1965). She was daughter of Gilbert El-liott-Murray-Kynynmound, 4th Earl of Minto and Mary Caroline Grey (Sybil's aunt). Her second husband John Jacob Astor, 1st Baron Astor of Hever, was son of William Waldorf Astor; he was brother-in-law to Nancy Astor.

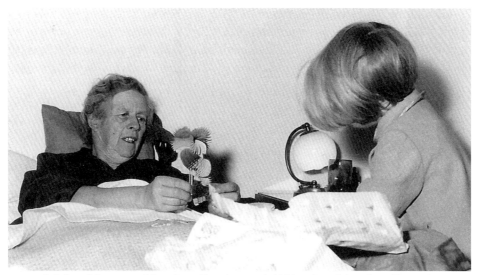

Sybil with her granddaughter Caroline mid-1950s. (Boyd family collection).

By far the most dramatic event, however, was the burglary at Harry's flat in Kinnerton Street, London, when Sybil (aged 76) was staying there in 1958. Harry and Sybil were held at knifepoint by three Irishmen who broke in. Sybil was woken in the night by a noise:

> I got up put on the light and my dressing gown, and went out of my room to see Harry standing in his pyjamas at the top of the stairs with two masked men behind him. Harry, with the utmost calmness, came forward and said, 'There is absolutely nothing to worry about, go back to bed.' This I did and he came in and sat on my bed and one of the men with a trilby hat right over his eyes and his face completely covered joined us. They warned us not to try and move or break a window.

Their guest, Sean Plunkett, however succeeded in locking the burglars, Harry and Sybil into her room, ran off in his silk pyjamas and bare feet and summoned help. Sybil commented dryly: 'It has been another experience in one's life, not one which H and I wish to be repeated too often!'

In July 1958, Mabel Grey, Sybil's sister-in-law, died. They had known each other for over 50 years. The world must indeed have seemed to closing in with the death of her friends. Her life became centred on visits by her grandchildren, great nieces and great nephews. On 15 July 1962 she held a party at Burley to celebrate her 80th birthday.

The following year, on 2 April 1963, her brother Charlie, 5th Earl Grey, died.

In January 1964, her son Harry married Jennifer Berry.

In January 1965, on the death of Winston Churchill, I remember Sybil aged 82 joining the mourners frail but determined, filing past his lying in state in Westminster Great Hall.

She spent much of her remaining energy and passion on her garden, giving an open day for the public in 1966. When she died flowers from her garden were used to decorate the church.

On March 14, 1966 she attended her sister Evy's 80th birthday party, where she was full of life, gay in spirit and interested in other in people despite her crippling arthritis. Another of her favourite cousins, Angus McDonnell, died in April that year.

Sybil in a reclining chair in the garden at Burley Grange. (Boyd family collection).

Less than two months later, on 4 June 1966, Sybil died just short of her 84th birthday. Friends spoke of her brave fight against lameness and growing incapacity, but the end was unexpected and a merciful release. Her friend and doctor, Margery Blackie, and her assistant Mussette Majendie, visited her at Burley and Sybil died the same evening peacefully in her sleep. Cerebral haemorrhage and arteriosclerosis were given as the cause of death.

Dr Blackie wrote to Sybil's sister Evy:

I can't tell you how sorry I am for all of you over Sybil, but how wonderful it was for her to go like that. She felt she was deteriorating and couldn't cope much longer and she was longing to die.

I can't tell you how thankful I am that Musette and I were there. We had such a lovely afternoon with Sybil on Friday and drove her all round the New Forest after tea, planted her carnations for her and had a lovely talk and then I went very thoroughly into her health and was able to reassure her, and she went to bed so peacefully. She drank her coffee sometime and I think then lay down and knew nothing more. She hadn't struggled to reach the bell or anything, and I don't think she ever knew a thing. It was exactly what she would have wished and I think my being there helped Nellie. I know how much you will miss her but I'm sure this is what she would have chosen.

A great friend of Molly's wrote to her about Sybil's death: 'How wonderful the "Bon Dieu" spared her any further suffering – It would have been terrible if she lived, paralysed and perhaps unable to speak, after the stroke and she, of all people I know, deserved a peaceful death.'

Remembering Sybil

Over a hundred people wrote letters of condolence, speaking of their sorrow at Sybil's death – her oldest friends like Dorothy Halifax and Hilda Grenfell, her nieces Molly Howick, Lindy Pollen and Nancy Morse, grandnieces and nephews, friends and neighbours from her years at Lowood in the Scottish Borders, new neighbours and friends from Burley, some even writing from America. All remembered her unique capacity to listen and empathise with people of all ages and from all walks of life, her enthusiasm, her wisdom and clear headed advice, and above all the vibrant love and friendship she gave to them.

They remembered a woman who was kind, with a great zest for life, courageous even in the face of disability and illness, wise and joyously gay in spirit. Mab Jones, whom Sybil had comforted on the death of Mab's husband Bertram, remembered, 'her joy in all loveliness and her ready sympathy, her laughter and the splendid clarity of her vision and the wholesome astringency she put into her advice that was so good for one. She has bound her friends in a sort of goodly fellowship.'

Her friend Doushka Landale, apparently a Russian émigré married into a distinguished Scottish family, wrote to Molly: ' She is not one who would wish to be mourned, but when someone like your mother goes something of life goes too, and my little world is a very poor one today.' She remembered 'a friend who filled so much of what was missing in my life.'

Reggie Grenfell, her nephew and husband of Joyce Grenfell, remembered her sometimes hilarious sense of fun and mischief, as when she loosed a live donkey into his downstairs bedroom at Howick where he was sleeping with his brother Harry.

Lindy Pollen, her niece, recalled how Sybil had dressed her in army uniform to get her a ride in a staff car when she visited Sybil in France in 1919, and how 'we laughed a good deal and always enjoyed being together.'

People remembered her love of gardens and the flowers that decked the church for her funeral, all cut from her garden at Burley, making it look 'more like a wedding than a funeral.'

My aunt Mickey Leschallas remembered how she threw herself into celebrating Christmas: 'I shall always think of her as she would like to be remembered, surrounded by her grandchildren in a sea of paper and string, happily undoing parcels and sharing their delight in each present.'

Nellie Barlow, her faithful housekeeper, helpmeet and companion, wrote: 'I feel very proud to have lived so closely with someone so wonderful as she was. She was the most understanding person I have ever met, and her thoughts were always of what she could do for others, while making light of her own pain and discomfort.'

Sybil's niece, Nancy Morse said of her: 'Her intense love of, and enthusiasm for, life and people and their concerns gave a special patina to everything she said and did – so that being with her was always a refreshment and stimulus, and one was warmed and revitalised and somehow made to glow by her flame.'

Even today, 50 years after her death, her great nephews and nieces and her grandchildren remember someone devoted to and interested in each of them, who never made them feel they were in the presence of an old person or that there was a gap in years between them. They remembered her for the paper hats and swords she made them, and for the wonderful stories she told of her life.

I remember her above all as loving and sympathetic, who taught me to paint and who tried unsuccessfully to pass on to me her love of cricket – when she tried to teach me to catch a ball I am afraid that I replied 'Sorry granny, I'm not that sort of boy.'

One should remember too the contradictory and complex sides of her character and story – the young girl growing up in a conventional Victorian family but who didn't marry until the age of 40; who enjoyed nothing better than sports and physical challenges such as fishing for salmon in the remote wilderness of Canada. A woman who happily embraced the danger of travelling to a war zone in far away Imperial Russia, and who faced the hazards and chaos of the Revolution when soldiers burst in to threaten her and her staff with guns and bayonets. An attractive woman who may have felt that she had some of the character of a man, but who came across to all who knew her as warm, caring, sympathetic and supportive. Someone who was the product of a patrician liberal tradition and who shared her father's support for the progressive Cooperative Movement, but who notably did not sympathise with the suffragettes, the greatest women's movement of her time.

Sybil was an aristocrat's daughter who nevertheless identified with and loved the democratic inclusiveness of Canada where anyone could succeed if they worked hard. A person who helped run a modern military hospital in wartime Russia but who nevertheless believed in a questionable cure based on intoning the slogan 'in every way I am getting better and better'.

A woman whose warmest friendships were with a range of strong and independent women who shared her outlook on the world. A complex character who left others with a glowing memory of what it was to be an engaged, loving, interested and sympathetic human being.

Very simplified GREY family tree

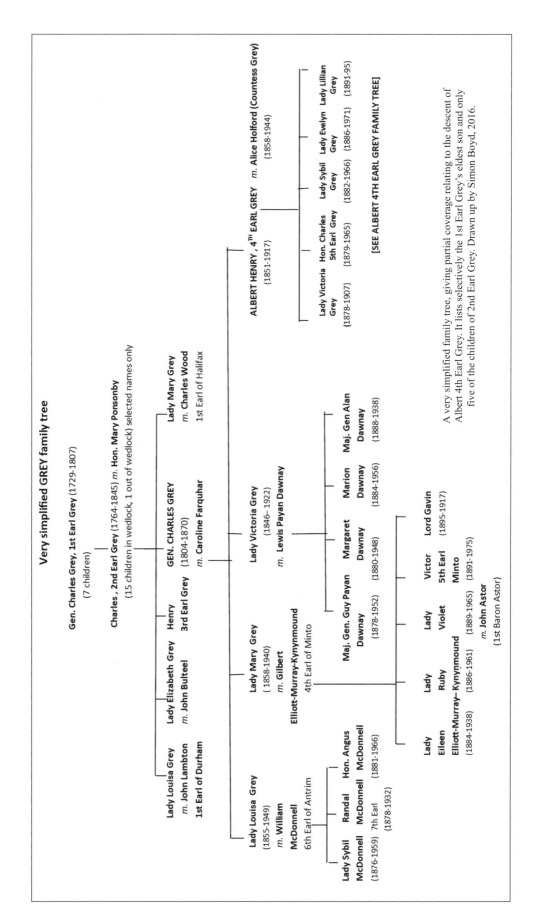

Gen. Charles Grey, 1st Earl Grey (1729-1807)
(7 children)

Charles , 2nd Earl Grey (1764-1845) *m.* **Hon. Mary Ponsonby**
(15 children in wedlock, 1 out of wedlock) selected names only

Lady Louisa Grey
m. John Lambton
1st Earl of Durham

Lady Elizabeth Grey
m. John Bulteel

Henry
3rd Earl Grey

GEN. CHARLES GREY
(1804-1870)
m. **Caroline Farquhar**

Lady Mary Grey
m. Charles Wood
1st Earl of Halifax

ALBERT HENRY , 4ᵀᴴ EARL GREY
(1851-1917)
m. **Alice Holford (Countess Grey)**
(1858-1944)

Lady Victoria
Grey
(1878-1907)

Hon. Charles
5th Earl Grey
(1879-1965)

Lady Sybil
Grey
(1882-1966)

Lady Evelyn
Grey
(1886-1971)

Lady Lillian
Grey
(1891-95)

[SEE ALBERT 4TH EARL GREY FAMILY TREE]

Lady Mary Grey
(1858-1940)
m. Gilbert
Elliott-Murray-Kynynmound
4th Earl of Minto

Lady Victoria Grey
(1846- 1922)
m. Lewis Payan Dawnay

Maj. Gen. Guy Payan
Dawnay
(1878-1952)

Margaret
Dawnay
(1880-1948)

Marion
Dawnay
(1884-1956)

Maj. Gen Alan
Dawnay
(1888-1938)

Lady Louisa Grey
(1855-1949)
m. **William**
McDonnell
6th Earl of Antrim

Lady Sybil
McDonnell
(1876-1959)

Randal
McDonnell
7th Earl
(1878-1932)

Hon. Angus
McDonnell
(1881-1966)

Lady
Eileen
Elliott-Murray– Kynynmound
(1884-1938)

Lady
Ruby
Violet
(1886-1961)

Lady
Violet
(1889-1965)
m. John Astor
(1st Baron Astor)

Victor
5th Earl
Minto
(1891-1975)

Lord Gavin
(1895-1917)

A very simplified family tree, giving partial coverage relating to the descent of Albert 4th Earl Grey. It lists selectively the 1st Earl Grey's eldest son and only five of the children of 2nd Earl Grey. Drawn up by Simon Boyd, 2016.

Albert 4th Earl Grey's family tree

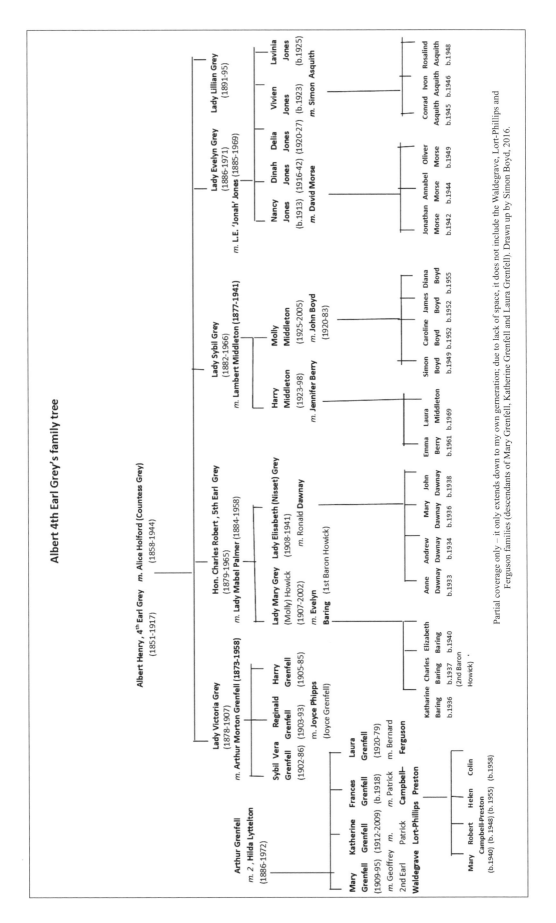

Partial coverage only – it only extends down to my own gemeration; due to lack of space, it does not include the Waldegrave, Lort-Phillips and Ferguson families (descendants of Mary Grenfell, Katherine Grenfell and Laura Grenfell). Drawn up by Simon Boyd, 2016.

Alice Holford's family tree

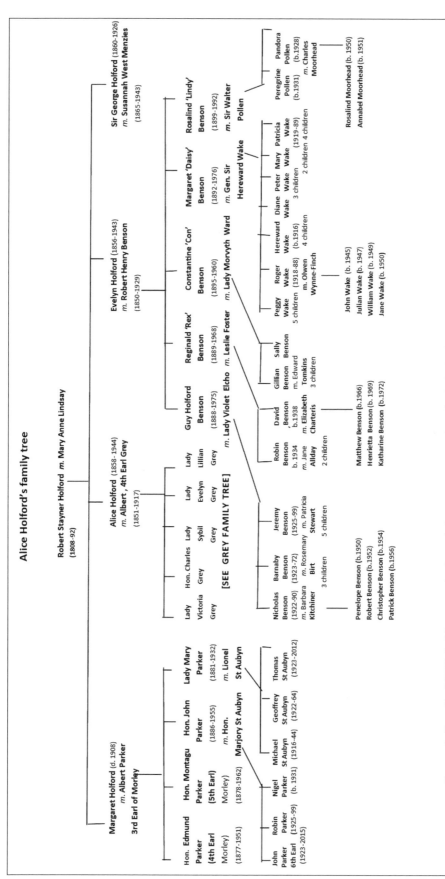

Drawn up by Simon Boyd (2016). Partial coverage only – it extends down to my own generation and omits the details of several Parker, St Aubyn, Benson, Wake and Pollen families.

Author's Note

I remember my grandmother speaking of her time in Russia, most particularly about Rasputin, his hypnotic eyes, his murder and how he would predict and engineer 'accidents' which occurred in the Emperor's palace, thereby helping to cement his influence over the Tsarina. But the full scope of what she did and achieved in Russia in the First World War only struck me later. As a young man, my mother told me that I should write an account of my grandmother's story in Russia.

The story of the Anglo-Russian Hospital has been well told by others particularly Michael Harmer, son of W. D. Harmer, a senior surgeon with the Anglo-Russian Hospital, in his book *The Forgotten Hospital*. Michael Harmer had access to a wide range of my grandmother's letters and diaries, as well as to the papers of others such as Lady Muriel Paget. His account put the history of the Anglo-Russian Hospital on the map and told the story right through to the last remnants of the hospital travelling home with Lady Muriel Paget in an extraordinary journey across Russia to Vladivostok on the Pacific coast, and back home via Japan and the USA.

Other books have included part of the story – e.g. Wilfrid Blunt's biography of Lady Paget entitled *Lady Muriel*, as well as the edited letters of Countess Olga Poutiatine, published as *War and Revolution*, edited by George Alexander Lensen, and the biography of Sir Geoffrey Jefferson, entitled *So that was life*.

My interest was particularly aroused when we found my grandmother's letters and diaries in a large battered green travel trunk in a cold damp backroom. Although the envelopes were in poor condition, some covered with mould, the letters inside were all intact. My sister Caroline and I typed them up (although they were already accompanied by contemporary copies typed on an old manual typewriter).

It was only when the task of typing up Lady Sybil's letters from Russia was finished that I discovered another set of letters – from Sybil's mother Countess Alice Grey, writing from England giving news of the home front in the First World War. There were also a host of other letters and diaries in the trunk – Sybil's diary of her trip to the Yukon in 1909 with her father, the Governor General of Canada; her mother Alice's diary of their round the world trip at the start of 1914; Sybil's letters from Grand Metis, the haven on the St Lawrence owned by Sybil's friend Elsie Reford; Sybil's papers from her time in charge of the Women's Legion of female ambulance drivers in France in 1919-20; and finally the diaries she kept of her visit with her husband Lambert Middleton to South America in 1927 and a set of letters and diaries she wrote in Kenya nearly 30 years later in 1956.

Suddenly it was possible to think of a full scale biography covering the whole of my grandmother's life, rather than just focusing on the time spent in Russia. I was also helped immeasurably by the discovery of my grandmother's earliest letters from the age of twelve in the archives belonging to the Howick Hall Trust, held at the Durham University special collections library.

Seeing and experiencing the places someone has lived in helps one to get a sense of their life and times. In the course of researching the book I have made trips to France and Belgium to see the battlefields of the First World War; to St Petersburg to experience the elegance and decadence and the extraordinary violence of that beautiful city's history; to Canada, to visit Ottawa and Quebec, the site of the colonial government over which Earl Grey presided as Governor General, as well as to Sybil's beloved Grand Metis. I have been to Romania seeking the elusive site of a field hospital in the green Carpathians; as well as visiting the Ukraine to see the beautiful Pecherska Lavra (Monastery) which my grandmother visited in 1916. I have also been lucky enough to visit some of the houses where Sybil and her relatives lived – Howick Hall, her childhood family home in Northumberland; Saltram in Devon, home of her cousins the Parkers; Westonbirt, her uncle's home in Gloucestershire; Lowood, the family home she made in the Scottish Borders with her husband Lambert Middleton; and of course Burley Grange in Hampshire where I knew her and where she died. I have also been privileged to visit some of the 'official' homes she knew – Rideau Hall and the Citadelle, the residences of the Governor Generals of Canada; and in St Petersburg, the Beloselsky-Belozersky Palace that she converted into a hospital.

I was also personally interested in my grandmother's visits to South Africa and to Kenya, and in her father's time as Administrator of Rhodesia at the time of the Matabele War. I have never visited South Africa, but I have lived in both the Sudan and in Nigeria and have visited the beautiful countries of Kenya, Uganda and Tanzania. In these diaries and letters, I believe it is possible to trace in miniature the evolution from the colonial British Empire, through its heyday to the final impetus towards decolonisation and independence in countries like Kenya.

For me it has also been a personal journey rediscovering my family's history, politics and social milieu and the world into which Sybil was born, its values and beliefs dominated by the British Empire, and how that world changed continuously in the course of her life.

What I hope emerges is a picture of a young girl growing up in late Victorian England, coming of age in the Edwardian era, and experiencing the thrill of travelling widely and learning about the world, before taking on the challenge of serving her country in Russia during the First World War and in France just after the war. The book reflects her interest in hospital administration and medical aid in the war, as well as in unconventional therapy, and her love of the open air life and wild places, before settling down to motherhood at the relatively late age of 40 in 1922. It is told largely through her own words, through her diaries and letters.

Russian names and spelling

SPELLINGS: In the chapter on Russia I have adopted a mix of spellings. Lady Sybil Grey tended to use anglicised spellings of her day – so she uses the suffix – 'off' as in Homiakoff and the suffix – 'eff' as in Kieff. I prefer and have tried to use the more modern forms (Homiakov, Kiev, etc). Occasionally Sybil uses Czar for the more usual Tsar.

Other names are variably spelt, e.g. 'Mr Poluvtsov' (one of the heads of the Russian Red Cross in Petrograd who worked with the Anglo-Russian Hospital in 1916). Sybil's earliest letters from Petrograd spell him as 'Mr Polotsoff' or 'Mr Poluvtzoff'. Michael Harmer lists him as 'Mr Polutsov'. It is possible that his real name was 'A. Polontzev' one of the names inscribed on the base of the Ikon that he and others in the Russian Red Cross presented to the Anglo-Russian Hospital.

Other names misspelt by Sybil Grey include 'Count Pouchkine' another Russian Red Cross official. His name (inscribed on the base of the Ikon) was 'Count A. C. Musiu-Pushkin'.

Often Sybil was transcribing a name she had only heard or only seen written in Cyrillic – when she travelled with the Field Hospital she wrote 'I don't know how these place names would be spelt in English [i.e. in Latin script] – I have only seen them written in Russian [i.e. in Cyrillic script].'

Back at home in Howick, the Grey's typist also struggled to interpret Sybil's handwriting and misspellings – so for example Sybil's 'Professor Shevkoonenko' is transcribed as 'Professor Sherkoovenko'. The name was probably 'Shevchenko' (a Ukrainian surname).

DATES: Imperial Russia used the Julian calendar which lagged thirteen days behind the Georgian calendar used in the rest of Europe (and which has since been adopted in Russia). So Sybil's letters characteristically list both dates at the top of her letters, sometimes rather haphazardly.

I have preferred the use of the modern European (Gregorian) calendar, as it makes it possible to compare dates in Sybil's letters from Russia with those say of her mother Alice in England.

A NOTE ON TITLES: Lady Sybil Grey was a Lady in her own right as daughter of an Earl. When she married Lambert Middleton she of course became Lady Sybil Middleton, just as her sisters had become Lady Vera Grenfell and Lady Evelyn Jones.

I have referred to their mother as Countess Alice Grey which was her position as wife of Earl Grey but she would more normally have been referred to as Lady Grey. Usually I refer to them by their Christian names, as they would themselves.

Acknowledgements

I wish to thank the following for their help and encouragement:

I was given immense help by Mike Harkness and the Durham University Library, Special Collections Library, which houses the Grey family papers. They enabled me to track down my grandmother's earliest letters aged ten in 1892 and those describing her youth and young womanhood in late Victorian and Edwardian Britain, together with her early visits to Italy and Malta, and her first visit to Africa with her parents in 1912.

In particular my thanks are due to my cousin Charles Baring, 2nd Lord Howick of Glendale, who showed me round Howick and generously allowed me to use letters and photographs belonging to the Howick Hall Trust at the Durham University Library. Thanks are also due to Richard Davies of the Brotherton Library, University of Leeds, which houses the papers of W. D. Harmer, and to the British Red Cross that holds the archive of the Anglo-Russian Hospital, for allowing the use of their photographs.

I am also grateful for the help and hospitality I received while researching Sybil's life with her parents in Canada, in particular from Alexander Reford, great grandson of Elsie Reford whose home at Grand Metis on the St Lawrence my grandmother visited many times. Alexander generously welcomed my wife Julia and me to Estevan Lodge and the Reford Gardens and showed us his archive. Also in Canada, my thanks are due to David Mendel for his stimulating overview of the history of Quebec and Canada; and to Kayley Kimball and Jean Matheson of the National Library and Archive of Canada (LAC) for their help and assistance in researching the wonderful LAC archives in Ottawa.

I am deeply grateful to my cousin Vivien Asquith, Sybil's niece, who kindly showed me the Jones family photograph collection and talked about her mother Evy and her father 'Jonah' Jones, as well as her recollections of Sybil. I am also indebted to my cousins, Anne Dawnay for her support and encouragement and for sharing her memories of my grandmother and Kenya; and Laura de Wesselow for sharing her collection of Middleton family photographs.

Nick Rollin, Ted Holt and Eloise Grey all helped greatly with their constructive comments on reading early drafts of chapters. In particular I wish to thank my friend and former colleague Jo Warrior for reading the synopsis and draft chapters and for her sympathetic and incisive advice on how to improve the book.

My heartfelt thanks go to my wife Julia for help and support at every stage of writing and research of this project and for putting up with the setbacks which it has sometimes involved as well sharing in the endless exciting discoveries. And also my sisters Caroline and Diana and to my brother James, with whom I share the ownership of my grandmother's copyright, for their forbearance and encouragement, and above all to Caroline who retyped my grandmother's letters from Russia.

I am greatly indebted to Lynette Owen, former Rights Director of Pearson, for her help and guidance on the intricacies of rights and copyright law.

I much appreciate the help and support of the descendants of those who worked as Lady Sybil's colleagues in the Anglo-Russian Hospital, Petrograd, particularly William and Juliet Harmer (grandchildren of W. D. Harmer) for the use of photographs and the map of the Eastern Front from their father Michael Harmer's excellent book *The Forgotten Hospital,* and for permission to use Lady Sybil's letter about the murder of Rasputin. Also, Hatty Free (great granddaughter of Lady Paget), Simon Jefferson (grandson of Sir Geoffrey Jefferson) and others, together with Dr Pauline Monro, who helped us to share in, and bring alive, and celebrate the centenary of the Anglo-Russian Hospital in 2016 at its former home at the Beloselsky-Belozersky Palace, St Petersburg, and in London at the Royal College of Nursing.

I am also grateful to Avril Meakin of the Howick Heritage Group for her interest in Lady Sybil and all things to do with Howick's history and for helping to conserve the superb Howick Hall Hospital photograph album, and to Christopher Arnander for information about his grandfather, David Lindsay, 27th Earl of Crawford and 10th Earl of Balcarres; and to my cousins Robert Campbell-Preston and David Benson for telling me about their families.

My thanks are also due to Lucy Hughes Hallett and Rory Maclean for a very challenging Arvon writing course at the Hurst in Shropshire; to Julie Summers for encouragement and help; and to the tutors at Madingley Hall for their insights on life writing; and to all those who have helped me tell my grandmother's story. Any errors or failure to take good advice is down to me alone.

Above all my thanks go to my grandmother, 'Burley Granny' as we knew her, and to my mother, Molly Boyd, who told to me many of the stories about her.

Simon Boyd, December 2017

Sources and thanks

Use of copyright material and other material

I am grateful to my cousin Lord Howick and the Howick Hall Trustees for the use of letters by Lady Sybil Grey and photographs held in the Grey Papers, at the Durham University Library, Special Collections, and for use of copyright material from the Howick Hall Hospital photograph album (digitised by Northumberland Archives). I am also indebted to my cousins Anne Dawnay, Vivien Asquith and Laura de Wesselow for use of their collections of photographs; and to Alexander Reford, the British Red Cross, the National Trust, the Library and Archives of Canada, the Yukon Archives and to many others for permission to use copyright and other material listed below.

Text materials used from Durham University Library, Special Collections files:

GRE 218/3: (May 1894-Dec 1902) Lady Sybil Grey (SG) to parents from Glenarm Castle, Ireland, May 1894; from Howick, March 1897. SG to mother from Malta, Dec. 1902, Jan. 1903

GRE 216/3 Part 1: SG to father from Ottawa, re mother's attack of scarlet fever, 4, 5, 6 July 1909. SG to father from Lockinge, 6 Dec. 1909, re House of Lords debate on Budget, re suffragettes and re forthcoming 1910 election.

GRE 216/3. Part 2: SG from Bradford re 1910 election, 14 Jan.1909.

GRE 208/2: Victoria (Vera) Grey from Ottawa to SG re her visit to Canada, 3 Dec 1899, 14 Dec 1899, 18 Jan 1900, 1 Feb1900.

GRE 213/3: SG from Howick to parents, 16 July 1892, 26 Nov. 1892; 13 July 1894. SG from Dorchester House to parents, 5 March 1896, 26 March 1896. SG from Howick to parents, 9 April, 17 April and 24 April 1896, 1 May 1896. SG from Dorchester House, 8 May, 15 May, 29 May 1896; 6 June, 12 June 1896. SG from Newells, Horsham, 3 July, 24 July 1896. SG from Saltram, 27 Aug. 1896, 18 Sept 1896, 6 Nov., 11 Dec., 18 Dec., 24 Dec.. SG from Saltram, 1 Jan., 15 Jan., 29 Jan., 18 Feb. 1897. SG from Howick, 12 March, 26, March 1897, 2 April, 16 April, 23 April, 30 April 1897, 23 July, 30 July 1897. SG from Villa Palmieri, Florence, April 17, 1899. SG from Hotel Bristol, Rome, 5 May 1899. SG from 1 Connaught Place, Hyde Park, 29 June 1899. SG from 1 Connaught Place, 10 July, 12 July, 21 July 1900. SG to mother from Howick, 27 July 1900. SG from 22 South Street, London, 12 April 1901.

GRE 289/4: Various correspondence between Lambert Middleton, Dissington Hall, to Earl Grey re loan and finance, 1910-11.

Other letters in the 4th Earl Grey collection: Violet Markham to Earl Grey, re SG, March 1908. Arthur Sladden to Earl Grey re financial losses, June 1910. SG description of ball given for Hilda Grenfell, Roehampton House, June 1910.

Robin Benson to Earl Grey on avoiding possibility of Arthur Grenfell bankruptcy, Aug. 1902.

Lady Muriel Paget telegram to Countess Grey re wounding of Lady Sybil, 8 July 1916. Earl Grey to Mansfield re illness and death of Lady Victoria, 20 Jan 1907 and Feb. 1907. Earl Grey telegrams to Mansfield at Howick re Lady Victoria's illness and death, Feb 1907.

SG at 22 South Street, re Prince's visit to Dorchester House and Jubilee illuminations, 19 June 1897. SG at Dorchester House, re the Queen's Jubilee procession through London and Review of Fleet, 2 July 1897.

Lady Sybil Grey letters from Southern Africa to Lady Wantage and to Charlie Howick, July-Aug. 1912.

The Newcastle Chronicle on Earl Grey's recruitment speech, Aug. 1914.

Illustrations from Howick Hall Trust collections:
Pictures from Howick Hall Hospital photograph album (1915-16).

Pictures from Durham Univ Special collections: Albert 4th Earl Grey and family, 1880s; Earl Grey and Party on train in Canada; 'The Empire is my country.'

Boyd Family text collection:
Lady Sybil Grey diary of trip to Yukon, Canada, July-Sept.,1909.

Letters from Earl Grey and SG on trip to Yukon 1909.

Countess Alice Grey, diary of Round the World Trip, Jan.-May 1914.

Lady Sybil Grey letters from Russia (Oct, 1915-June 1916; Oct. 1916-March 1917).

Lady Sybil Grey diary of Revolution (Feb.-March 1917).

Countess Alice Grey letters from England to SG in Russia, (Oct. 1915-March 1917).

Lady Muriel Paget letters to SG, Aug. 1915 and Dec. 1916.

Letters to SG from friends in Russia (Lintott, Brooke, Garstin, Poutiatine, Buchanan et al.) after her departure, 1917.

Lady Sybil Grey letters from London Feb.-Sept.1918 re Dorchester House Hospital et al.

Lady Sybil Grey letters from France re visit to Paris in early 1919, and re her service as Commandant of the Women's Legion in France, Aug. 1919- April 1920.

Lady Sybil Grey letters from Grand Metis, Canada, re her visits in 1920 and in June 1936.

Lady Sybil Grey letters from Nancy, France, Feb.-April 1922, re visit to Emile Coué.

Lady Sybil Middleton (SM) letters and full year diaries, 1927-1965.

Lady Sybil Middleton letters from South Africa (1950) and letters and diary from Kenya (Feb.-March 1956).

Letters of condolence on the death of Lady Sybil Middleton, to Evy Jones and Molly Boyd from Nancy Morse, Dr Margery Blackie et al.

Other sources, Text:
Letters of Countess Alice Grey and Lady Evelyn Grey to Elsie Reford, on death of Vera, Feb.1907 – Reford Family Collection

Earl Grey and Countess Alice Grey letters to children from Rhodesia, 1896 – Howick Hall Trust (quoted in Graham Sims, *Albert 4th Earl Grey, Paladin of Empire*, Central Africa Historical Association,1970).

Letter from Lady Sybil Middleton to Lady Halifax re General Strike, 1926 – Borthwick Institute, University of York.

Letter from SG to father re murder of Rasputin, 1916 – by permission of William Harmer and references from *The Forgotten Hospital* by Michael Harmer (Springwood Books, 1982) as indicated by on-page notes.

Description of life at Buckhurst Park, from *Kleinwort Benson* (Oxford University Press, 1997) – by permission of Jehanne Wake.

Countess Olga Poutiatine, letters 1916, quoted in George Lensen, *War and Revolution* (Diplomatic Press, 1971) – Harry Ransom Center, University of Texas at Austin.

Robert Bruce-Lockhart, from *Memoirs of a British Agent* (Macmillan) – by permission of PLSclear.

Lord Selborne on the threat of the German Navy, quoted from Margaret MacMillan, *The War that Ended Peace* (Profile Books, 2013, by permission of Random House).

Mark Gardner, letter to his sister, 1916 – by permission of Richard Gardner.

Sydney Daily Telegraph, on Earl Grey's speech in Sydney, 30 March 1914.
The National Review, 1919: Leopold Maxse's article 'A Fateful Breakfast'.
The British Journal of Nursing, 16 Oct. 1915, on SG's appointment.
R H Hubbard, *Rideau Hall* (Queen's Printer, Ottawa, 1968, crown copyright).
Dr Thompson and Dr Graham Aspland, unpublished letters to SG re Stary Ply, 1916.
Sir George Buchanan, *My Mission to Russia* (Cassell & Co, 1923).
Harold Begbie, *Albert Fourth Earl Grey, A Last Word* (Hodder & Stoughton, 1918)
World War Two newspapers (source unknown) pasted in SG's diaries, 1940-45.
Avril Meakin, *Howick – People, Places, Flora, Fauna, Seasons and Celebrations* (Howick Heritage Group, 2012).
Christopher Arnander, *Private Lord Crawford's Great War Diaries* (Pen & Sword, 2013)

Illustrations:

Holfords of Westonbirt Trust – photographs of Westonbirt greenhouses, and of Dorchester House.
Reford Family Collection – photographs of Estevan Lodge and of Elsie Reford.
The National Trust – Saltram House 1850s; Stag Lodge 1894.
The Library and Archives of Canada (LAC) – Earl Grey and Countess Grey; Lady Victoria Grey; Lady Sybil Grey (photographed by Topley); Parade for the Service for King Edward VII's funeral, Ottawa. Yatch Bacchante. Lady Evelyn Grey.
John Massey Stewart and Mary Evans Picture Library – photograph of Nevsky Prospekt, Petrograd.
Library of Congress – Countess Grey and her daughters on the Vaterland, 1914.
The Yukon Archives – Earl Grey and party on Solomon's Dome, Dawson, 1909.
William Harmer and the Leeds Russian Archive (Brotherton Library, University of Leeds) –The Imperial family visiting the Anglo-Russian Hospital, 1916 [MS 781/6]; Staff outside the ARH; Field Hospital Parade. Map of The Eastern Front, (from Michael Harmer's, *The Forgotten Hospital*, Springwood Books, 1982).
The British Red Cross Museums and Archives – The holy Ikon given to the ARH; Young Cossack; Blessing of the Field Hospital; Field Hospital at camp.
Laura de Wesselow, for permission to use photographs – Valetta Palace album Jan. 1903; Women's Legion staff cars and ambulances, 1919-20; Women's Legion Christmas card, 1919; Sybil, Molly and Harry at Eton, 1930s; Sybil portrait, 1941, by Molly Bishop; Sybil at Harry's wedding, 1964; Burley Grange.
Anne Dawnay, for permission to use photographs – Sybil on safari in Kenya, 1956; Sybil and party at Government House, Mombasa; Anne Dawnay with three lion cubs.
Boyd family collection – Howick Hall print; Robert Stayner Holford; Albert 4th Earl Grey at Howick; promotional brochure on Honolulu; photograph of surfers; Sybil Grey's WO Passbook; Charlie Grey in uniform; the Dmitry Palace, 1916; Sybil's sketch map of the Anglo-Russian Hospital; Queen Alexandra's letter to Earl Grey; postcard of the Pecherska Lavra, Kiev; Sybil Grey's awards and medals; Sybil Grey in the uniform of the Women's Legion; Father Neptune certificate, 1927; Lambert Middleton on deck; Rio de Janeiro Bay, photographed by Sybil; Molly and Harry in the Lowood garden; Sybil in 1930s; Lambert Middleton; Molly Middleton; John Boyd; Sybil at Molly's wedding.
Vivien Asquith for permission to use the photograph of her father, L. E. 'Jonah' Jones, on his return from captivity in WW1.

Websites such as Wikipedia and Peerage.com and others have been invaluable sources of information.

Bibliography

Books

A Crown of Maples – Constitutional Monarchy in Canada (Department of Canadian Heritage, 2012)

Christopher Arvander (ed): *Private Lord Crawford's Great War Diaries – from Medical Orderly to Cabinet Minister* (Pen & Sword, 2013)

Catherine Bailey: *Black Diamonds – The Rise and Fall of an English Dynasty* (Penguin, 2008).

Harold Begbie: *Albert, Fourth Earl Grey – A Last Word* (Hodder & Stoughton, 1918)

Anthony Cave Brown: *'C' – The Secret Life of Sir Stewart Menzies, Spymaster to Winston Churchill* (Collier Books, 1989)

Wilfrid Blunt: *Lady Muriel* (Methuen, 1962)

R H Bruce-Lockhart: *Memoirs of a British Agent* (Macmillan, 1974)

John Buchan: Francis and Riversdale Grenfell – a Memoir (Nelson, 1920)

George Buchanan, Sir: *My Mission to Russia* (Cassell, 1923)

Frances Campbell-Preston (edited by Hugo Vickers): *The Rich Spoils of Time* (The Dovecote Press, 1988)

Charles Douglas-Home: *Evelyn Baring – The Last Proconsul* (Collins, 1978)

Orlando Figes: *A People's Tragedy – The Russian Revolution 1891-1924* (Pimlico, 1996)

Denis Norman Garstin: *Friendly Russia* (T F Unwin, 1915)

Michael Harmer: *The Forgotten Hospital* (Springwood Books, 1982)

R H Hubbard: *Rideau Hall – An Illustrated History of Government House, Ottawa* (Roger Duhamel, Queen's Printer, Ottawa, 1967)

L E Jones: *A Victorian Boyhood* (Macmillan); *An Edwardian Youth* (Macmillan); *Georgian Afternoon* (Rupert Hart Davis).

Sean Lang: *Why the First World War Broke Out* (Searching Finance, 2014)

George Alexander Lensen: *War and Revolution – Excerpts from the Letters and Diaries of Countess Olga Poutiatine* (The Diplomatic Press, 1971)

Elizabeth Longford, Lady: *Louisa, Lady in Waiting* (Jonathan Cape, 1979)

Margaret MacMillan: *The War that Ended Peace* (Profile Books, 2013)

Avril Meakin: *Howick's Seven Tales of the Unexpected* (2104) and *Howick: People, Places, Flora, Fauna, Seasons and Celebrations* (Howick Heritage Group, 2012)

James Morris: *Heaven's Command* (Pax Britannica Trilogy) (Faber & Faber, 1973)

Jeremy Paxman: *Great Britain's Great War* (Viking, Penguin, 2013)

Alexander Reford: *The Reford Gardens – Elsie's Paradise* (Les Edition de l'Hommes, 2004)

Harold Shukman: *Rasputin* (Sutton Publishing, 1997)

Graham Sims: *Albert, Fourth Earl Grey, Paladin of Empire* (Central African Historical Association, Salisbury, 1970)

Jehanne Wake: *Kleinwort Benson – The History of Two Families in Banking* (OUP, 1997)

Michael Waterhouse: *Edwardian Requiem – A Life of Sir Edward Grey* (Biteback Publishing, 2014)

Journals
Anglo-Russian Hospital Report, 1917 (Drs Fleming and Jefferson)
History Today online (Vol 59, issue 1, November 2009)
Christopher Danziger: *The Prince, the Spy and the Mad Monk* (Oxford Today, Vol. 29, No. 1, 2016)
Sybil Grey, Lady: *Sidelights on the Russian Revolution* (The National Review, 1918?)
Leopold Maxse: *A Fateful Breakfast* (The National Review, August 1918)
Keith Neilson: *Joy Rides –British Intelligence and Propaganda in Russia, 1914-17* (The Historical Journal, 24, 4, 1981)

Websites etc
Peerage.com
Wikipedia.com

Radio Programme
Every Day in Every Way, presented by Gillian Darby, 30.12.2012

Index